Acknowledgements

The publishers would like to thank the
Telegraph Colour Library
for permission to reproduce
the photograph on page 8.

Cover image:
Tom Van Sant / Geosphere Project, Santa Monica,
Science Photo Library.

The illustrations are by Chapman Bounford,
Hard Lines, and Gary Hinks.

The page design is by Adrian Smith.

Oil spillage data is from
*Oil Pollution Survey around the Coast
of the United Kingdom, 1995*
by kind permission of the publishers,
ACOPS (Advisory Committee on Protection of the Sea).

THE OXFORD Practical ATLAS

D0552188

OXFORD
UNIVERSITY PRESS

Great Clarendon Street, Oxford OX2 6DP

Oxford University Press is a department of the University of Oxford.
It furthers the University's objective of excellence in research, scholarship,
and education by publishing worldwide in

Oxford New York

Auckland Bangkok Buenos Aires Cape Town Chennai
Dar es Salaam Delhi Hong Kong Istanbul Karachi Kolkata
Kuala Lumpur Madrid Melbourne Mexico City Mumbai Nairobi
São Paulo Shanghai Taipei Tokyo Toronto

with an associated company in Berlin

Oxford is a registered trade mark of Oxford University Press
in the UK and in certain other countries

© Oxford University Press 2003

Database right Oxford University Press (maker)

First published 2003

© Maps copyright Oxford University Press

British Library Cataloguing in Publication Data

Data available

ISBN 0 19 832067 1 (hardback)   ISBN 0 19 832066 3 (paperback)

1 3 5 7 9 10 8 6 4 2

Printed in Italy

02461

Editorial Adviser

Patrick Wiegand

Oxford University Press

2 **Contents** The World, The British Isles

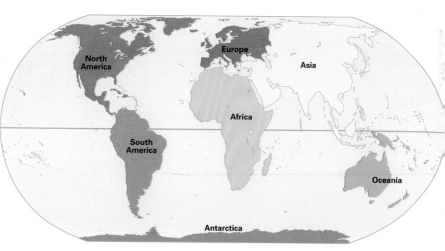

The World

Countries _____ 4–5

Land and Water _____ 6–7

Climate and Ecosystems _____ 8–9

Earthquakes and Volcanoes _____ 10–11

Population _____ 12–13

Development and Interdependence _____ 14–15

Environment and Pollution _____ 16–17

The British Isles

Countries _____ 18

Land and Water _____ 19

Climate _____ 20–21

Population _____ 22

Farming and Industry _____ 23

Energy _____ 24

Communications _____ 25

Pollution _____ 26

Scenery and Conservation _____ 27

Topographic map _____ 28

Orkney and Shetland Islands _____ 29

Scottish Highlands and Islands _____ 30–31

Northern Ireland _____ 32

Southern Scotland _____ 33

Northern England _____ 34–35

Wales _____ 36

English West Midlands _____ 37

South East England _____ 38–39

South West England _____ 40–41

Maps that show general features of regions, countries or continents are called **topographic maps**. These maps are shown with a light band of colour in the contents list.

For example:

South West England

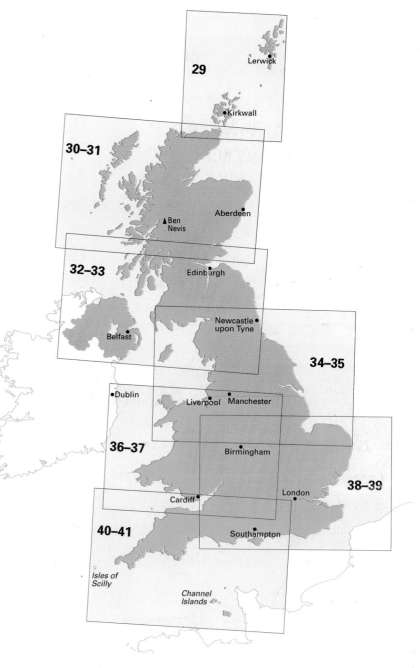

Contents Continents and Poles 3

Europe

Topographic map 42–43
European Union 43
Wealth 43
Climate and Ecosystems 44
Farming, Energy, and Minerals 45
Industry and Environmental issues 46
Population 47
France 48
Benelux, Germany, Alps 49
Spain and Portugal 50
Italy 51

Asia

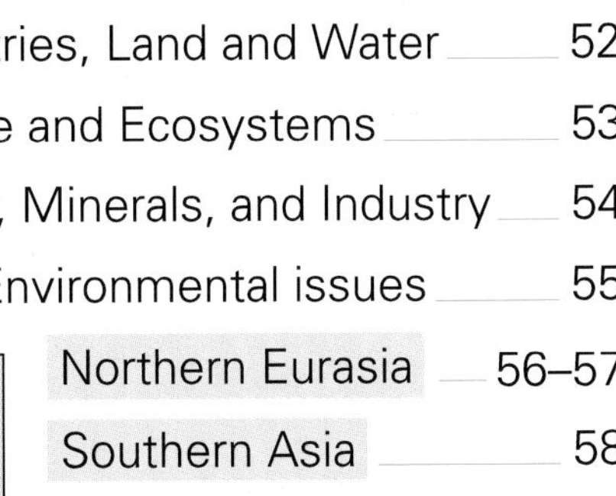

Countries, Land and Water 52
Climate and Ecosystems 53
Farming, Energy, Minerals, and Industry 54
Population and Environmental issues 55

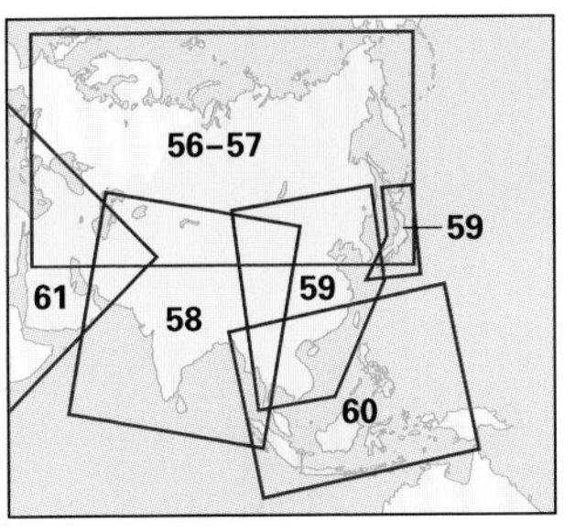
56–57
59
61
58
59
60

Northern Eurasia 56–57
Southern Asia 58
China and Japan 59
South East Asia 60
The Middle East and North Africa 61

Africa

Countries, Land and Water 62
Climate and Ecosystems 63
Farming, Energy, Minerals, and Industry 64
Population and Environmental issues 65

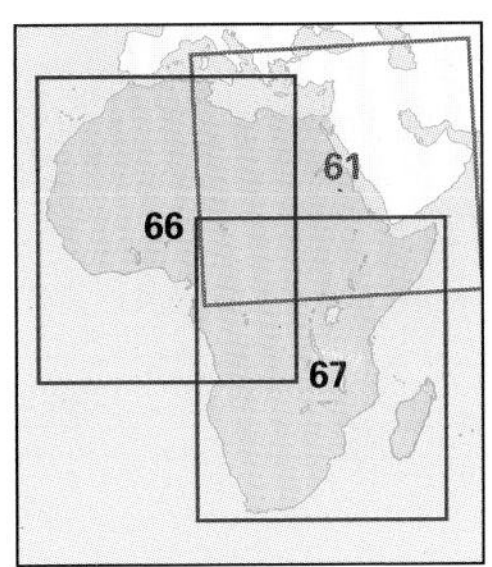
61
66
67

North and West Africa 66
South and East Africa 67

Oceania

Countries, Land and Water 68
Climate and Ecosystems 69
Farming, Energy, Minerals, and Industry 70
Population and Environmental issues 71
Australia 72
New Zealand 73

North America

Countries, Land and Water 74
Climate and Ecosystems 75
Farming, Energy, Minerals, and Industry 76
Population and Environmental issues 77

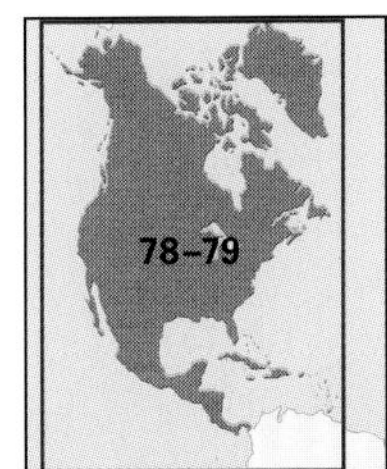
78–79

Canada, Greenland, USA, Mexico and the Caribbean 78–79

South America

Countries, Land and Water 80
Climate and Ecosystems 81
Farming, Energy, Minerals, and Industry 82
Population and Environmental issues 83

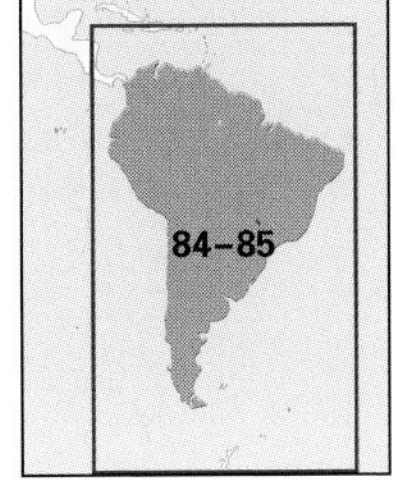
84–85

South America 84–85

The Poles

The Arctic Ocean 86
Antarctica 86

Index 87-96

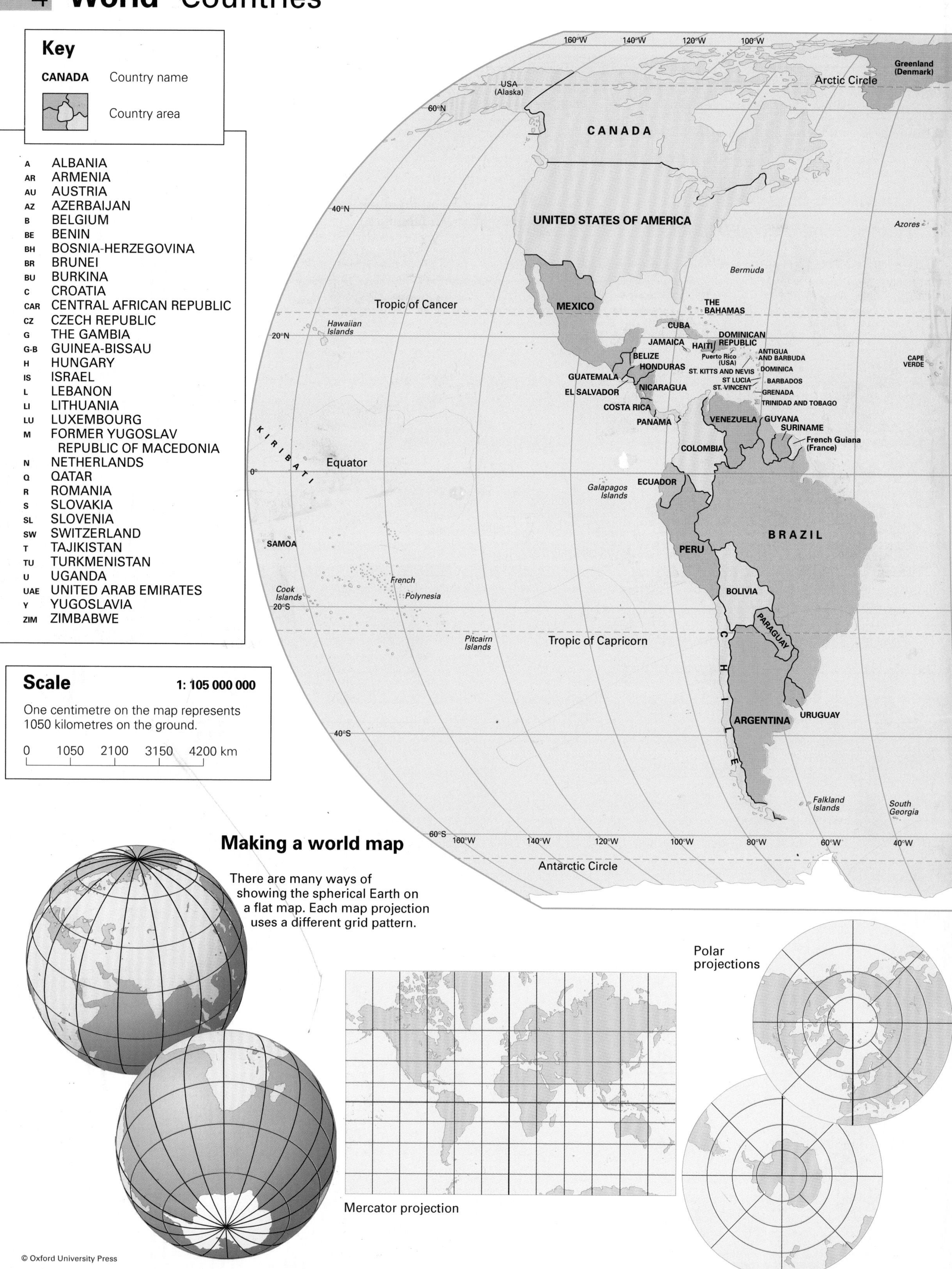

Key

CANADA   Country name

Country area

A	ALBANIA
AR	ARMENIA
AU	AUSTRIA
AZ	AZERBAIJAN
B	BELGIUM
BE	BENIN
BH	BOSNIA-HERZEGOVINA
BR	BRUNEI
BU	BURKINA
C	CROATIA
CAR	CENTRAL AFRICAN REPUBLIC
CZ	CZECH REPUBLIC
G	THE GAMBIA
G-B	GUINEA-BISSAU
H	HUNGARY
IS	ISRAEL
L	LEBANON
LI	LITHUANIA
LU	LUXEMBOURG
M	FORMER YUGOSLAV REPUBLIC OF MACEDONIA
N	NETHERLANDS
Q	QATAR
R	ROMANIA
S	SLOVAKIA
SL	SLOVENIA
SW	SWITZERLAND
T	TAJIKISTAN
TU	TURKMENISTAN
U	UGANDA
UAE	UNITED ARAB EMIRATES
Y	YUGOSLAVIA
ZIM	ZIMBABWE

Scale
1: 105 000 000

One centimetre on the map represents 1050 kilometres on the ground.

0   1050   2100   3150   4200 km

Making a world map

There are many ways of showing the spherical Earth on a flat map. Each map projection uses a different grid pattern.

Mercator projection

Polar projections

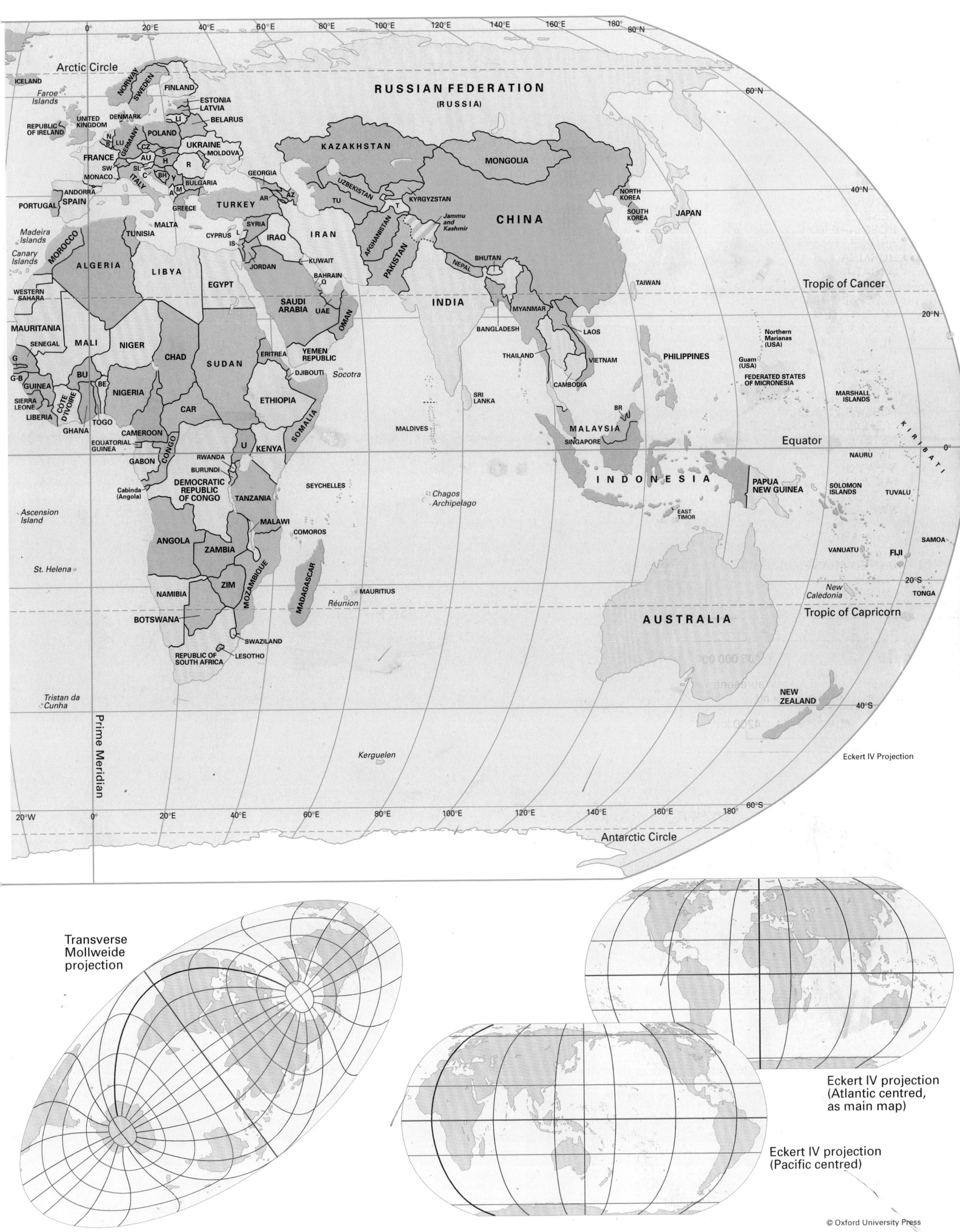

Arctic Circle

ICELAND
Faroe Islands
REPUBLIC OF IRELAND
UNITED KINGDOM
PORTUGAL
SPAIN
ANDORRA
Madeira Islands
Canary Islands
MOROCCO
WESTERN SAHARA
MAURITANIA
SENEGAL
G — GUINEA
G-B
GUINEA
SIERRA LEONE
LIBERIA
COTE D'IVOIRE
GHANA
TOGO
BE
BU
MALI
NIGER
NIGERIA
CAMEROON
EQUATORIAL GUINEA
GABON
CONGO
CHAD
CAR
DEMOCRATIC REPUBLIC OF CONGO
Cabinda (Angola)
ANGOLA
NAMIBIA
BOTSWANA
REPUBLIC OF SOUTH AFRICA
LESOTHO
SWAZILAND
ZIM
ZAMBIA
MOZAMBIQUE
MALAWI
TANZANIA
RWANDA
BURUNDI
U
KENYA
SOMALIA
ETHIOPIA
DJIBOUTI
ERITREA
SUDAN
LIBYA
EGYPT
ALGERIA
TUNISIA
MALTA
Socotra

NORWAY
SWEDEN
FINLAND
DENMARK
ESTONIA
LATVIA
LI
BELARUS
POLAND
UKRAINE
MOLDOVA
GERMANY
N
LU
B
FRANCE
MONACO
ITALY
SW
C
CZ
AU
SL
H
R
BULGARIA
GREECE
CYPRUS
TURKEY
SYRIA
IS
L
IRAQ
JORDAN
SAUDI ARABIA
KUWAIT
BAHRAIN Q
UAE
OMAN
YEMEN REPUBLIC
GEORGIA
AR
AZ
TU
UZBEKISTAN
IRAN
AFGHANISTAN
PAKISTAN
KYRGYZSTAN
T
Jammu and Kashmir
NEPAL
BHUTAN
INDIA
BANGLADESH
MYANMAR
SRI LANKA
MALDIVES
KAZAKHSTAN
RUSSIAN FEDERATION (RUSSIA)
MONGOLIA
CHINA
NORTH KOREA
SOUTH KOREA
JAPAN
TAIWAN
LAOS
THAILAND
VIETNAM
CAMBODIA
PHILIPPINES
MALAYSIA
SINGAPORE
INDONESIA
BR
EAST TIMOR
PAPUA NEW GUINEA
Northern Marianas (USA)
Guam (USA)
FEDERATED STATES OF MICRONESIA
MARSHALL ISLANDS
NAURU
SOLOMON ISLANDS
TUVALU
KIRIBATI
VANUATU
FIJI
SAMOA
TONGA
New Caledonia
AUSTRALIA
NEW ZEALAND

SEYCHELLES
Chagos Archipelago
MADAGASCAR
COMOROS
MAURITIUS
Réunion

Ascension Island
St. Helena
Tristan da Cunha

Prime Meridian

Kerguelen

Tropic of Cancer
Equator
Tropic of Capricorn
Antarctic Circle

60°N
40°N
20°N
0°
20°S
40°S
60°S
80°N

0° 20°E 40°E 60°E 80°E 100°E 120°E 140°E 160°E 180°
20°W 0° 20°E 40°E 60°E 80°E 100°E 120°E 140°E 160°E 180°

Eckert IV Projection

Transverse Mollweide projection

Eckert IV projection (Atlantic centred, as main map)

Eckert IV projection (Pacific centred)

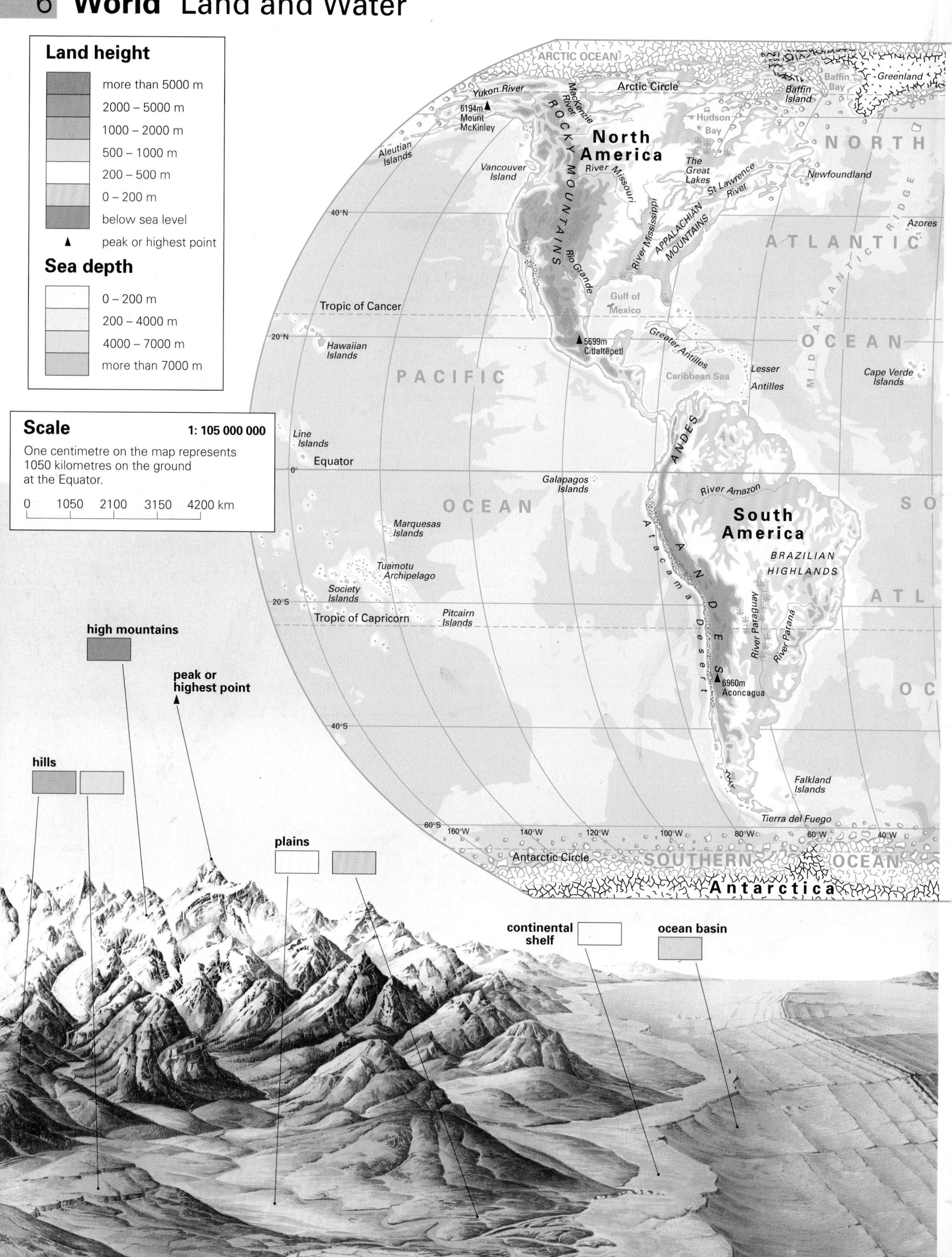

Land height

- more than 5000 m
- 2000 – 5000 m
- 1000 – 2000 m
- 500 – 1000 m
- 200 – 500 m
- 0 – 200 m
- below sea level
- ▲ peak or highest point

Sea depth

- 0 – 200 m
- 200 – 4000 m
- 4000 – 7000 m
- more than 7000 m

Scale

1: 105 000 000

One centimetre on the map represents
1050 kilometres on the ground
at the Equator.

0   1050   2100   3150   4200 km

high mountains

peak or
highest point

hills

plains

continental
shelf

ocean basin

ARCTIC OCEAN

Arctic Circle

Greenland

Baffin
Bay

Baffin
Island

NORTH

Yukon River

Mackenzie
River

ROCKY MOUNTAINS

6194m ▲
Mount
McKinley

Aleutian
Islands

Vancouver
Island

Hudson
Bay

The
Great
Lakes

St Lawrence
River

Newfoundland

North
America

River Missouri

River Mississippi

APPALACHIAN
MOUNTAINS

ATLANTIC

Azores

40°N

Rio Grande

20°N

Tropic of Cancer

Gulf of
Mexico

5699m ▲
Citlaltépetl

Greater Antilles

Caribbean Sea

Lesser
Antilles

Cape Verde
Islands

OCEAN

MID ATLANTIC RIDGE

PACIFIC

Hawaiian
Islands

Line
Islands

Equator

0°

Galapagos
Islands

ANDES

River Amazon

South
America

BRAZILIAN
HIGHLANDS

SO

Marquesas
Islands

OCEAN

ATL

Tuamotu
Archipelago

Society
Islands

20°S

Pitcairn
Islands

Tropic of Capricorn

Atacama Desert

A N D E S

River Paraguay

River Paraná

OC

40°S

6960m ▲
Aconcagua

Falkland
Islands

160°W   140°W   120°W   100°W   80°W   60°W   40°W

60°S

Tierra del Fuego

Antarctic Circle

SOUTHERN   OCEAN

Antarctica

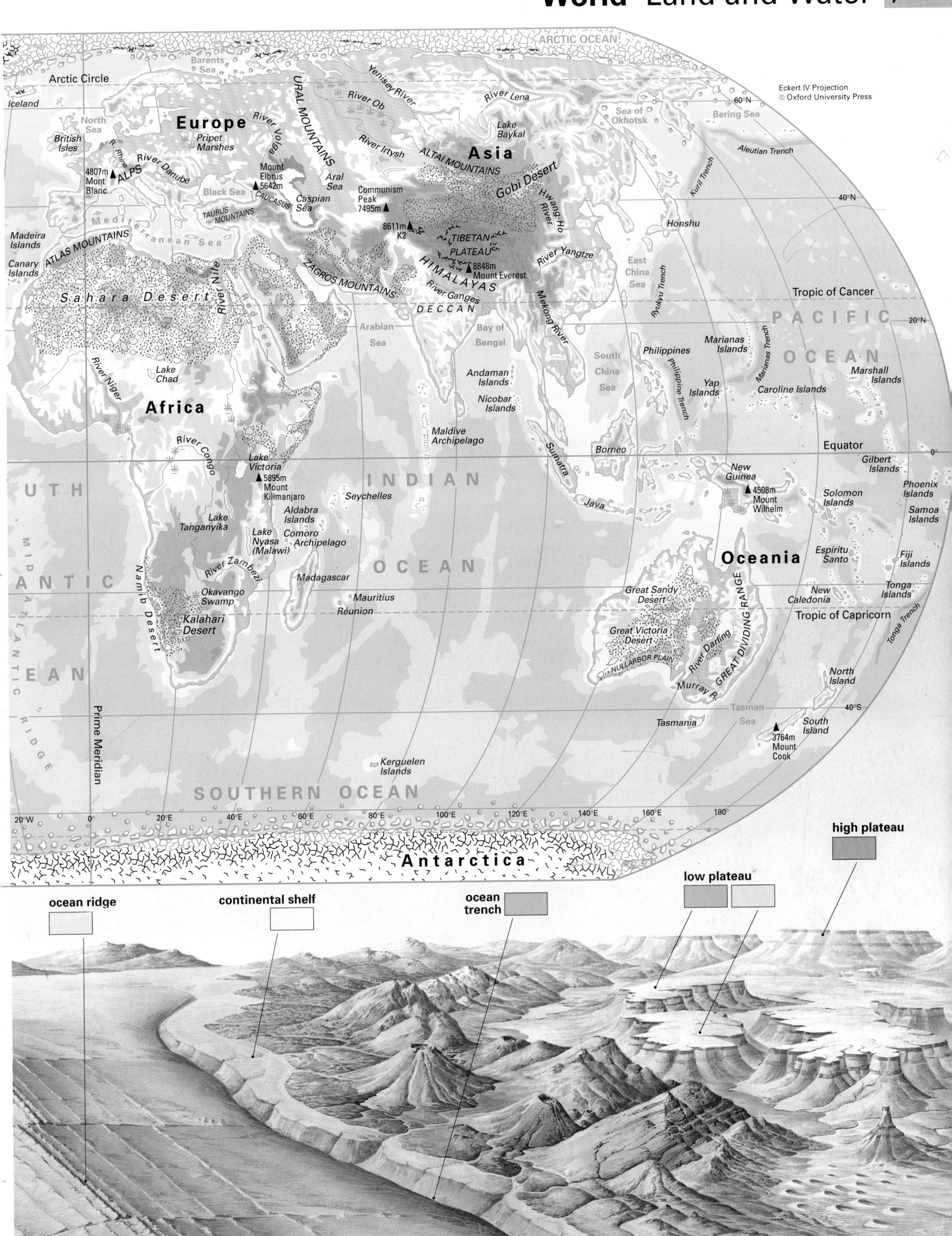
Eckert IV Projection
© Oxford University Press
ARCTIC OCEAN
Arctic Circle
Iceland
Barents Sea
North Sea
British Isles
Europe
Pripet Marshes
R. Rhine
River Danube
ALPS
4807m Mont Blanc
River Volga
Mount Elbrus 5642m
CAUCASUS
Black Sea
TAURUS MOUNTAINS
Mediterranean Sea
Caspian Sea
Aral Sea
URAL MOUNTAINS
Yenisey River
River Ob
River Irtysh
River Lena
Lake Baykal
Sea of Okhotsk
Bering Sea
Aleutian Trench
Kuril Trench
Asia
ALTAI MOUNTAINS
Gobi Desert
Communism Peak 7495m
8611m K2
TIBETAN PLATEAU
Hwang-Ho River
River Yangtze
HIMALAYAS
8848m Mount Everest
River Ganges
DECCAN
ZAGROS MOUNTAINS
Honshu
East China Sea
Ryukyu Trench
Tropic of Cancer
PACIFIC OCEAN
Madeira Islands
Canary Islands
ATLAS MOUNTAINS
Sahara Desert
River Nile
Red Sea
Arabian Sea
Bay of Bengal
Mekong River
South China Sea
Philippines
Philippine Trench
Marianas Islands
Marianas Trench
Yap Islands
Caroline Islands
Marshall Islands
River Niger
Lake Chad
Africa
Andaman Islands
Nicobar Islands
Maldive Archipelago
Sumatra
Borneo
Equator
Gilbert Islands
River Congo
Lake Victoria
5895m Mount Kilimanjaro
INDIAN OCEAN
Seychelles
New Guinea
4508m Mount Wilhelm
Java
Solomon Islands
Phoenix Islands
Samoa Islands
Lake Tanganyika
Aldabra Islands
Lake Nyasa (Malawi)
Comoro Archipelago
River Zambezi
Oceania
Espíritu Santo
Fiji Islands
Namib Desert
Okavango Swamp
Madagascar
Mauritius
Réunion
Kalahari Desert
Great Sandy Desert
GREAT DIVIDING RANGE
New Caledonia
Tonga Islands
Tropic of Capricorn
Tonga Trench
Great Victoria Desert
NULLARBOR PLAIN
River Darling
Murray R.
North Island
Tasman Sea
Tasmania
South Island
3764m Mount Cook
MID ATLANTIC RIDGE
SOUTH ATLANTIC OCEAN
Prime Meridian
Kerguelen Islands
SOUTHERN OCEAN
Antarctica
60°N
40°N
20°N
0°
40°S
20°W
0°
20°E
40°E
60°E
80°E
100°E
120°E
140°E
160°E
180°
ocean ridge
continental shelf
ocean trench
low plateau
high plateau

Deciduous and
mixed forest

Evergreen trees
and shrubs
(Mediterranean)

Desert

Semi-desert

Tropical rain
forest

Tropical grasslands
(savannah)

A Meteosat view of
the Earth recorded
by a geostationary satellite
positioned 36 000 km above
the intersection of the
Prime Meridian and the Equator

Climatic regions

Hot tropical rainy

rain all year

monsoon

dry in winter

Very dry

with no reliable rain

with a little rain

**Influenced by the sea:
warm summers, mild winters**

with dry summers
(Mediterranean type)

with dry winters

with no dry season

Cool

with dry winters

rain all year

Cold polar

no warm season
and fairly dry

Mountain

height of the land strongly
affects the climate

Ecosystems

Vegetation types are those which
would occur naturally without
interference by people

Coniferous forest

cone bearing trees

Deciduous and mixed forest

leaf shedding and
coniferous tress

Tropical rain forest

many species of lush,
tall trees

Tropical grasslands (savannah)

tall grass parkland
with scattered trees

Thorn forest

low trees and shrubs with
spines or thorns

Evergreen trees and shrubs

plants and small trees
with leathery leaves

Temperate grasslands

prairies, steppes,
pampas and veld

Semi-desert

short grasses and
drought-resistant scrub

Desert

sand and stones,
very little vegetation

Tundra

moss and lichen,
with few trees

Ice

no vegetation

Mountains

thin soils, steep slopes
and high altitude affects
type of vegetation

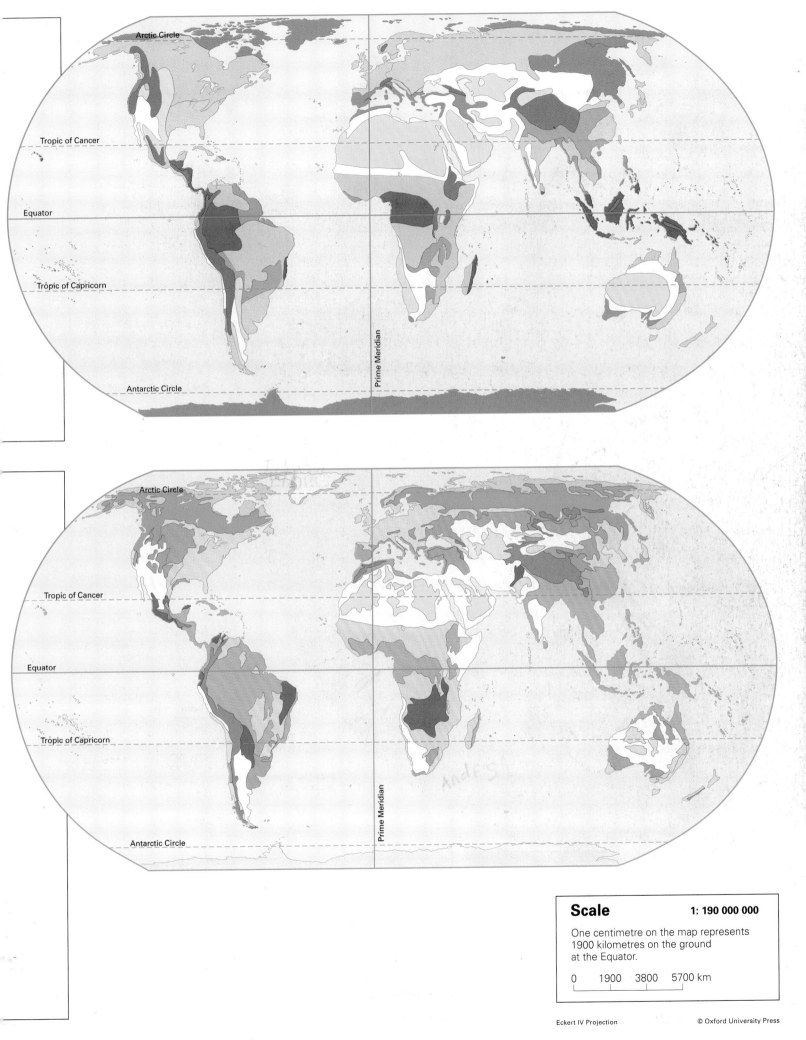

Scale 1: 190 000 000

One centimetre on the map represents
1900 kilometres on the ground
at the Equator.

0   1900   3800   5700 km

Eckert IV Projection   © Oxford University Press

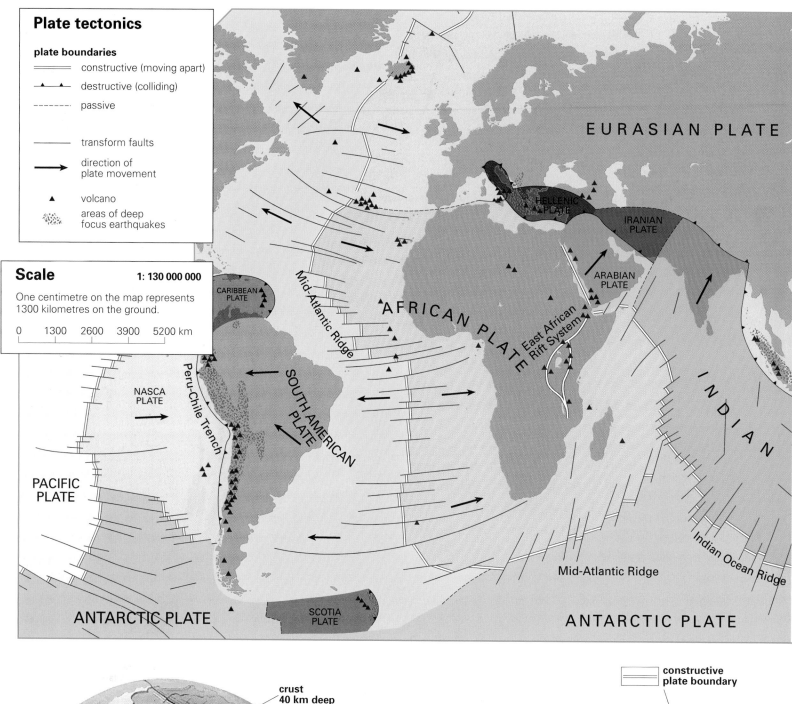

Plate tectonics

plate boundaries

‖‖‖‖‖	constructive (moving apart)
▲—▲—▲	destructive (colliding)
– – – –	passive
———	transform faults
→	direction of plate movement
▲	volcano
⣿⣿⣿	areas of deep focus earthquakes

Scale   1: 130 000 000

One centimetre on the map represents 1300 kilometres on the ground.

0   1300   2600   3900   5200 km

EURASIAN PLATE

HELLENIC PLATE

IRANIAN PLATE

ARABIAN PLATE

CARIBBEAN PLATE

Mid-Atlantic Ridge

AFRICAN PLATE

East African Rift System

NASCA PLATE

Peru-Chile Trench

SOUTH AMERICAN PLATE

INDIAN

PACIFIC PLATE

Mid-Atlantic Ridge

Indian Ocean Ridge

ANTARCTIC PLATE

SCOTIA PLATE

ANTARCTIC PLATE

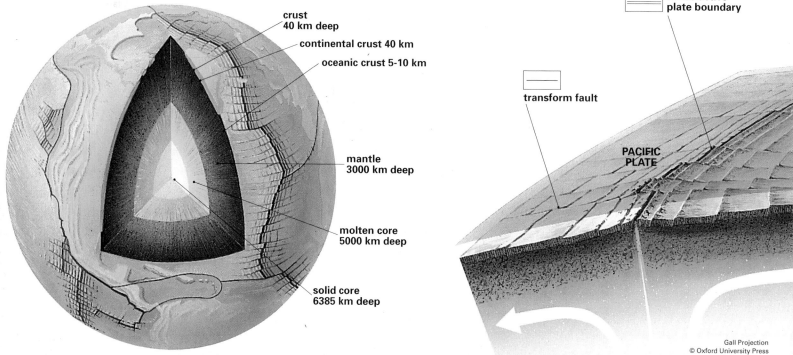

crust 40 km deep

continental crust 40 km

oceanic crust 5-10 km

mantle 3000 km deep

molten core 5000 km deep

solid core 6385 km deep

constructive plate boundary

transform fault

PACIFIC PLATE

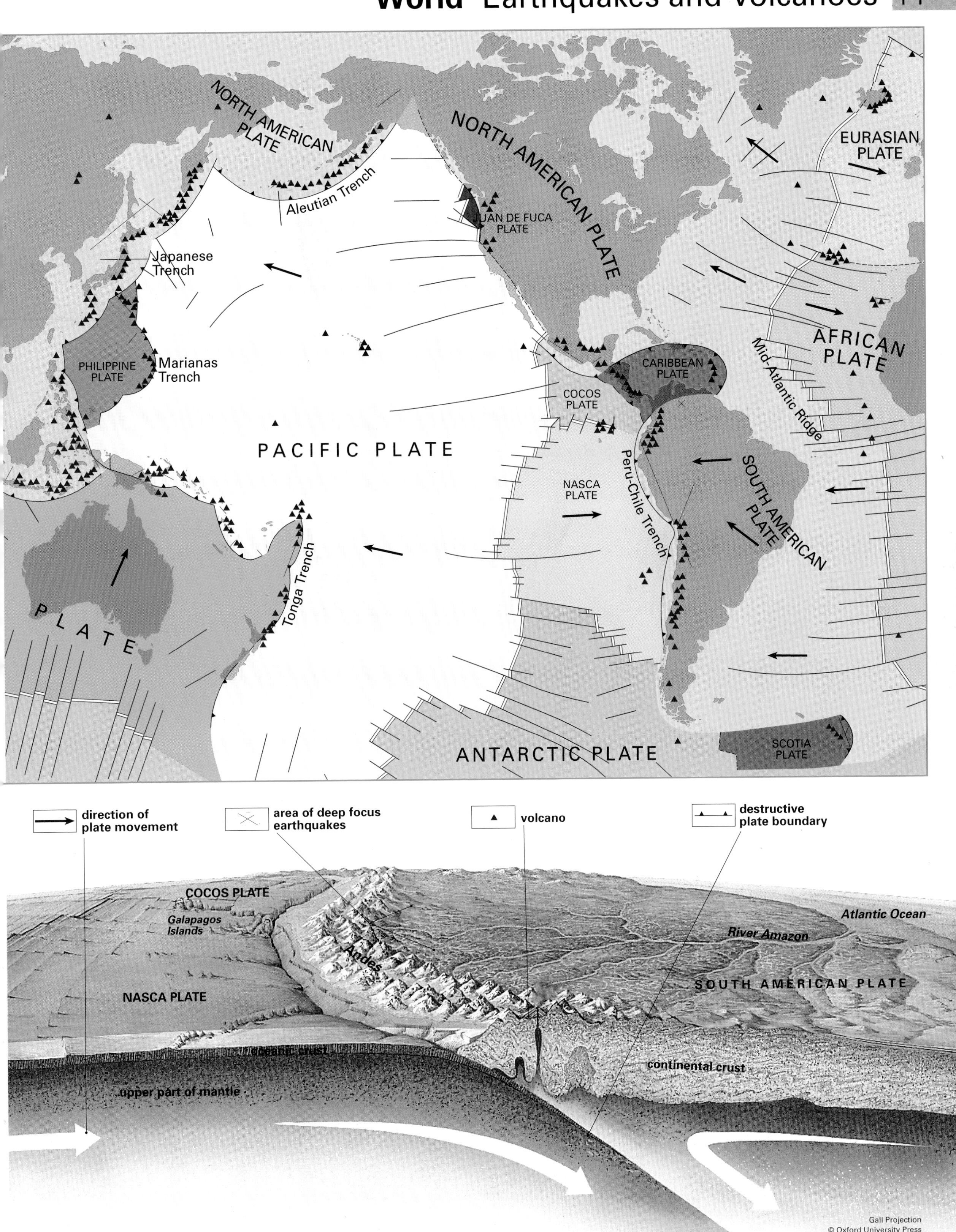

NORTH AMERICAN PLATE

NORTH AMERICAN PLATE

EURASIAN PLATE

Aleutian Trench

JUAN DE FUCA PLATE

Japanese Trench

AFRICAN PLATE

PHILIPPINE PLATE

Marianas Trench

CARIBBEAN PLATE

COCOS PLATE

Mid-Atlantic Ridge

PACIFIC PLATE

NASCA PLATE

Peru-Chile Trench

SOUTH AMERICAN PLATE

PLATE

Tonga Trench

ANTARCTIC PLATE

SCOTIA PLATE

direction of plate movement

area of deep focus earthquakes

volcano

destructive plate boundary

COCOS PLATE

Galapagos Islands

Atlantic Ocean

River Amazon

Andes

NASCA PLATE

SOUTH AMERICAN PLATE

oceanic crust

continental crust

upper part of mantle

Gall Projection

© Oxford University Press

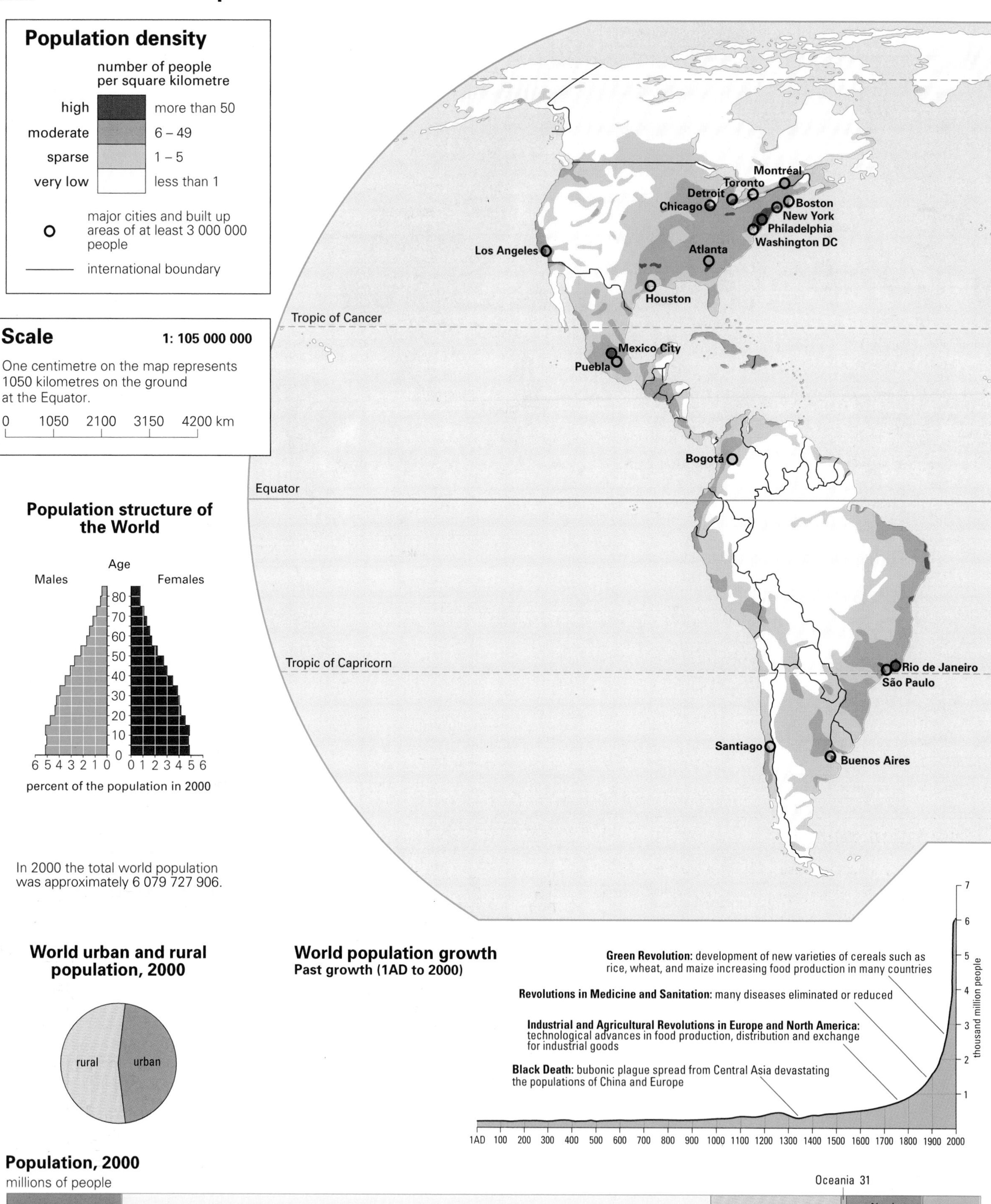

Population density

number of people per square kilometre

high		more than 50
moderate		6 – 49
sparse		1 – 5
very low		less than 1

○ major cities and built up areas of at least 3 000 000 people

—— international boundary

Scale

1: 105 000 000

One centimetre on the map represents 1050 kilometres on the ground at the Equator.

0   1050   2100   3150   4200 km

Population structure of the World

Age

Males   Females

80
70
60
50
40
30
20
10
0

6 5 4 3 2 1 0   0 1 2 3 4 5 6

percent of the population in 2000

In 2000 the total world population was approximately 6 079 727 906.

World urban and rural population, 2000

rural   urban

World population growth
Past growth (1AD to 2000)

Green Revolution: development of new varieties of cereals such as rice, wheat, and maize increasing food production in many countries

Revolutions in Medicine and Sanitation: many diseases eliminated or reduced

Industrial and Agricultural Revolutions in Europe and North America: technological advances in food production, distribution and exchange for industrial goods

Black Death: bubonic plague spread from Central Asia devastating the populations of China and Europe

thousand million people

1AD 100 200 300 400 500 600 700 800 900 1000 1100 1200 1300 1400 1500 1600 1700 1800 1900 2000

Population, 2000
millions of people

Oceania 31

Europe 729	Asia 3688	Africa 805	North America 481	South America 347

Land areas
thousands of square kilometres

Europe 10 498	Asia 44 387	Africa 30 335	Oceania 8503	North America 24 241	South America 17 832	Antarctica 13 340

Tropic of Cancer

Equator

Tropic of Capricorn

Montréal
Toronto
Detroit
Chicago
Boston
New York
Philadelphia
Washington DC
Los Angeles
Atlanta
Houston
Mexico City
Puebla
Bogotá
Rio de Janeiro
São Paulo
Santiago
Buenos Aires

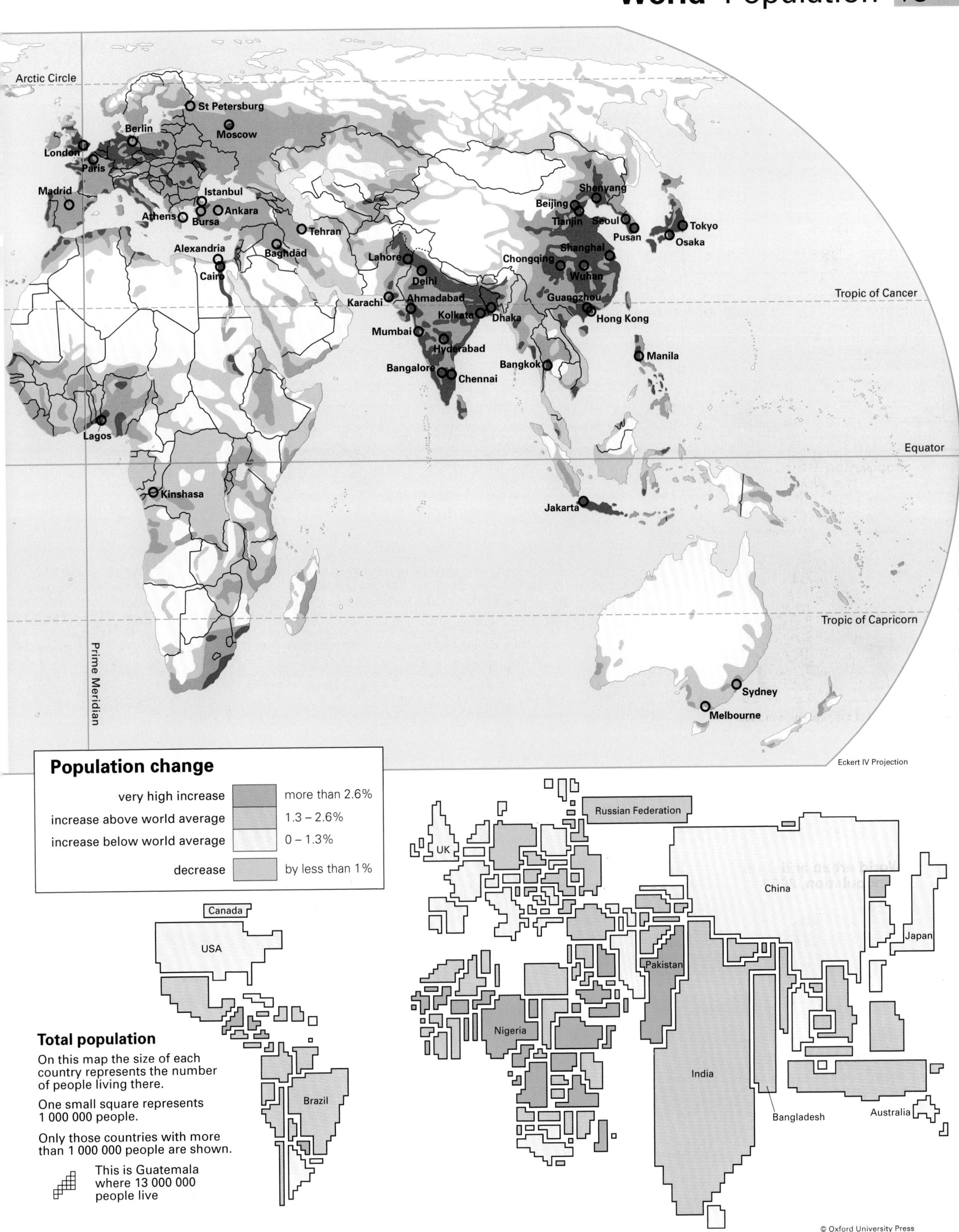

Arctic Circle

St Petersburg
Berlin
Moscow
London
Paris
Madrid
Istanbul
Athens
Ankara
Bursa
Tehran
Shenyang
Beijing
Tianjin
Seoul
Pusan
Tokyo
Osaka
Alexandria
Baghdad
Lahore
Chongqing
Shanghai
Cairo
Delhi
Wuhan
Tropic of Cancer
Karachi
Ahmadabad
Guangzhou
Mumbai
Kolkata
Dhaka
Hong Kong
Hyderabad
Bangkok
Manila
Bangalore
Chennai
Lagos
Equator
Kinshasa
Jakarta
Tropic of Capricorn
Prime Meridian
Sydney
Melbourne

Eckert IV Projection

Population change

very high increase	more than 2.6%
increase above world average	1.3 – 2.6%
increase below world average	0 – 1.3%
decrease	by less than 1%

Total population

On this map the size of each country represents the number of people living there.

One small square represents 1 000 000 people.

Only those countries with more than 1 000 000 people are shown.

This is Guatemala where 13 000 000 people live

Russian Federation
UK
China
Japan
Canada
USA
Pakistan
Nigeria
India
Brazil
Bangladesh
Australia

© Oxford University Press

Purchasing power

Purchasing Power Parity (PPP), 2000 in $ US

Based on Gross Domestic Product (GDP) per person, adjusted for the local cost of living.

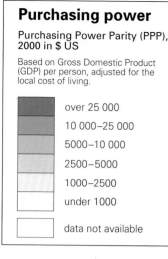

- over 25 000
- 10 000–25 000
- 5000–10 000
- 2500–5000
- 1000–2500
- under 1000
- data not available

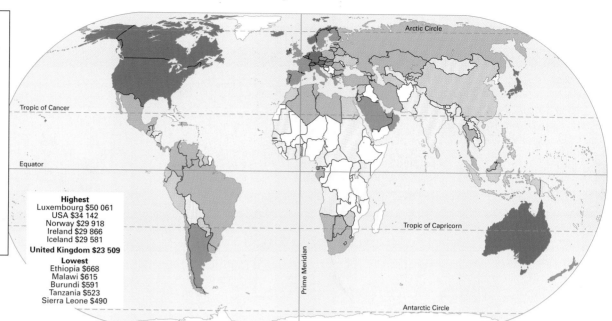

Highest
Luxembourg $50 061
USA $34 142
Norway $29 918
Ireland $29 866
Iceland $29 581
United Kingdom $23 509
Lowest
Ethiopia $668
Malawi $615
Burundi $591
Tanzania $523
Sierra Leone $490

Givers and receivers of aid, 2000 in $ US

Givers
- over $100 per person
- $50–$100 per person
- $25–$50 per person
- **countries neither giving nor receiving**

Receivers
- under $10 per person
- $10–$100 per person
- over $100 per person
- data not available

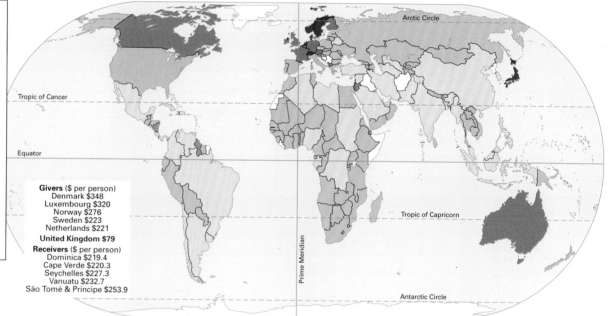

Givers ($ per person)
Denmark $348
Luxembourg $320
Norway $276
Sweden $223
Netherlands $221
United Kingdom $79
Receivers ($ per person)
Dominica $219.4
Cape Verde $220.3
Seychelles $227.3
Vanuatu $232.7
São Tomé & Principe $253.9

Life expectancy

Average number of years a baby born in 2000 can expect to live

- over 70 years
- 65–70 years
- 60–65 years
- 55–60 years
- under 55 years
- data not available

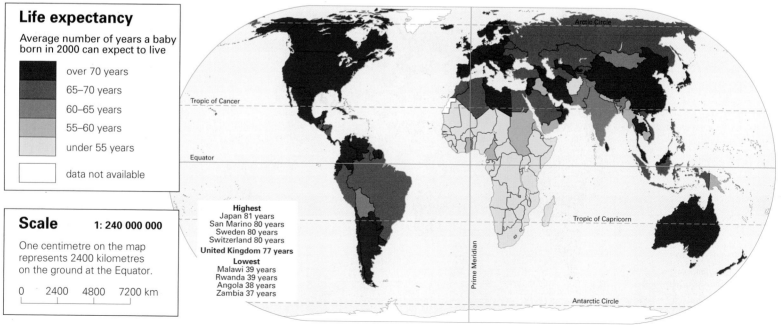

Highest
Japan 81 years
San Marino 80 years
Sweden 80 years
Switzerland 80 years
United Kingdom 77 years
Lowest
Malawi 39 years
Rwanda 39 years
Angola 38 years
Zambia 37 years

Scale

1: 240 000 000

One centimetre on the map represents 2400 kilometres on the ground at the Equator.

0   2400   4800   7200 km

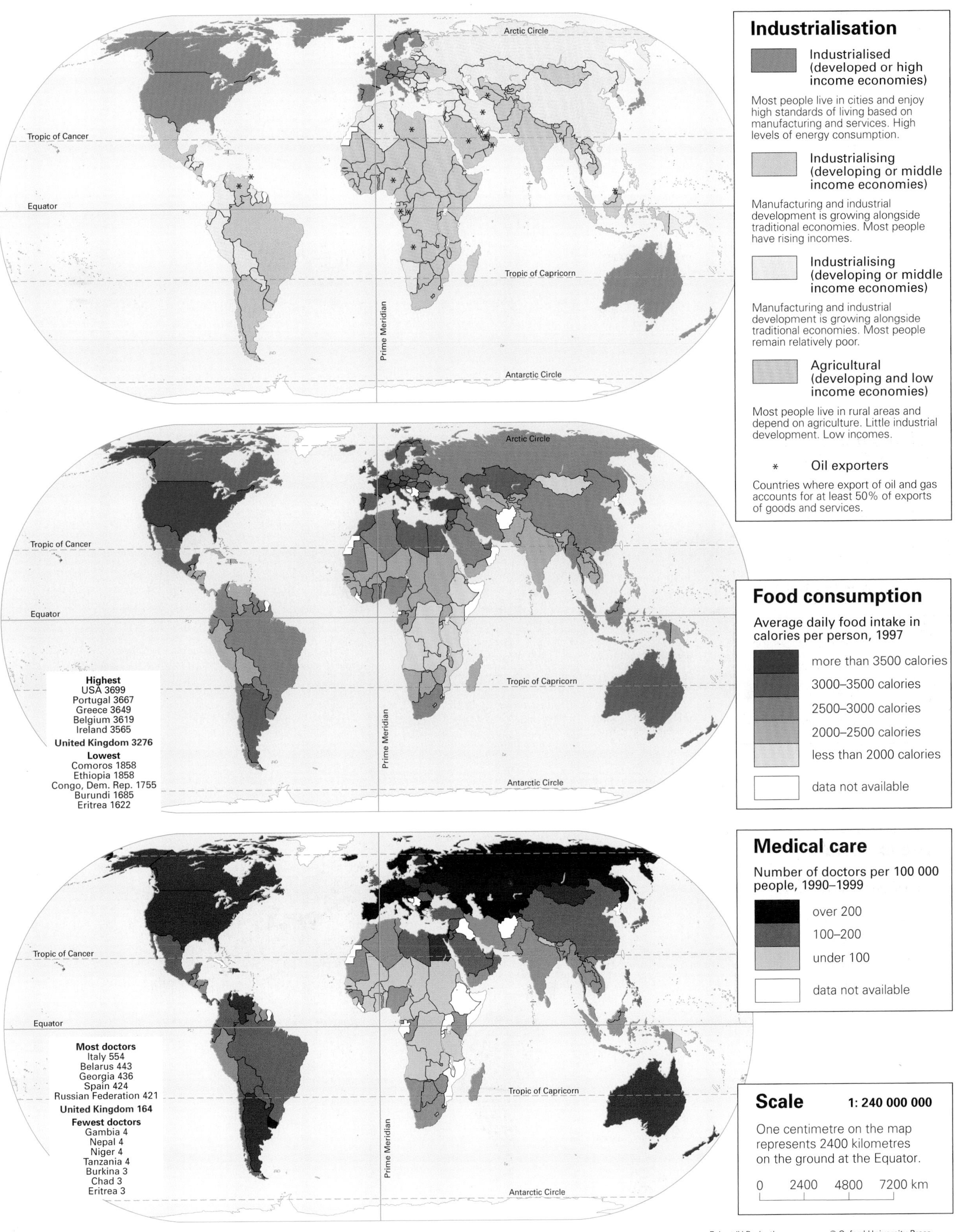

Industrialisation

Industrialised (developed or high income economies)

Most people live in cities and enjoy high standards of living based on manufacturing and services. High levels of energy consumption.

Industrialising (developing or middle income economies)

Manufacturing and industrial development is growing alongside traditional economies. Most people have rising incomes.

Industrialising (developing or middle income economies)

Manufacturing and industrial development is growing alongside traditional economies. Most people remain relatively poor.

Agricultural (developing and low income economies)

Most people live in rural areas and depend on agriculture. Little industrial development. Low incomes.

* Oil exporters

Countries where export of oil and gas accounts for at least 50% of exports of goods and services.

Highest
USA 3699
Portugal 3667
Greece 3649
Belgium 3619
Ireland 3565
United Kingdom 3276
Lowest
Comoros 1858
Ethiopia 1858
Congo, Dem. Rep. 1755
Burundi 1685
Eritrea 1622

Food consumption

Average daily food intake in calories per person, 1997

more than 3500 calories
3000–3500 calories
2500–3000 calories
2000–2500 calories
less than 2000 calories
data not available

Most doctors
Italy 554
Belarus 443
Georgia 436
Spain 424
Russian Federation 421
United Kingdom 164
Fewest doctors
Gambia 4
Nepal 4
Niger 4
Tanzania 4
Burkina 3
Chad 3
Eritrea 3

Medical care

Number of doctors per 100 000 people, 1990–1999

over 200
100–200
under 100
data not available

Scale   1: 240 000 000

One centimetre on the map represents 2400 kilometres on the ground at the Equator.

0   2400   4800   7200 km

Eckert IV Projection   © Oxford University Press

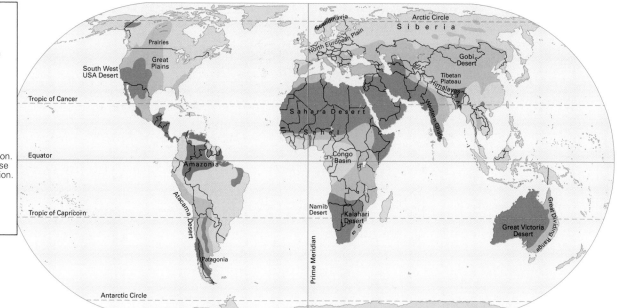

Water

Surplus

Enough water to support vegetation and crops without irrigation.

large surplus

surplus

Deficiency

Not enough water to support vegetation and crops without irrigation. After long periods of deficiency, these areas may lose their natural vegetation.

deficiency

chronic deficiency

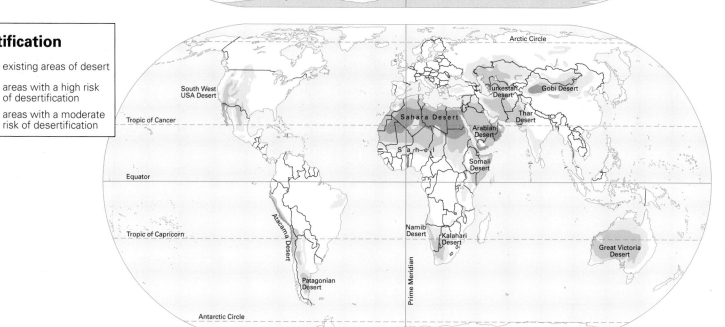

Desertification

existing areas of desert

areas with a high risk of desertification

areas with a moderate risk of desertification

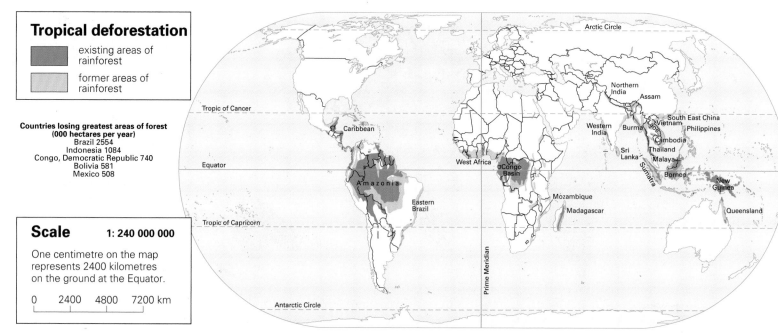

Tropical deforestation

existing areas of rainforest

former areas of rainforest

Countries losing greatest areas of forest
(000 hectares per year)
Brazil 2554
Indonesia 1084
Congo, Democratic Republic 740
Bolivia 581
Mexico 508

Scale   1: 240 000 000

One centimetre on the map represents 2400 kilometres on the ground at the Equator.

0   2400   4800   7200 km

Eckert IV Projection

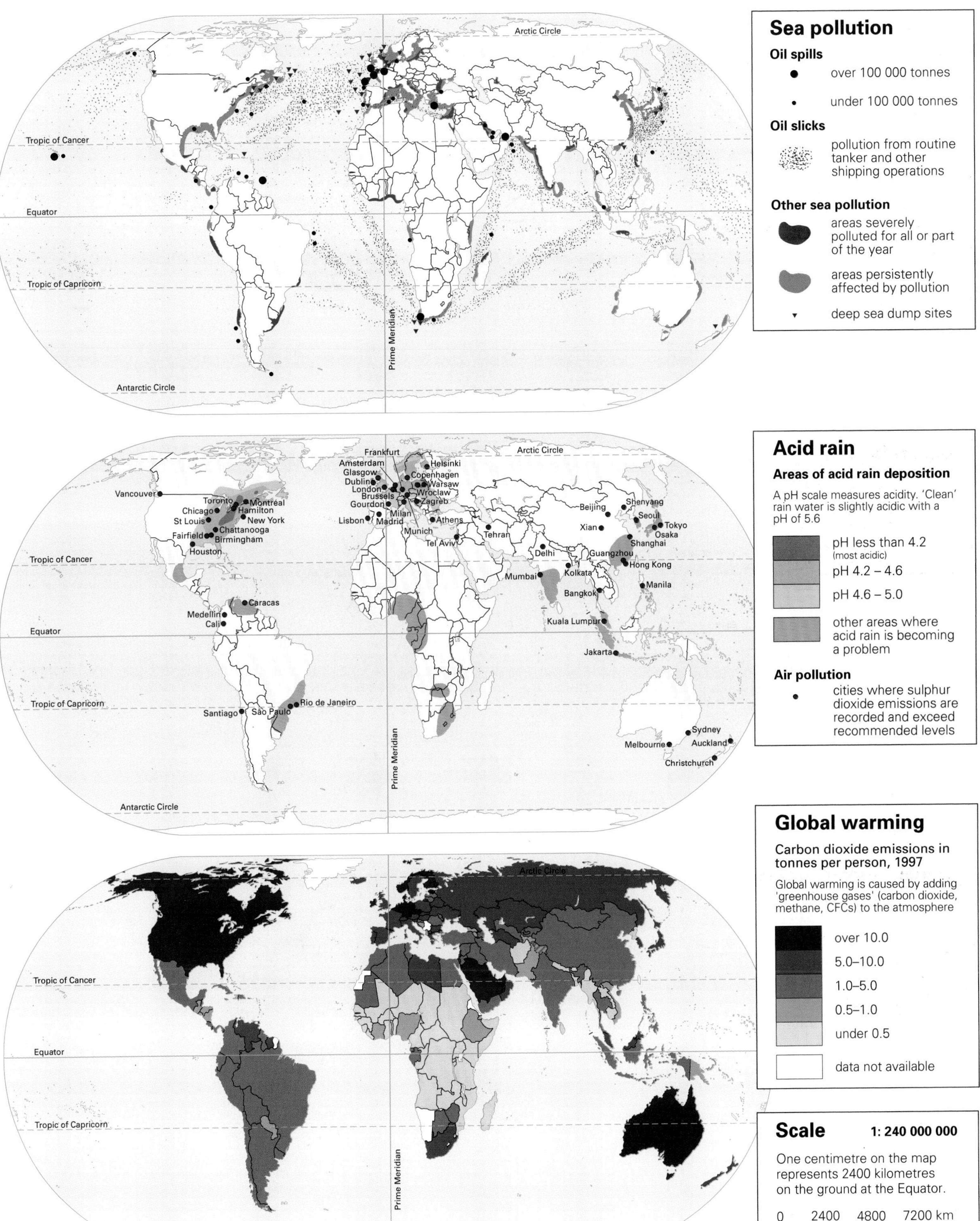

Sea pollution

Oil spills

●   over 100 000 tonnes

·   under 100 000 tonnes

Oil slicks

pollution from routine tanker and other shipping operations

Other sea pollution

areas severely polluted for all or part of the year

areas persistently affected by pollution

▼   deep sea dump sites

Acid rain

Areas of acid rain deposition

A pH scale measures acidity. 'Clean' rain water is slightly acidic with a pH of 5.6

pH less than 4.2 (most acidic)

pH 4.2 – 4.6

pH 4.6 – 5.0

other areas where acid rain is becoming a problem

Air pollution

·   cities where sulphur dioxide emissions are recorded and exceed recommended levels

Global warming

Carbon dioxide emissions in tonnes per person, 1997

Global warming is caused by adding 'greenhouse gases' (carbon dioxide, methane, CFCs) to the atmosphere

over 10.0

5.0–10.0

1.0–5.0

0.5–1.0

under 0.5

data not available

Scale   1: 240 000 000

One centimetre on the map represents 2400 kilometres on the ground at the Equator.

0   2400   4800   7200 km

Eckert IV Projection

© Oxford University Press

Key

- ·—·—·—· international boundary
- ------- national boundary

Scale

1: 4 500 000

One centimetre on the map represents
45 kilometres on the ground.

0   45   90   135   180 km

Key to districts in Northern Ireland

1	Belfast	14	Fermanagh
2	Newtownabbey	15	Omagh
3	Carrickfergus	16	Cookstown
4	Castlereagh	17	Magherafelt
5	North Down	18	Strabane
6	Ards	19	Londonderry
7	Down	20	Limavady
8	Newry & Mourne	21	Coleraine
9	Banbridge	22	Ballymoney
10	Lisburn	23	Moyle
11	Craigavon	24	Ballymena
12	Armagh	25	Larne
13	Dungannon	26	Antrim

Key to unitary authorities in Scotland

1	West Dunbartonshire	9	Falkirk
2	East Dunbartonshire	10	West Lothian
3	North Lanarkshire	11	City of Edinburgh
4	Glasgow City	12	Midlothian
5	East Renfrewshire	13	East Lothian
6	Renfrewshire	14	North Ayrshire
7	Inverclyde	15	East Ayrshire
8	Clackmannanshire	16	Dundee City

United Kingdom

Republic of Ireland

England is divided into counties
and some new unitary authorities.
Wales and Scotland are divided
into unitary authorities.
Northern Ireland is divided
into districts.

The Republic of Ireland is
divided into counties.

Key to unitary authorities in Wales

1	Cardiff	8	Caerphilly
2	The Vale of Glamorgan	9	Blaenau Gwent
3	Bridgend	10	Monmouthshire
4	Swansea	11	Conwy
5	Neath Port Talbot	12	Denbighshire
6	Rhondda Cynon Taff	13	Flintshire
7	Merthyr Tydfil	14	Wrexham

Key to unitary authorities in England

1	Hartlepool	10	Bristol
2	Stockton-on-Tees	11	North Somerset
3	Middlesbrough	12	Bath and North East Somerset
4	Redcar and Cleveland	13	Luton
5	East Riding of Yorkshire	14	Milton Keynes
6	City of Kingston upon Hull	15	Leicester City
7	North Lincolnshire	16	Swindon
8	North East Lincolnshire	17	Windsor & Maidenhead
9	South Gloucestershire		

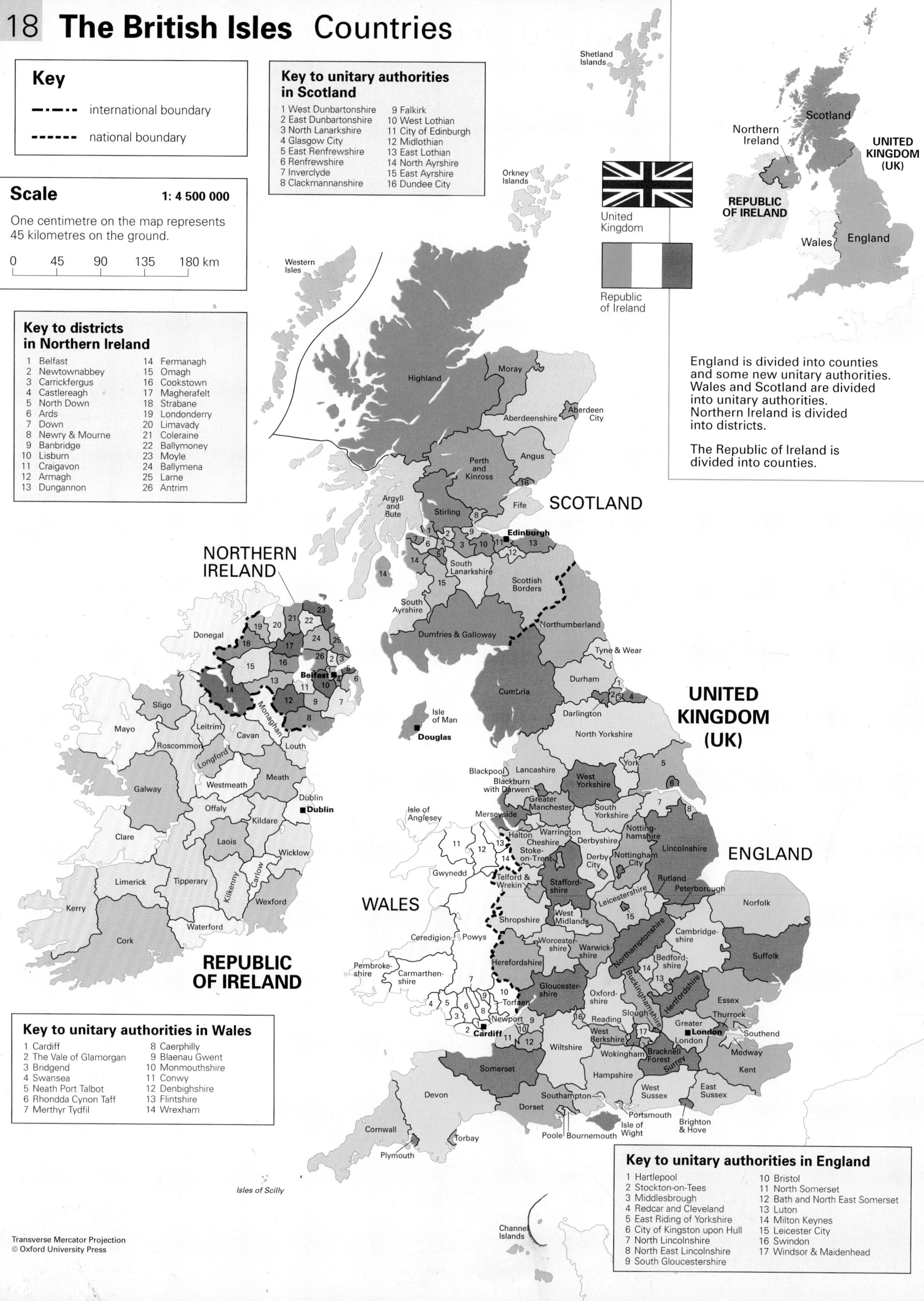

Transverse Mercator Projection
© Oxford University Press

The British Isles Land and Water

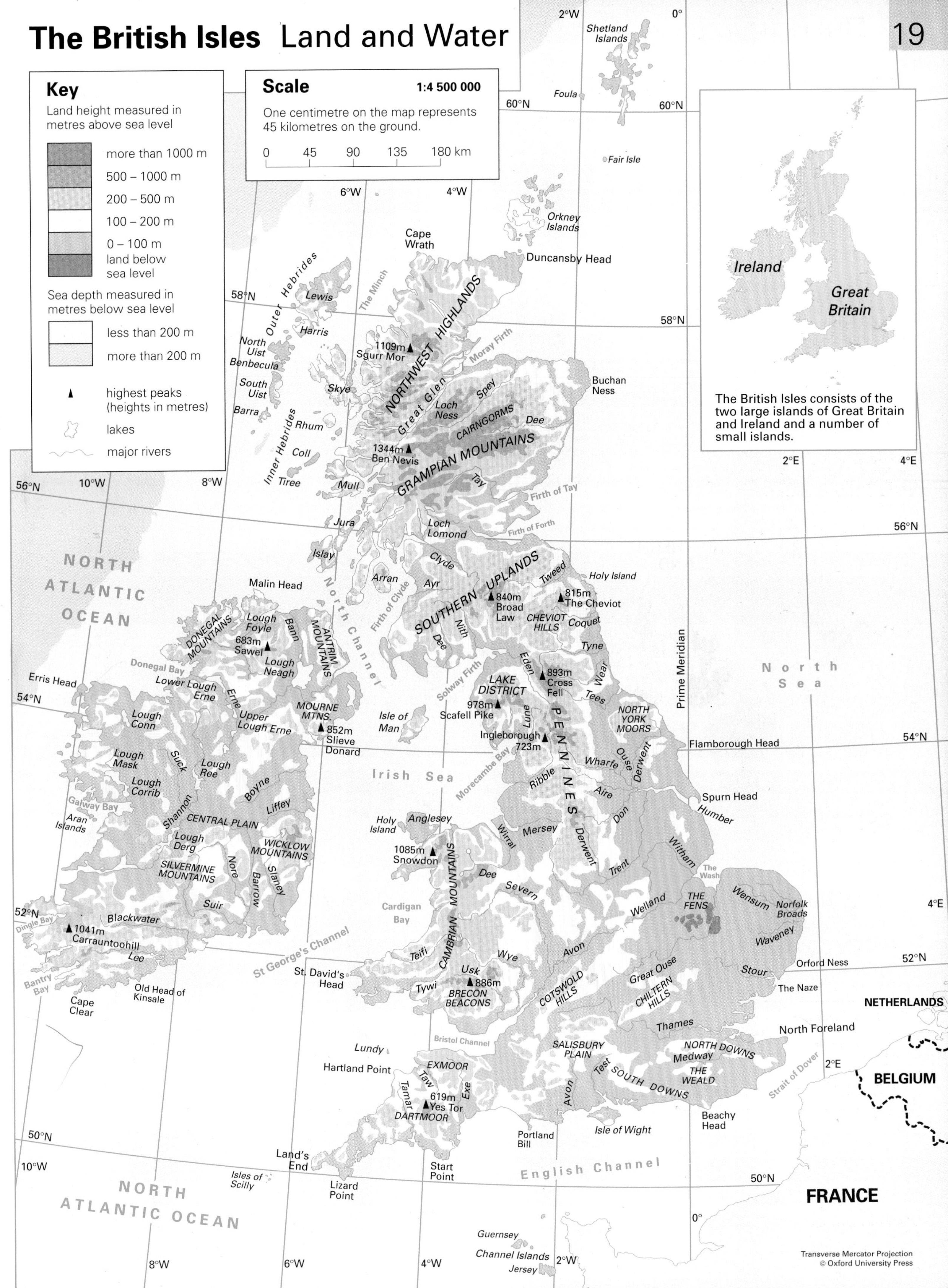

Key

Land height measured in metres above sea level

- more than 1000 m
- 500 – 1000 m
- 200 – 500 m
- 100 – 200 m
- 0 – 100 m
- land below sea level

Sea depth measured in metres below sea level

- less than 200 m
- more than 200 m

▲ highest peaks (heights in metres)

lakes

major rivers

Scale   1:4 500 000

One centimetre on the map represents 45 kilometres on the ground.

0   45   90   135   180 km

The British Isles consists of the two large islands of Great Britain and Ireland and a number of small islands.

Ireland   *Great Britain*

Transverse Mercator Projection
© Oxford University Press

Average surface temperature

- 16–18°C
- 14–16°C
- 12–14°C
- 10–12°C
- 8–10°C
- 6–8°C
- 4–6°C
- 2–4°C
- 0–2°C
- –2–0°C

• climate recording stations for which graphs are shown

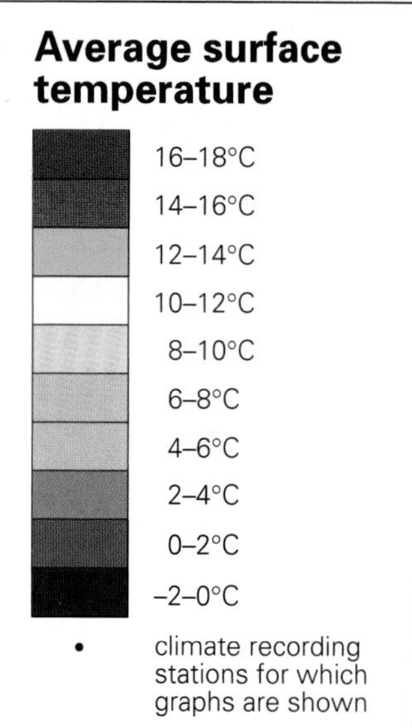

Scale   1: 8 000 000

One centimetre on the map represents 80 kilometres on the ground.

0   80   160   240 km

January temperature

Edinburgh (134m)

Belfast (17m)

Cambridge (12m)

Cardiff (61m)

July temperature

Edinburgh (134m)

Belfast (17m)

Cambridge (12m)

Cardiff (61m)

Belfast (17m)
Temperature in degrees Celsius
Rainfall in millimetres
J F M A M J J A S O N D

Edinburgh (134m)
Temperature in degrees Celsius
Rainfall in millimetres
J F M A M J J A S O N D

Cardiff (61m)
Temperature in degrees Celsius
Rainfall in millimetres
J F M A M J J A S O N D

Cambridge (12m)
Temperature in degrees Celsius
Rainfall in millimetres
J F M A M J J A S O N D

Transverse Mercator Projection
© Oxford University Press

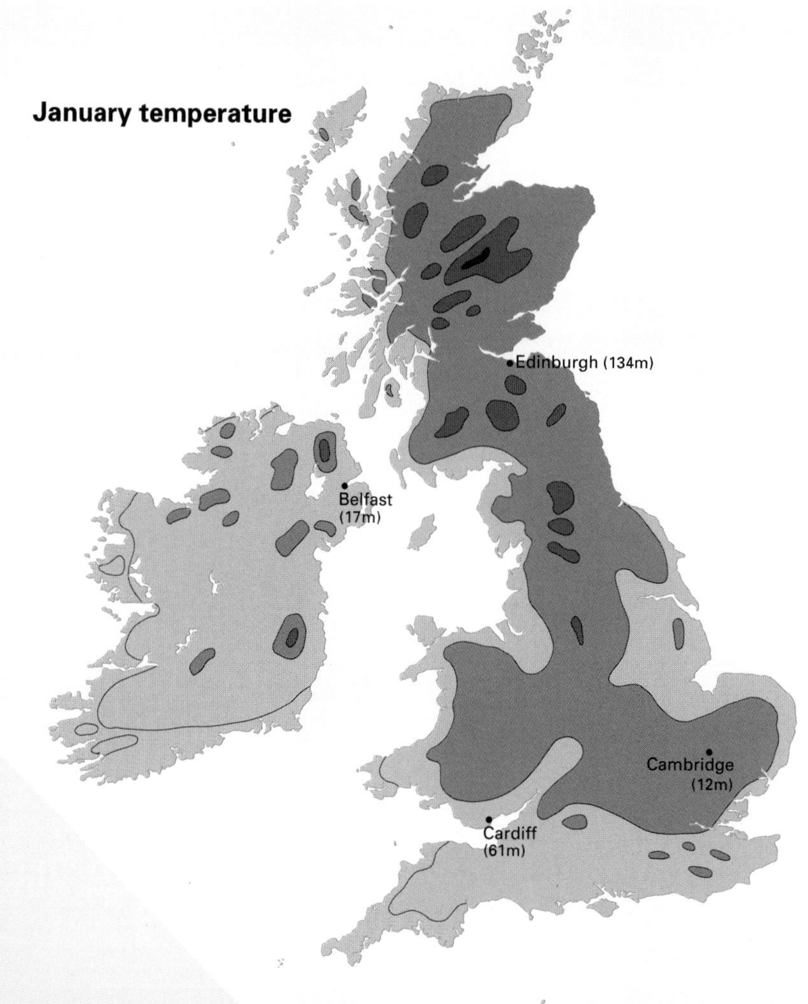

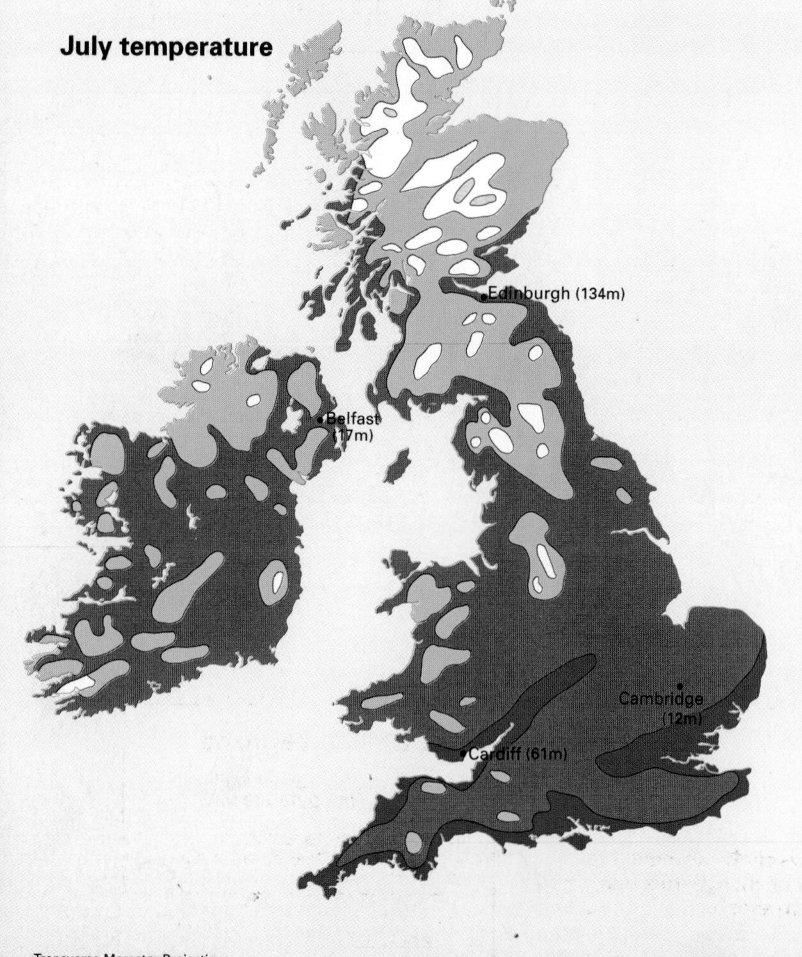

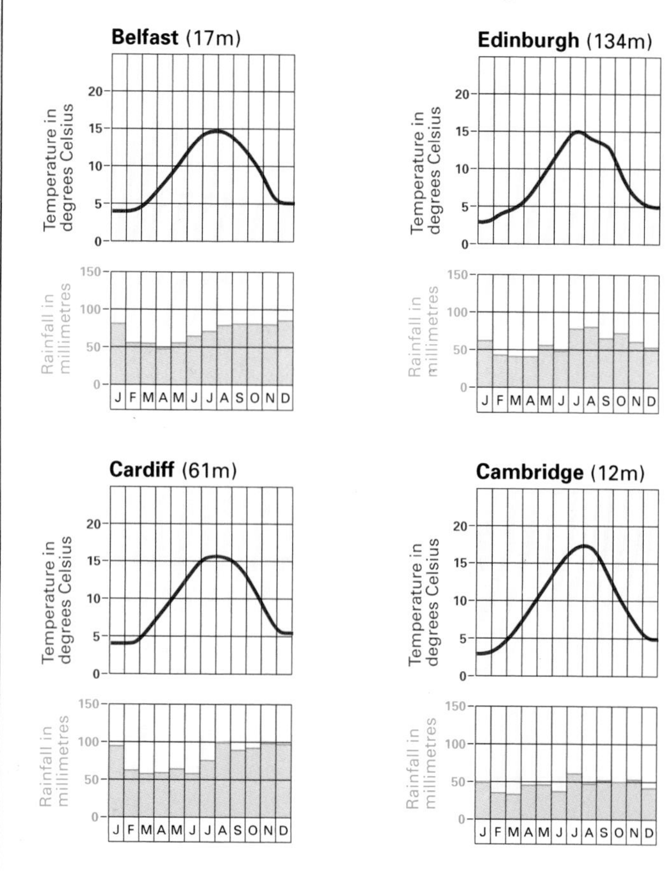

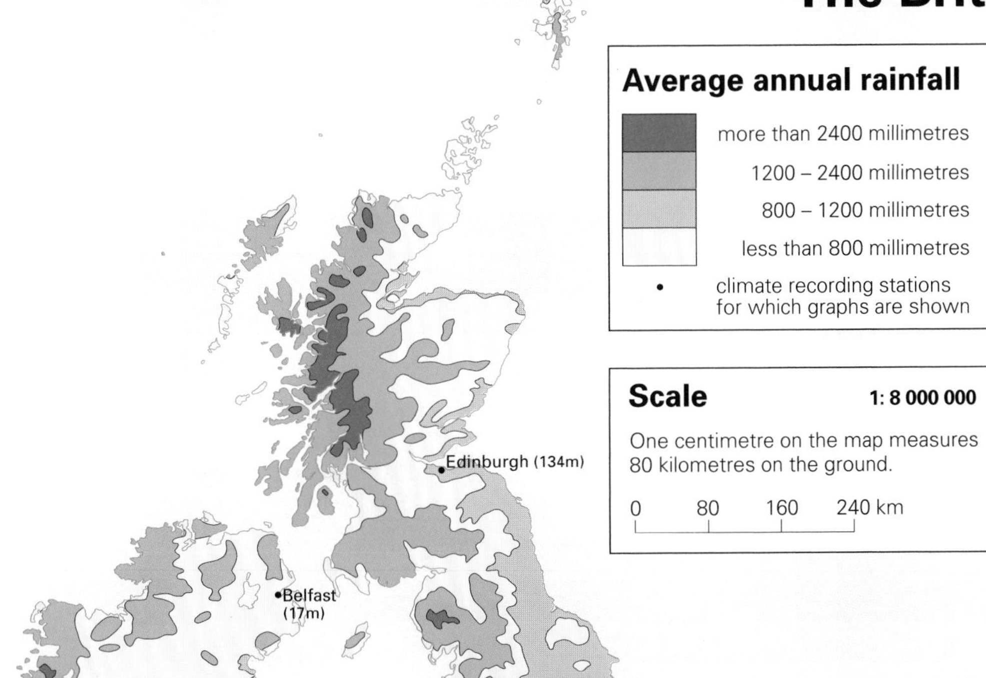

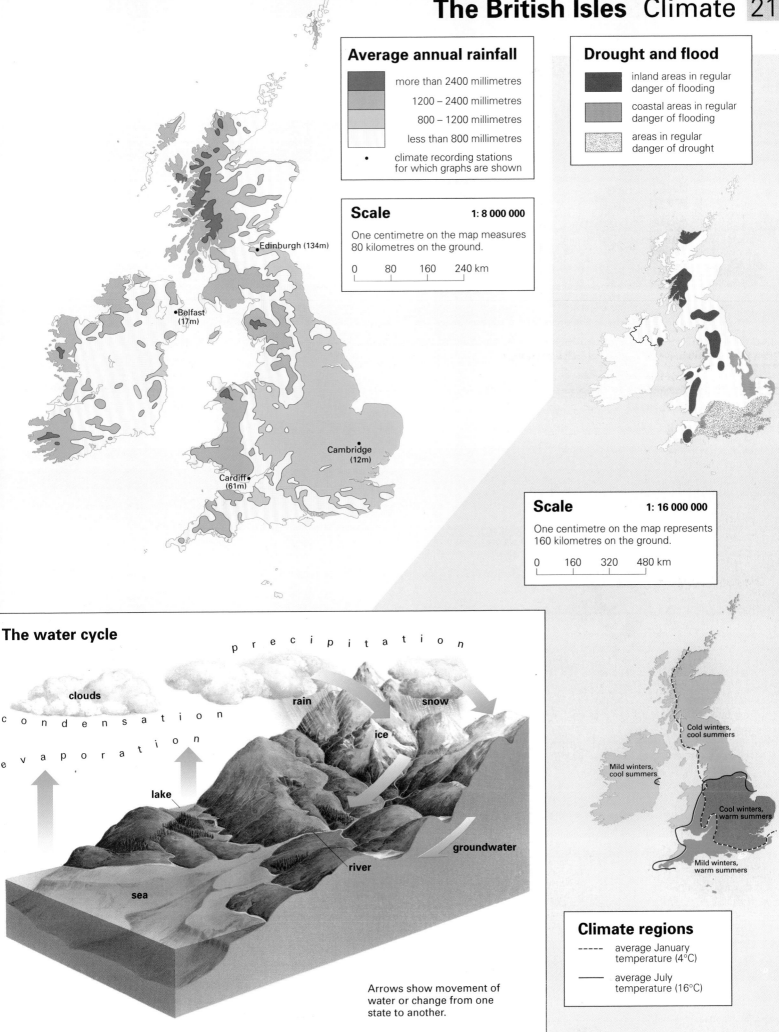

Average annual rainfall

- more than 2400 millimetres
- 1200 – 2400 millimetres
- 800 – 1200 millimetres
- less than 800 millimetres
- • climate recording stations for which graphs are shown

Drought and flood

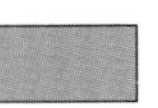

- inland areas in regular danger of flooding
- coastal areas in regular danger of flooding
- areas in regular danger of drought

Scale 1: 8 000 000

One centimetre on the map measures 80 kilometres on the ground.

0   80   160   240 km

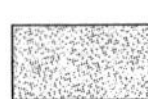

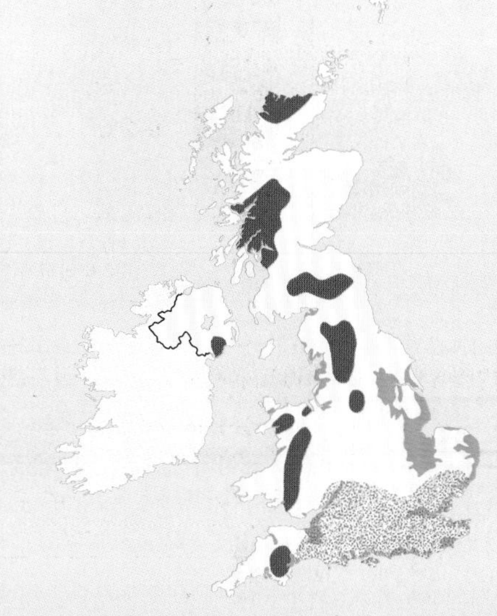

Scale 1: 16 000 000

One centimetre on the map represents 160 kilometres on the ground.

0   160   320   480 km

•Edinburgh (134m)

•Belfast (17m)

Cambridge (12m)

Cardiff• (61m)

The water cycle

precipitation

clouds

condensation

evaporation

rain

snow

ice

lake

groundwater

river

sea

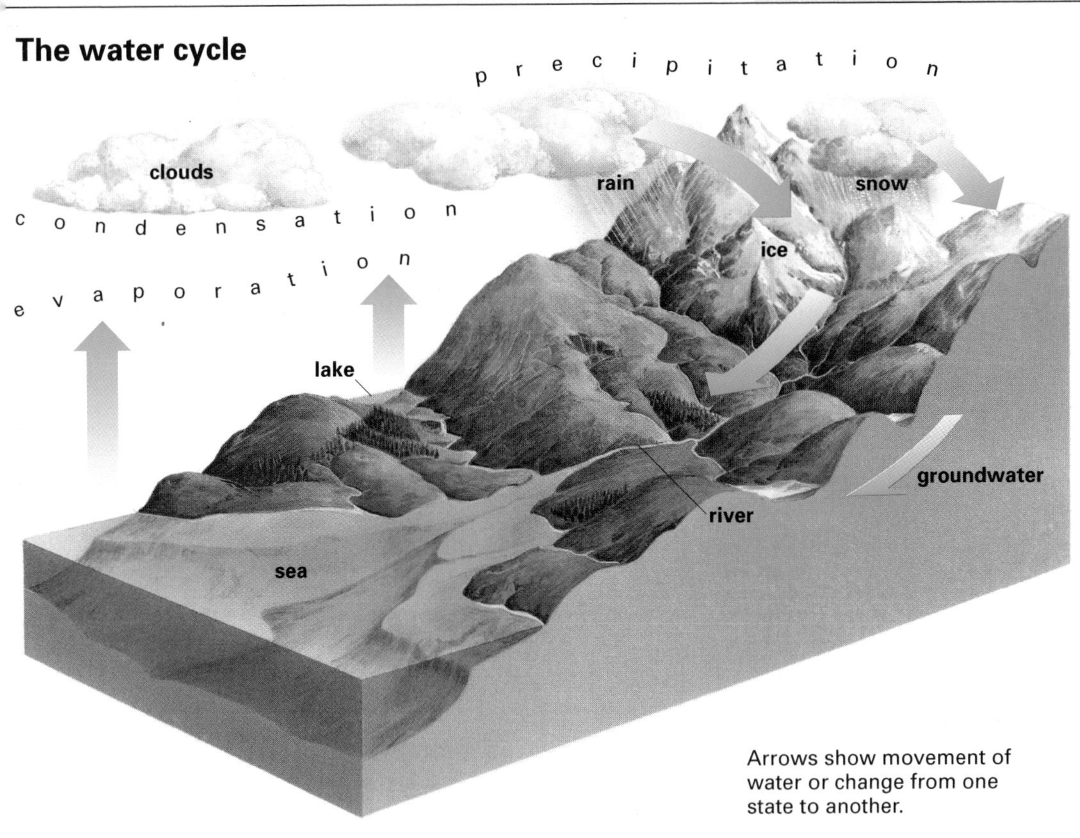

Arrows show movement of water or change from one state to another.

Cold winters, cool summers

Mild winters, cool summers

Cool winters, warm summers

Mild winters, warm summers

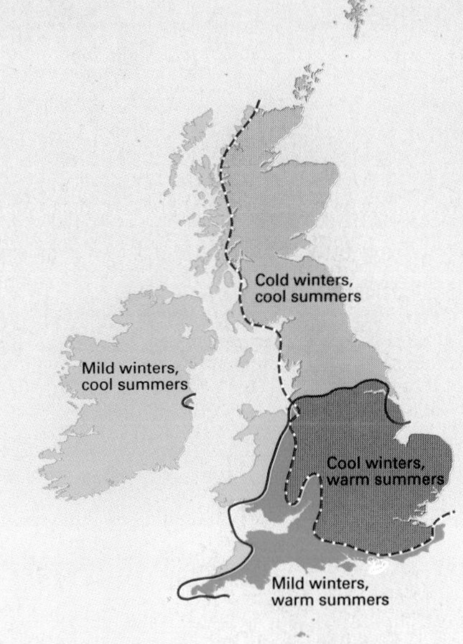

Climate regions

----- average January temperature (4°C)

——— average July temperature (16°C)

Transverse Mercator Projection
© Oxford University Press

Population structure of the United Kingdom

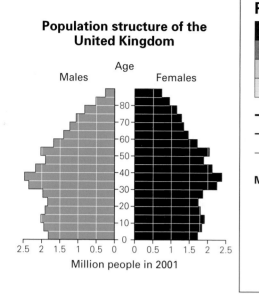

Age

Males   Females

80
70
60
50
40
30
20
10
0

2.5 2 1.5 1 0.5 0 | 0 0.5 1 1.5 2 2.5

Million people in 2001

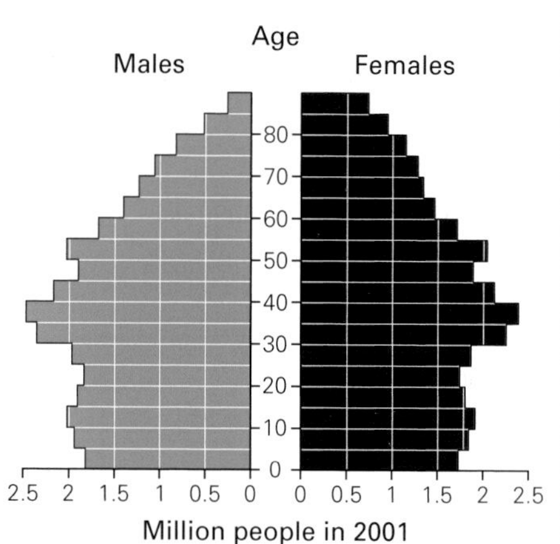

Population density

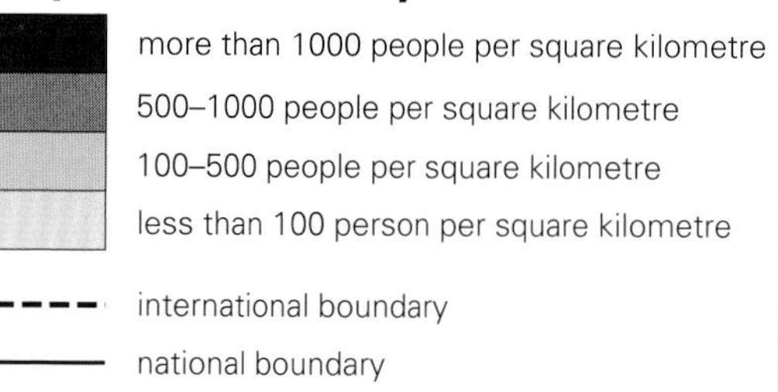

■ more than 1000 people per square kilometre
■ 500–1000 people per square kilometre
■ 100–500 people per square kilometre
□ less than 100 person per square kilometre

- - - - international boundary
―――― national boundary
―――― county, unitary authority, or district boundary

Major cities

● with more than 6 million people
● with 1 million people
• with between 400 000 and 1 million people
· with between 100 000 and 400 000 people

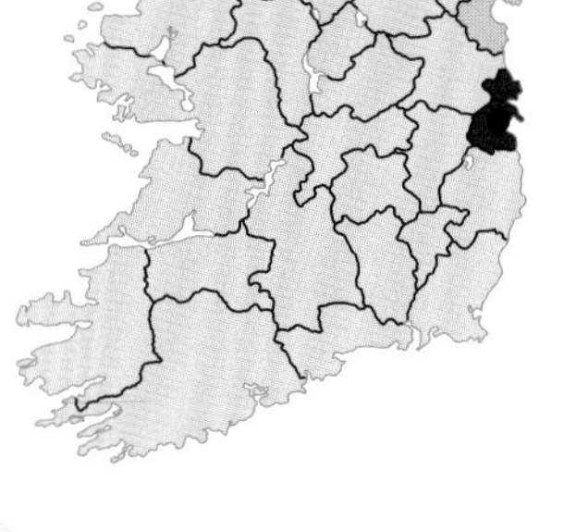

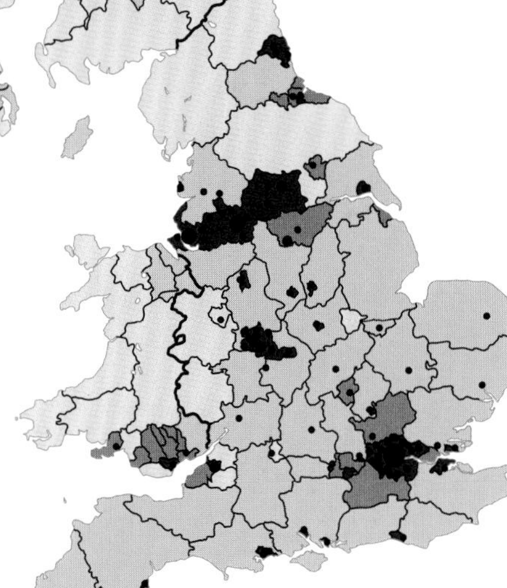

Scale   1: 8 000 000

One centimetre on the map represents 80 kilometres on the ground.

0   80   160   240 km

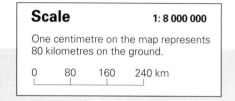

British Isles population data

United Kingdom	Overall population density 243 people per square kilometre
Republic of Ireland	Overall population density 54 people per square kilometre

Total population 2001

England	50.0 million people
Wales	2.9 million people
Scotland	5.1 million people
Northern Ireland	1.7 million people
United Kingdom	59.7 million people
Republic of Ireland	3.8 million people

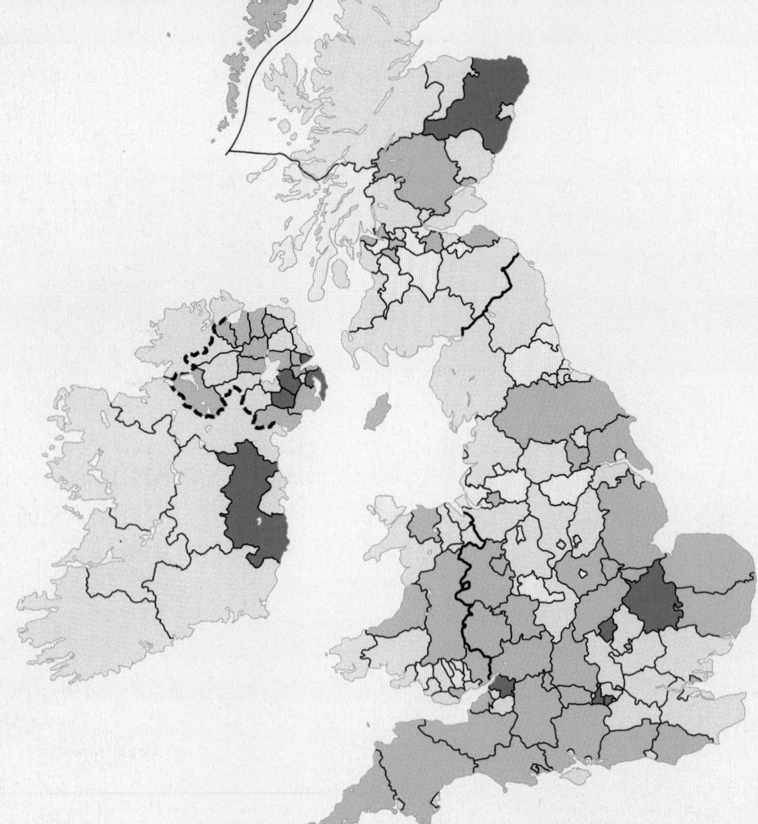

Population change

Change in population in each county, region or district, 1981 – 1999

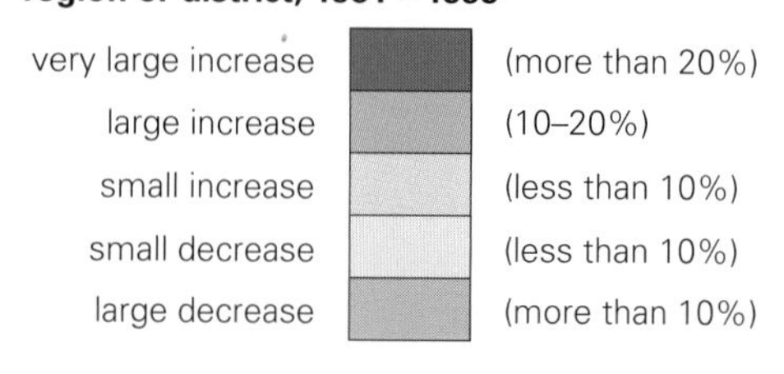

very large increase	■	(more than 20%)
large increase	■	(10–20%)
small increase	■	(less than 10%)
small decrease	□	(less than 10%)
large decrease	■	(more than 10%)

- - - - international boundary
―――― national boundary
―――― county, unitary authority, or district boundary

Transverse Mercator Projection
© Oxford University Press

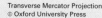

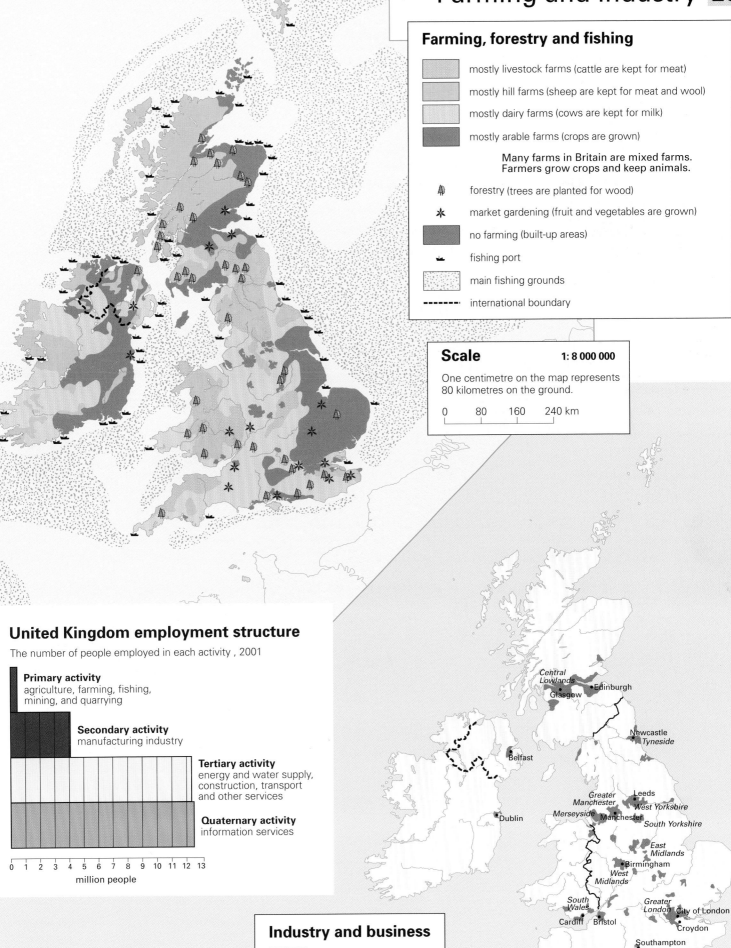

Farming, forestry and fishing

mostly livestock farms (cattle are kept for meat)

mostly hill farms (sheep are kept for meat and wool)

mostly dairy farms (cows are kept for milk)

mostly arable farms (crops are grown)

Many farms in Britain are mixed farms. Farmers grow crops and keep animals.

forestry (trees are planted for wood)

market gardening (fruit and vegetables are grown)

no farming (built-up areas)

fishing port

main fishing grounds

- - - - - international boundary

Scale

1: 8 000 000

One centimetre on the map represents 80 kilometres on the ground.

0   80   160   240 km

United Kingdom employment structure

The number of people employed in each activity , 2001

Primary activity
agriculture, farming, fishing, mining, and quarrying

Secondary activity
manufacturing industry

Tertiary activity
energy and water supply, construction, transport and other services

Quaternary activity
information services

0 1 2 3 4 5 6 7 8 9 10 11 12 13
million people

Industry and business

major industrial area

office and business centre

- - - - - international boundary

——— national boundary

Central Lowlands
Glasgow
Edinburgh
Belfast
Newcastle
Tyneside
Dublin
Greater Manchester
Merseyside
Manchester
Leeds
West Yorkshire
South Yorkshire
East Midlands
Birmingham
West Midlands
South Wales
Cardiff
Bristol
Greater London
City of London
Croydon
Southampton

Transverse Mercator Projection
© Oxford University Press

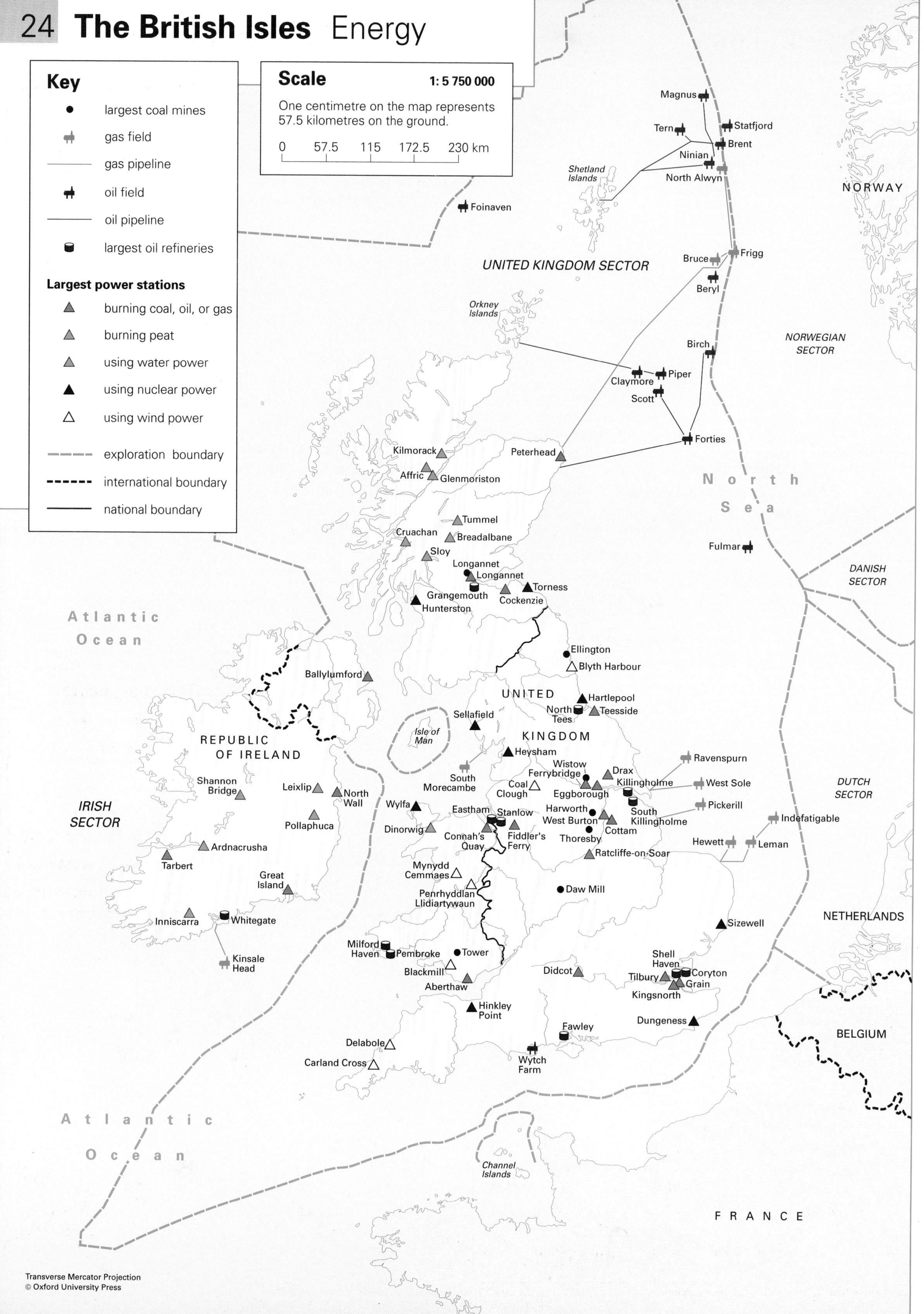

Key

- ● largest coal mines
- ⛏ gas field
- — gas pipeline
- ⛏ oil field
- — oil pipeline
- ⬤ largest oil refineries

Largest power stations

- ▲ burning coal, oil, or gas
- ▲ burning peat
- ▲ using water power
- ▲ using nuclear power
- △ using wind power

- – – – exploration boundary
- ▪▪▪▪ international boundary
- —— national boundary

Scale   1: 5 750 000

One centimetre on the map represents 57.5 kilometres on the ground.

0   57.5   115   172.5   230 km

UNITED KINGDOM SECTOR

Magnus
Tern
Statfjord
Brent
Ninian
North Alwyn
Shetland Islands
NORWAY

Foinaven

Bruce
Frigg
Beryl

Orkney Islands

NORWEGIAN SECTOR

Birch
Claymore
Piper
Scott

Kilmorack
Affric
Glenmoriston
Peterhead
Forties

North Sea

Tummel
Cruachan
Breadalbane
Sloy
Longannet
Longannet
Torness
Grangemouth
Cockenzie
Hunterston

Fulmar

DANISH SECTOR

Atlantic Ocean

Ballylumford

Ellington
Blyth Harbour

UNITED

Sellafield
Isle of Man

KINGDOM

Hartlepool
North Tees
Teesside

REPUBLIC OF IRELAND

Heysham

Ravenspurn

Shannon Bridge
Leixlip
North Wall
South Morecambe
Wistow
Ferrybridge
Drax
Killingholme
West Sole

IRISH SECTOR

Pollaphuca
Wylfa
Eastham
Stanlow
Coal Clough
Eggborough
Harworth
West Burton
Cottam
South Killingholme
Pickerill

Ardnacrusha
Dinorwig
Connah's Quay
Fiddler's Ferry
Thoresby
Ratcliffe-on-Soar
Hewett
Leman
Indefatigable

DUTCH SECTOR

Tarbert

Great Island
Mynydd Cemmaes
Daw Mill
Inniscarra
Whitegate
Penrhyddlan Llidiartywaun
Sizewell

NETHERLANDS

Kinsale Head
Milford Haven
Pembroke
Tower
Shell Haven
Tilbury
Coryton
Grain
Blackmill
Didcot
Kingsnorth

Aberthaw
Hinkley Point
Fawley
Dungeness

BELGIUM

Delabole
Carland Cross
Wytch Farm

Atlantic Ocean

Channel Islands

FRANCE

The British Isles

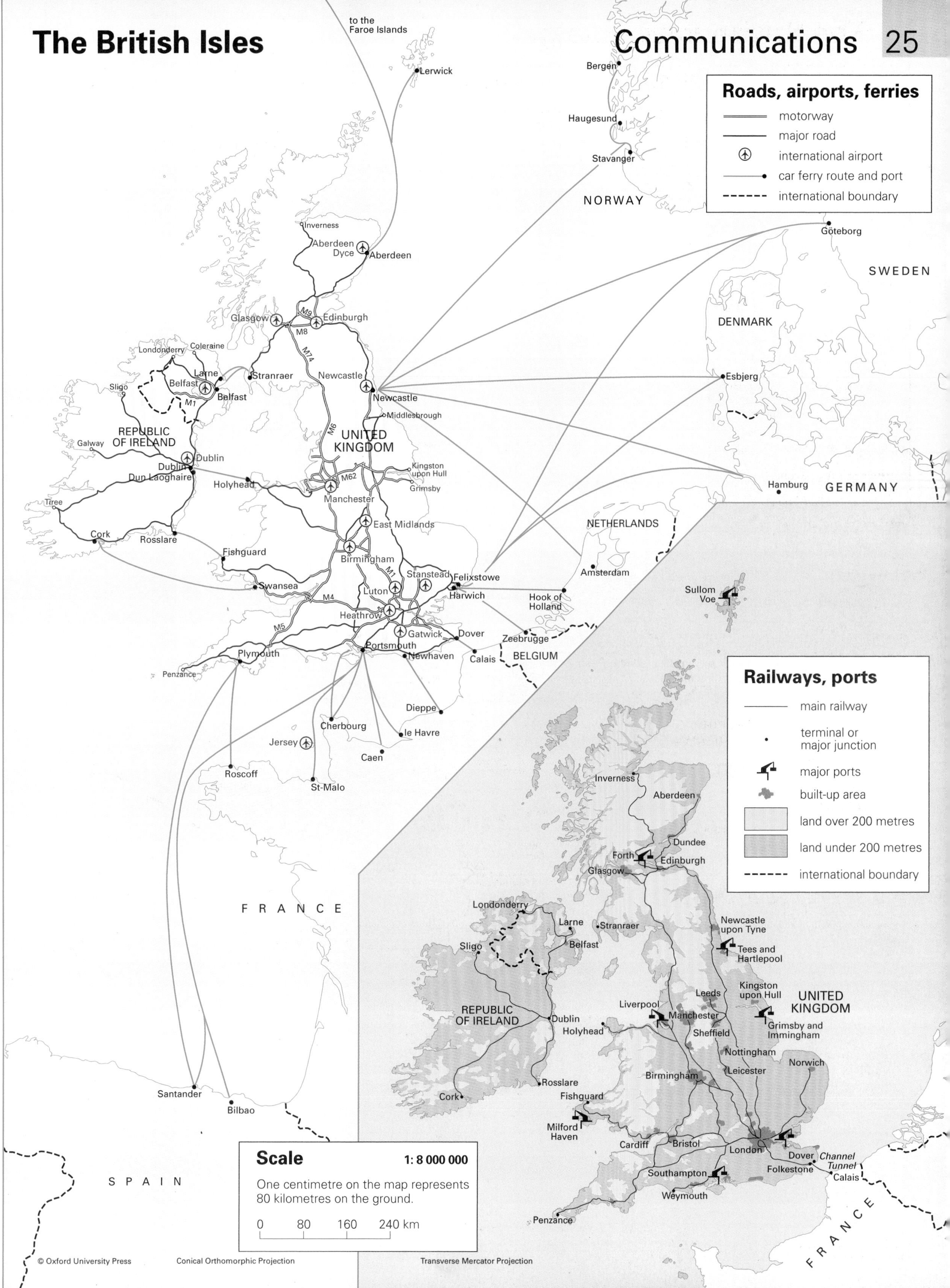

Roads, airports, ferries

	motorway
	major road
✈	international airport
●—	car ferry route and port
---	international boundary

Railways, ports

	main railway
•	terminal or major junction
⚓	major ports
	built-up area
	land over 200 metres
	land under 200 metres
---	international boundary

Scale   1 : 8 000 000

One centimetre on the map represents
80 kilometres on the ground.

0   80   160   240 km

© Oxford University Press   Conical Orthomorphic Projection   Transverse Mercator Projection

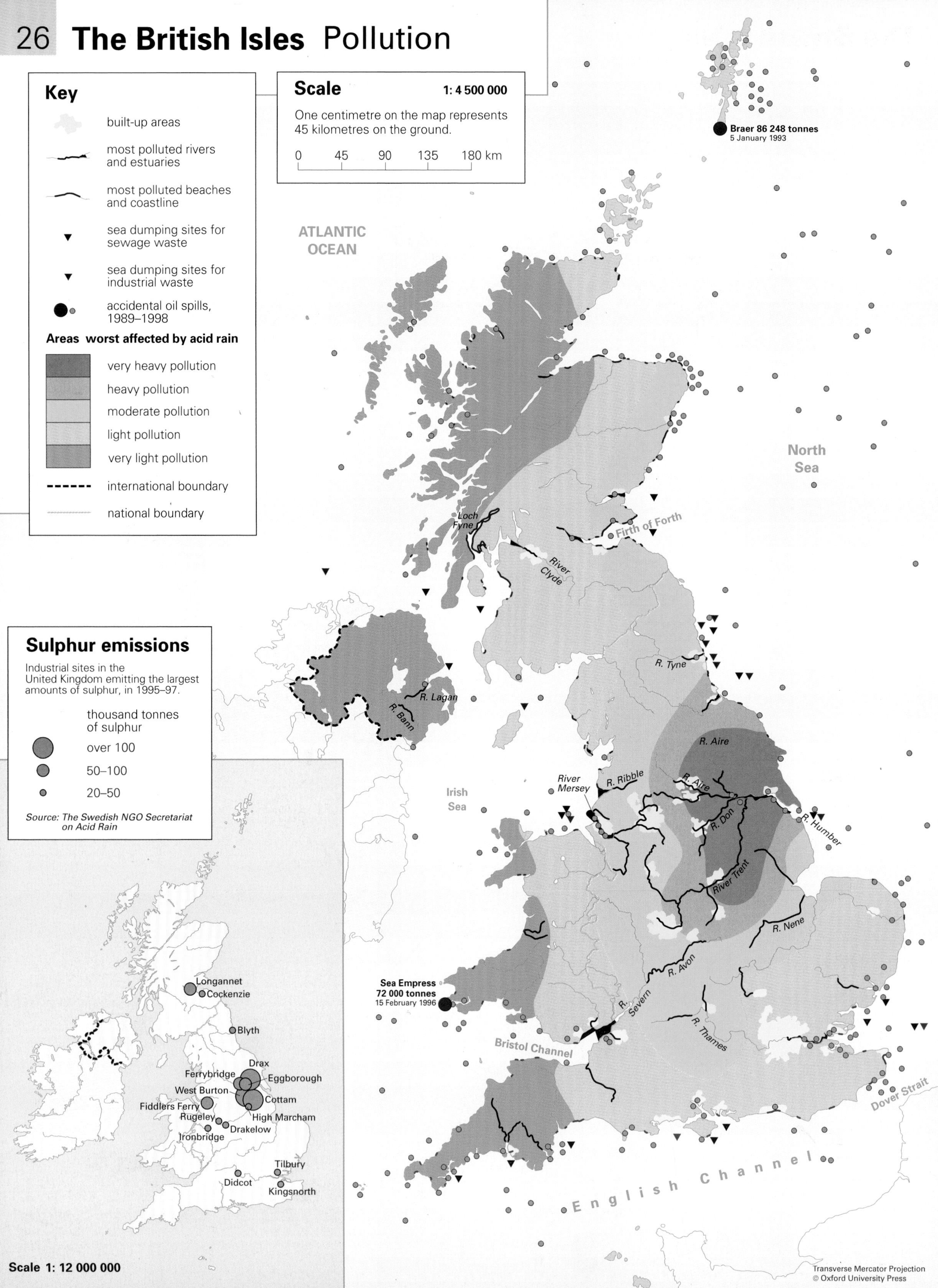

Key

- built-up areas
- most polluted rivers and estuaries
- most polluted beaches and coastline
- ▼ sea dumping sites for sewage waste
- ▼ sea dumping sites for industrial waste
- ● ○ accidental oil spills, 1989–1998

Areas worst affected by acid rain

- very heavy pollution
- heavy pollution
- moderate pollution
- light pollution
- very light pollution
- ----- international boundary
- ········ national boundary

Scale

1: 4 500 000

One centimetre on the map represents 45 kilometres on the ground.

| 0 | 45 | 90 | 135 | 180 km |

Sulphur emissions

Industrial sites in the United Kingdom emitting the largest amounts of sulphur, in 1995–97.

thousand tonnes of sulphur

- ⬤ over 100
- ● 50–100
- • 20–50

Source: The Swedish NGO Secretariat on Acid Rain

Scale 1: 12 000 000

Longannet
Cockenzie
Blyth
Drax
Ferrybridge
Eggborough
West Burton
Cottam
Fiddlers Ferry
High Marcham
Rugeley
Drakelow
Ironbridge
Tilbury
Didcot
Kingsnorth

ATLANTIC OCEAN

Braer 86 248 tonnes
5 January 1993

North Sea

Loch Fyne
Firth of Forth
River Clyde
R. Tyne
R. Lagan
R. Bann
R. Aire
River Mersey
R. Ribble
R. Aire
River Trent
R. Don
R. Humber
R. Nene
Irish Sea
R. Avon
R. Severn
R. Thames
Dover Strait

Sea Empress 72 000 tonnes
15 February 1996

Bristol Channel

English Channel

Transverse Mercator Projection
© Oxford University Press

National Parks

National Park
land over 200 metres
land under 200 metres
major built-up area
international boundary
national boundary

World Heritage Sites

Sites and monuments of world-wide natural (★) and cultural heritage (★), considered to be of such exceptional interest and value that their protection is agreed by international cooperation.

Scale 1: 8 000 000

One centimetre on the map represents 80 kilometres on the ground.

0 80 160 240 km

Other protected areas

Areas of Outstanding Natural Beauty (England, Wales, Northern Ireland); National Scenic Areas (Scotland)

Heritage Coast (England and Wales); Coastal Conservation Zones (Scotland); Conservation designated coast (Northern Ireland);

major built-up area

international boundary

national boundary

Transverse Mercator Projection

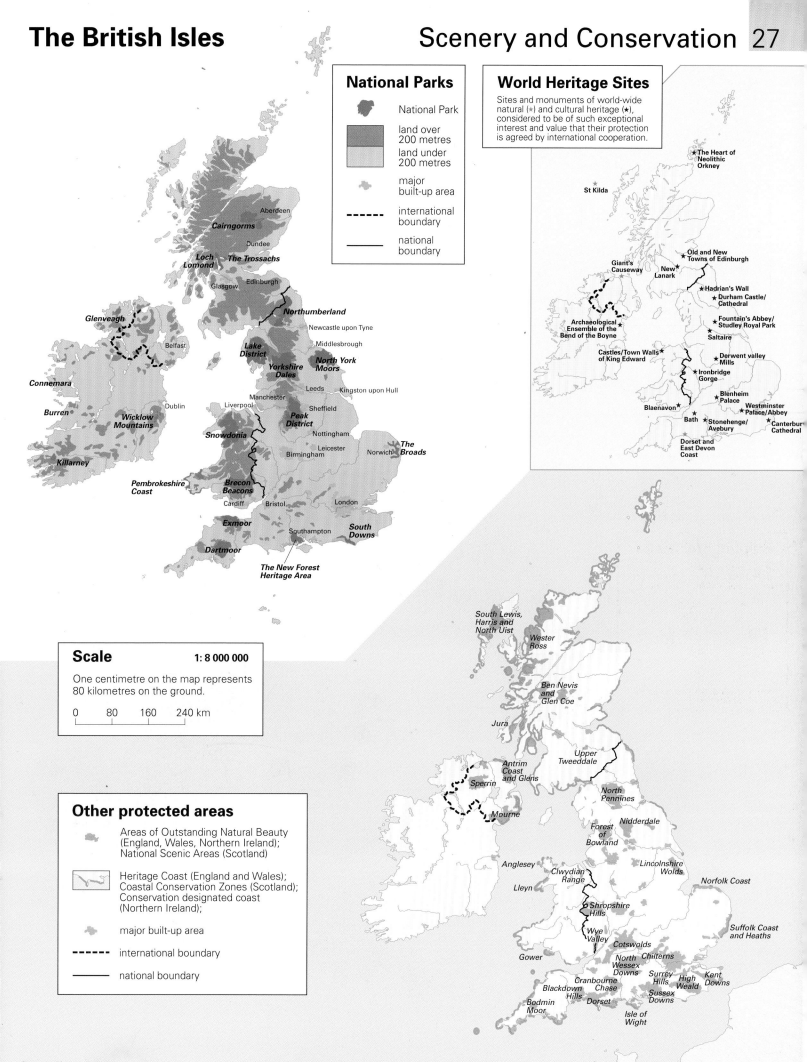

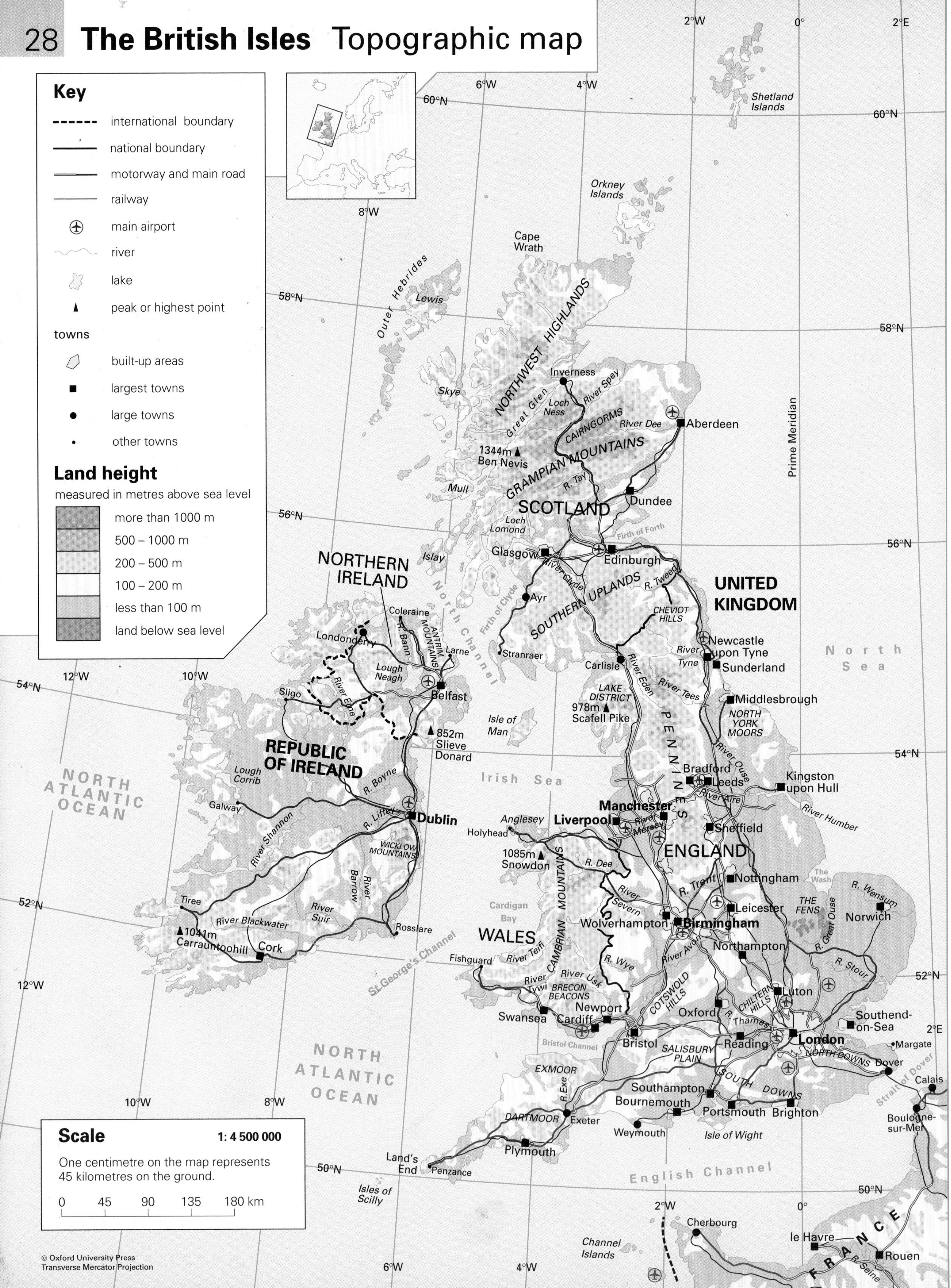

Key

- – – – – international boundary
- ———— national boundary
- motorway and main road
- ———— railway
- ✈ main airport
- ~~~ river
- lake
- ▲ peak or highest point

towns

- built-up areas
- ■ largest towns
- ● large towns
- • other towns

Land height

measured in metres above sea level

- more than 1000 m
- 500 – 1000 m
- 200 – 500 m
- 100 – 200 m
- less than 100 m
- land below sea level

Scale 1: 4 500 000

One centimetre on the map represents 45 kilometres on the ground.

0   45   90   135   180 km

© Oxford University Press
Transverse Mercator Projection

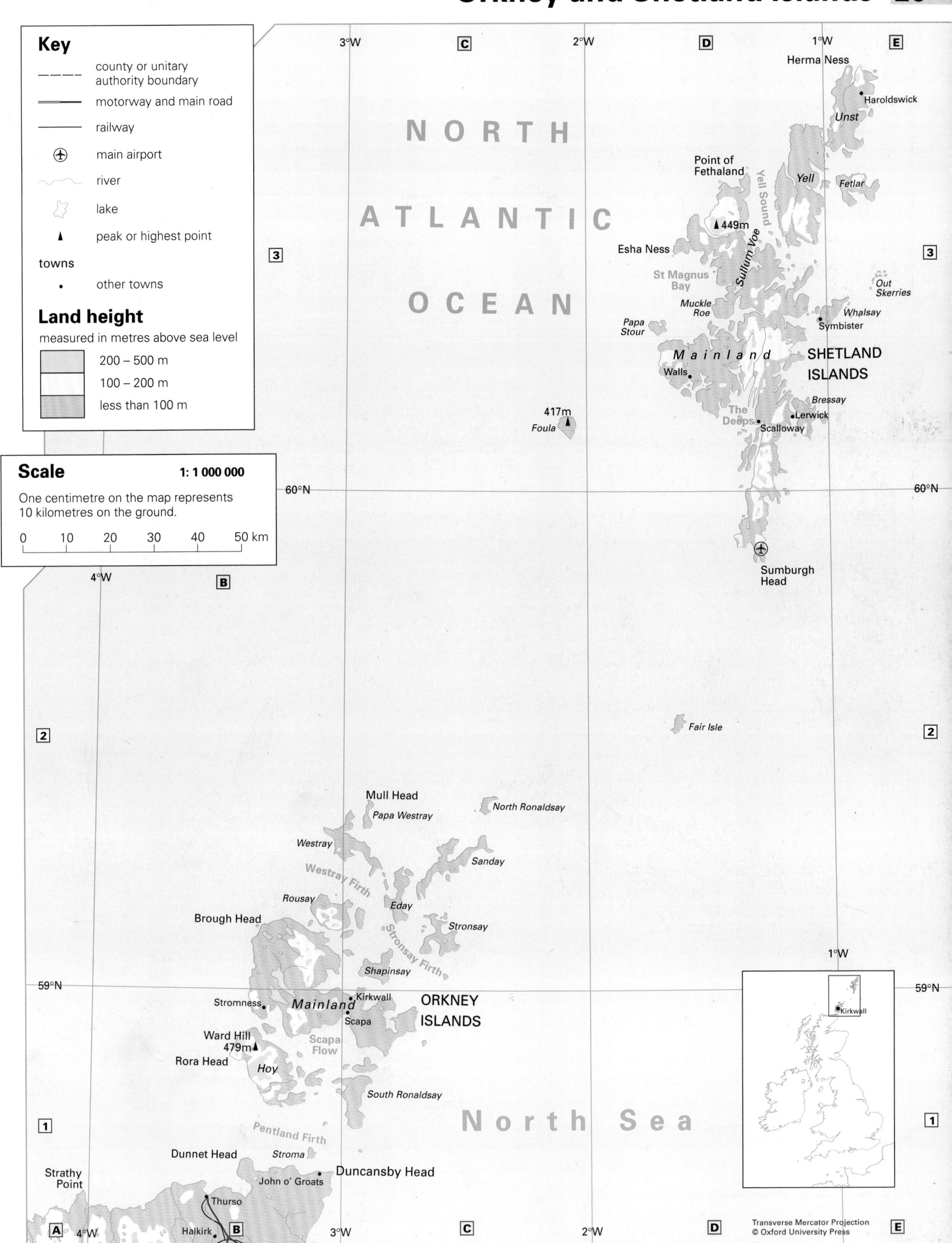

Key

- - - - county or unitary authority boundary

───── motorway and main road

──A── railway

⊕ main airport

river

lake

▲ peak or highest point

towns

• other towns

Land height

measured in metres above sea level

200 – 500 m
100 – 200 m
less than 100 m

Scale   1: 1 000 000

One centimetre on the map represents
10 kilometres on the ground.

0 10 20 30 40 50 km

NORTH ATLANTIC OCEAN

SHETLAND ISLANDS

Herma Ness
Haroldswick
Unst
Point of Fethaland
Yell
Fetlar
▲ 449m
Esha Ness
Sullum Voe
Yell Sound
Out Skerries
St Magnus Bay
Whalsay
Symbister
Muckle Roe
Papa Stour
Mainland
Walls
Bressay
The Deeps
Lerwick
Scalloway
417m ▲
Foula

Sumburgh Head

Fair Isle

Mull Head
Papa Westray
North Ronaldsay
Westray
Sanday
Westray Firth
Rousay
Eday
Brough Head
Stronsay
Stronsay Firth
Shapinsay
ORKNEY ISLANDS
Stromness
Kirkwall
Mainland
Scapa
Ward Hill 479m ▲
Scapa Flow
Rora Head
Hoy
South Ronaldsay

North Sea

Pentland Firth
Dunnet Head
Stroma
Strathy Point
Duncansby Head
John o' Groats
Thurso
Halkirk

Kirkwall

Transverse Mercator Projection
© Oxford University Press

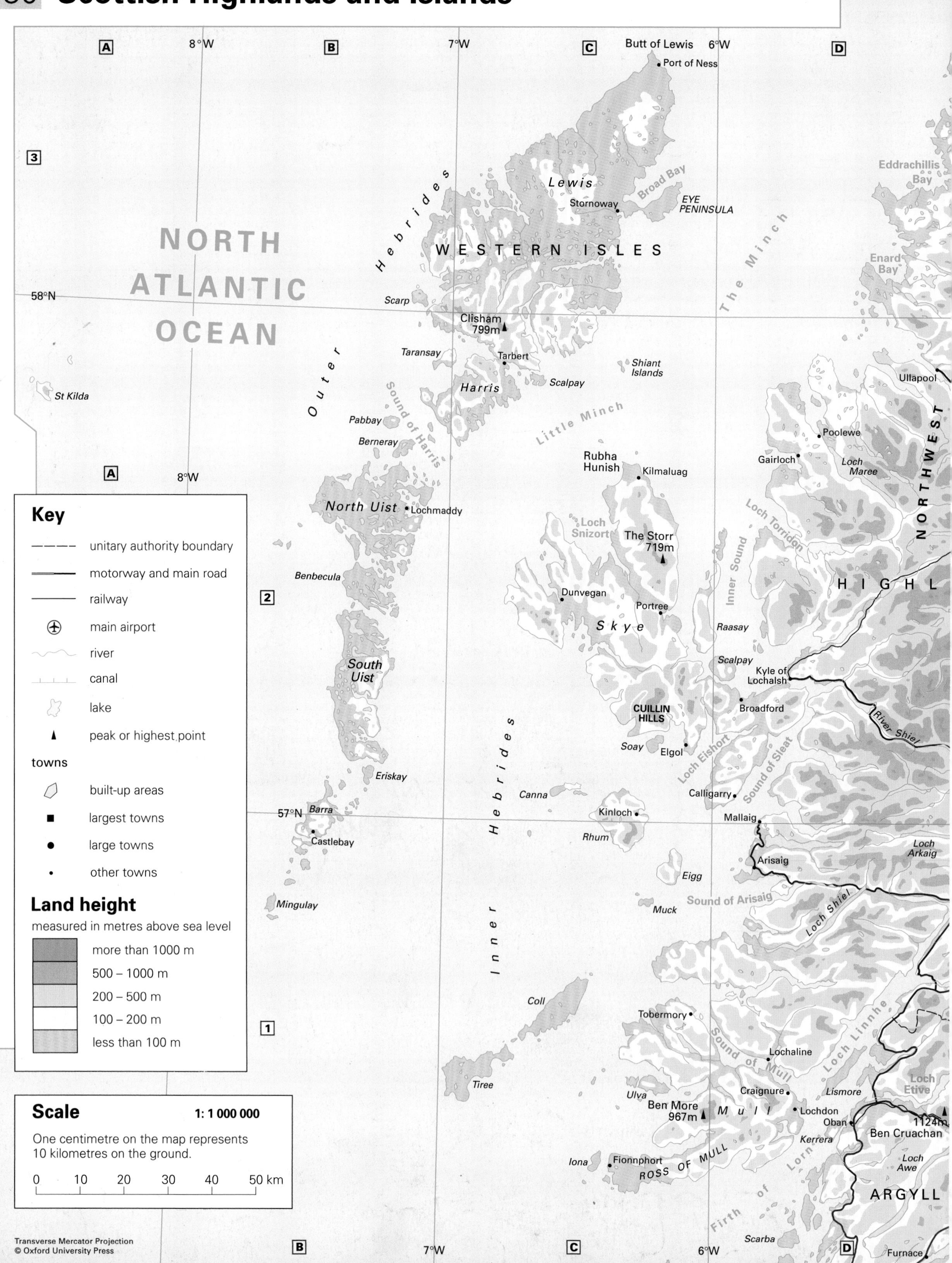

A 8°W | B 7°W | C Butt of Lewis 6°W | D

NORTH ATLANTIC OCEAN

58°N

57°N

Butt of Lewis
Port of Ness

Lewis
Stornoway
Broad Bay
EYE PENINSULA

WESTERN ISLES

Eddrachillis Bay
Enard Bay
The Minch

Scarp
Clisham 799m
Taransay
Tarbert
Scalpay
Shiant Islands
Harris
Pabbay
Berneray
Sound of Harris
Outer Hebrides
Little Minch

St Kilda

Ullapool
Poolewe
Gairloch
Loch Maree
NORTHWEST
Loch Torridon

Rubha Hunish
Kilmaluag
Loch Snizort
The Storr 719m
Dunvegan
Portree
Skye
Raasay
Scalpay
Kyle of Lochalsh
Broadford
HIGHL

North Uist · Lochmaddy
Benbecula
South Uist
Eriskay
Barra
Castlebay
Mingulay

Inner Sound

CUILLIN HILLS
Soay
Elgol
Loch Eishort
Sound of Sleat
Calligarry
River Shiel

Canna
Kinloch
Rhum
Mallaig
Arisaig
Loch Arkaig
Sound of Arisaig
Loch Shiel

Inner Hebrides

Eigg
Muck

Coll

Tobermory
Lochaline
Craignure
Lismore
Loch Linnhe
Ulva
Ben More 967m
Mull
Lochdon
Oban
Kerrera
Ben Cruachan 1124m
Loch Awe
Loch Etive

Tiree

Iona
Fionnphort
ROSS OF MULL
Firth of Lorn
Scarba
Furnace
ARGYLL

Key

----- unitary authority boundary

──── motorway and main road

──── railway

⊕ main airport

〜 river

canal

lake

▲ peak or highest point

towns

built-up areas

■ largest towns

● large towns

· other towns

Land height

measured in metres above sea level

more than 1000 m

500 – 1000 m

200 – 500 m

100 – 200 m

less than 100 m

Scale

1: 1 000 000

One centimetre on the map represents
10 kilometres on the ground.

0 10 20 30 40 50 km

Transverse Mercator Projection
© Oxford University Press

Scottish Highlands and Islands

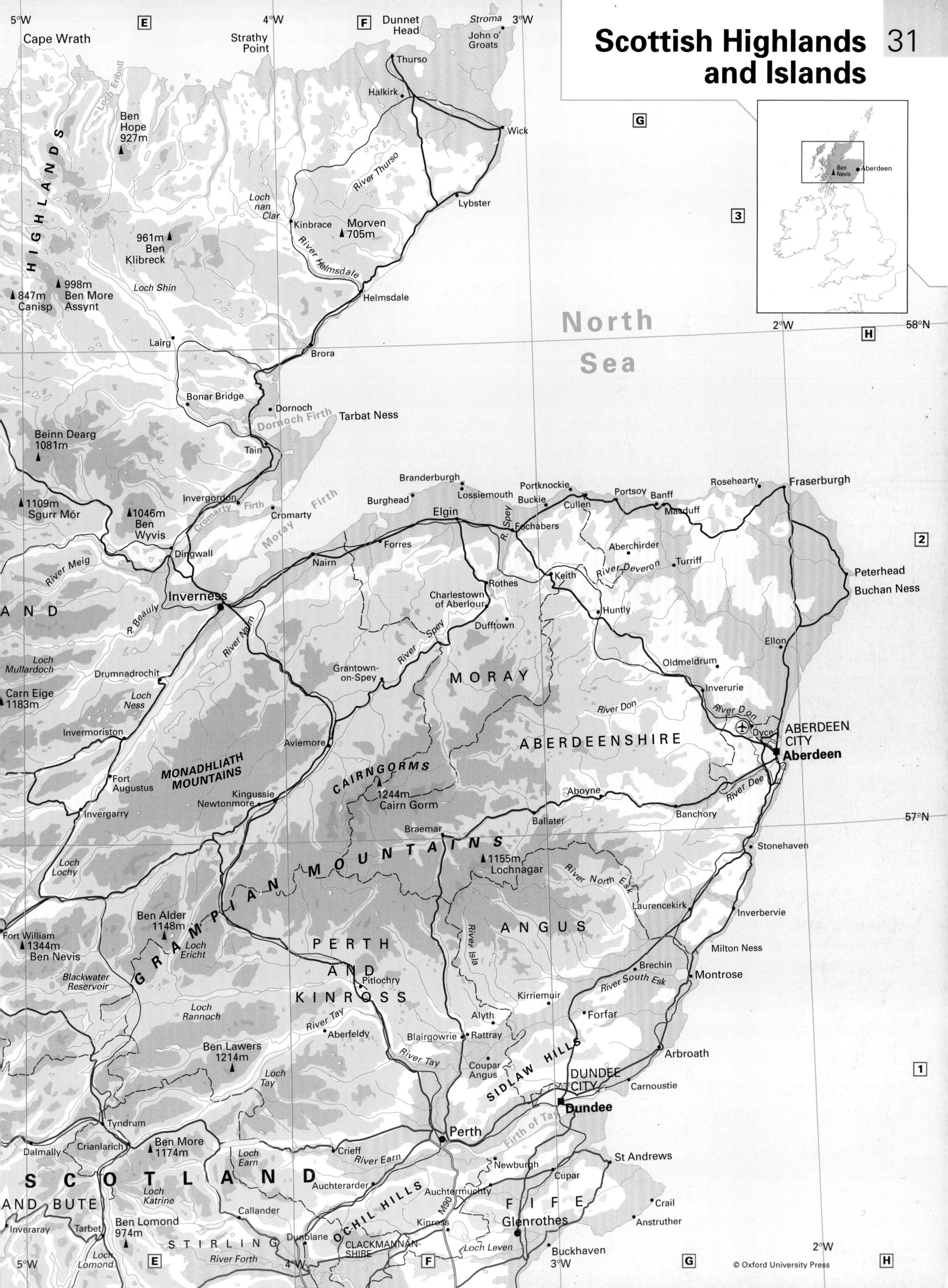
5°W
4°W
3°W
2°W
58°N
57°N
E
F
G
H
1
2
3
Cape Wrath
Strathy Point
Dunnet Head
Stroma
John o' Groats
Thurso
Halkirk
Wick
Loch Eriboll
Ben Hope 927m
HIGHLANDS
River Thurso
Loch nan Clar
Kinbrace
Morven 705m
Lybster
961m Ben Klibreck
River Helmsdale
998m Ben More Assynt
847m Canisp
Loch Shin
Helmsdale
North Sea
Lairg
Brora
Bonar Bridge
Dornoch
Dornoch Firth
Tarbat Ness
Beinn Dearg 1081m
Tain
Branderburgh
Lossiemouth
Portknockie
Buckie
Cullen
Portsoy
Banff
Macduff
Rosehearty
Fraserburgh
1109m Sgurr Mór
1046m Ben Wyvis
Invergordon
Cromarty Firth
Cromarty
Moray Firth
Burghead
Elgin
R. Spey
Fochabers
Dingwall
River Meig
Forres
Nairn
Aberchirder
Turriff
River Deveron
Keith
Rothes
Peterhead
Buchan Ness
Inverness
AND
Charlestown of Aberlour
R. Beauly
River Nairn
Dufftown
Huntly
River Spey
Loch Mullardoch
Drumnadrochit
Grantown-on-Spey
MORAY
Ellon
Oldmeldrum
Inverurie
Carn Eige 1183m
Loch Ness
River Don
Dyce
ABERDEEN CITY
Aberdeen
Invermoriston
Aviemore
ABERDEENSHIRE
MONADHLIATH MOUNTAINS
CAIRNGORMS
Fort Augustus
Kingussie
Newtonmore
1244m Cairn Gorm
Aboyne
River Dee
Invergarry
Ballater
Banchory
Braemar
Stonehaven
GRAMPIAN MOUNTAINS
1155m Lochnagar
River North Esk
Loch Lochy
Laurencekirk
Inverbervie
Fort William
1344m Ben Nevis
Ben Alder 1148m
Loch Ericht
PERTH AND KINROSS
ANGUS
River Isla
Milton Ness
Brechin
Montrose
Blackwater Reservoir
Pitlochry
River South Esk
Kirriemuir
Loch Rannoch
River Tay
Aberfeldy
Alyth
Forfar
Blairgowrie
Rattray
Ben Lawers 1214m
Coupar Angus
SIDLAW HILLS
Arbroath
Loch Tay
DUNDEE CITY
Carnoustie
Dundee
Tyndrum
Perth
Firth of Tay
Dalmally
Crianlarich
Ben More 1174m
Crieff
River Earn
Loch Earn
Newburgh
St Andrews
SCOTLAND
Auchterarder
Cupar
Loch Katrine
OCHIL HILLS
Auchtermuchty
AND BUTE
FIFE
Crail
Callander
Glenrothes
Anstruther
Inveraray
Tarbet
Ben Lomond 974m
Kinross
M90
Dunblane
STIRLING
CLACKMANNANSHIRE
Loch Leven
Buckhaven
Loch Lomond
River Forth
Ben Nevis
Aberdeen

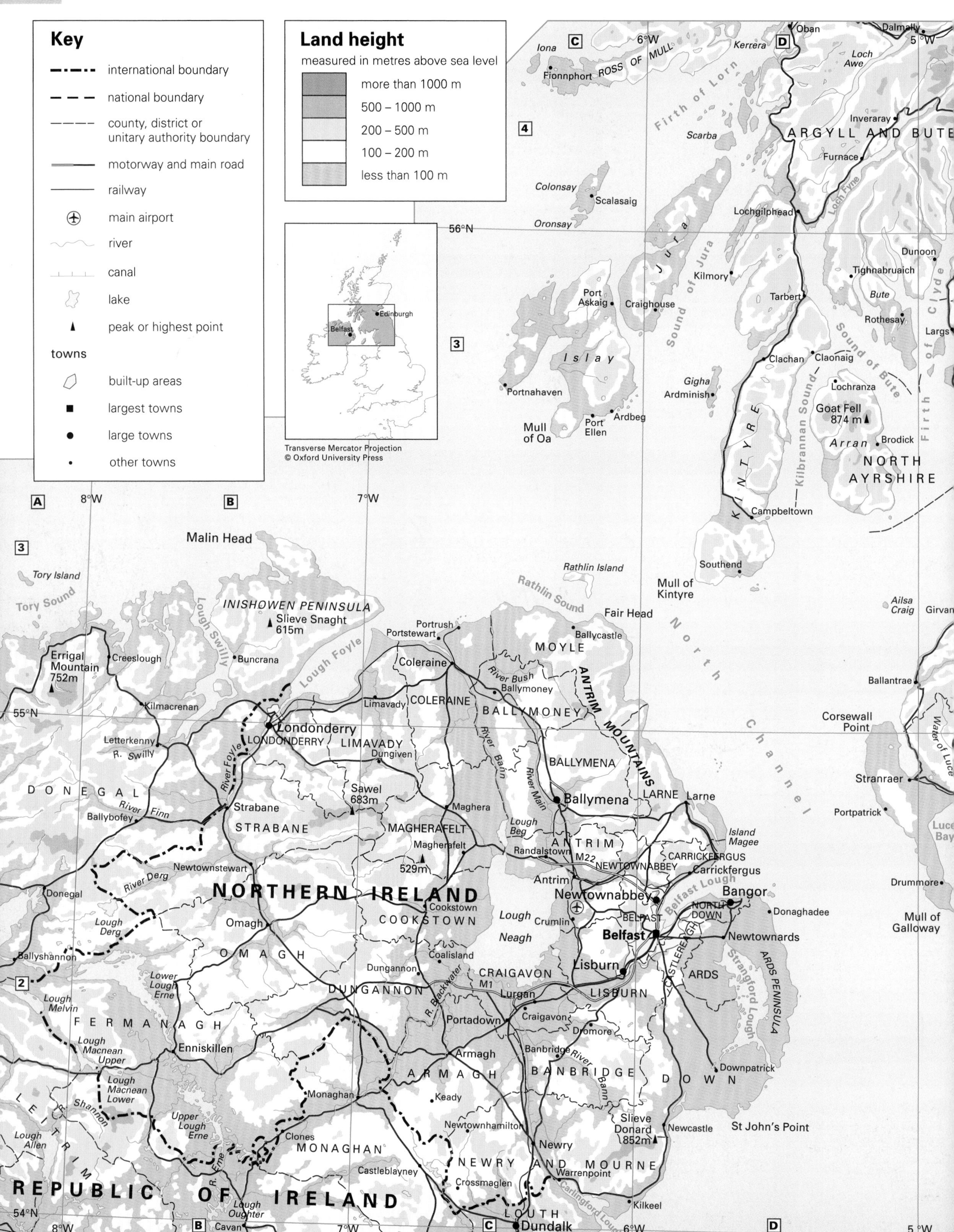

Key

—·—·—	international boundary
— — —	national boundary
— ·· — ·· —	county, district or unitary authority boundary
	motorway and main road
	railway
✈	main airport
	river
	canal
	lake
▲	peak or highest point

towns

	built-up areas
■	largest towns
●	large towns
•	other towns

Land height

measured in metres above sea level

	more than 1000 m
	500 – 1000 m
	200 – 500 m
	100 – 200 m
	less than 100 m

Transverse Mercator Projection
© Oxford University Press

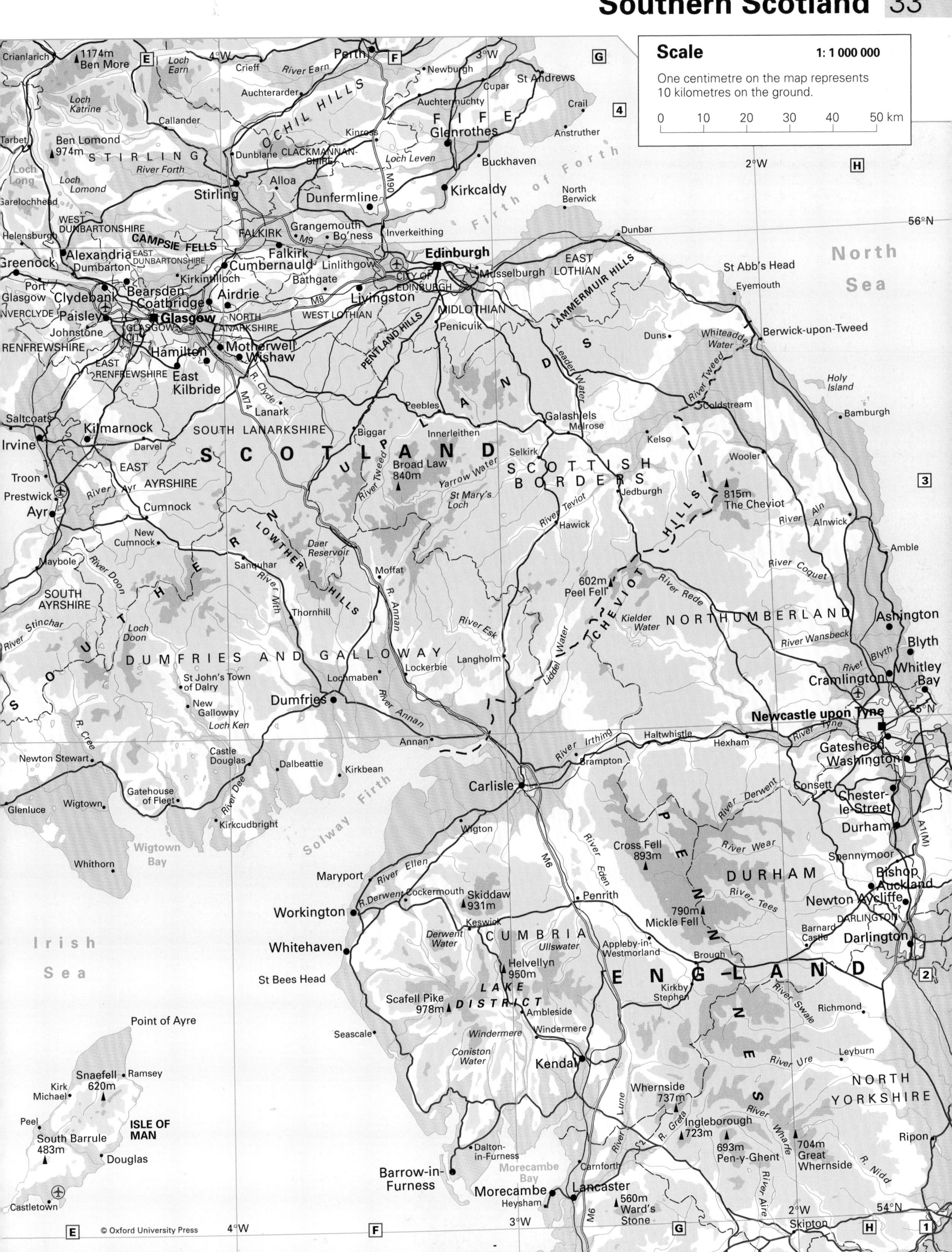

Scale   1: 1 000 000

One centimetre on the map represents
10 kilometres on the ground.

0   10   20   30   40   50 km

© Oxford University Press

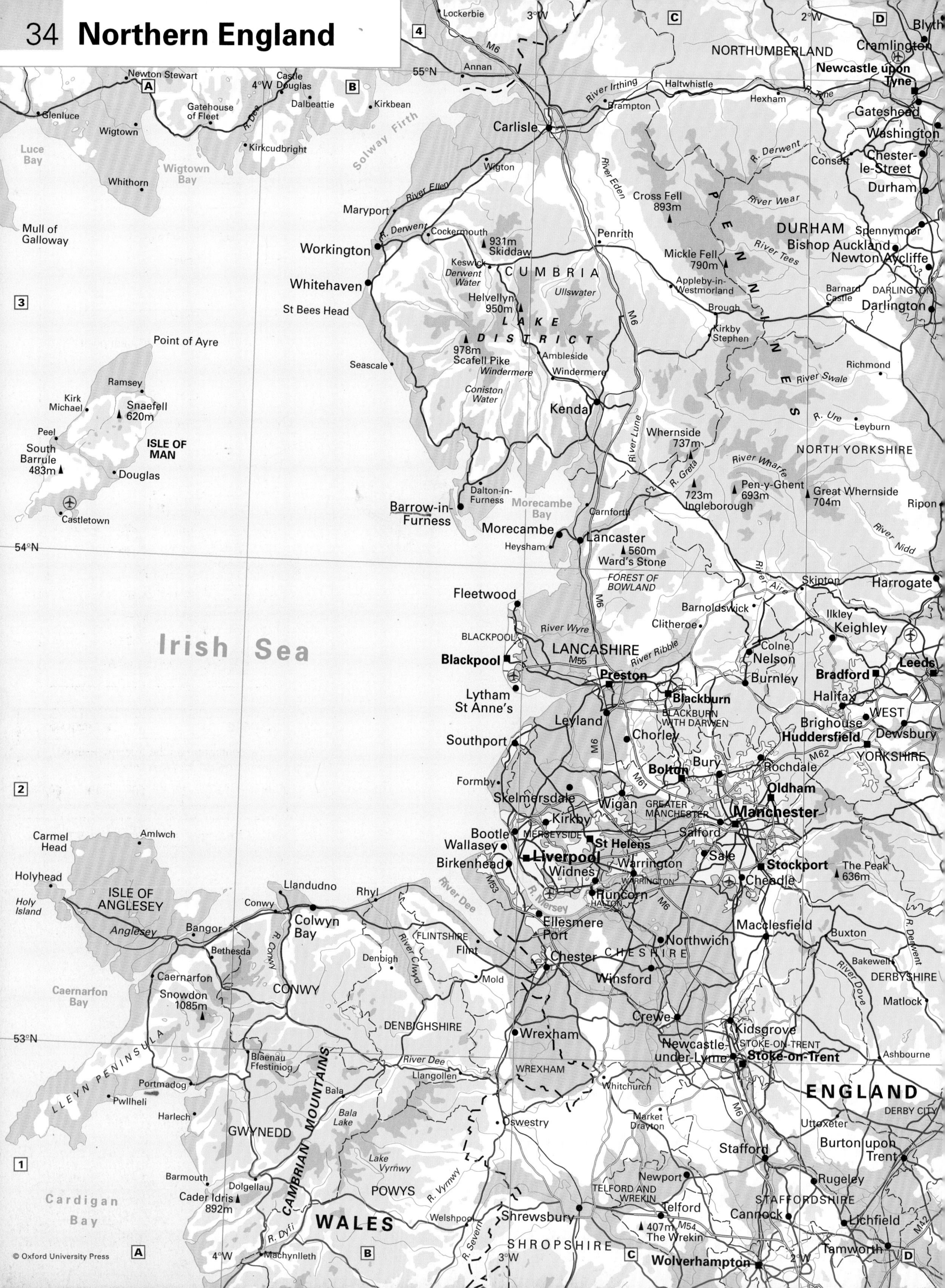

Lockerbie · 3°W · C · 2°W · D · Blyth

NORTHUMBERLAND · Cramlington

M6 · Annan · Newcastle upon Tyne

55°N · River Irthing · Haltwhistle · Brampton · Hexham · R. Tyne · Gateshead

Carlisle · River Irthing · Washington

Newton Stewart · 4°W · Castle Douglas · Dalbeattie · Kirkbean · Consett · Chester-le-Street

Glenluce · Gatehouse of Fleet · Kirkcudbright · R. Dee · Solway Firth · Durham

Wigtown · River Ellen · Wigton · Penrith · Cross Fell 893m · DURHAM · Spennymoor

Whithorn · Wigtown Bay · Maryport · Cockermouth · 931m Skiddaw · River Wear · Bishop Auckland

Luce Bay · R. Derwent · Keswick · Derwent Water · Mickle Fell 790m · Newton Aycliffe

Mull of Galloway · Workington · CUMBRIA · Appleby-in-Westmorland · Barnard Castle · DARLINGTON

Whitehaven · St Bees Head · Helvellyn 950m · Ullswater · Brough · Darlington

LAKE · Kirkby Stephen · Richmond

Point of Ayre · DISTRICT · 978m Scafell Pike · Ambleside · River Swale

Ramsey · Seascale · Windermere · Windermere · NORTH YORKSHIRE

Kirk Michael · Snaefell 620m · Coniston Water · Kendal · R. Ure · Leyburn

Peel · ISLE OF MAN · Whernside 737m · River Wharfe

South Barrule 483m · Douglas · Dalton-in-Furness · Morecambe Bay · Carnforth · 723m Ingleborough · Pen-y-Ghent 693m · Great Whernside 704m · Ripon

Castletown · Barrow-in-Furness · Morecambe · Lancaster · River Nidd

54°N · Heysham · Ward's Stone 560m · River Aire · Skipton · Harrogate

Fleetwood · FOREST OF BOWLAND · Barnoldswick · Ilkley · Keighley

River Wyre · Clitheroe · Colne · Bradford · Leeds

Irish Sea · BLACKPOOL · LANCASHIRE · River Ribble · Nelson

Blackpool · M55 · Preston · Burnley · Halifax · WEST

Lytham St Anne's · Blackburn · BLACKBURN WITH DARWEN · Brighouse · Dewsbury

Leyland · Chorley · Huddersfield · YORKSHIRE

Southport · M6 · Bury · Rochdale · M62

Formby · Skelmersdale · Wigan · GREATER MANCHESTER · Bolton · Oldham

Kirkby · MERSEYSIDE · St Helens · Salford · Manchester

Bootle · Wallasey · Liverpool · Warrington · Sale · Stockport · The Peak 636m

Birkenhead · Widnes · WARRINGTON · Cheadle

Llandudno · Rhyl · River Dee · Runcorn · HALTON · M6 · Macclesfield · Buxton

Carmel Head · Amlwch · Conwy · Colwyn Bay · Ellesmere Port · Northwich · R. Derwent

Holyhead · ISLE OF ANGLESEY · FLINTSHIRE · Flint · CHESHIRE · Bakewell

Holy Island · Anglesey · Bangor · Denbigh · Chester · Winsford · DERBYSHIRE

Caernarfon Bay · Caernarfon · Mold · Crewe · Matlock

Snowdon 1085m · CONWY · Kidsgrove · STOKE-ON-TRENT

53°N · DENBIGHSHIRE · Wrexham · Newcastle-under-Lyme · Stoke-on-Trent · Ashbourne

LLEYN PENINSULA · Blaenau Ffestiniog · River Dee · WREXHAM · Whitchurch · ENGLAND

Portmadog · Llangollen · Oswestry · Market Drayton · DERBY CITY

Pwllheli · Harlech · GWYNEDD · Bala · Uttoxeter · Burton upon Trent

Barmouth · Dolgellau · CAMBRIAN MOUNTAINS · Bala Lake · POWYS · Lake Vyrnwy · Newport · TELFORD AND WREKIN · Stafford · Rugeley · STAFFORDSHIRE

Cader Idris 892m · R. Vyrnwy · Telford · Cannock · Lichfield

Cardigan Bay · R. Dyfi · Welshpool · Shrewsbury · 407m The Wrekin · M54

WALES · Machynlleth · 4°W · B · 3°W · SHROPSHIRE · Wolverhampton · C · Tamworth · 2°W · D

© Oxford University Press

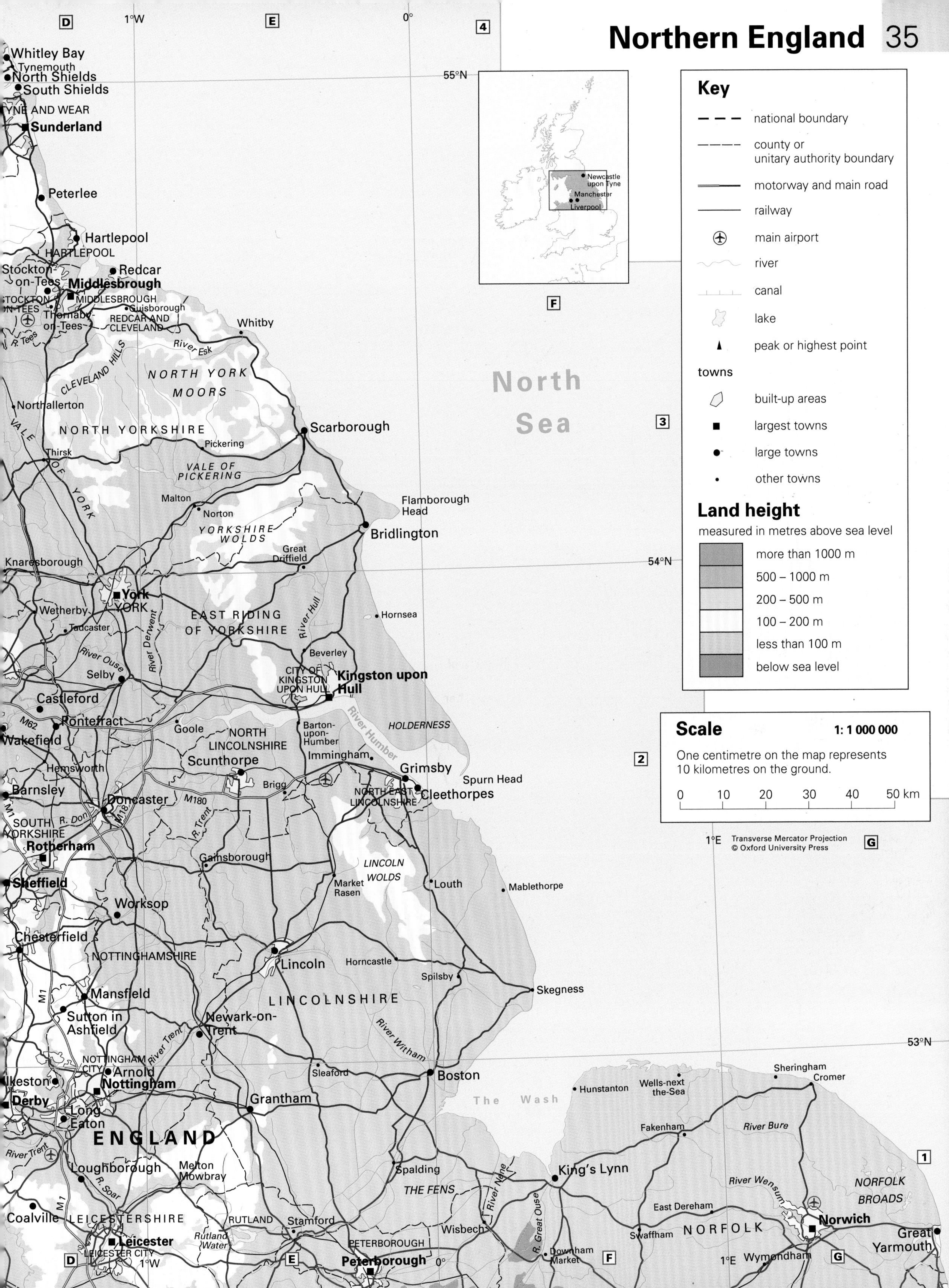

Key

- – – – national boundary
- – · – · county or unitary authority boundary
- motorway and main road
- railway
- ✈ main airport
- river
- canal
- lake
- ▲ peak or highest point

towns

- built-up areas
- ■ largest towns
- ● large towns
- · other towns

Land height

measured in metres above sea level

- more than 1000 m
- 500 – 1000 m
- 200 – 500 m
- 100 – 200 m
- less than 100 m
- below sea level

Scale   1: 1 000 000

One centimetre on the map represents
10 kilometres on the ground.

0   10   20   30   40   50 km

Transverse Mercator Projection
© Oxford University Press

North
Sea

D 1°W E 0° 4
55°N

Newcastle
upon Tyne
Manchester
Liverpool

F

Whitley Bay
Tynemouth
North Shields
South Shields
TYNE AND WEAR
Sunderland
Peterlee
Hartlepool
HARTLEPOOL
Stockton-on-Tees
STOCKTON-ON-TEES
Redcar
Middlesbrough
MIDDLESBROUGH
Thornaby-on-Tees
Guisborough
REDCAR AND CLEVELAND
R. Tees
CLEVELAND HILLS
Whitby
River Esk
NORTH YORK MOORS
Northallerton
NORTH YORKSHIRE
VALE OF YORK
Thirsk
Pickering
Scarborough
VALE OF PICKERING
Malton
Norton
YORKSHIRE WOLDS
Flamborough Head
Knaresborough
Great Driffield
Bridlington
54°N
Wetherby
York
YORK
River Ouse
Taucaster
River Derwent
EAST RIDING OF YORKSHIRE
River Hull
Hornsea
Selby
Beverley
CITY OF KINGSTON UPON HULL
Kingston upon Hull
Castleford
M62
Pontefract
Goole
NORTH LINCOLNSHIRE
Barton-upon-Humber
River Humber
HOLDERNESS
Wakefield
Hemsworth
Scunthorpe
Immingham
Barnsley
Brigg
Grimsby
Spurn Head
Doncaster
M180
NORTH EAST LINCOLNSHIRE
Cleethorpes
SOUTH YORKSHIRE
R. Don
M18
R. Trent
Rotherham
Gainsborough
LINCOLN WOLDS
Sheffield
Market Rasen
Louth
Mablethorpe
Worksop
Chesterfield
NOTTINGHAMSHIRE
Lincoln
Horncastle
Mansfield
Spilsby
Skegness
Sutton in Ashfield
LINCOLNSHIRE
Newark-on-Trent
River Witham
53°N
NOTTINGHAM CITY
Arnold
River Trent
Sleaford
Boston
Sheringham
Cromer
Ilkeston
Nottingham
Sleaford
Hunstanton
Wells-next-the-Sea
Derby
Long Eaton
Grantham
The Wash
Fakenham
River Bure
River Trent
ENGLAND
Spalding
King's Lynn
River Wensum
NORFOLK BROADS
Loughborough
Melton Mowbray
R. Soar
THE FENS
River Nene
East Dereham
G
Coalville LEICESTERSHIRE
RUTLAND
Stamford
R. Great Ouse
Wisbech
Swaffham
NORFOLK
Norwich
Great Yarmouth
Leicester
Rutland Water
PETERBOROUGH
Downham Market
Wymondham
LEICESTER CITY 1°W
Peterborough
D E 0° F 1°E G

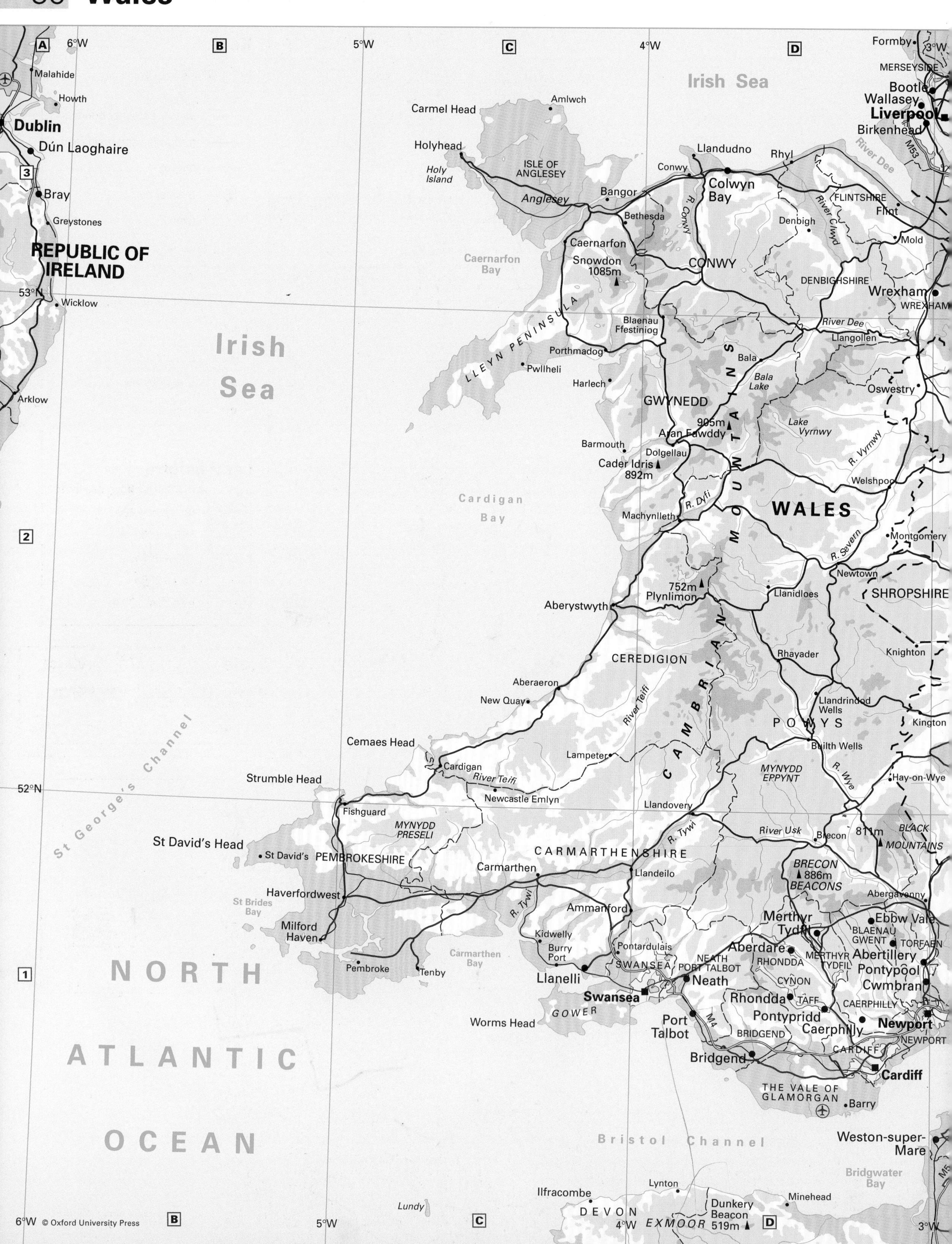

Formby
MERSEYSIDE
Malahide
Howth
Irish Sea
Bootle
Wallasey
Liverpool
Birkenhead
Dublin
Dún Laoghaire
Carmel Head
Amlwch
Llandudno
Conwy
Rhyl
Bray
Holyhead
ISLE OF ANGLESEY
Colwyn Bay
R. Conwy
FLINTSHIRE
Flint
River Dee
Greystones
Holy Island
Anglesey
Bangor
Bethesda
CONWY
Denbigh
River Clwyd
Mold
REPUBLIC OF IRELAND
Caernarfon
Snowdon 1085m
DENBIGHSHIRE
Wrexham
WREXHAM
53°N
Wicklow
Caernarfon Bay
Blaenau Ffestiniog
Bala
Llangollen
Oswestry
Porthmadog
River Dee
Pwllheli
LLEYN PENINSULA
Harlech
Bala Lake
Arklow
Irish Sea
GWYNEDD
Lake Vyrnwy
905m Aran Fawddy
MOUNTAINS
Barmouth
Dolgellau
R. Vyrnwy
Cader Idris 892m
Welshpool
Cardigan Bay
Machynlleth
R. Dyfi
WALES
Montgomery
Newtown
752m Plynlimon
Llanidloes
SHROPSHIRE
Aberystwyth
R. Severn
2
CAMBRIAN
Rhayader
Knighton
CEREDIGION
Aberaeron
Llandrindod Wells
New Quay
River Teifi
POWYS
Kington
Cemaes Head
Lampeter
Builth Wells
Cardigan
River Teifi
MYNYDD EPPYNT
Strumble Head
Newcastle Emlyn
R. Wye
Hay-on-Wye
52°N
Fishguard
Llandovery
Brecon
811m BLACK MOUNTAINS
St David's Head
MYNYDD PRESELI
River Usk
CARMARTHENSHIRE
BRECON BEACONS 886m
Abergavenny
St David's PEMBROKESHIRE
Carmarthen
Llandeilo
Haverfordwest
R. Tywi
Merthyr Tydfil
Ebbw Vale
St Brides Bay
Ammanford
BLAENAU GWENT TORFAEN
Milford Haven
Kidwelly
Pontardulais
NEATH PORT TALBOT
Aberdare
RHONDDA
MERTHYR TYDFIL
Abertillery
Pontypool Cwmbran
Pembroke
Tenby
Burry Port
SWANSEA
Neath
CYNON
Rhondda
TAFF
CAERPHILLY
1
Swansea
Pontypridd
Caerphilly
Newport
Carmarthen Bay
GOWER
Port Talbot
M4
BRIDGEND
CARDIFF
NEWPORT
Worms Head
Bridgend
Cardiff
NORTH
THE VALE OF GLAMORGAN
Barry
ATLANTIC
Weston-super-Mare
OCEAN
Bristol Channel
Bridgwater Bay
Lynton
Minehead
Lundy
Ilfracombe
Dunkery Beacon 519m
DEVON
EXMOOR

St George's Channel

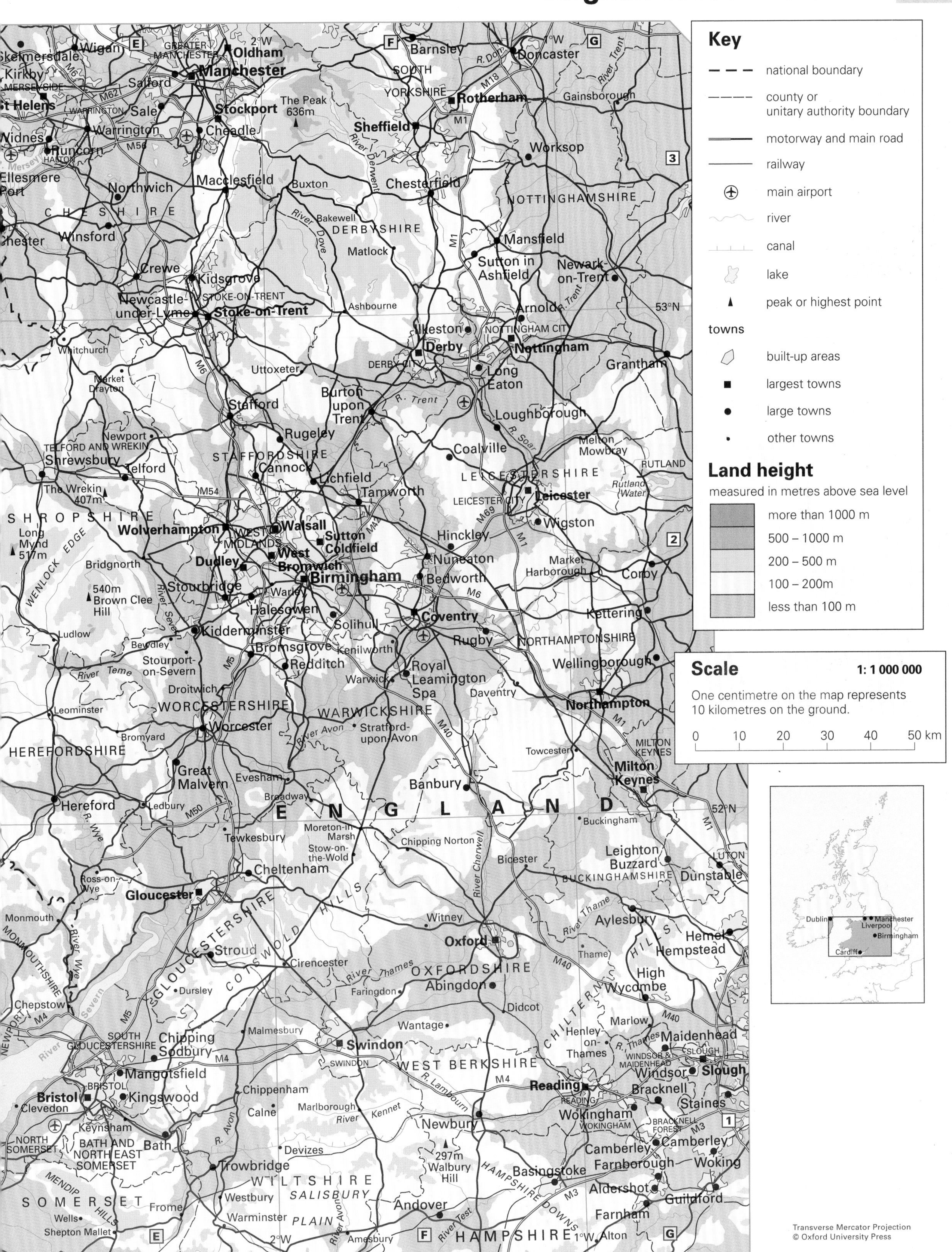

Key

– – – national boundary

– – – county or unitary authority boundary

—— motorway and main road

—— railway

✈ main airport

river

canal

lake

▲ peak or highest point

towns

built-up areas

■ largest towns

● large towns

• other towns

Land height

measured in metres above sea level

more than 1000 m

500 – 1000 m

200 – 500 m

100 – 200m

less than 100 m

Scale   1: 1 000 000

One centimetre on the map represents
10 kilometres on the ground.

0   10   20   30   40   50 km

Transverse Mercator Projection
© Oxford University Press

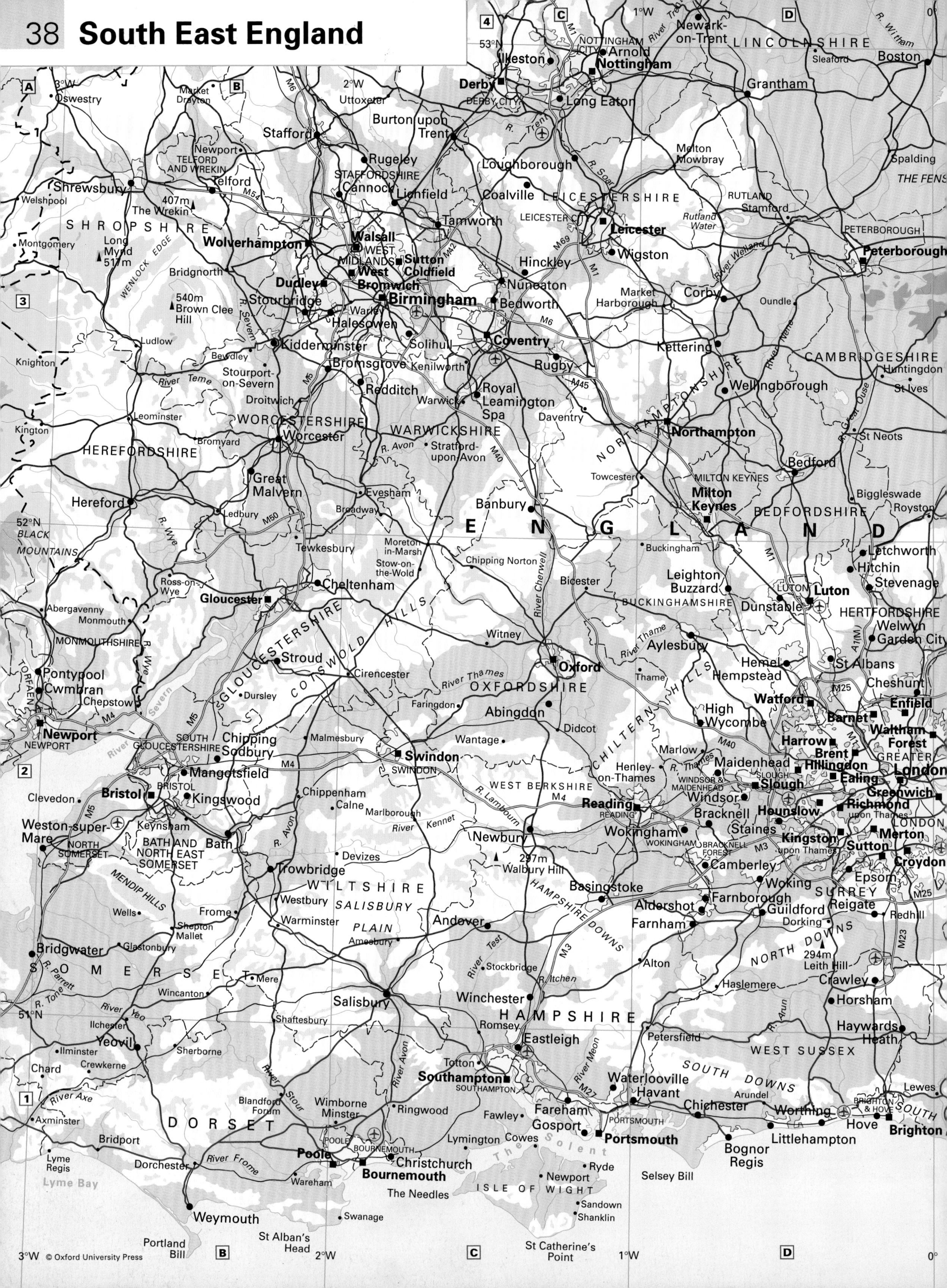
Newark-on-Trent
LINCOLNSHIRE
R. Witham
Sleaford
Boston
53°N
NOTTINGHAM CITY
Arnold
Nottingham
Ilkeston
Derby
DERBY CITY
Long Eaton
Grantham
Oswestry
Market Drayton
2°W
Uttoxeter
Burton upon Trent
R. Trent
Stafford
Newport
TELFORD AND WREKIN
Rugeley
Melton Mowbray
Spalding
THE FENS
Loughborough
R. Soar
Shrewsbury
Telford
STAFFORDSHIRE
Cannock
Lichfield
Coalville
LEICESTERSHIRE
RUTLAND
Stamford
Welshpool
407m
The Wrekin
M54
Tamworth
LEICESTER CITY
Rutland Water
SHROPSHIRE
Leicester
PETERBOROUGH
Montgomery
Long Mynd 517m
Wolverhampton
Walsall
WEST MIDLANDS
Sutton Coldfield
M42
M69
Wigston
Peterborough
River Welland
WENLOCK EDGE
Bridgnorth
Dudley
West Bromwich
Hinckley
Nuneaton
M1
Market Harborough
Corby
Oundle
540m
Brown Clee Hill
R. Severn
Stourbridge
Warley
Halesowen
Birmingham
Bedworth
M6
Coventry
Ludlow
Kidderminster
Solihull
Kettering
River Nene
CAMBRIDGESHIRE
Huntingdon
Knighton
Bewdley
Stourport-on-Severn
River Teme
Bromsgrove
Kenilworth
Rugby
M45
NORTHAMPTONSHIRE
Wellingborough
St Ives
Droitwich
Redditch
M5
Warwick
Royal Leamington Spa
Daventry
Kington
Leominster
WORCESTERSHIRE
WARWICKSHIRE
Northampton
R. Great Ouse
St Neots
HEREFORDSHIRE
Bromyard
Worcester
R. Avon
Stratford-upon-Avon
M40
Bedford
Great Malvern
Towcester
MILTON KEYNES
Milton Keynes
Evesham
Biggleswade
Hereford
R. Wye
Ledbury
M50
Broadway
Banbury
BEDFORDSHIRE
Royston
52°N
BLACK MOUNTAINS
ENGLAND
Tewkesbury
Moreton-in-Marsh
Stow-on-the-Wold
Chipping Norton
River Cherwell
Buckingham
Letchworth
Hitchin
Ross-on-Wye
Cheltenham
Bicester
Leighton Buzzard
LUTON
Luton
Stevenage
Abergavenny
Monmouth
Gloucester
BUCKINGHAMSHIRE
Dunstable
HERTFORDSHIRE
Welwyn Garden City
MONMOUTHSHIRE
GLOUCESTERSHIRE
COTSWOLD HILLS
Witney
River Thame
Aylesbury
A1(M)
TORFAEN
Pontypool
Cwmbran
Stroud
Cirencester
River Thames
Oxford
Thame
CHILTERN HILLS
Hemel Hempstead
St Albans
Cheshunt
Chepstow
Dursley
OXFORDSHIRE
M25
Watford
Enfield
Newport
NEWPORT
M4
Faringdon
Abingdon
High Wycombe
Barnet
Waltham Forest
SOUTH GLOUCESTERSHIRE
Chipping Sodbury
Malmesbury
Didcot
Wantage
M40
Harrow
Brent
GREATER LONDON
London
River Severn
Swindon
SWINDON
Marlow
R. Thames
Maidenhead
Hillingdon
Ealing
Mangotsfield
Henley-on-Thames
WINDSOR & MAIDENHEAD
SLOUGH
Slough
Clevedon
Bristol
BRISTOL
Kingswood
Chippenham
WEST BERKSHIRE
R. Lambourn
Windsor
Greenwich
Calne
Marlborough
Reading
READING
Bracknell
Hounslow
Richmond upon Thames
Weston-super-Mare
Keynsham
River Kennet
Wokingham
WOKINGHAM
Staines
Merton
Kingston upon Thames
NORTH SOMERSET
BATH AND NORTH EAST SOMERSET
Bath
R. Avon
Newbury
BRACKNELL FOREST
M3
Sutton
Croydon
Devizes
297m
Walbury Hill
Camberley
Epsom
MENDIP HILLS
Trowbridge
WILTSHIRE
HAMPSHIRE DOWNS
Basingstoke
Woking
SURREY
Westbury
SALISBURY PLAIN
Aldershot
Farnborough
Guildford
Reigate
Wells
Frome
Warminster
Andover
Farnham
Dorking
Redhill
Shepton Mallet
Amesbury
River Test
NORTH DOWNS
M23
Bridgwater
Glastonbury
Stockbridge
Alton
294m
Leith Hill
SOMERSET
R. Parrett
Mere
R. Itchen
Crawley
R. Tone
Wincanton
Salisbury
Winchester
Haslemere
51°N
River Yeo
Ilchester
Shaftesbury
HAMPSHIRE
Horsham
Romsey
R. Arun
Haywards Heath
Yeovil
Ilminster
Sherborne
Eastleigh
River Meon
Petersfield
WEST SUSSEX
Chard
Crewkerne
River Stour
River Avon
Totton
Southampton
SOUTHAMPTON
SOUTH DOWNS
M27
Waterlooville
Havant
River Axe
Blandford Forum
Wimborne Minster
Ringwood
Arundel
Lewes
Axminster
DORSET
Fawley
Fareham
Gosport
PORTSMOUTH
Chichester
Worthing
BRIGHTON & HOVE
Hove
Brighton
SOUTH
Bridport
POOLE
BOURNEMOUTH
Lymington
Cowes
The Solent
Portsmouth
Littlehampton
Lyme Regis
Dorchester
River Frome
Poole
Christchurch
Bournemouth
Ryde
Bognor Regis
Selsey Bill
Lyme Bay
Wareham
Newport
ISLE OF WIGHT
The Needles
Sandown
Shanklin
Weymouth
Swanage
Portland Bill
St Alban's Head
St Catherine's Point
3°W
2°W
1°W
0°
A
B
C
D
1
2
3
4

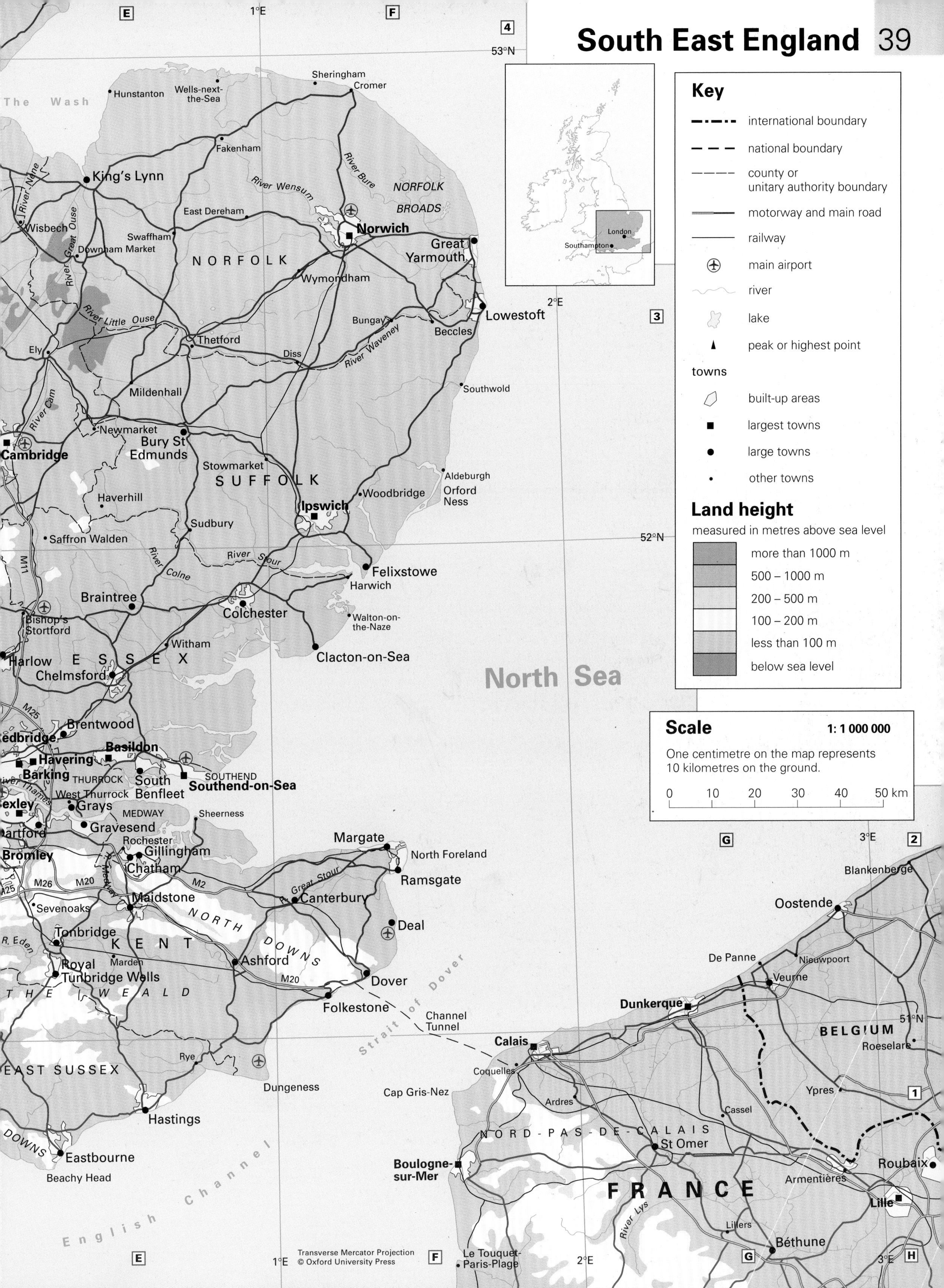

Key

- — ·· — ·· — international boundary
- – – – national boundary
- – · – · – county or unitary authority boundary
- ═══ motorway and main road
- ——— railway
- ⊕ main airport
- river
- lake
- ▲ peak or highest point

towns

- built-up areas
- ■ largest towns
- ● large towns
- • other towns

Land height

measured in metres above sea level

- more than 1000 m
- 500 – 1000 m
- 200 – 500 m
- 100 – 200 m
- less than 100 m
- below sea level

Scale   1: 1 000 000

One centimetre on the map represents
10 kilometres on the ground.

| 0 | 10 | 20 | 30 | 40 | 50 km |

Transverse Mercator Projection
© Oxford University Press

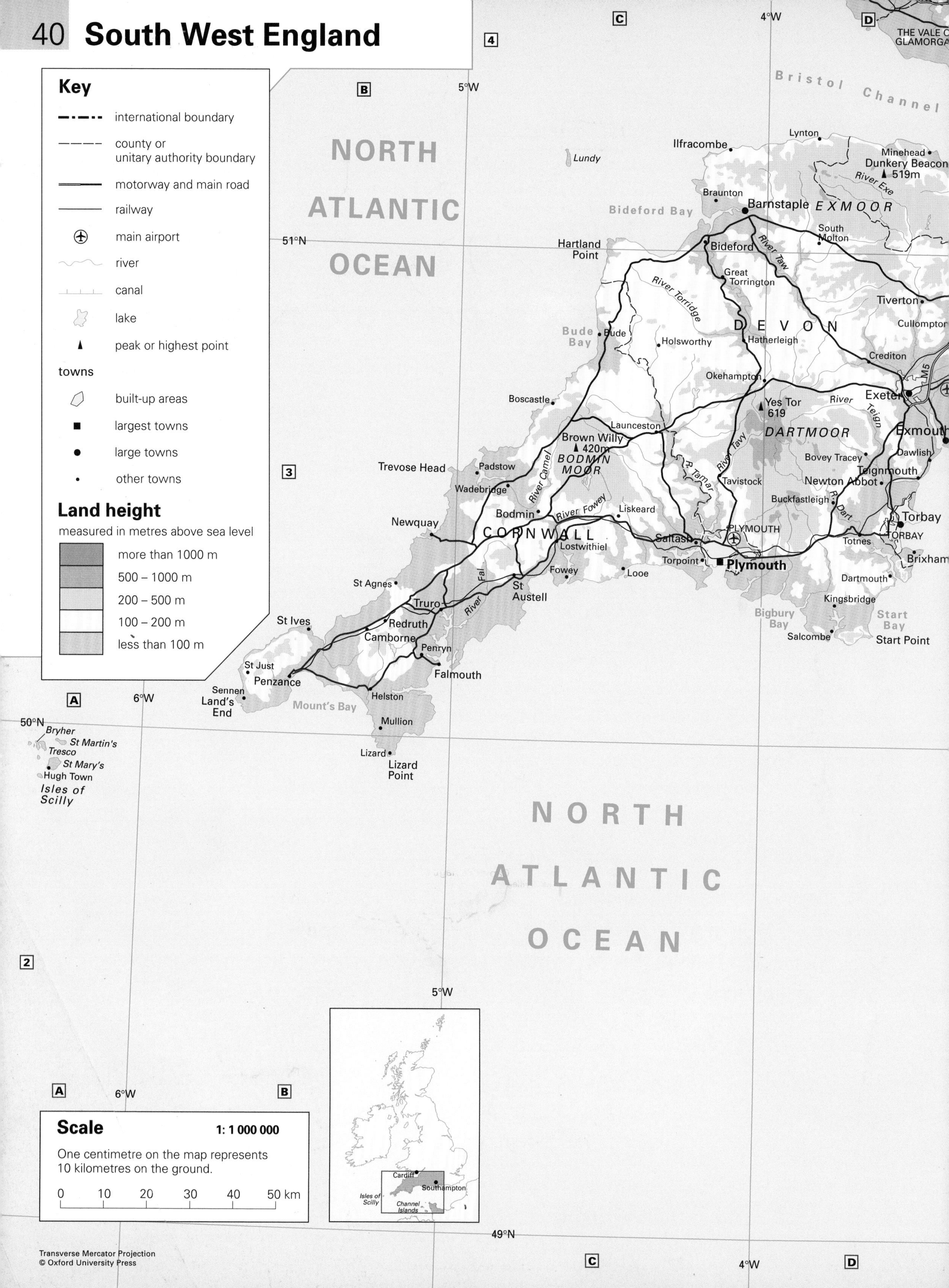

Key

- ·—··—··— international boundary
- ––––– county or unitary authority boundary
- ═══ motorway and main road
- —— railway
- ✈ main airport
- ～ river
- ⊣⊢ canal
- 🝙 lake
- ▲ peak or highest point

towns
- ⬠ built-up areas
- ■ largest towns
- ● large towns
- • other towns

Land height

measured in metres above sea level

- more than 1000 m
- 500 – 1000 m
- 200 – 500 m
- 100 – 200 m
- less than 100 m

NORTH ATLANTIC OCEAN

NORTH ATLANTIC OCEAN

Bristol Channel

THE VALE OF GLAMORGAN

Lundy

Ilfracombe
Lynton
Minehead
Dunkery Beacon ▲ 519m
River Exe
Braunton
Bideford Bay
Barnstaple
EXMOOR
South Molton
Hartland Point
Bideford
River Taw
Great Torrington
Tiverton
River Torridge
DEVON
Cullompton
Bude Bay
Bude
Holsworthy
Hatherleigh
Crediton
Boscastle
Okehampton
Exeter
M5
Launceston
Yes Tor 619 ▲
River Teign
Exmouth
Brown Willy ▲ 420m
BODMIN MOOR
DARTMOOR
Dawlish
Trevose Head
Padstow
R. Tavy
Bovey Tracey
Teignmouth
Wadebridge
River Camel
R. Lyd
R. Tamar
Tavistock
Newton Abbot
Newquay
Bodmin
River Fowey
Liskeard
Buckfastleigh
CORNWALL
Saltash
PLYMOUTH
R. Dart
Torbay
St Agnes
Lostwithiel
TORBAY
St Austell
Fowey
Torpoint
Totnes
Brixham
Truro
River Fal
Looe
Plymouth
Dartmouth
Redruth
Camborne
Penryn
Kingsbridge
Start Bay
St Ives
Bigbury Bay
Salcombe
St Just
Falmouth
Start Point
Sennen
Penzance
Helston
Land's End
Mount's Bay
Mullion
Bryher
St Martin's
Tresco
St Mary's
Hugh Town
Isles of Scilly
Lizard
Lizard Point

Scale   1: 1 000 000

One centimetre on the map represents 10 kilometres on the ground.

0   10   20   30   40   50 km

Cardiff
Southampton
Isles of Scilly
Channel Islands

51°N · 50°N · 49°N · 6°W · 5°W · 4°W

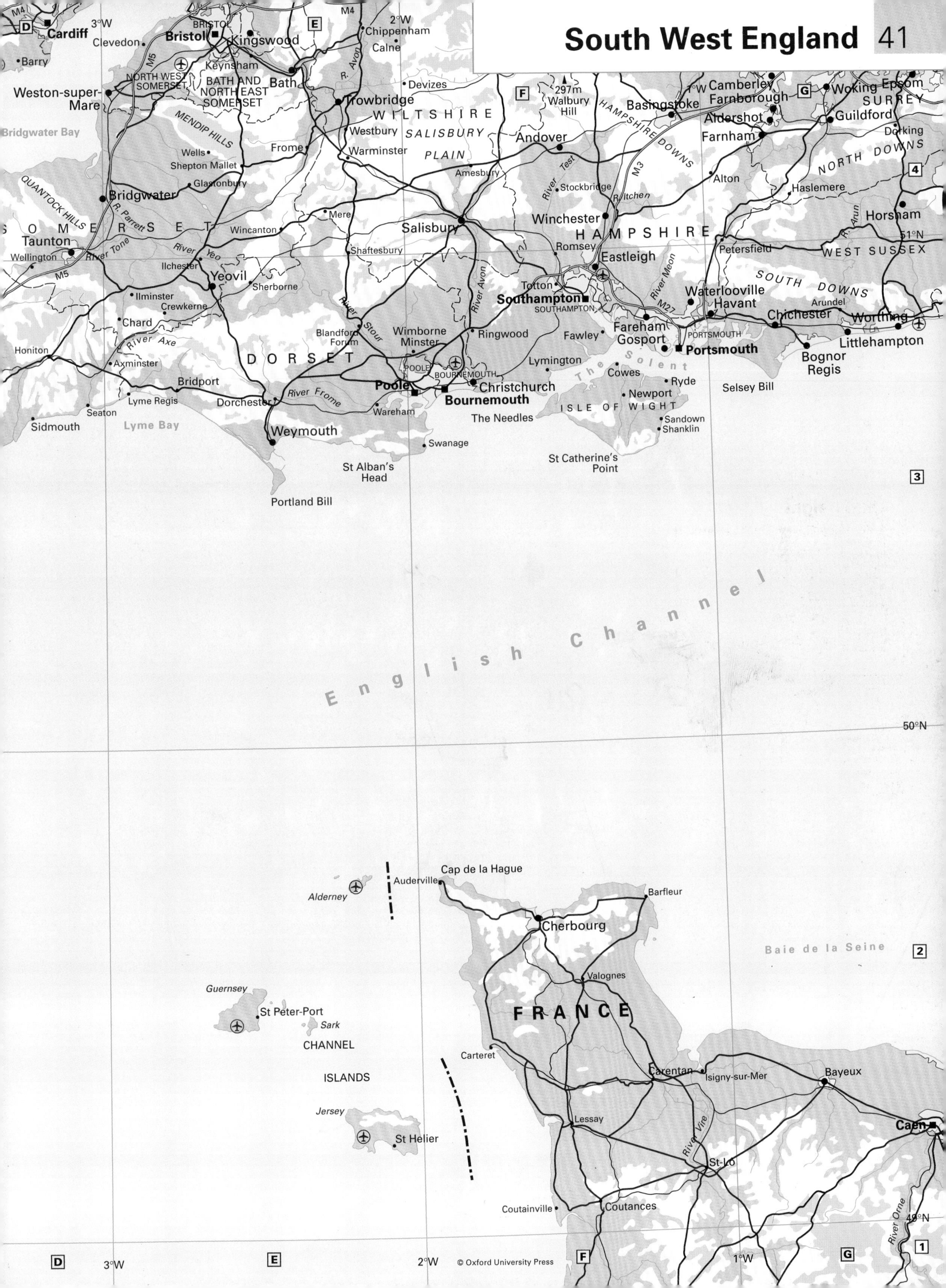

English Channel

SOMERSET

Cardiff
Barry
Clevedon
BRISTOL
Bristol
Kingswood
Chippenham
Calne
Keynsham
BATH AND NORTH EAST SOMERSET
Bath
Weston-super-Mare
NORTH WEST SOMERSET
Trowbridge
Devizes
Bridgwater Bay
MENDIP HILLS
Wells
Shepton Mallet
Glastonbury
WILTSHIRE
Westbury
Frome
SALISBURY PLAIN
Warminster
297m
Walbury Hill
Basingstoke
Camberley
Farnborough
Aldershot
Woking
Epsom
SURREY
Guildford
Dorking
Andover
Farnham
QUANTOCK HILLS
Bridgwater
R. Parrett
Taunton
Wellington
Mere
Amesbury
Stockbridge
River Test
Winchester
Alton
Haslemere
HAMPSHIRE DOWNS
NORTH DOWNS
4
Horsham
51°N
River Tone
Ilchester
Wincanton
Salisbury
Shaftesbury
Romsey
R. Itchen
HAMPSHIRE
Petersfield
WEST SUSSEX
River Yeo
Yeovil
Sherborne
Eastleigh
SOUTH DOWNS
Ilminster
Crewkerne
Totton
SOUTHAMPTON
Southampton
Waterlooville
Havant
Arundel
Chichester
Worthing
Chard
River Avon
Wimborne Minster
Ringwood
Fawley
Fareham
Gosport
PORTSMOUTH
Littlehampton
River Axe
Blandford Forum
River Stour
Lymington
Cowes
Portsmouth
Bognor Regis
Honiton
Axminster
Bridport
DORSET
The Solent
Ryde
Selsey Bill
Lyme Regis
Dorchester
River Frome
POOLE
Poole
Christchurch
Bournemouth
ISLE OF WIGHT
Newport
Sandown
Shanklin
Seaton
Sidmouth
Lyme Bay
Wareham
The Needles
St Catherine's Point
3
Weymouth
St Alban's Head
Swanage

Portland Bill

50°N

English Channel

Cap de la Hague
Auderville
Barfleur
Alderney
Cherbourg
Baie de la Seine
2
Valognes
Guernsey
St Peter-Port
Sark
FRANCE
CHANNEL
Carteret
Bayeux
ISLANDS
Lessay
Carentan
Isigny-sur-Mer
Jersey
St Helier
Caen
River Vire
St-Lo
Coutainville
Coutances
River Orne
49°N
1

D   3°W   E   2°W   © Oxford University Press   F   1°W   G   1

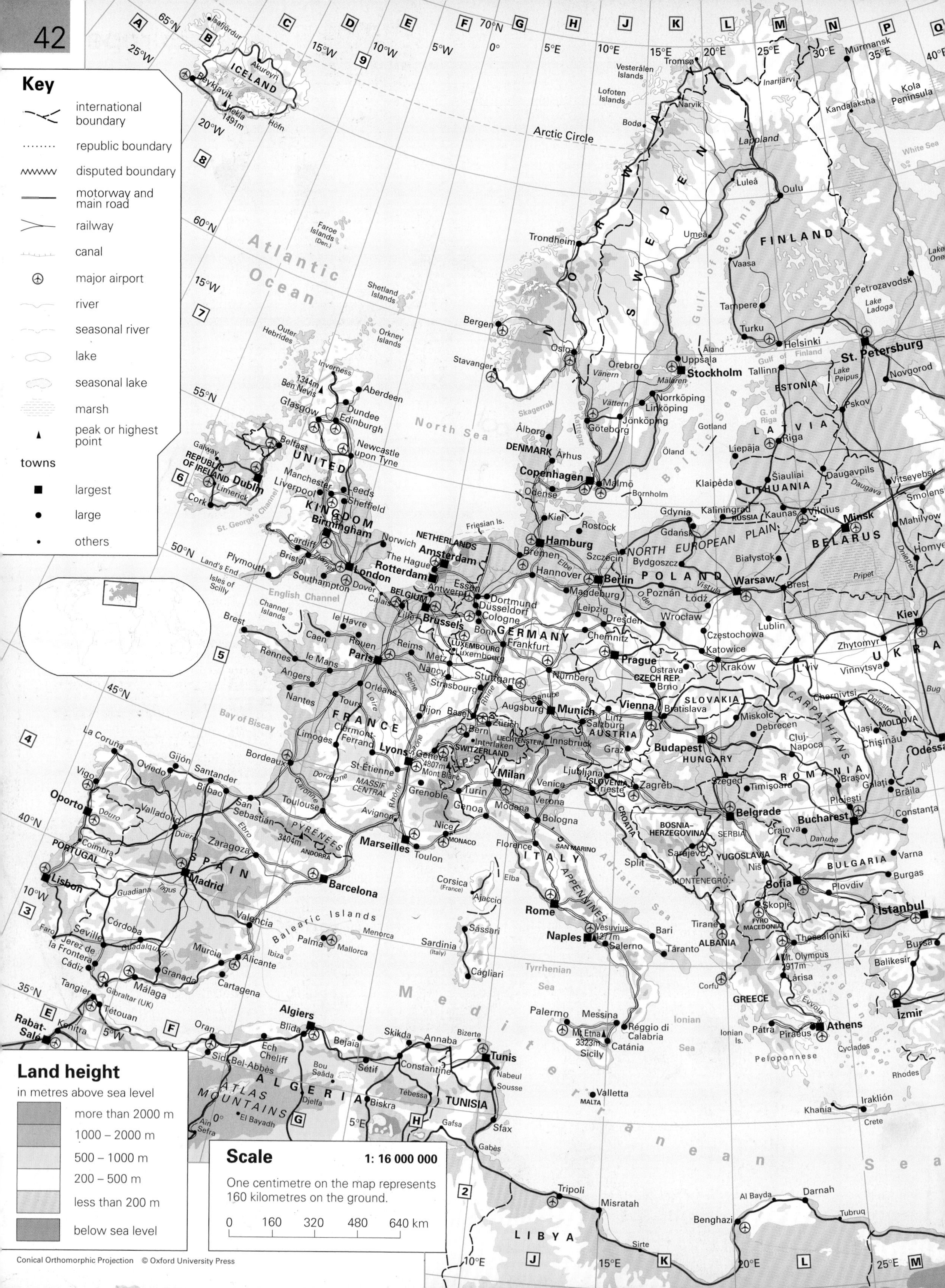
Key
international boundary
republic boundary
disputed boundary
motorway and main road
railway
canal
major airport
river
seasonal river
lake
seasonal lake
marsh
peak or highest point
towns
largest
large
others
Land height
in metres above sea level
more than 2000 m
1000 – 2000 m
500 – 1000 m
200 – 500 m
less than 200 m
below sea level
Scale
1: 16 000 000
One centimetre on the map represents 160 kilometres on the ground.
0 160 320 480 640 km
Conical Orthomorphic Projection
© Oxford University Press
65°N
60°N
55°N
50°N
45°N
40°N
35°N
70°N
25°W
20°W
15°W
10°W
5°W
0°
5°E
10°E
15°E
20°E
25°E
30°E
35°E
40°E
Arctic Circle
ICELAND
Reykjavík
Akureyri
Ísafjörður
Hekla 1491m
Höfn
Faroe Islands (Den.)
Atlantic Ocean
Shetland Islands
Orkney Islands
Outer Hebrides
North Sea
Skagerrak
Kattegat
Baltic Sea
Gulf of Bothnia
Gulf of Finland
G. of Riga
White Sea
Kola Peninsula
Lake Onega
Lake Ladoga
Lake Peipus
Vesterålen Islands
Lofoten Islands
NORWAY
SWEDEN
FINLAND
Lappland
Inarijärvi
Tromsø
Narvik
Bodø
Murmansk
Kandalaksha
Luleå
Oulu
Umeå
Vaasa
Trondheim
Tampere
Turku
Helsinki
Petrozavodsk
St. Petersburg
Novgorod
Åland
Bergen
Oslo
Stavanger
Örebro
Vänern
Vättern
Mälaren
Uppsala
Stockholm
Tallinn
ESTONIA
Pskov
Norrköping
Linköping
Jönköping
Göteborg
Gotland
Öland
LATVIA
Riga
Liepāja
Ålborg
DENMARK
Århus
Copenhagen
Malmö
Odense
Bornholm
Klaipėda
Šiauliai
Daugavpils
Daugava
LITHUANIA
Vitsyebsk
Smolensk
Kaunas
Vilnius
Kaliningrad
RUSSIA
Minsk
Mahilyow
BELARUS
Homyel
Dnieper
Pripet
Inverness
Aberdeen
1344m Ben Nevis
Glasgow
Dundee
Edinburgh
Newcastle upon Tyne
Belfast
Galway
REPUBLIC OF IRELAND
Dublin
Limerick
Cork
UNITED KINGDOM
Manchester
Liverpool
Leeds
Sheffield
Birmingham
St. George's Channel
Cardiff
Bristol
Norwich
London
Southampton
Dover
Plymouth
Land's End
Isles of Scilly
English Channel
Channel Islands
Thames
Friesian Is.
NETHERLANDS
Amsterdam
The Hague
Rotterdam
BELGIUM
Antwerp
Brussels
Calais
Lille
Essen
Dortmund
Düsseldorf
Cologne
Bonn
LUXEMBOURG
Luxembourg
Kiel
Rostock
Hamburg
Bremen
Elbe
Hannover
Magdeburg
Berlin
Leipzig
Dresden
GERMANY
Frankfurt
Chemnitz
Gdynia
Gdańsk
Szczecin
Bydgoszcz
NORTH EUROPEAN PLAIN
Białystok
POLAND
Poznań
Oder
Vistula
Łódź
Warsaw
Brest
Wrocław
Lublin
Częstochowa
Katowice
Kraków
Prague
Ostrava
Brno
CZECH REP.
Kiev
Zhytomyr
Vinnytsya
UKRAINE
L'viv
Bug
Brest
le Havre
Caen
Rouen
Rennes
le Mans
Angers
Paris
Reims
Metz
Nancy
Strasbourg
Stuttgart
Nürnberg
Danube
Augsburg
Munich
Seine
Loire
Orléans
Tours
Nantes
Bay of Biscay
FRANCE
Dijon
Basel
Rhine
Zürich
Bern
Interlaken
LIECHTENSTEIN
SWITZERLAND
Innsbruck
Salzburg
Linz
AUSTRIA
Vienna
Bratislava
SLOVAKIA
Graz
Miskolc
Debrecen
Budapest
HUNGARY
Cluj-Napoca
CARPATHIANS
Chernivtsi
Dniester
MOLDOVA
Iaşi
Chişinău
Odessa
Limoges
Clermont-Ferrand
Lyons
Geneva
4807m Mont Blanc
ALPS
Saône
Rhône
St-Étienne
MASSIF CENTRAL
Dordogne
Grenoble
Bordeaux
Garonne
Toulouse
Avignon
Marseilles
Toulon
Nice
MONACO
Turin
Milan
Genoa
Venice
Verona
Modena
Bologna
Ljubljana
SLOVENIA
Trieste
Zagreb
CROATIA
Szeged
Timişoara
ROMANIA
Braşov
Galati
Brăila
Ploieşti
Bucharest
Constanta
Danube
Belgrade
SERBIA
BOSNIA-HERZEGOVINA
Sarajevo
YUGOSLAVIA
MONTENEGRO
Niš
Craiova
BULGARIA
Varna
Burgas
Sofia
Plovdiv
İstanbul
La Coruña
Gijón
Oviedo
Santander
Bilbao
San Sebastián
Vigo
Oporto
Douro
Valladolid
Duero
Ebro
PYRÉNÉES
3404m
ANDORRA
Zaragoza
Coimbra
PORTUGAL
Lisbon
Tagus
Madrid
SPAIN
Barcelona
Guadiana
Córdoba
Valencia
Seville
Faro
Jerez de la Frontera
Cádiz
Guadalquivir
Granada
Málaga
Murcia
Alicante
Cartagena
Gibraltar (UK)
Tangier
Tétouan
Rabat-Salé
Kenitra
Balearic Islands
Menorca
Mallorca
Palma
Ibiza
Corsica (France)
Ajaccio
Elba
Florence
SAN MARINO
ITALY
APPENNINES
Adriatic Sea
Split
Rome
Sardinia (Italy)
Sássari
Cágliari
Naples
Vesuvius 1277m
Salerno
Bari
Táranto
Tyrrhenian Sea
Palermo
Messina
Mt Etna 3323m
Sicily
Catánia
Réggio di Calabria
Ionian Sea
Ionian Is.
Tirane
ALBANIA
Corfu
Skopje
FYRO MACEDONIA
Thessaloniki
Mt. Olympus 2917m
Lárisa
GREECE
Pátra
Piraeus
Athens
Peloponnese
Cyclades
Aegean Sea
Bursa
Balıkesir
İzmir
Rhodes
Iraklión
Khania
Crete
Mediterranean Sea
Oran
Algiers
Blida
Bejaia
Skikda
Annaba
Bizerte
Tunis
Constantine
Sétif
Sidi Bel-Abbès
Ech Cheliff
Bou Saâda
ALGERIA
ATLAS MOUNTAINS
Djelfa
Biskra
Tébessa
TUNISIA
Nabeul
Sousse
Sfax
Gafsa
Gabès
Ain Sefra
El Bayadh
Valletta
MALTA
Tripoli
Misratah
LIBYA
Sirte
Benghazi
Al Bayda
Darnah
Tubruq

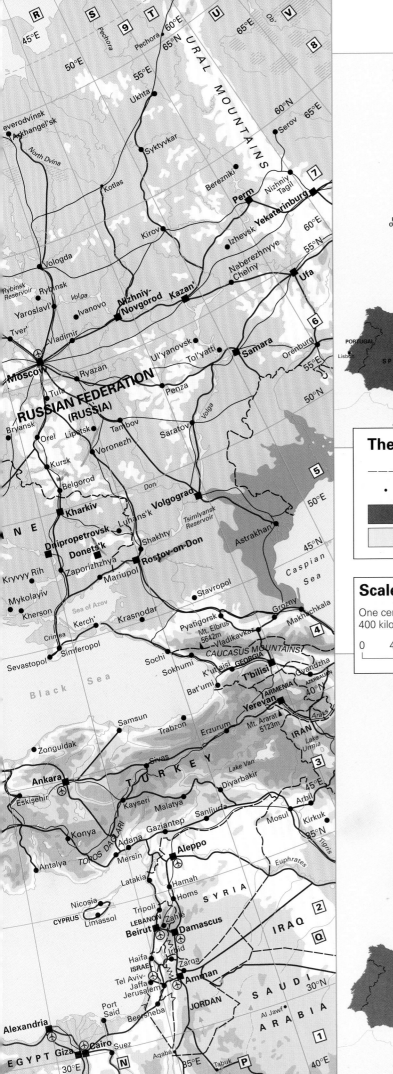

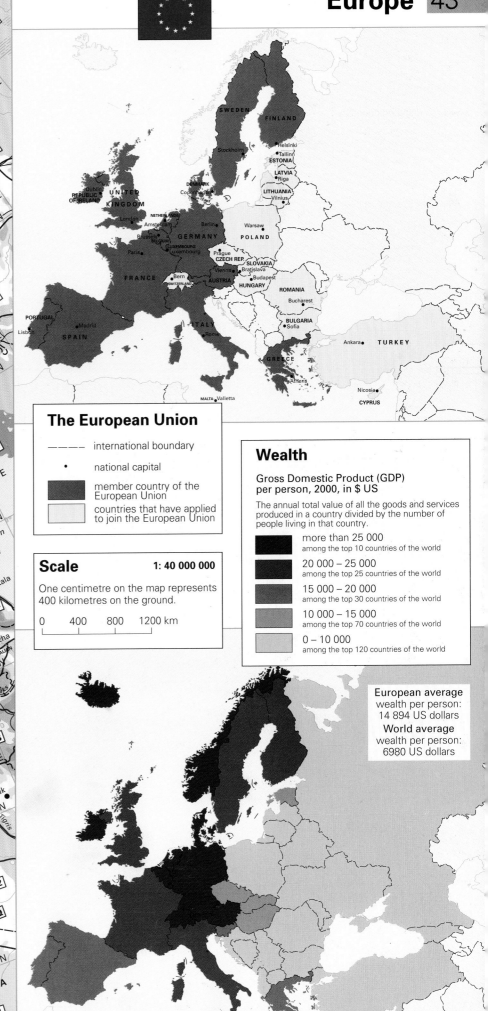

The European Union

--- international boundary

• national capital

member country of the European Union

countries that have applied to join the European Union

Scale

1: 40 000 000

One centimetre on the map represents 400 kilometres on the ground.

0   400   800   1200 km

Wealth

Gross Domestic Product (GDP) per person, 2000, in $ US

The annual total value of all the goods and services produced in a country divided by the number of people living in that country.

more than 25 000
among the top 10 countries of the world

20 000 – 25 000
among the top 25 countries of the world

15 000 – 20 000
among the top 30 countries of the world

10 000 – 15 000
among the top 70 countries of the world

0 – 10 000
among the top 120 countries of the world

European average
wealth per person:
14 894 US dollars

World average
wealth per person:
6980 US dollars

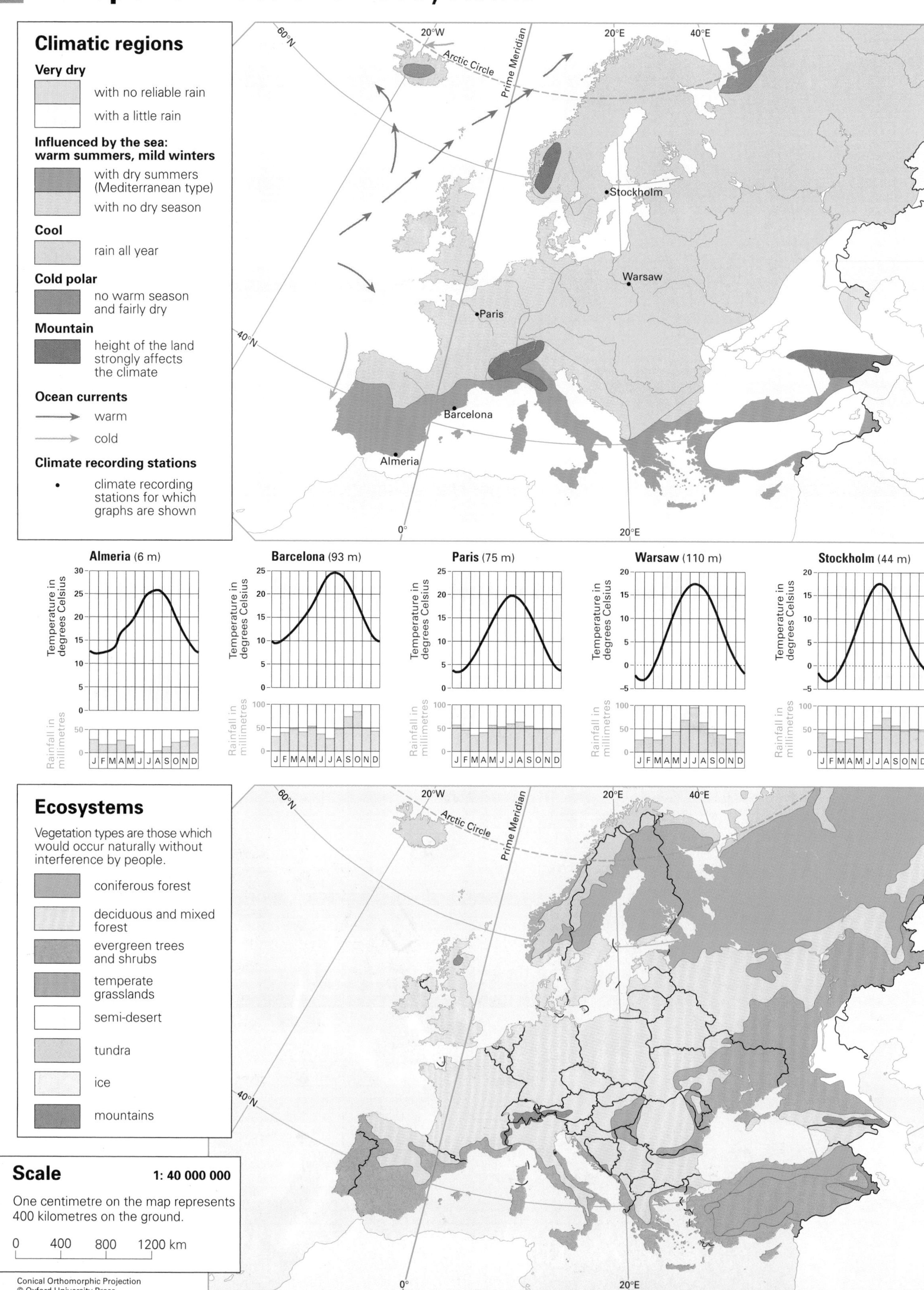

Climatic regions

Very dry

with no reliable rain

with a little rain

Influenced by the sea: warm summers, mild winters

with dry summers (Mediterranean type)

with no dry season

Cool

rain all year

Cold polar

no warm season and fairly dry

Mountain

height of the land strongly affects the climate

Ocean currents

→ warm

→ cold

Climate recording stations

• climate recording stations for which graphs are shown

Almeria (6 m)

Barcelona (93 m)

Paris (75 m)

Warsaw (110 m)

Stockholm (44 m)

Temperature in degrees Celsius

Rainfall in millimetres

J F M A M J J A S O N D

Ecosystems

Vegetation types are those which would occur naturally without interference by people.

coniferous forest

deciduous and mixed forest

evergreen trees and shrubs

temperate grasslands

semi-desert

tundra

ice

mountains

Scale
1: 40 000 000

One centimetre on the map represents 400 kilometres on the ground.

0 400 800 1200 km

Conical Orthomorphic Projection
© Oxford University Press

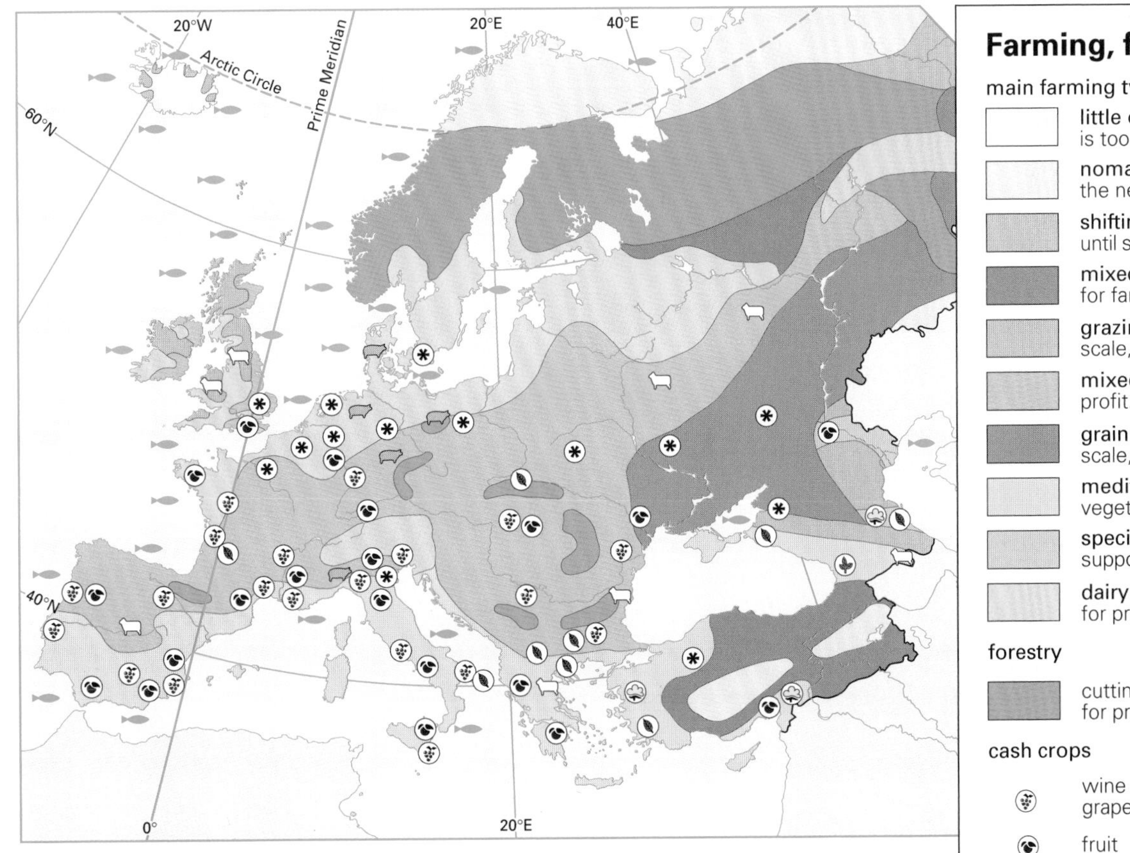

Farming, forestry, and fishing

main farming types

little or no farming : because the area is too cold or otherwise harsh.

nomadic herding : animals provide all the needs of the wandering families.

shifting cultivation : small areas farmed until soils exhausted, then family moves.

mixed subsistence : crops and animals for family food.

grazing and stock rearing : on a large scale, for profit.

mixed farming : animals and crops for profit.

grain farming : mostly wheat, on a large scale, for profit.

mediterranean farming : cereals, animals, vegetables, fruit, wine sold for profit.

specialized horticulture : often supported by irrigation.

dairy farming : milk, butter, and cheese for profit.

forestry

cutting and replacement of timber for profit

cash crops

🍇	wine grapes	🍃	tea	🍂	tobacco
🍒	fruit	✳	sugar	⊕	cotton

animal products

🐑	wool	🐖	meat	🐟	fish

Almeria
Mean annual rainfall: 233 mm   Mean January temperature: 12.0°C   Mean July temperature: 25.0°C

Barcelona
Mean annual rainfall: 587 mm   Mean January temperature: 9.5°C   Mean July temperature: 24.5°C

Paris
Mean annual rainfall: 589 mm   Mean January temperature: 3.5°C   Mean July temperature: 20.0°C

Warsaw
Mean annual rainfall: 525 mm   Mean January temperature: -3.0°C   Mean July temperature: 19.5°C

Stockholm
Mean annual rainfall: 524 mm   Mean January temperature: -3.0°C   Mean July temperature: 18.0°C

Scale   1: 40 000 000

One centimetre on the map represents 400 kilometres on the ground.

0   400   800   1200 km

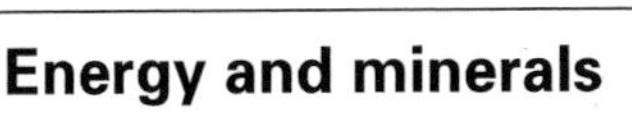

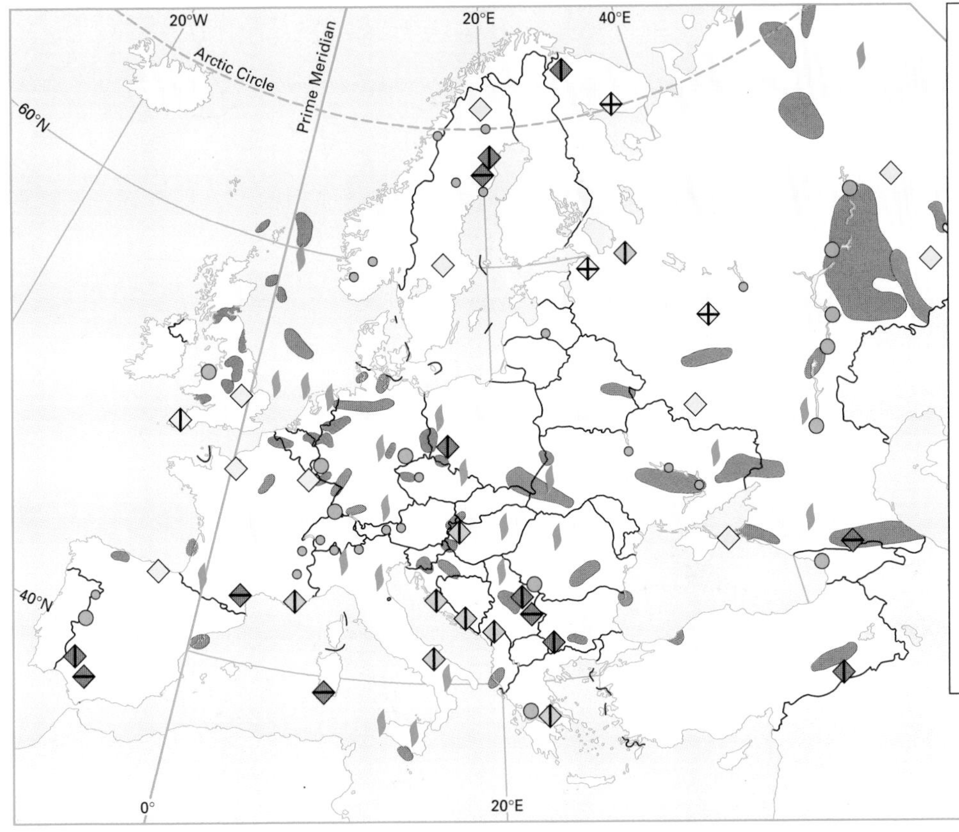

Energy and minerals

energy

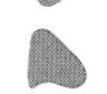

coalfield

oil field (with associated gas, and sometimes off shore)

gas field

hydro-electric power stations

● largest (over 1000 megawatts)

· smaller (500 – 1000 megawatts)

minerals (main mining areas)

◇ iron ore

◈ silver

⬦ tin

◈ copper

⬦ bauxite

⊕ phosphates

Conical Orthomorphic Projection
© Oxford University Press

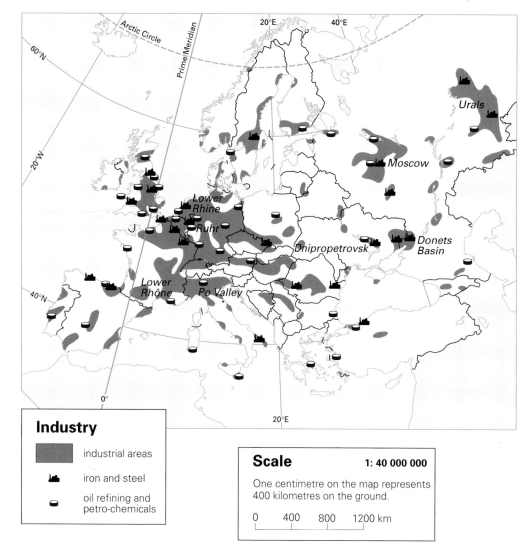

Population structure of the United Kingdom

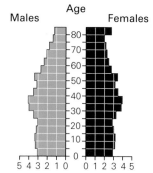

Age
Males / Females

5 4 3 2 1 0 0 1 2 3 4 5

percent of total population in 2000
Total population : 59.5 million

Population structure of France

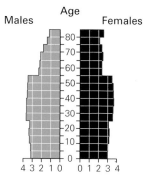

Age
Males / Females

4 3 2 1 0 0 1 2 3 4

percent of total population in 2000
Total population : 59.3 million

Industry

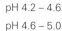

industrial areas

iron and steel

oil refining and petro-chemicals

Scale   1: 40 000 000

One centimetre on the map represents 400 kilometres on the ground.

0   400   800   1200 km

Environmental issues

sea pollution

areas severely polluted for all or part of the year

areas persistently affected by pollution

▼   deep sea dump sites

✱   major oil spills (over 100 000 tonnes)

∗   major oil spills (under 100 000 tonnes)

acid rain

A pH scale measures acidity. Unaffected rain water is slightly acidic with a pH of 5.6

pH less than 4.2 (most acidic)

pH 4.2 – 4.6

pH 4.6 – 5.0

air pollution

◇   cities where sulphur dioxide emissions are recorded and exceed recommended levels

industrial sites emitting the largest amounts of sulphur

◯   over 200 000 tonnes

◯   100 000 – 200 000 tonnes

○   50 000 – 100 000 tonnes

○   30 000 – 50 000 tonnes

global warming
addition of greenhouse gases in tonnes of carbon per person
(look at the world map on page 17)

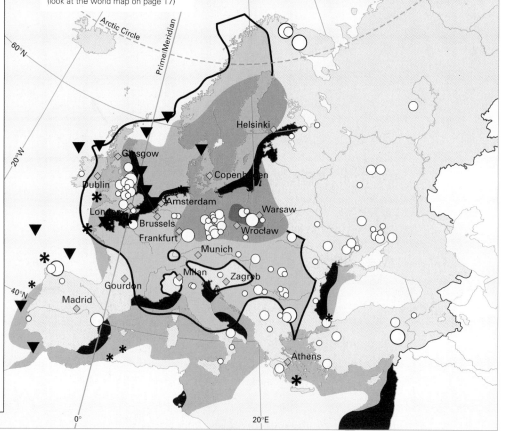

Conical Orthomorphic Projection
© Oxford University Press

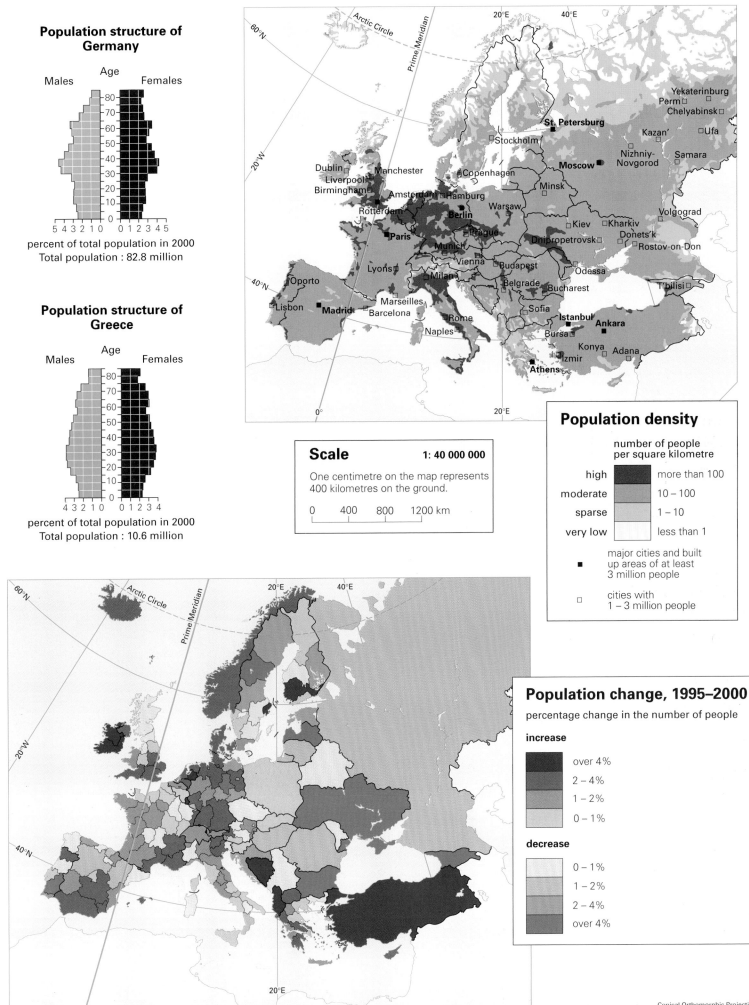

Population structure of Germany

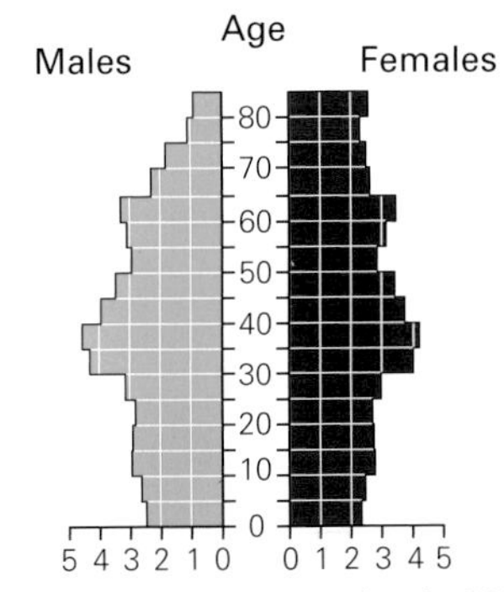

Males — Age — Females

5 4 3 2 1 0   0 1 2 3 4 5

percent of total population in 2000
Total population : 82.8 million

Population structure of Greece

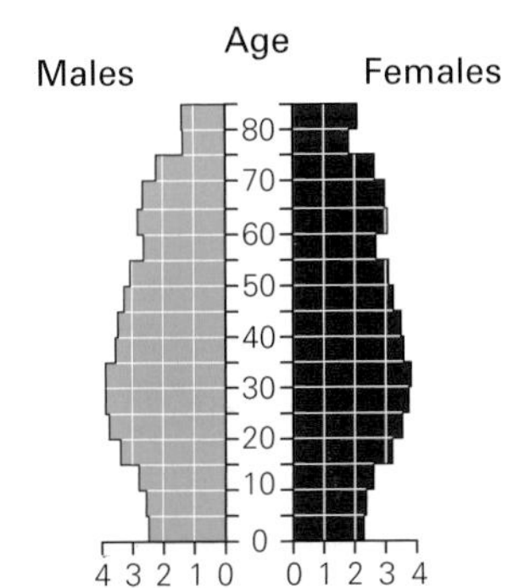

Males — Age — Females

4 3 2 1 0   0 1 2 3 4

percent of total population in 2000
Total population : 10.6 million

Scale   1: 40 000 000

One centimetre on the map represents
400 kilometres on the ground.

0   400   800   1200 km

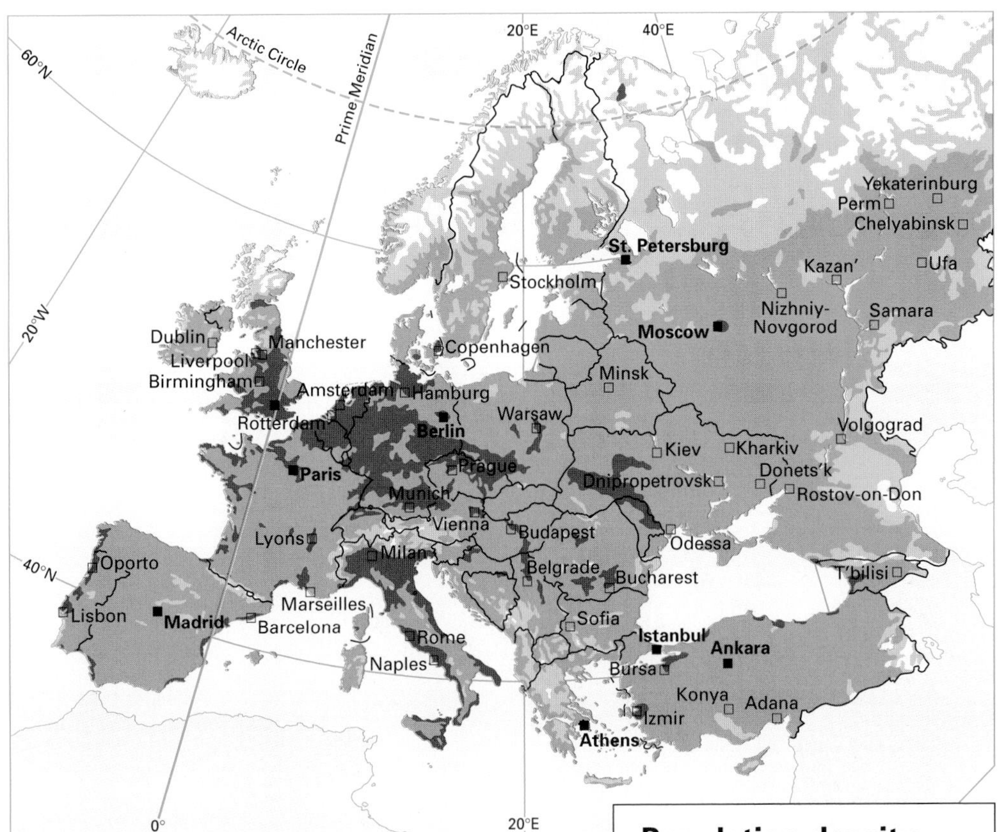

Population density

number of people
per square kilometre

high	more than 100
moderate	10 – 100
sparse	1 – 10
very low	less than 1

■ major cities and built up areas of at least 3 million people

□ cities with 1 – 3 million people

Population change, 1995–2000

percentage change in the number of people

increase

over 4%
2 – 4%
1 – 2%
0 – 1%

decrease

0 – 1%
1 – 2%
2 – 4%
over 4%

Conical Orthomorphic Projection
© Oxford University Press

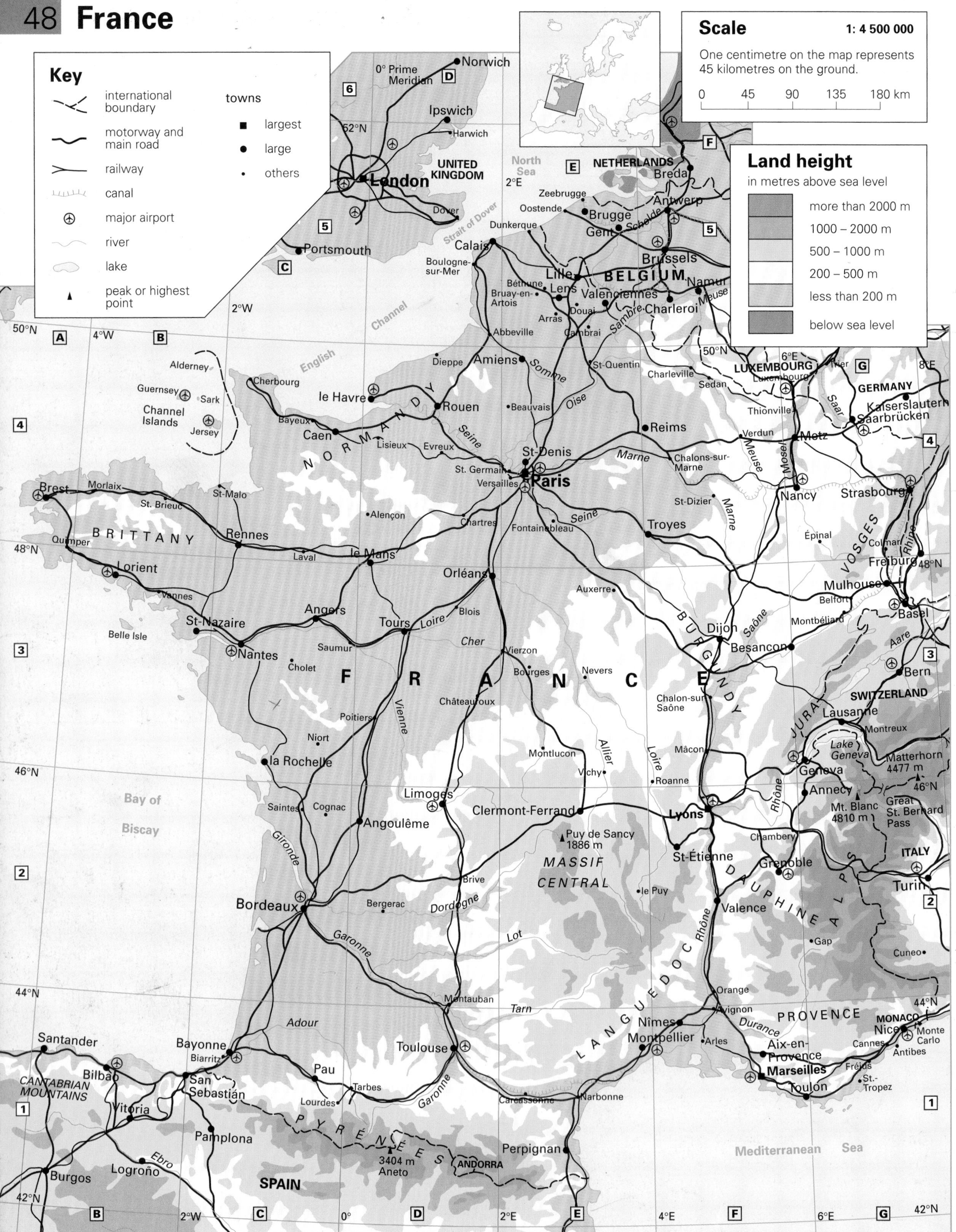

Conical Orthomorphic Projection   © Oxford University Press

Key

international boundary		towns	
motorway and main road		■	largest
railway		●	large
canal		·	others
✈	major airport		
river			
lake			
▲	peak or highest point		

Land height

in metres above sea level

- more than 2000 m
- 1000 – 2000 m
- 500 – 1000 m
- 200 – 500 m
- less than 200 m
- below sea level

Scale

1: 4 500 000

One centimetre on the map represents 45 kilometres on the ground.

0   45   90   135   180 km

Conical Orthomorphic Projection   © Oxford University Press

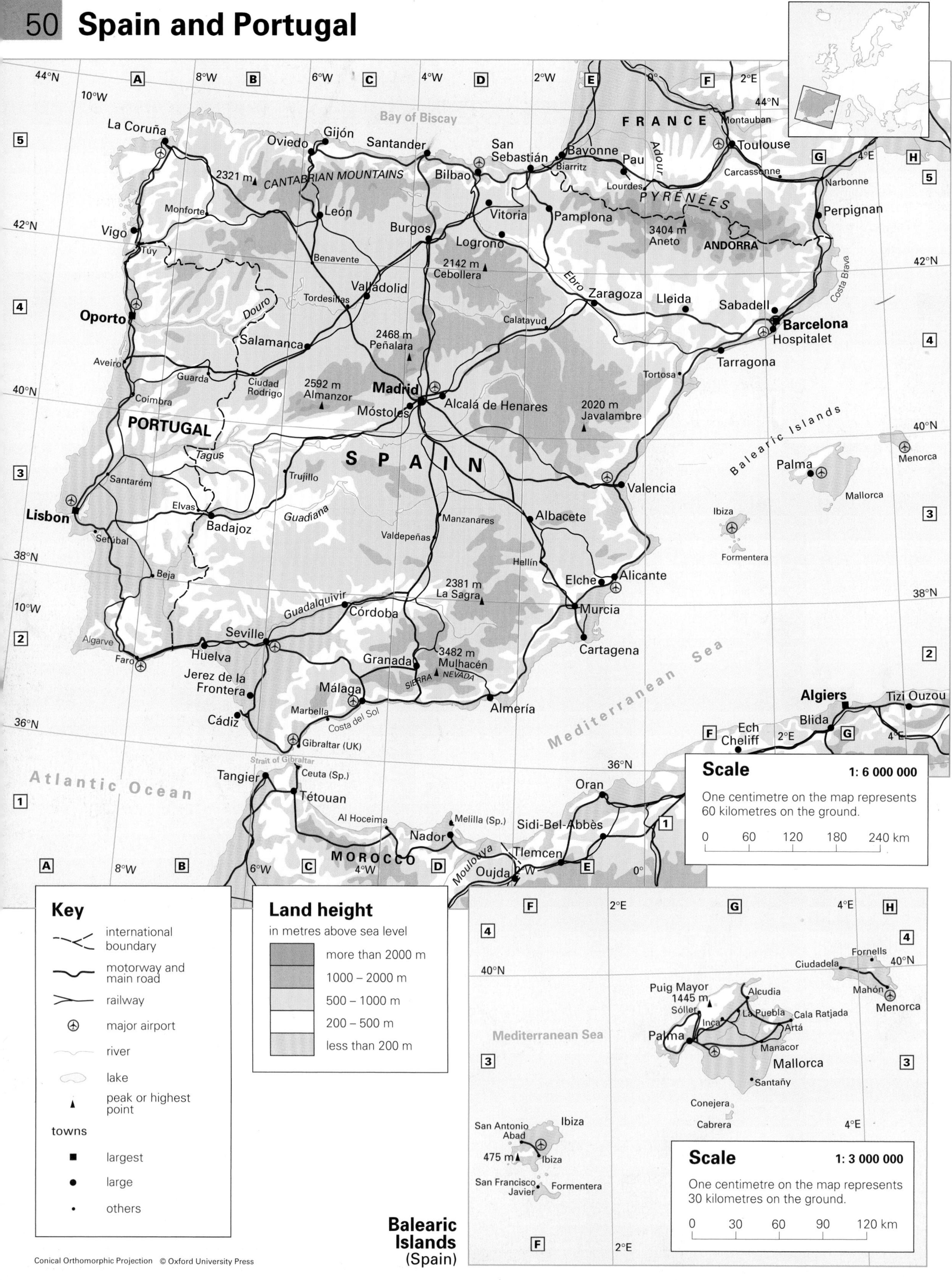

Key

- ⌇⌇ international boundary
- ⌇ motorway and main road
- ⌇ railway
- ⊕ major airport
- ⌇ river
- ⬭ lake
- ▲ peak or highest point

towns

- ■ largest
- ● large
- · others

Land height

in metres above sea level

- more than 2000 m
- 1000 – 2000 m
- 500 – 1000 m
- 200 – 500 m
- less than 200 m

Scale 1: 6 000 000

One centimetre on the map represents 60 kilometres on the ground.

0 60 120 180 240 km

Scale 1: 3 000 000

One centimetre on the map represents 30 kilometres on the ground.

0 30 60 90 120 km

Balearic Islands (Spain)

Conical Orthomorphic Projection © Oxford University Press

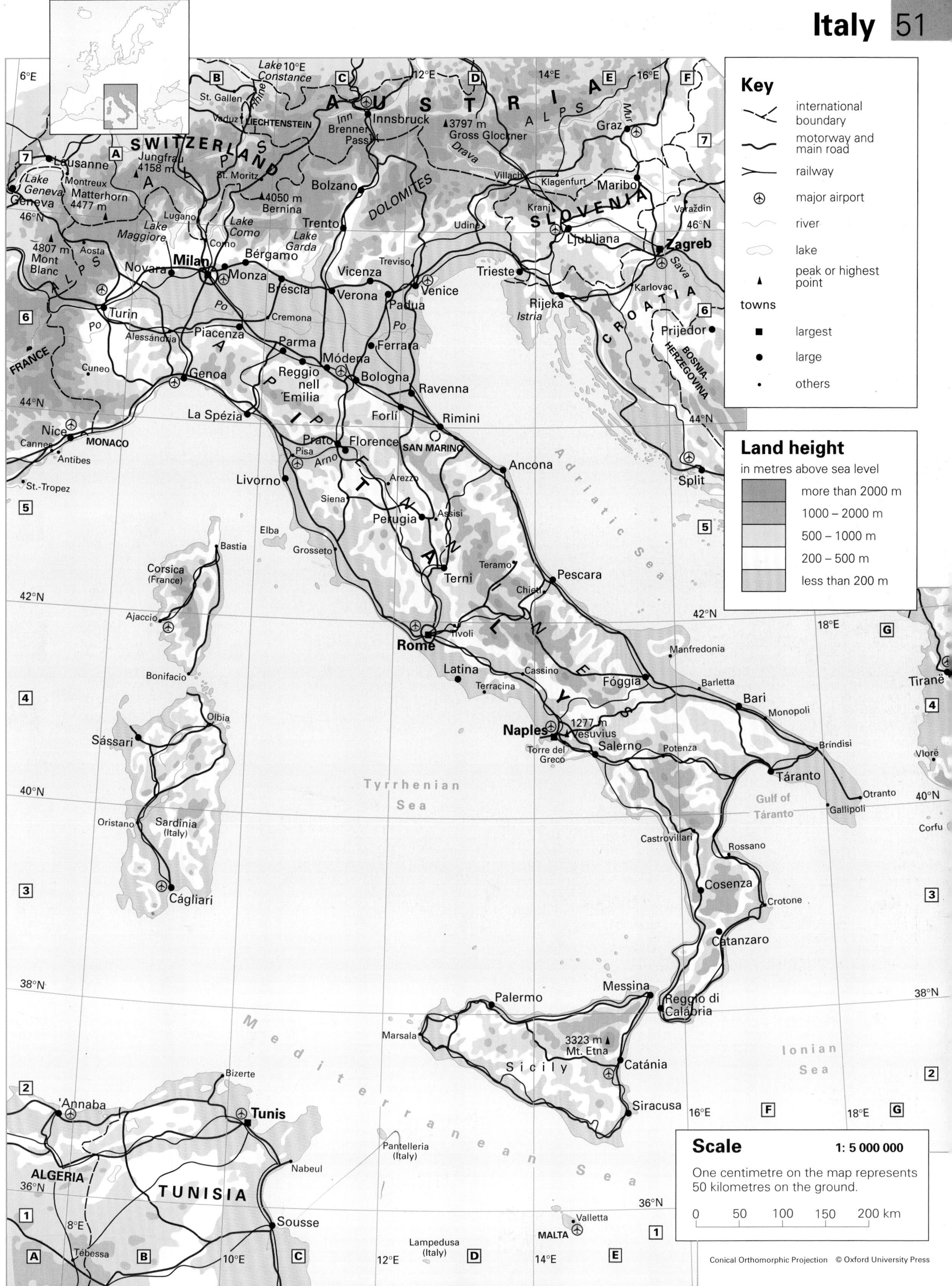

Key

- ⤬ international boundary
- ⌇ motorway and main road
- ⤲ railway
- ⊕ major airport
- ≈ river
- ◌ lake
- ▲ peak or highest point

towns
- ■ largest
- ● large
- · others

Land height
in metres above sea level

- more than 2000 m
- 1000 – 2000 m
- 500 – 1000 m
- 200 – 500 m
- less than 200 m

Scale   1: 5 000 000

One centimetre on the map represents 50 kilometres on the ground.

0   50   100   150   200 km

Conical Orthomorphic Projection   © Oxford University Press

SWITZERLAND · Lausanne · Montreux · Matterhorn 4477 m · Lake Geneva · Geneva · Jungfrau 4158 m · St. Moritz · 4050 m · Bernina · Lugano · Lake Como · Como · Mont Blanc 4807 m · Aosta · Novara · Milan · Monza · Bérgamo · Bréscia · Turin · Po · Piacenza · Alessándria · Cuneo · Genoa · Parma · Módena · Reggio nell 'Emilia · Bologna · La Spézia · Cremona · Ferrara

FRANCE · Nice · MONACO · Cannes · Antibes · St.-Tropez · Bastia · Corsica (France) · Ajaccio · Bonifacio · Sássari · Olbia · Oristano · Sardínia (Italy) · Cágliari

St. Gallen · Vaduz · LIECHTENSTEIN · Lake Constance · Rhine · Inn · Brenner Pass · Innsbruck · 3797 m Gross Glockner · Drava · Villach · Klagenfurt · Maribor · Bolzano · DOLOMITES · Trento · Trento · Udine · SLOVENIA · Kranj · Ljubljana · Zagreb · Trieste · Rijeka · Istria · Karlovac · Varaždin · Sava · CROATIA · Prijedor · BOSNIA-HERZEGOVINA

Vicenza · Verona · Padua · Venice · Treviso

AUSTRIA · ALPS · Graz · Mur

Po · Arno · Pisa · Prato · Florence · Livorno · Elba · Grosseto · Siena · Arezzo · Perugia · Assisi · SAN MARINO · Forlí · Rimini · Ravenna · Ancona · Adriatic Sea · Split

Teramo · Terni · Chieti · Pescara · Manfredonia · Tivoli · Rome · Latina · Terracina · Cassino · Fóggia · Barletta · Bari · Monopoli · Bríndisi · Tiranë · Vlorë · ALBANIA · Corfu · Otranto · Gallipoli · Táranto · Gulf of Táranto

Naples · 1277 m Vesuvius · Torre del Greco · Salerno · Potenza · Castrovillari · Rossano · Cosenza · Crotone · Catanzaro

Tyrrhenian Sea

Mediterranean Sea

Palermo · Marsala · Messina · Reggio di Calábria · Sicily · 3323 m Mt. Etna · Catánia · Siracusa · Ionian Sea

Pantelleria (Italy) · Nabeul · Tunis · TUNISIA · ALGERIA · 'Annaba · Bizerte · Sousse · Tébessa · Lampedusa (Italy) · Valletta · MALTA

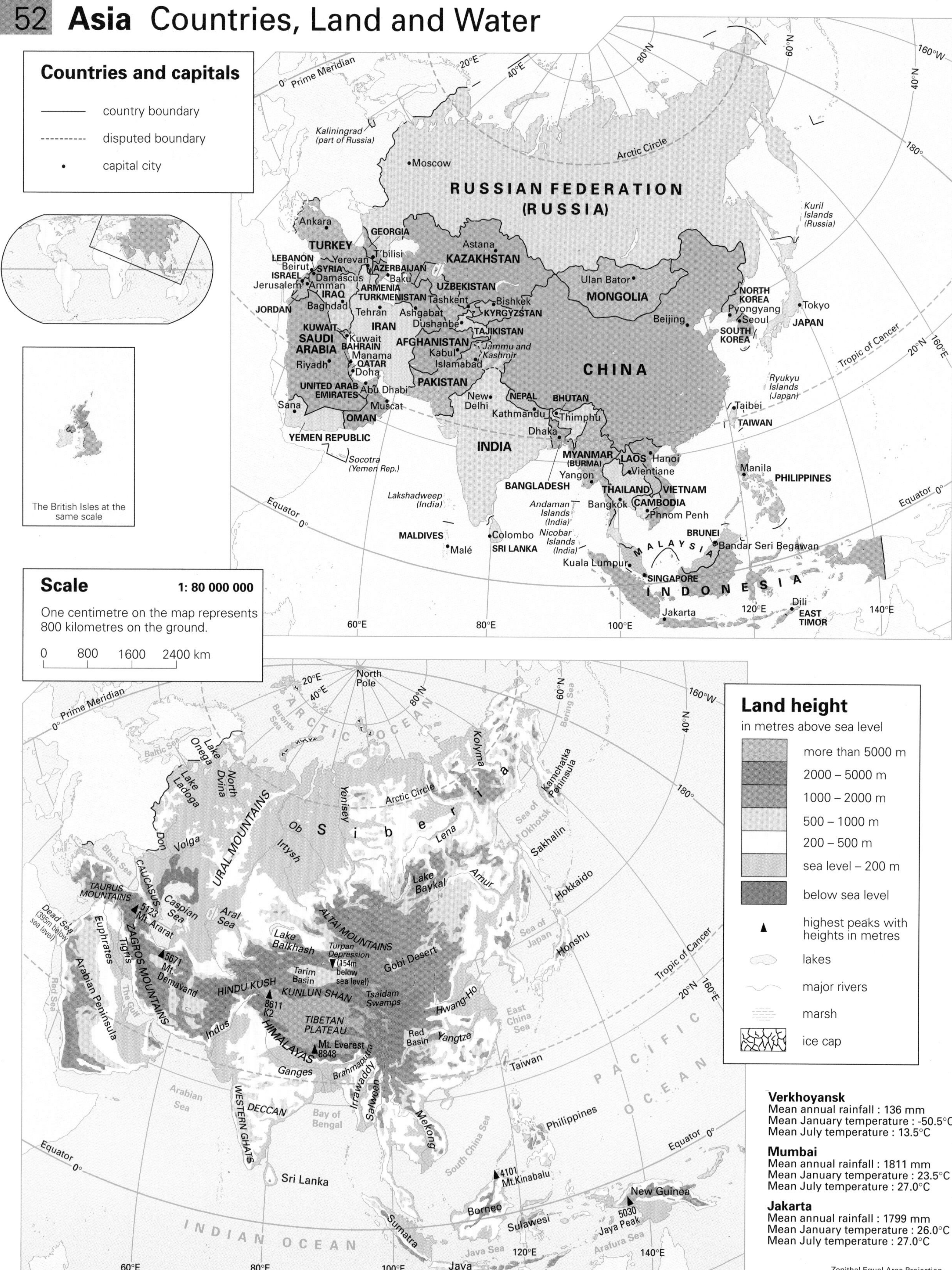

Countries and capitals

	country boundary
- - - -	disputed boundary
•	capital city

The British Isles at the same scale

Scale 1: 80 000 000

One centimetre on the map represents 800 kilometres on the ground.

0   800   1600   2400 km

Land height

in metres above sea level

- more than 5000 m
- 2000 – 5000 m
- 1000 – 2000 m
- 500 – 1000 m
- 200 – 500 m
- sea level – 200 m
- below sea level
- ▲ highest peaks with heights in metres
- lakes
- major rivers
- marsh
- ice cap

Verkhoyansk
Mean annual rainfall : 136 mm
Mean January temperature : -50.5°C
Mean July temperature : 13.5°C

Mumbai
Mean annual rainfall : 1811 mm
Mean January temperature : 23.5°C
Mean July temperature : 27.0°C

Jakarta
Mean annual rainfall : 1799 mm
Mean January temperature : 26.0°C
Mean July temperature : 27.0°C

Zenithal Equal Area Projection
© Oxford University Press

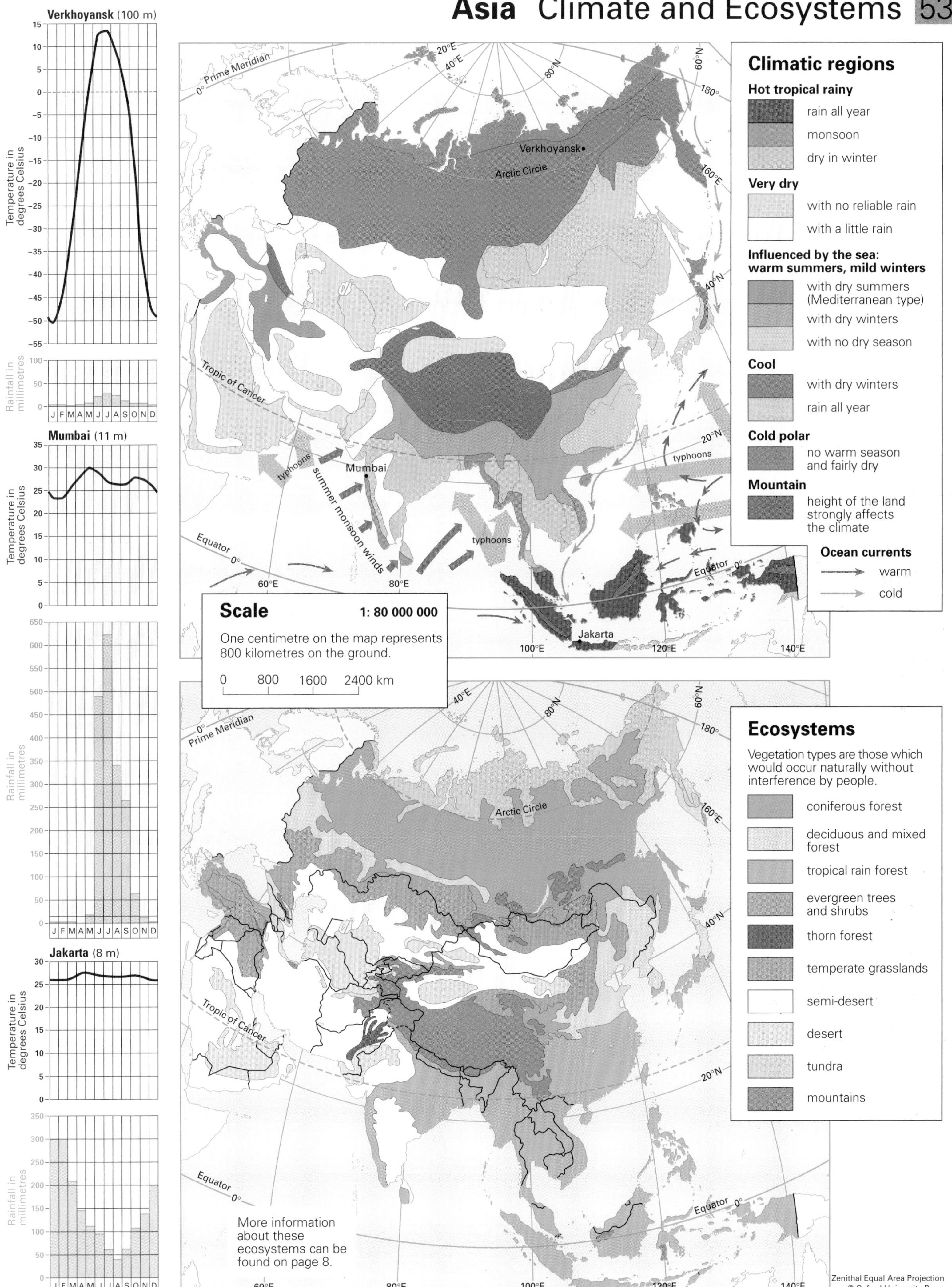

Verkhoyansk (100 m)

Temperature in degrees Celsius

Rainfall in millimetres

J F M A M J J A S O N D

Mumbai (11 m)

Temperature in degrees Celsius

Rainfall in millimetres

J F M A M J J A S O N D

Jakarta (8 m)

Temperature in degrees Celsius

Rainfall in millimetres

J F M A M J J A S O N D

Scale   1: 80 000 000

One centimetre on the map represents 800 kilometres on the ground.

0   800   1600   2400 km

Climatic regions

Hot tropical rainy
- rain all year
- monsoon
- dry in winter

Very dry
- with no reliable rain
- with a little rain

Influenced by the sea: warm summers, mild winters
- with dry summers (Mediterranean type)
- with dry winters
- with no dry season

Cool
- with dry winters
- rain all year

Cold polar
- no warm season and fairly dry

Mountain
- height of the land strongly affects the climate

Ocean currents
- warm
- cold

Ecosystems

Vegetation types are those which would occur naturally without interference by people.

- coniferous forest
- deciduous and mixed forest
- tropical rain forest
- evergreen trees and shrubs
- thorn forest
- temperate grasslands
- semi-desert
- desert
- tundra
- mountains

More information about these ecosystems can be found on page 8.

Zenithal Equal Area Projection
© Oxford University Press

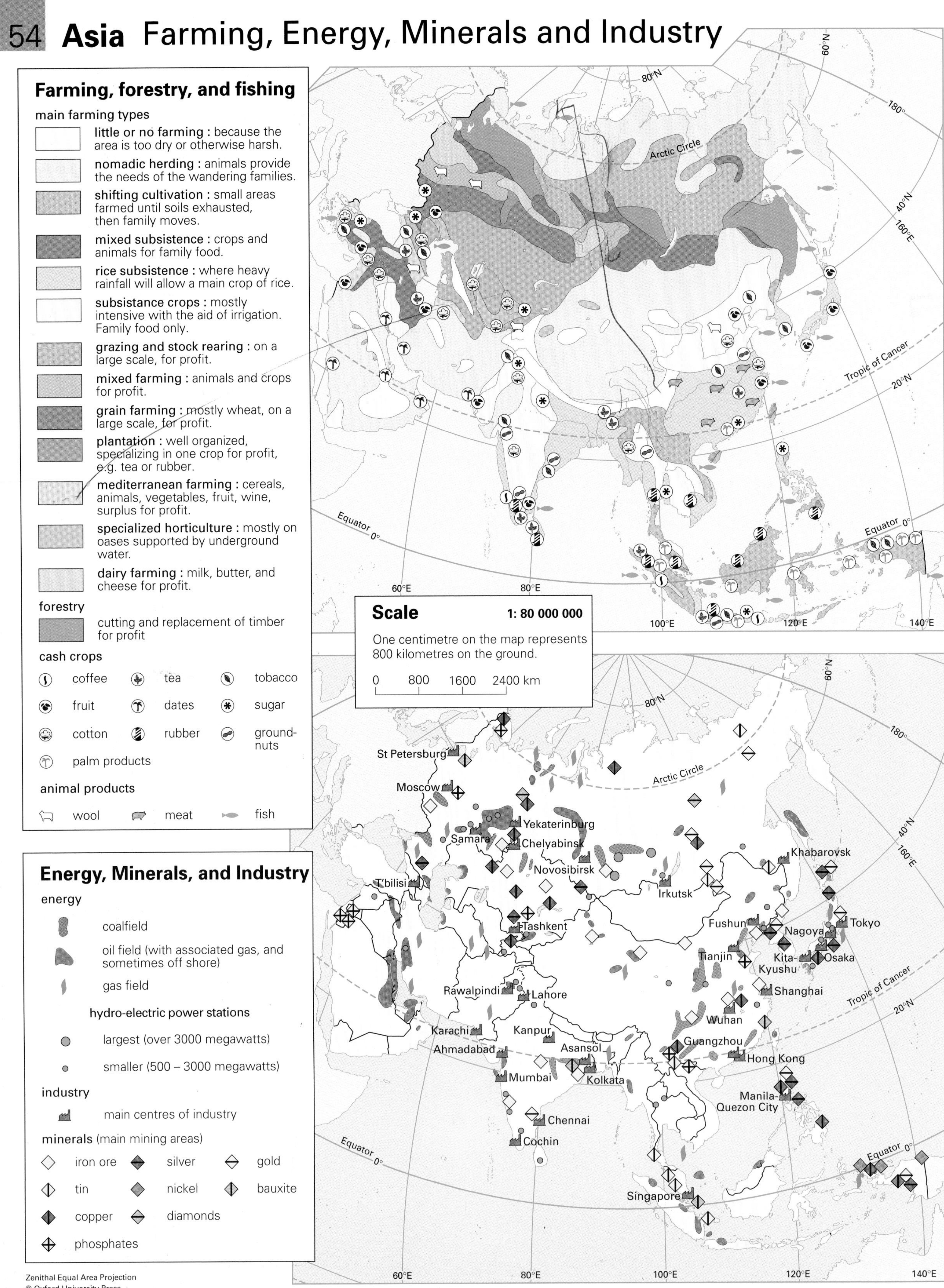

Farming, forestry, and fishing

main farming types

	little or no farming : because the area is too dry or otherwise harsh.
	nomadic herding : animals provide the needs of the wandering families.
	shifting cultivation : small areas farmed until soils exhausted, then family moves.
	mixed subsistence : crops and animals for family food.
	rice subsistence : where heavy rainfall will allow a main crop of rice.
	subsistance crops : mostly intensive with the aid of irrigation. Family food only.
	grazing and stock rearing : on a large scale, for profit.
	mixed farming : animals and crops for profit.
	grain farming : mostly wheat, on a large scale, for profit.
	plantation : well organized, specializing in one crop for profit, e.g. tea or rubber.
	mediterranean farming : cereals, animals, vegetables, fruit, wine, surplus for profit.
	specialized horticulture : mostly on oases supported by underground water.
	dairy farming : milk, butter, and cheese for profit.

forestry

	cutting and replacement of timber for profit

cash crops

Ⓢ	coffee	🍃	tea		tobacco
	fruit	ⓣ	dates	✳	sugar
	cotton		rubber		ground-nuts
ⓣ	palm products				

animal products

🐑	wool		meat	🐟	fish

Energy, Minerals, and Industry

energy

	coalfield
	oil field (with associated gas, and sometimes off shore)
	gas field

hydro-electric power stations

●	largest (over 3000 megawatts)
•	smaller (500 – 3000 megawatts)

industry

🏭	main centres of industry

minerals (main mining areas)

◇	iron ore	◆	silver	◇	gold
◇	tin	◆	nickel	◇	bauxite
◆	copper	◇	diamonds		
⊕	phosphates				

Scale   1: 80 000 000

One centimetre on the map represents 800 kilometres on the ground.

0   800   1600   2400 km

Zenithal Equal Area Projection
© Oxford University Press

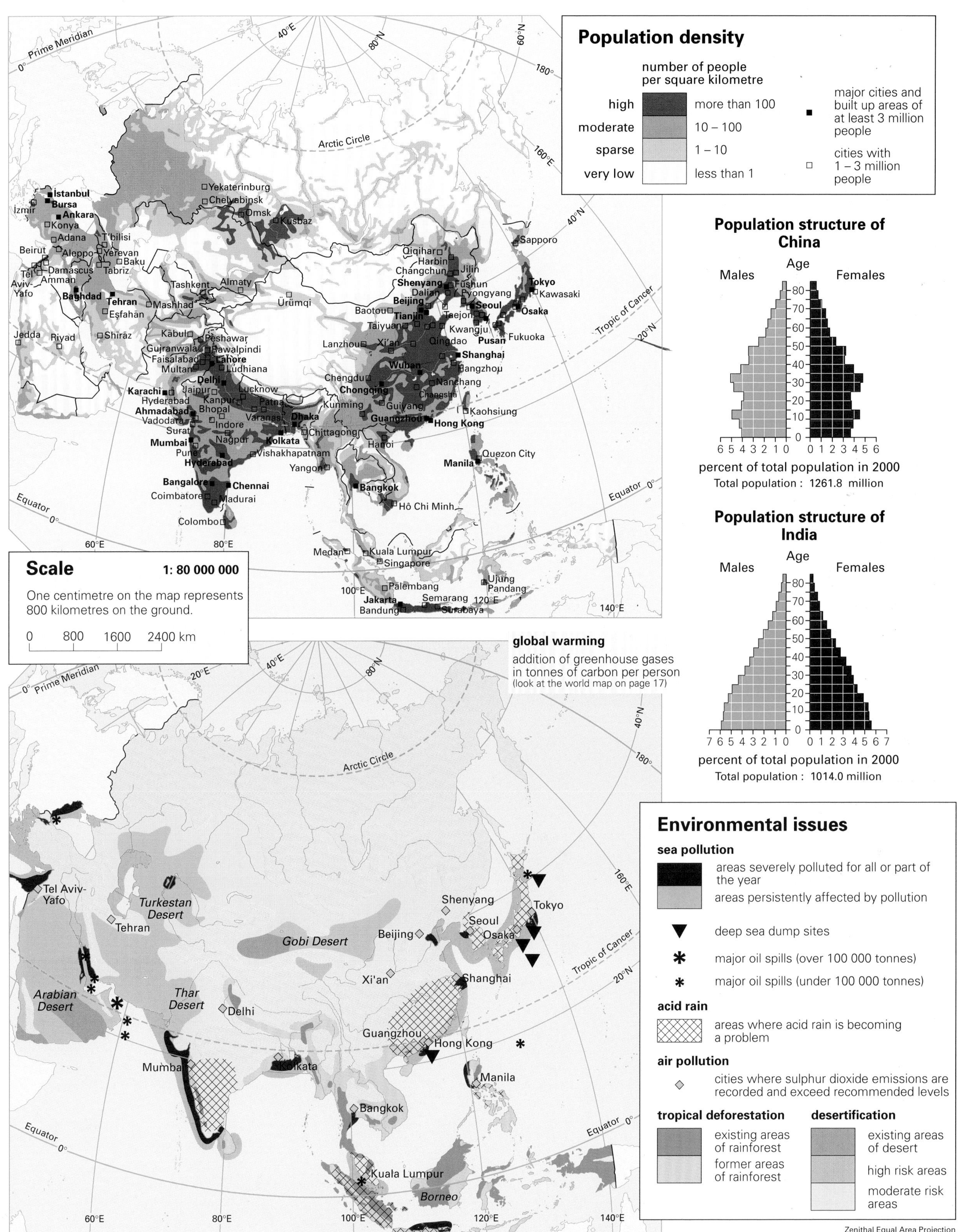

Population density

number of people per square kilometre

high	more than 100
moderate	10 – 100
sparse	1 – 10
very low	less than 1

■ major cities and built up areas of at least 3 million people

□ cities with 1 – 3 million people

Population structure of China

Males — Age — Females

percent of total population in 2000
Total population : 1261.8 million

Population structure of India

Males — Age — Females

percent of total population in 2000
Total population : 1014.0 million

Scale   1: 80 000 000

One centimetre on the map represents 800 kilometres on the ground.

0   800   1600   2400 km

global warming
addition of greenhouse gases in tonnes of carbon per person
(look at the world map on page 17)

Environmental issues

sea pollution

▮ areas severely polluted for all or part of the year

▯ areas persistently affected by pollution

▼ deep sea dump sites

✳ major oil spills (over 100 000 tonnes)

✲ major oil spills (under 100 000 tonnes)

acid rain

▨ areas where acid rain is becoming a problem

air pollution

◇ cities where sulphur dioxide emissions are recorded and exceed recommended levels

tropical deforestation

existing areas of rainforest

former areas of rainforest

desertification

existing areas of desert

high risk areas

moderate risk areas

Zenithal Equal Area Projection
© Oxford University Press

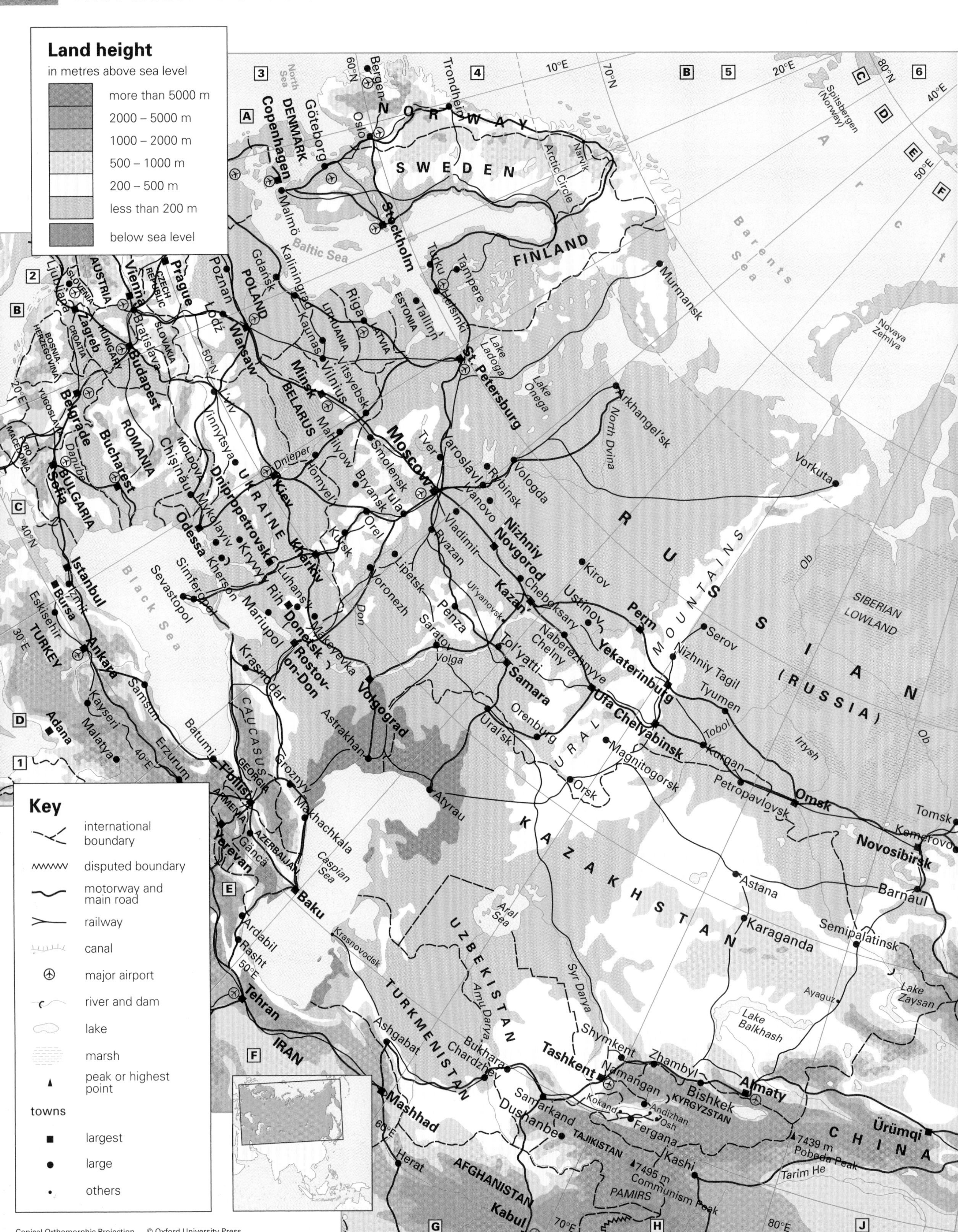

Land height

in metres above sea level

- more than 5000 m
- 2000 – 5000 m
- 1000 – 2000 m
- 500 – 1000 m
- 200 – 500 m
- less than 200 m
- below sea level

Key

- international boundary
- ᨿᨿᨿ disputed boundary
- motorway and main road
- railway
- canal
- ⊕ major airport
- river and dam
- lake
- marsh
- ▲ peak or highest point

towns

- ■ largest
- ● large
- • others

Conical Orthomorphic Projection   © Oxford University Press

Scale 1: 20 000 000

One centimetre on the map represents
200 kilometres on the ground.

0 200 400 600 800 km

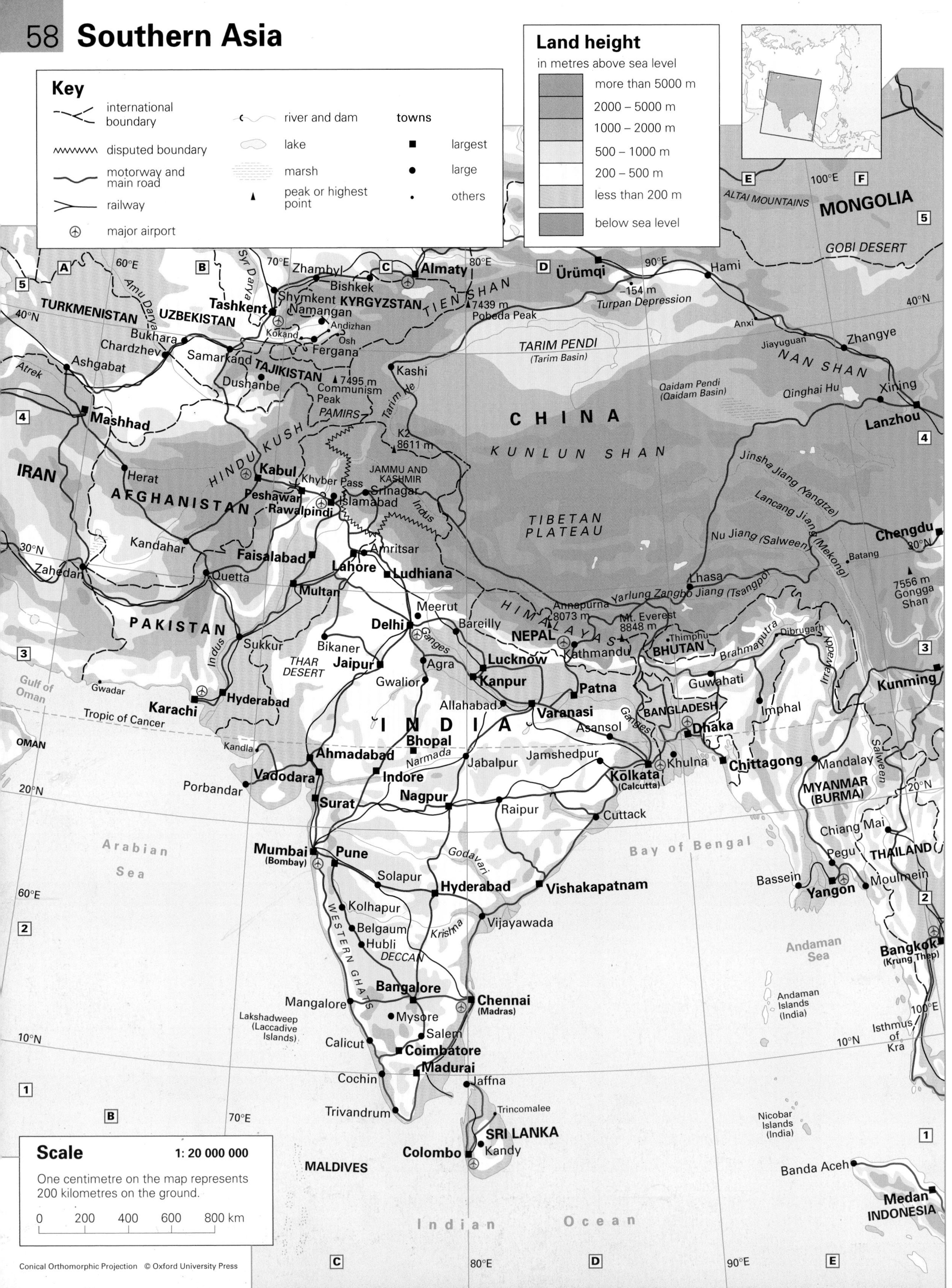

Key

				towns
international boundary		river and dam	■	largest
disputed boundary		lake	●	large
motorway and main road		marsh	·	others
railway		peak or highest point		
major airport				

Land height

in metres above sea level

- more than 5000 m
- 2000 – 5000 m
- 1000 – 2000 m
- 500 – 1000 m
- 200 – 500 m
- less than 200 m
- below sea level

Scale 1: 20 000 000

One centimetre on the map represents 200 kilometres on the ground.

0 200 400 600 800 km

Conical Orthomorphic Projection © Oxford University Press

© Oxford University Press

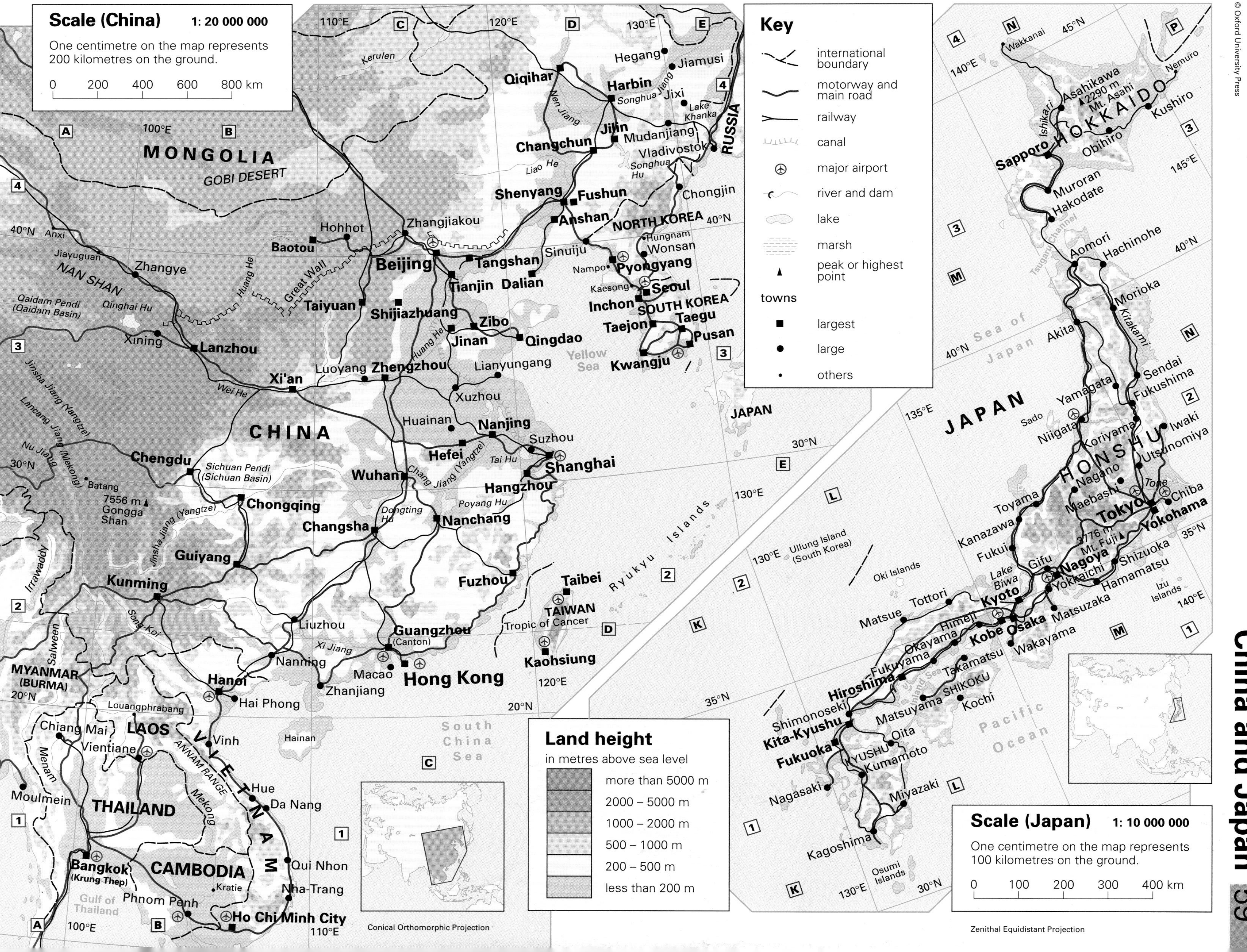

Scale (Japan) 1: 10 000 000

One centimetre on the map represents
100 kilometres on the ground.

0   100   200   300   400 km

Zenithal Equidistant Projection

Key

international boundary	
motorway and main road	
railway	
canal	
major airport	⊕
river and dam	
lake	
marsh	
peak or highest point	▲

towns
largest	■
large	●
others	·

Land height
in metres above sea level

more than 5000 m	
2000 – 5000 m	
1000 – 2000 m	
500 – 1000 m	
200 – 500 m	
less than 200 m	

Conical Orthomorphic Projection

Scale (China) 1: 20 000 000

One centimetre on the map represents
200 kilometres on the ground.

0   200   400   600   800 km

Map labels (selected):

HOKKAIDO, HONSHU, JAPAN, KYUSHU, SHIKOKU, Sapporo, Sendai, Tokyo, Yokohama, Nagoya, Kyoto, Osaka, Kobe, Hiroshima, Fukuoka, Kita-Kyushu, Nagasaki, Kagoshima, Sea of Japan, Pacific Ocean, Ryukyu Islands, Mt. Fuji 3776

RUSSIA, MONGOLIA, CHINA, NORTH KOREA, SOUTH KOREA, JAPAN, TAIWAN, MYANMAR (BURMA), LAOS, THAILAND, CAMBODIA, VIETNAM

Harbin, Qiqihar, Changchun, Jilin, Shenyang, Fushun, Anshan, Beijing, Tianjin, Tangshan, Dalian, Shijiazhuang, Taiyuan, Baotou, Hohhot, Lanzhou, Xining, Xi'an, Chengdu, Chongqing, Kunming, Guiyang, Changsha, Wuhan, Nanchang, Fuzhou, Guangzhou, Hong Kong, Macao, Shanghai, Nanjing, Hangzhou, Hefei, Zhengzhou, Luoyang, Jinan, Zibo, Qingdao, Taibei, Kaohsiung

Pyongyang, Seoul, Inchon, Taejon, Taegu, Pusan, Kwangju, Yellow Sea, South China Sea, Tropic of Cancer

Gobi Desert, Nan Shan, Qaidam Pendi (Qaidam Basin), Sichuan Pendi (Sichuan Basin), Great Wall, Huang He, Chang Jiang (Yangtze), Jinsha Jiang (Yangtze), Lancang Jiang (Mekong), Mekong, Irrawaddy, Salween, Gongga Shan 7556

Hanoi, Hai Phong, Da Nang, Qui Nhon, Nha-Trang, Ho Chi Minh City, Phnom Penh, Bangkok (Krung Thep), Vientiane, Gulf of Thailand

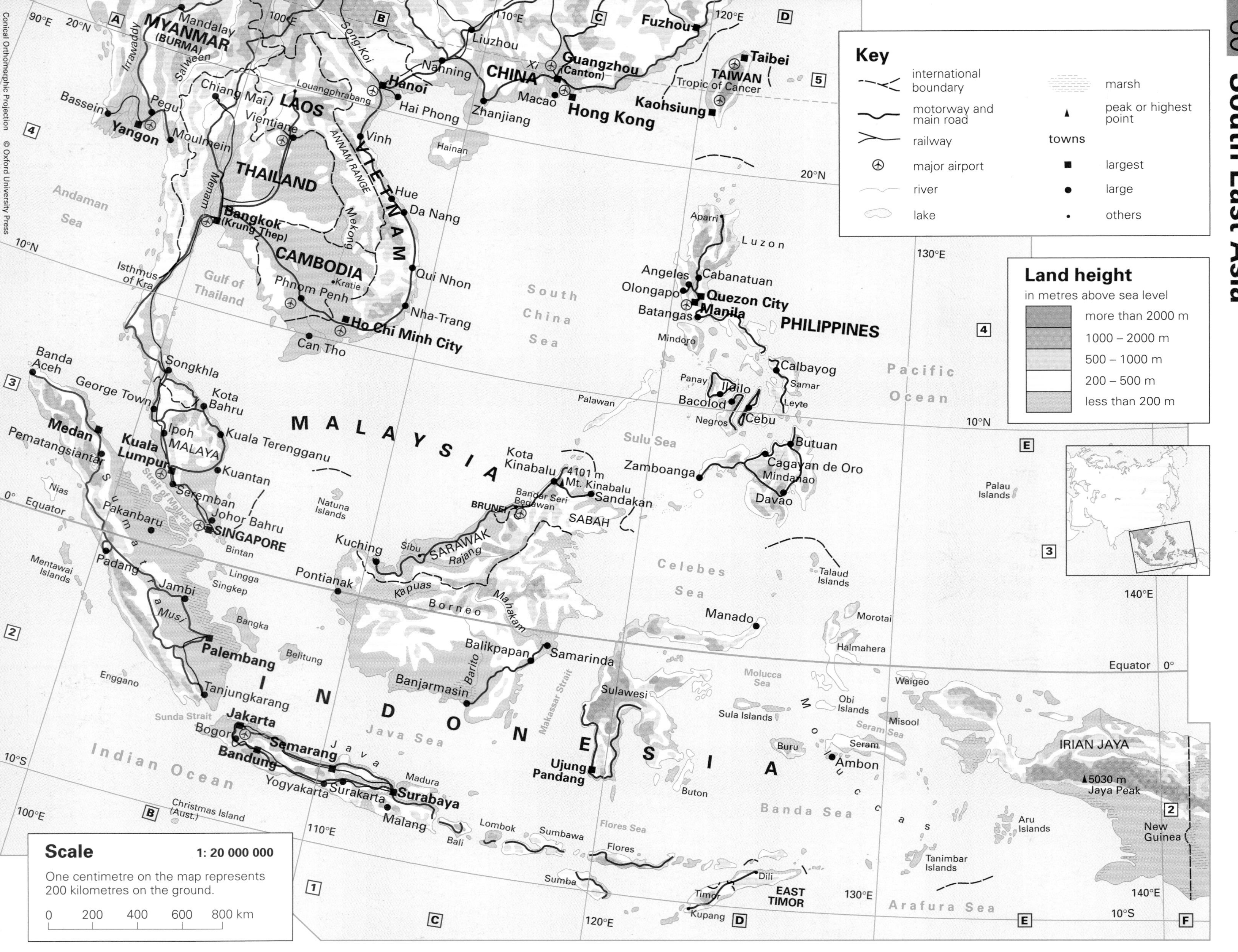

Key

marsh		peak or highest point
		towns
international boundary		largest
motorway and main road		large
railway		others
major airport		river
		lake

Land height
in metres above sea level

- more than 2000 m
- 1000 – 2000 m
- 500 – 1000 m
- 200 – 500 m
- less than 200 m

Scale

1 : 20 000 000

One centimetre on the map represents
200 kilometres on the ground.

0 200 400 600 800 km

Conical Orthomorphic Projection   © Oxford University Press

PHILIPPINES

Luzon

Aparri

Cabanatuan

Quezon City

Manila

Angeles

Olongapo

Batangas

Mindoro

Calbayog

Samar

Leyte

Iloilo

Cebu

Bacolod

Panay

Negros

Butuan

Cagayan de Oro

Mindanao

Davao

Zamboanga

Sulu Sea

Palawan

Sandakan

Mt. Kinabalu 4101 m

Kota Kinabalu

SABAH

Bandar Seri Begawan

BRUNEI

SARAWAK

Rajang

Sibu

Kuching

Borneo

Kapuas

Pontianak

Natuna Islands

MALAYSIA

Kuala Terengganu

Kuantan

Kota Bahru

Songkhla

George Town

Ipoh

MALAYA

Kuala Lumpur

Seremban

Johor Bahru

SINGAPORE

Bintan

Lingga

Singkep

Bangka

Belitung

Strait of Malacca

Medan

Pematangsiantar

Pekanbaru

Padang

Jambi

Palembang

INDONESIA

Musi

Tanjungkarang

Sunda Strait

Nias

Mentawai Islands

Enggano

Banda Aceh

Indian Ocean

Christmas Island (Aust.)

Jakarta

Bogor

Bandung

Java

Semarang

Surakarta

Yogyakarta

Surabaya

Malang

Madura

Bali

Java Sea

Lombok

Sumbawa

Sumba

Flores

Flores Sea

Bali

Ujung Pandang

Sulawesi

Samarinda

Mahakam

Balikpapan

Barito

Banjarmasin

Makassar Strait

Celebes Sea

Manado

Morotai

Halmahera

Molucca Sea

Obi Islands

Sula Islands

Seram

Seram Sea

Buru

Ambon

Banda Sea

Buton

Button

Tanimbar Islands

Aru Islands

Arafura Sea

Weigeo

Misool

IRIAN JAYA

New Guinea

Jaya Peak ▲5030 m

EAST TIMOR

Dili

Timor

Kupang

Talaud Islands

Palau Islands

Pacific Ocean

South China Sea

CHINA

Fuzhou

Guangzhou (Canton)

Xi

Macao

Zhanjiang

Hong Kong

Kaohsiung

Taibei

TAIWAN

Tropic of Cancer

Liuzhou

Nanning

Hainan

Hai Phong

Hanoi

Vinh

Song-Koi

Louangphrabang

Vientiane

Chiang Mai

LAOS

VIETNAM

Hue

Da Nang

Qui Nhon

Nha-Trang

Ho Chi Minh City

Can Tho

ANNAM RANGE

Mekong

Kratie

Phnom Penh

CAMBODIA

THAILAND

Bangkok (Krung Thep)

Menam

Gulf of Thailand

Isthmus of Kra

MYANMAR (BURMA)

Mandalay

Moulmein

Pegu

Yangon

Bassein

Irrawaddy

Salween

Andaman Sea

Equator

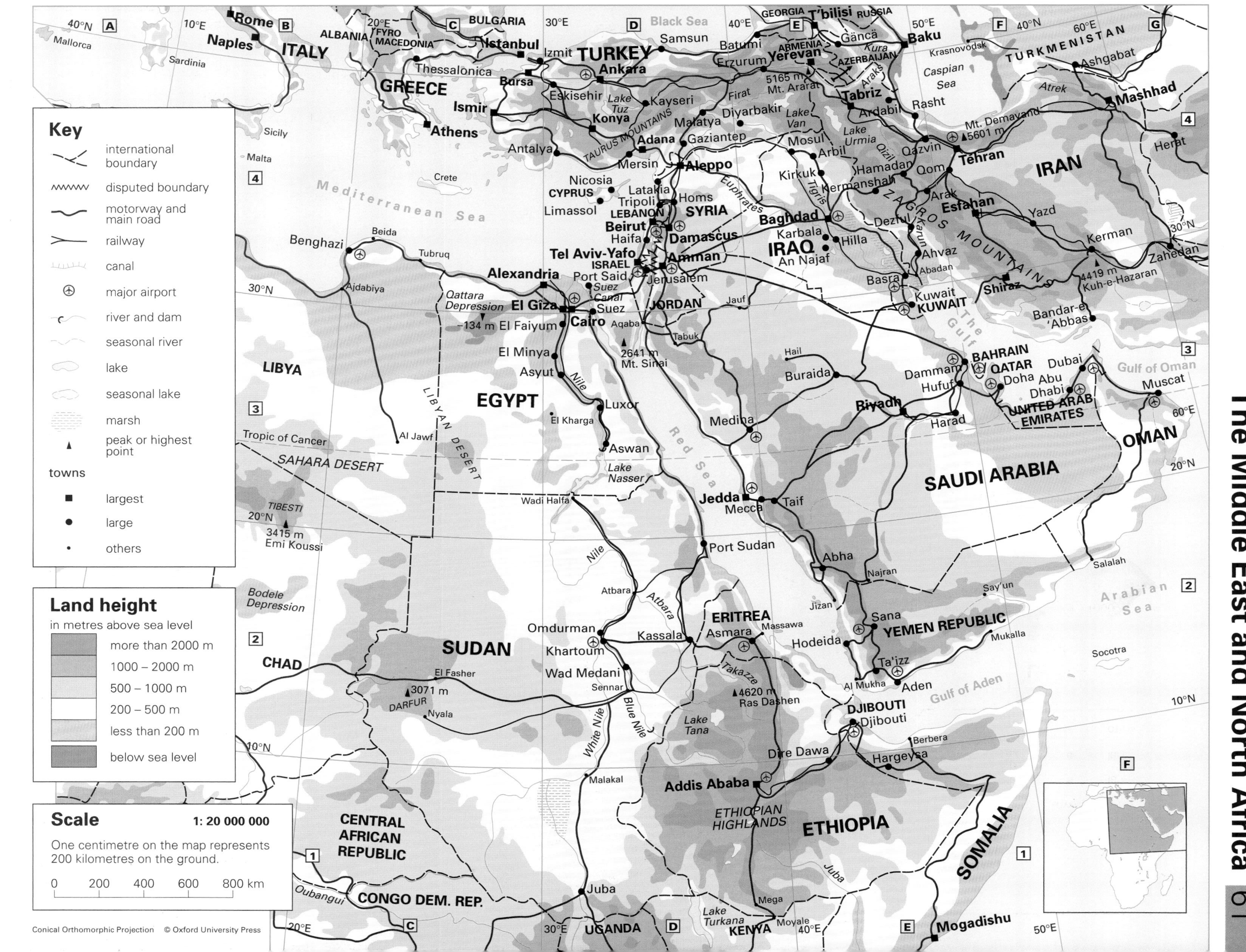

Key

Y	international boundary
Y	disputed boundary
wwww	motorway and main road
	railway
	canal
⊕	major airport
	river and dam
	seasonal river
	lake
	seasonal lake
	marsh
▲	peak or highest point

towns

■ largest

● large

• others

Land height

in metres above sea level

	more than 2000 m
	1000 – 2000 m
	500 – 1000 m
	200 – 500 m
	less than 200 m
	below sea level

Scale

1: 20 000 000

One centimetre on the map represents 200 kilometres on the ground.

0 200 400 600 800 km

Conical Orthomorphic Projection   © Oxford University Press

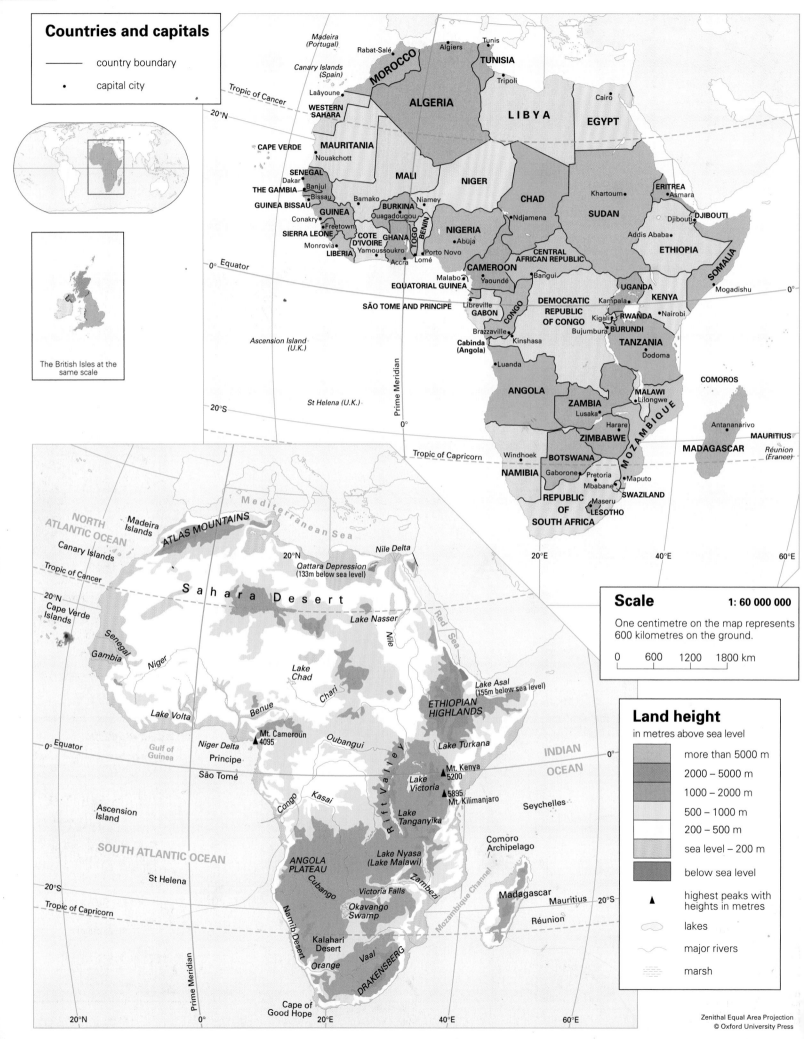

Countries and capitals

—— country boundary

• capital city

The British Isles at the same scale

Tropic of Cancer

20°N

MOROCCO
Rabat-Salé
Madeira (Portugal)
Canary Islands (Spain)
Laâyoune
WESTERN SAHARA
Algiers
TUNISIA
Tunis
Tripoli
ALGERIA
LIBYA
EGYPT
Cairo

CAPE VERDE
MAURITANIA
Nouakchott
MALI
NIGER
CHAD
SUDAN
Khartoum
ERITREA
Asmara
DJIBOUTI
Djibouti

SENEGAL
Dakar
THE GAMBIA
Banjul
Bamako
Niamey
Ndjamena
GUINEA BISSAU
Bissau
BURKINA
Ouagadougou
NIGERIA
Abuja
CENTRAL AFRICAN REPUBLIC
Addis Ababa
ETHIOPIA
GUINEA
Conakry
SIERRA LEONE
Freetown
COTE D'IVOIRE
GHANA
TOGO
BENIN
Porto Novo
Lomé
CAMEROON
Bangui
UGANDA
Kampala
KENYA
SOMALIA
Mogadishu
Monrovia
LIBERIA
Yamoussoukro
Accra

Equator 0°

Malabo
Yaoundé
EQUATORIAL GUINEA
SÃO TOME AND PRINCIPE
Libreville
GABON
CONGO
Brazzaville
DEMOCRATIC REPUBLIC OF CONGO
Kinshasa
Kigali
RWANDA
BURUNDI
Bujumbura
Nairobi
TANZANIA
Dodoma
Cabinda (Angola)
Luanda

COMOROS

ANGOLA
ZAMBIA
Lusaka
MALAWI
Lilongwe
Antananarivo
MADAGASCAR
MAURITIUS
Réunion (France)

20°S

ZIMBABWE
Harare
MOZAMBIQUE
Tropic of Capricorn
Windhoek
BOTSWANA
Gaborone
Pretoria
Maputo
SWAZILAND
NAMIBIA
Mbabane
REPUBLIC OF SOUTH AFRICA
Maseru
LESOTHO

Prime Meridian

Ascension Island (U.K.)

St Helena (U.K.)

Scale 1: 60 000 000

One centimetre on the map represents 600 kilometres on the ground.

0   600   1200   1800 km

NORTH ATLANTIC OCEAN
Madeira Islands
ATLAS MOUNTAINS
Mediterranean Sea
Nile Delta
Qattara Depression (133m below sea level)

Canary Islands
Tropic of Cancer
20°N
Cape Verde Islands
Sahara Desert
Lake Nasser
Nile
Red Sea

Senegal
Gambia
Niger
Lake Chad
Chari
Lake Asal (155m below sea level)

Lake Volta
Benue
Mt. Cameroun ▲ 4095
ETHIOPIAN HIGHLANDS

Gulf of Guinea
Niger Delta
Principe
São Tomé
Oubangui
Lake Turkana
INDIAN OCEAN
Equator 0°
0°
Mt. Kenya ▲ 5200
Ascension Island
Congo
Kasai
Rift Valley
Lake Victoria
▲ 5895 Mt. Kilimanjaro
Seychelles

SOUTH ATLANTIC OCEAN
Lake Tanganyika
Comoro Archipelago
Madagascar
Mauritius

St Helena
ANGOLA PLATEAU
Cubango
Lake Nyasa (Lake Malawi)
Zambezi
20°S
Victoria Falls
Mozambique Channel
Réunion
Namib Desert
Okavango Swamp
Kalahari Desert
Vaal
Orange
DRAKENSBERG

Tropic of Capricorn
Prime Meridian
Cape of Good Hope
20°N
0°
20°E
40°E
60°E

Land height

in metres above sea level

more than 5000 m

2000 – 5000 m

1000 – 2000 m

500 – 1000 m

200 – 500 m

sea level – 200 m

below sea level

▲ highest peaks with heights in metres

lakes

major rivers

marsh

Zenithal Equal Area Projection
© Oxford University Press

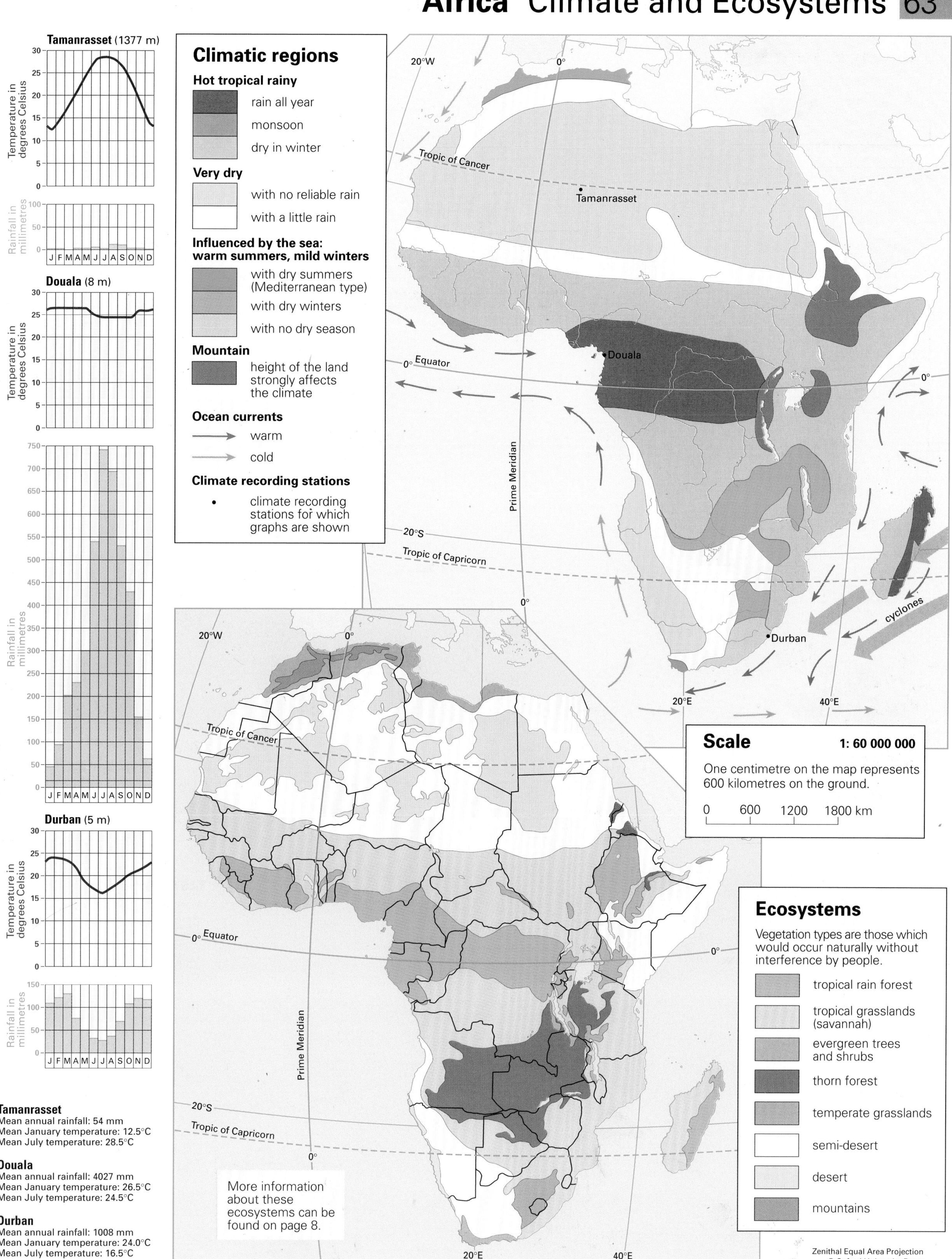

Tamanrasset (1377 m)

Temperature in degrees Celsius

Rainfall in millimetres

J F M A M J J A S O N D

Douala (8 m)

Temperature in degrees Celsius

Rainfall in millimetres

J F M A M J J A S O N D

Durban (5 m)

Temperature in degrees Celsius

Rainfall in millimetres

J F M A M J J A S O N D

Climatic regions

Hot tropical rainy

rain all year

monsoon

dry in winter

Very dry

with no reliable rain

with a little rain

Influenced by the sea: warm summers, mild winters

with dry summers (Mediterranean type)

with dry winters

with no dry season

Mountain

height of the land strongly affects the climate

Ocean currents

→ warm

→ cold

Climate recording stations

• climate recording stations for which graphs are shown

20°W 0° Tropic of Cancer Tamanrasset

0° Equator Douala

Prime Meridian

20°S Tropic of Capricorn

0° 0°

cyclones

Durban

20°E 40°E

Scale
1: 60 000 000

One centimetre on the map represents 600 kilometres on the ground.

0   600   1200   1800 km

20°W 0° Tropic of Cancer

0° Equator 0°

Prime Meridian

20°S Tropic of Capricorn

0° 20°E 40°E

More information about these ecosystems can be found on page 8.

Ecosystems

Vegetation types are those which would occur naturally without interference by people.

tropical rain forest

tropical grasslands (savannah)

evergreen trees and shrubs

thorn forest

temperate grasslands

semi-desert

desert

mountains

Tamanrasset
Mean annual rainfall: 54 mm
Mean January temperature: 12.5°C
Mean July temperature: 28.5°C

Douala
Mean annual rainfall: 4027 mm
Mean January temperature: 26.5°C
Mean July temperature: 24.5°C

Durban
Mean annual rainfall: 1008 mm
Mean January temperature: 24.0°C
Mean July temperature: 16.5°C

Zenithal Equal Area Projection
© Oxford University Press

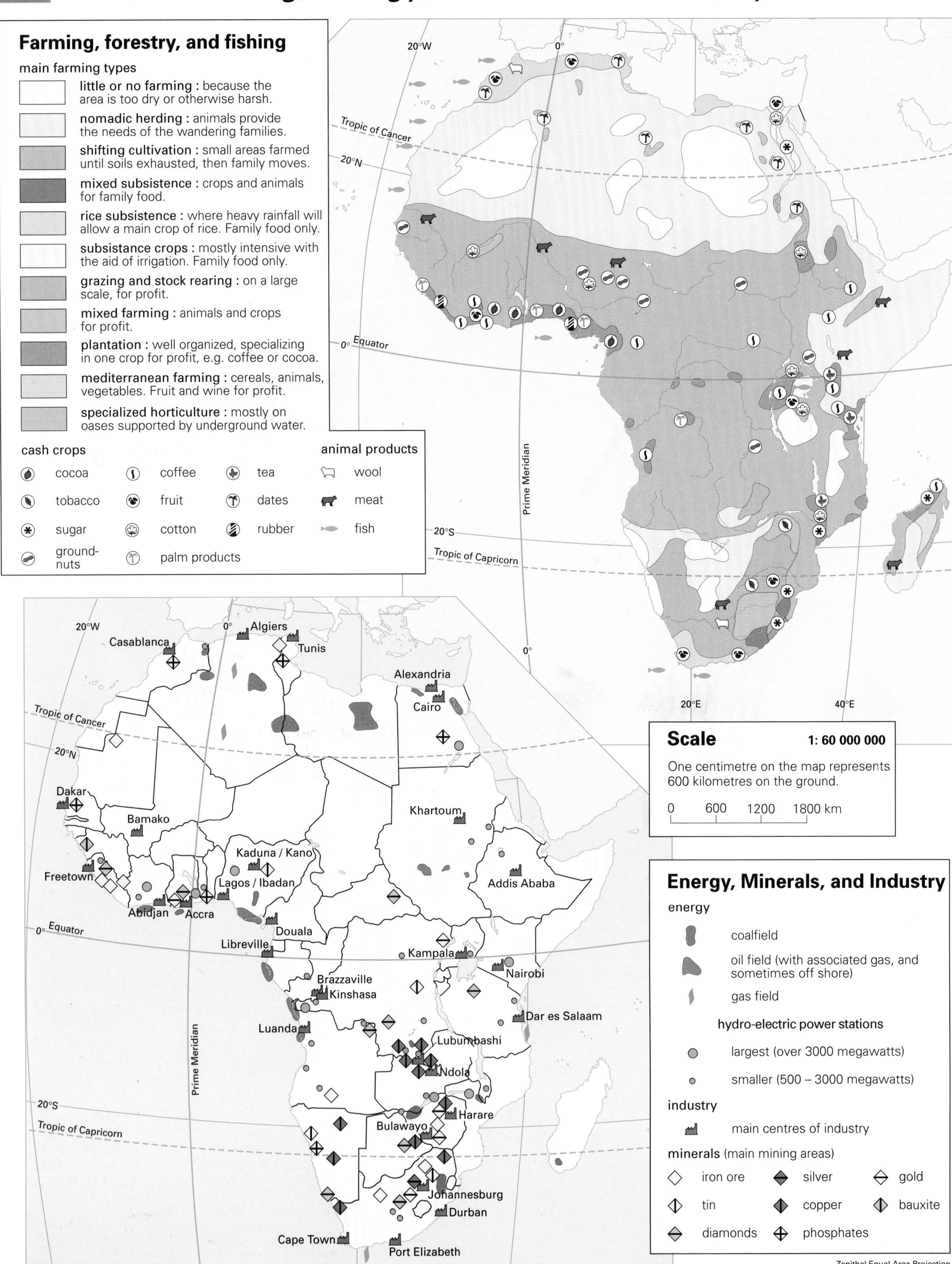

Farming, forestry, and fishing

main farming types

- **little or no farming** : because the area is too dry or otherwise harsh.
- **nomadic herding** : animals provide the needs of the wandering families.
- **shifting cultivation** : small areas farmed until soils exhausted, then family moves.
- **mixed subsistence** : crops and animals for family food.
- **rice subsistence** : where heavy rainfall will allow a main crop of rice. Family food only.
- **subsistance crops** : mostly intensive with the aid of irrigation. Family food only.
- **grazing and stock rearing** : on a large scale, for profit.
- **mixed farming** : animals and crops for profit.
- **plantation** : well organized, specializing in one crop for profit, e.g. coffee or cocoa.
- **mediterranean farming** : cereals, animals, vegetables. Fruit and wine for profit.
- **specialized horticulture** : mostly on oases supported by underground water.

cash crops

- cocoa
- tobacco
- sugar
- ground-nuts
- coffee
- fruit
- cotton
- palm products
- tea
- dates
- rubber

animal products

- wool
- meat
- fish

Scale   1: 60 000 000

One centimetre on the map represents 600 kilometres on the ground.

0   600   1200   1800 km

Energy, Minerals, and Industry

energy

- coalfield
- oil field (with associated gas, and sometimes off shore)
- gas field

hydro-electric power stations

- largest (over 3000 megawatts)
- smaller (500 – 3000 megawatts)

industry

- main centres of industry

minerals (main mining areas)

- iron ore
- tin
- diamonds
- silver
- copper
- phosphates
- gold
- bauxite

Zenithal Equal Area Projection
© Oxford University Press

Population density

number of people per square kilometre

high	more than 100
moderate	10 – 100
sparse	1 – 10
very low	less than 1

■ major cities and built up areas of at least 3 million people

□ cities with 1 – 3 million people

Population structure of Kenya

Males   Age   Females

percent of total population in 2000
Total population : 30.3 million

Population structure of Egypt

Males   Age   Females

percent of total population in 2000
Total population : 68.4 million

Scale   1 : 60 000 000

One centimetre on the map represents 600 kilometres on the ground.

0   600   1200   1800 km

Environmental issues

sea pollution

■ areas severely polluted for all or part of the year

areas persistently affected by pollution

▼ deep sea dump sites

✳ major oil spills (over 100 000 tonnes)

✳ major oil spills (under 100 000 tonnes)

acid rain

areas where acid rain is becoming a problem

tsetse fly

areas affected by the tsetse fly

tropical deforestation

existing areas of rainforest

former areas of rainforest

desertification

existing areas of desert

high risk areas

moderate risk areas

global warming

addition of greenhouse gases in tonnes of carbon per person
(look at the world map on page 17)

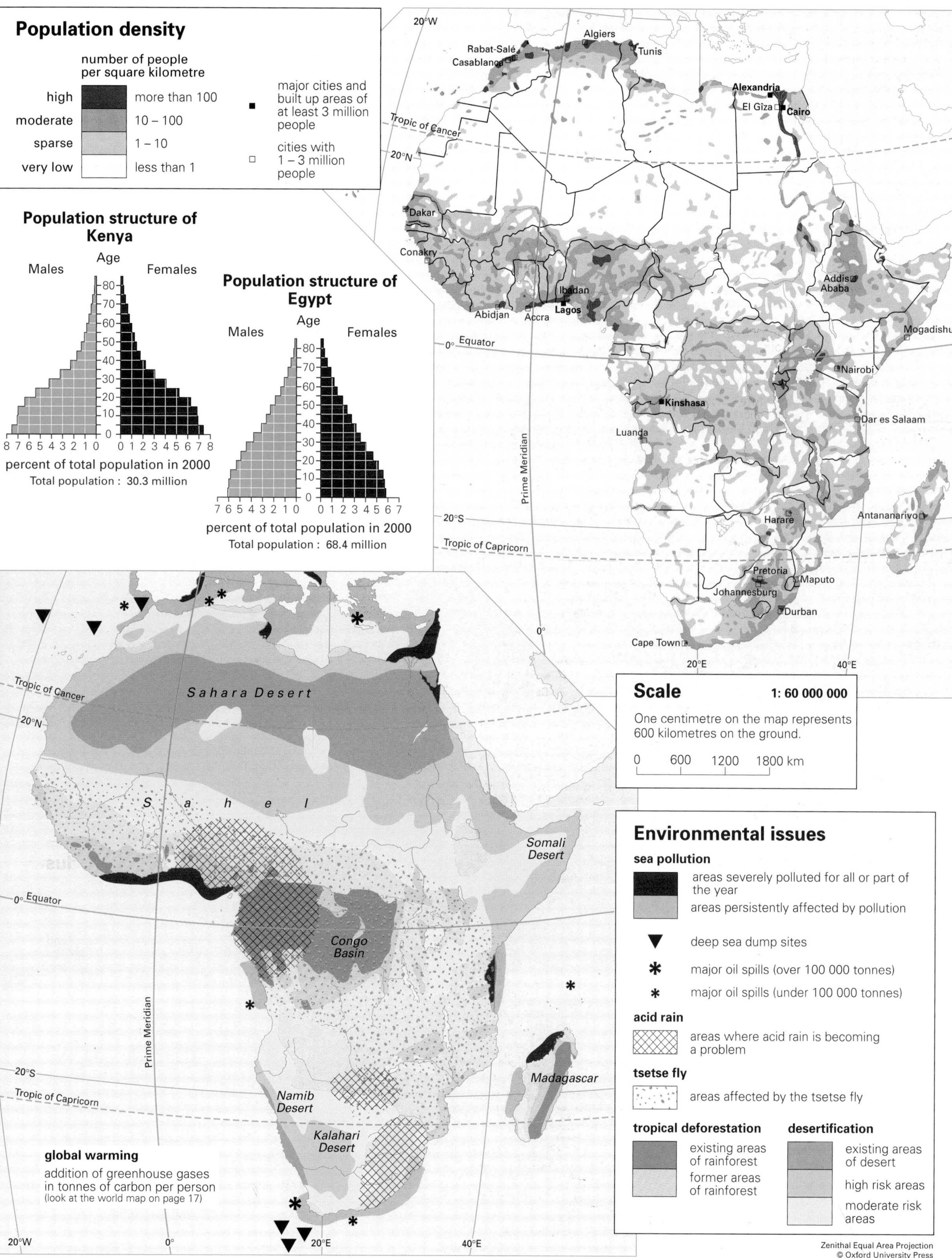

Sahara Desert

Sahel

Somali Desert

Congo Basin

Namib Desert

Kalahari Desert

Madagascar

Zenithal Equal Area Projection
© Oxford University Press

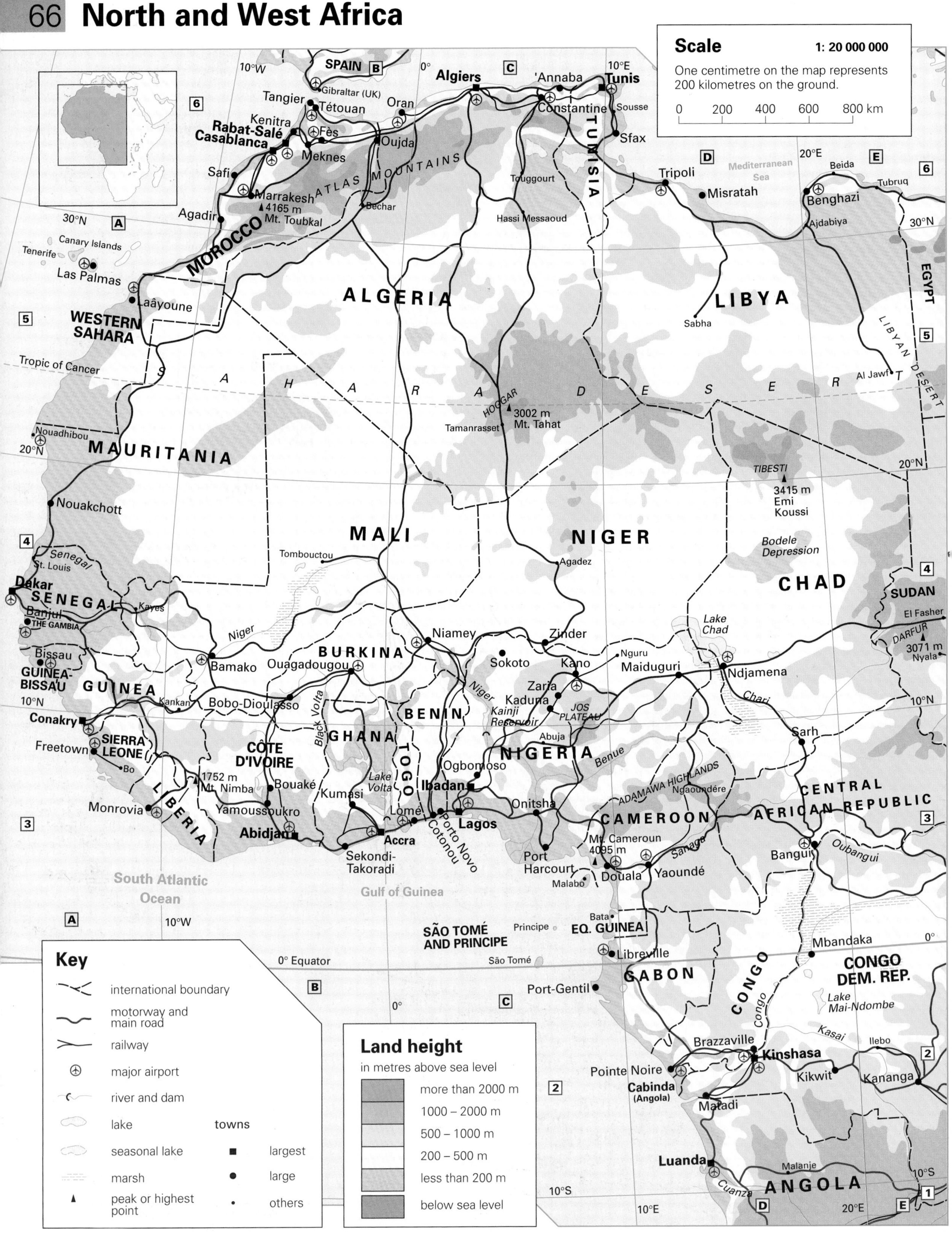

Scale 1: 20 000 000

One centimetre on the map represents 200 kilometres on the ground.

| 0 | 200 | 400 | 600 | 800 km |

Key

Symbol	Meaning
	international boundary
	motorway and main road
	railway
✈	major airport
	river and dam
	lake
	seasonal lake
	marsh
▲	peak or highest point

towns
- ■ largest
- ● large
- • others

Land height

in metres above sea level

- more than 2000 m
- 1000 – 2000 m
- 500 – 1000 m
- 200 – 500 m
- less than 200 m
- below sea level

Zenithal Equal Area Projection   © Oxford University Press

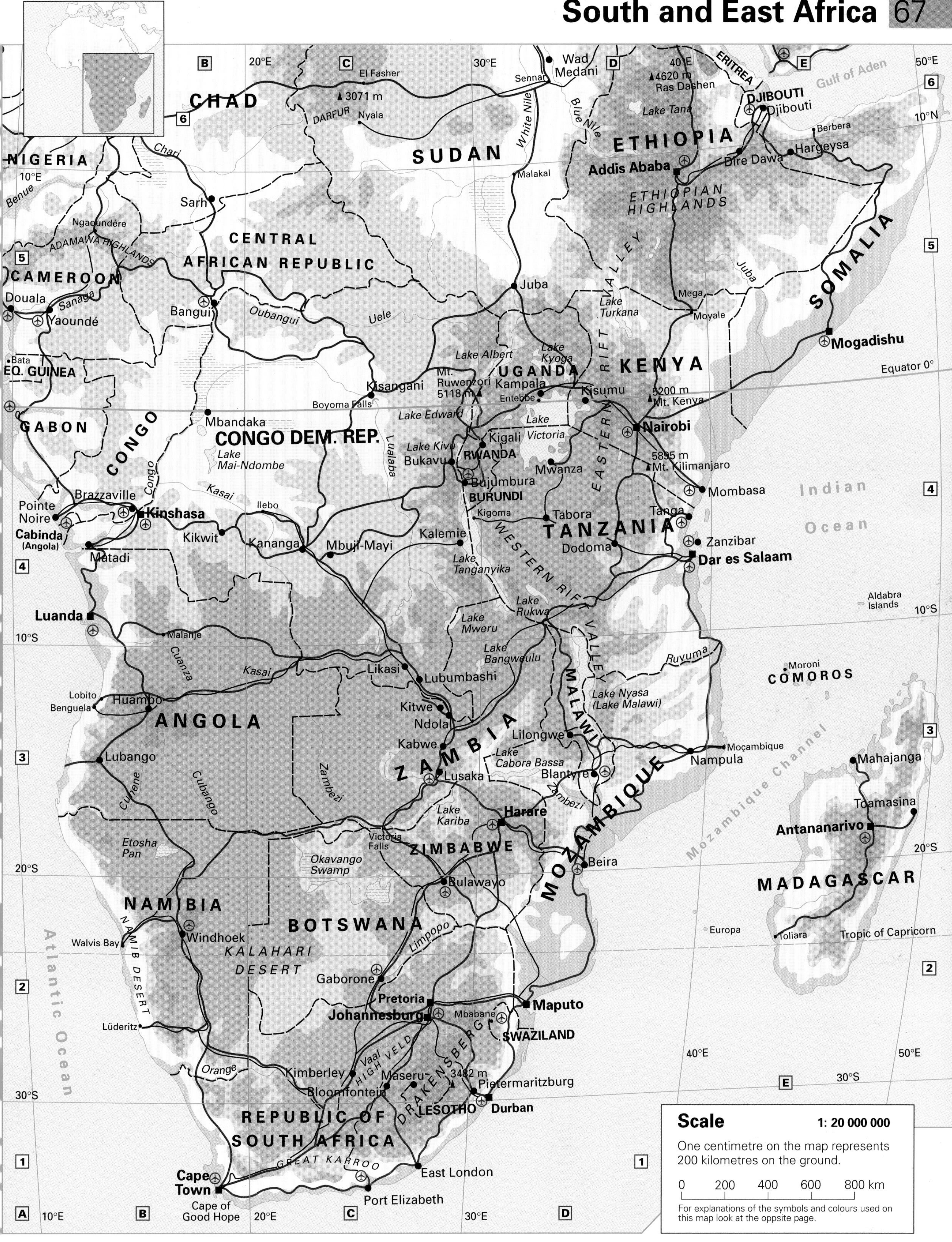

Scale 1: 20 000 000

One centimetre on the map represents
200 kilometres on the ground.

0   200   400   600   800 km

For explanations of the symbols and colours used on
this map look at the oppsite page.

Zenithal Equal Area Projection   © Oxford University Press

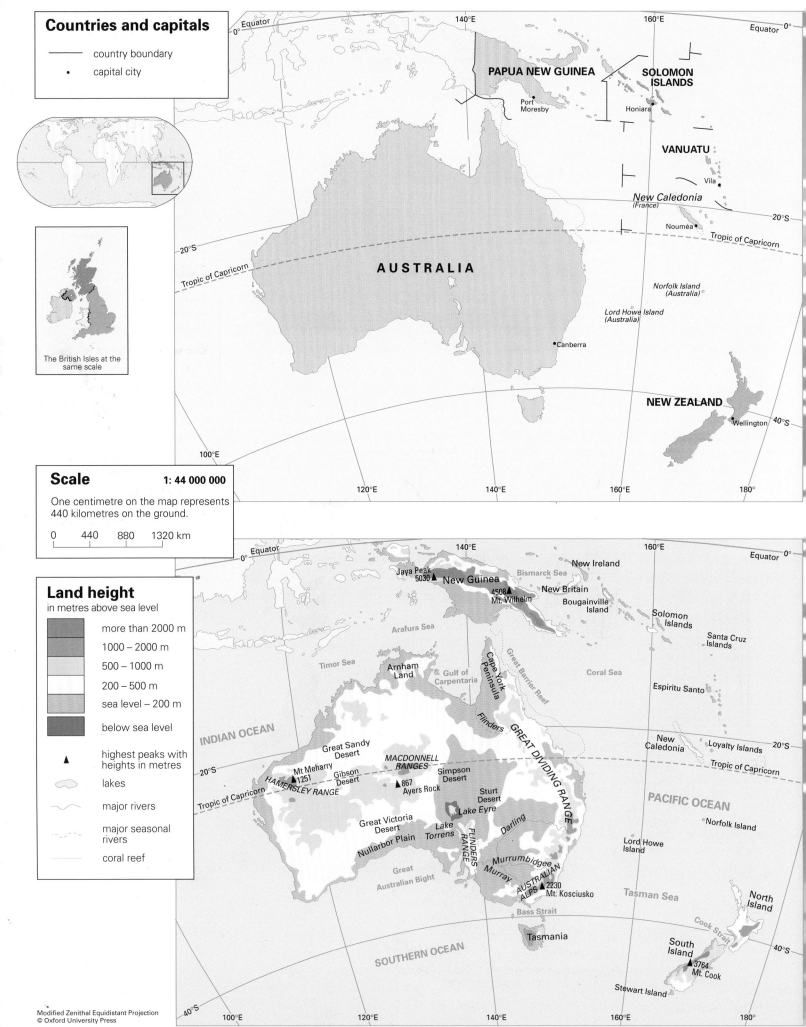

Countries and capitals

— country boundary

• capital city

The British Isles at the same scale

Equator 0°

140°E

160°E

Equator 0°

PAPUA NEW GUINEA

Port Moresby

SOLOMON ISLANDS

Honiara

VANUATU

Vila

New Caledonia (France)

Nouméa

Tropic of Capricorn

20°S

AUSTRALIA

Tropic of Capricorn

Norfolk Island (Australia)

Lord Howe Island (Australia)

•Canberra

NEW ZEALAND

Wellington

40°S

100°E

120°E

140°E

160°E

180°

Scale   1: 44 000 000

One centimetre on the map represents 440 kilometres on the ground.

0   440   880   1320 km

Land height

in metres above sea level

- more than 2000 m
- 1000 – 2000 m
- 500 – 1000 m
- 200 – 500 m
- sea level – 200 m
- below sea level

▲   highest peaks with heights in metres

lakes

major rivers

major seasonal rivers

coral reef

Equator 0°

140°E

160°E

Equator 0°

Jaya Peak 5030▲

New Guinea

Bismarck Sea

New Ireland

4508▲ Mt. Wilhelm

New Britain

Bougainville Island

Solomon Islands

Santa Cruz Islands

Arafura Sea

Coral Sea

Espiritu Santo

Timor Sea

Arnham Land

Gulf of Carpentaria

Cape York Peninsula

Great Barrier Reef

New Caledonia

Loyalty Islands

20°S

Tropic of Capricorn

INDIAN OCEAN

Great Sandy Desert

MACDONNELL RANGES

Flinders

GREAT DIVIDING RANGE

PACIFIC OCEAN

Mt Meharry 1251▲

HAMERSLEY RANGE

Gibson Desert

867▲ Ayers Rock

Simpson Desert

Sturt Desert

Norfolk Island

Great Victoria Desert

Lake Torrens

Lake Eyre

FLINDERS RANGE

Darling

Lord Howe Island

Nullarbor Plain

Murrumbidgee

Murray

AUSTRALIAN ALPS 2230▲ Mt. Kosciusko

Great Australian Bight

Tasman Sea

North Island

Bass Strait

Tasmania

SOUTHERN OCEAN

Cook Strait

South Island

3764▲ Mt. Cook

Stewart Island

40°S

100°E

120°E

140°E

160°E

180°

Modified Zenithal Equidistant Projection
© Oxford University Press

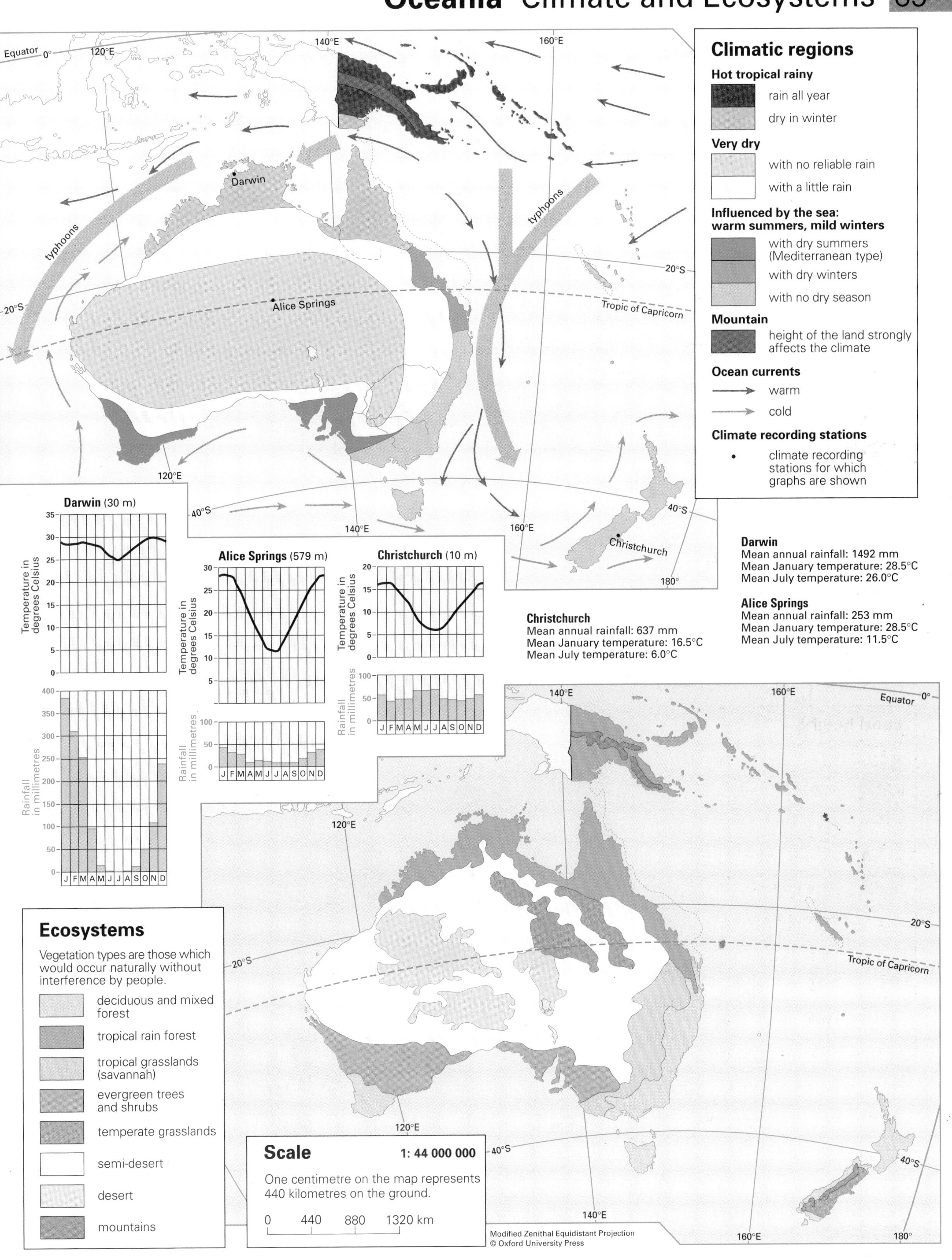

Climatic regions

Hot tropical rainy

rain all year

dry in winter

Very dry

with no reliable rain

with a little rain

Influenced by the sea: warm summers, mild winters

with dry summers (Mediterranean type)

with dry winters

with no dry season

Mountain

height of the land strongly affects the climate

Ocean currents

→ warm

→ cold

Climate recording stations

• climate recording stations for which graphs are shown

Darwin
Mean annual rainfall: 1492 mm
Mean January temperature: 28.5°C
Mean July temperature: 26.0°C

Alice Springs
Mean annual rainfall: 253 mm
Mean January temperature: 28.5°C
Mean July temperature: 11.5°C

Christchurch
Mean annual rainfall: 637 mm
Mean January temperature: 16.5°C
Mean July temperature: 6.0°C

Darwin (30 m)

Alice Springs (579 m)

Christchurch (10 m)

Ecosystems

Vegetation types are those which would occur naturally without interference by people.

deciduous and mixed forest

tropical rain forest

tropical grasslands (savannah)

evergreen trees and shrubs

temperate grasslands

semi-desert

desert

mountains

Scale 1: 44 000 000

One centimetre on the map represents 440 kilometres on the ground.

0   440   880   1320 km

Modified Zenithal Equidistant Projection
© Oxford University Press

Farming, forestry, and fishing

main farming types

little or no farming : because the area is too dry or otherwise harsh.

shifting cultivation : small areas farmed until soils exhausted, then family moves.

mixed subsistence : crops and animals for family food.

grazing and stock rearing : on a large scale, for profit.

intensive grazing : fattening of lambs, mainly for meat, and of beef cattle. All for profit.

mixed farming : animals and crops for profit.

grain farming : mostly wheat but also other cereals, for profit.

plantation : well organized, specializing in one crop for profit, e.g. sugar or cocoa.

specialized horticulture : mostly supported by irrigation.

dairy farming : milk, butter, and cheese for profit. Also lamb fattening in New Zealand.

forestry

forestry for profit

cash crops

cocoa		coffee		fruit	
sugar		cotton		rice	
palm products					

animal products

wool   meat   fish

area irrigated by the River Murray Scheme

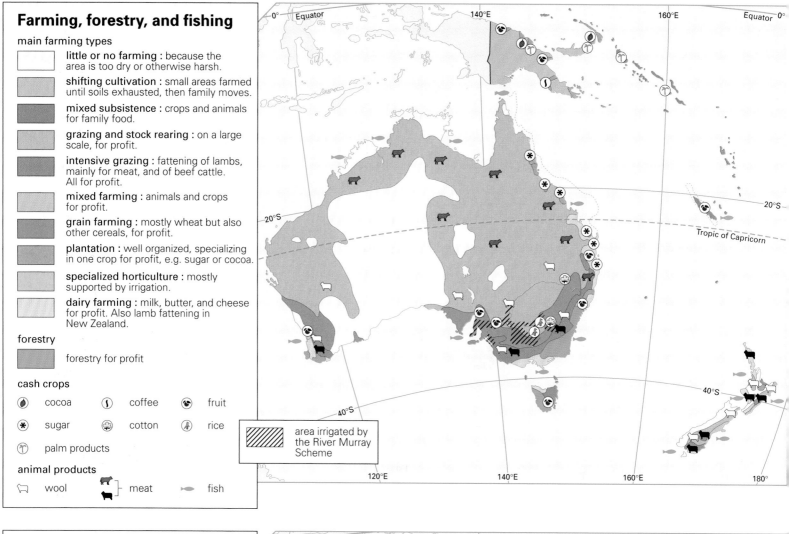

Energy, Minerals, and Industry

energy

coalfield

oil field (with associated gas, and sometimes off shore)

gas field

hydro-electric power stations

largest (over 3000 megawatts)

smaller (500 – 3000 megawatts)

industry

main centres of industry

minerals (main mining areas)

silver		gold		tin	
copper		bauxite		nickel	
zinc		lead		uranium	
diamonds		iron ore (iron sands in New Zealand)			

Australian underground water supplies

areas where artesian water is generally available

areas where artesian water is available in places

Scale   1: 44 000 000

One centimetre on the map represents 440 kilometres on the ground.

0   440   880   1320 km

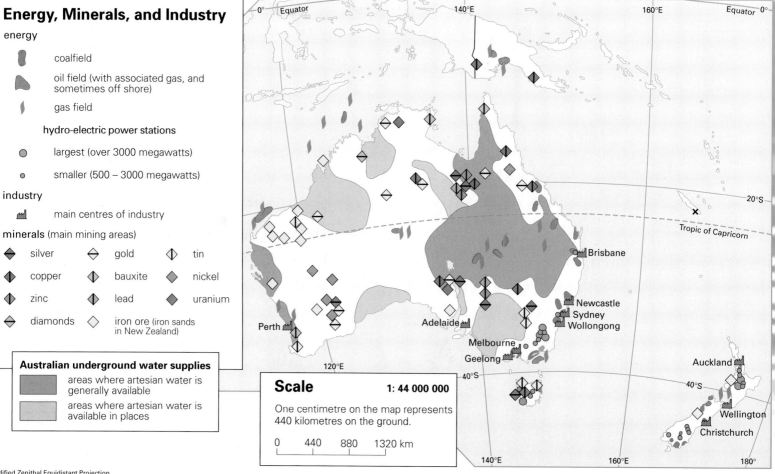

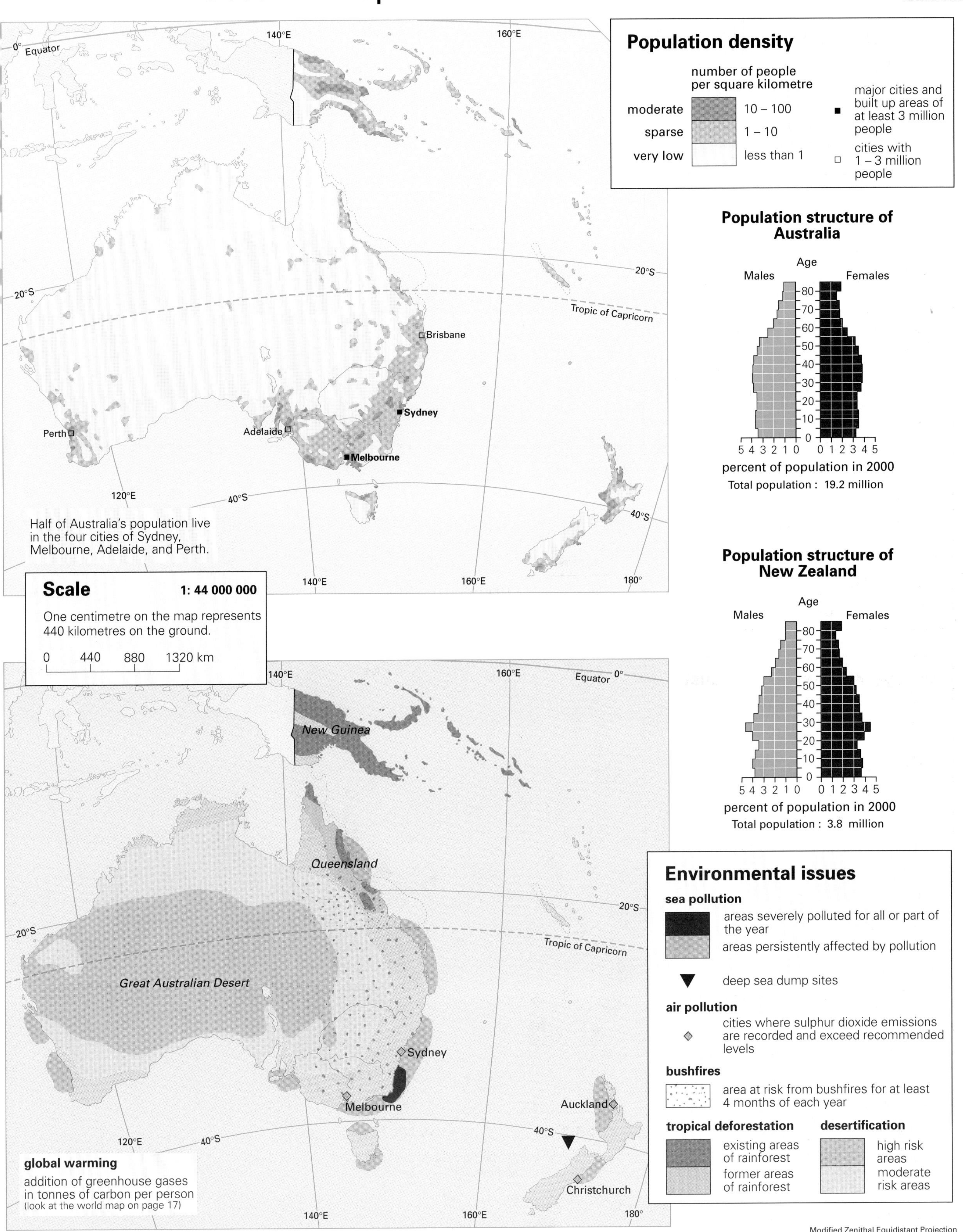

Population density

number of people
per square kilometre

moderate	10 – 100
sparse	1 – 10
very low	less than 1

■ major cities and built up areas of at least 3 million people

□ cities with 1 – 3 million people

Population structure of Australia

Age
Males — Females

80, 70, 60, 50, 40, 30, 20, 10, 0

5 4 3 2 1 0   0 1 2 3 4 5

percent of population in 2000

Total population : 19.2 million

Population structure of New Zealand

Age
Males — Females

80, 70, 60, 50, 40, 30, 20, 10, 0

5 4 3 2 1 0   0 1 2 3 4 5

percent of population in 2000

Total population : 3.8 million

Half of Australia's population live in the four cities of Sydney, Melbourne, Adelaide, and Perth.

Scale   1: 44 000 000

One centimetre on the map represents 440 kilometres on the ground.

0   440   880   1320 km

Equator
20°S
Tropic of Capricorn
40°S

Perth
Adelaide
Brisbane
Sydney
Melbourne

New Guinea
Queensland
Great Australian Desert
Sydney
Melbourne
Auckland
Christchurch

Environmental issues

sea pollution

■ areas severely polluted for all or part of the year

areas persistently affected by pollution

▼ deep sea dump sites

air pollution

◆ cities where sulphur dioxide emissions are recorded and exceed recommended levels

bushfires

area at risk from bushfires for at least 4 months of each year

tropical deforestation

existing areas of rainforest

former areas of rainforest

desertification

high risk areas

moderate risk areas

global warming

addition of greenhouse gases in tonnes of carbon per person
(look at the world map on page 17)

Modified Zenithal Equidistant Projection
© Oxford University Press

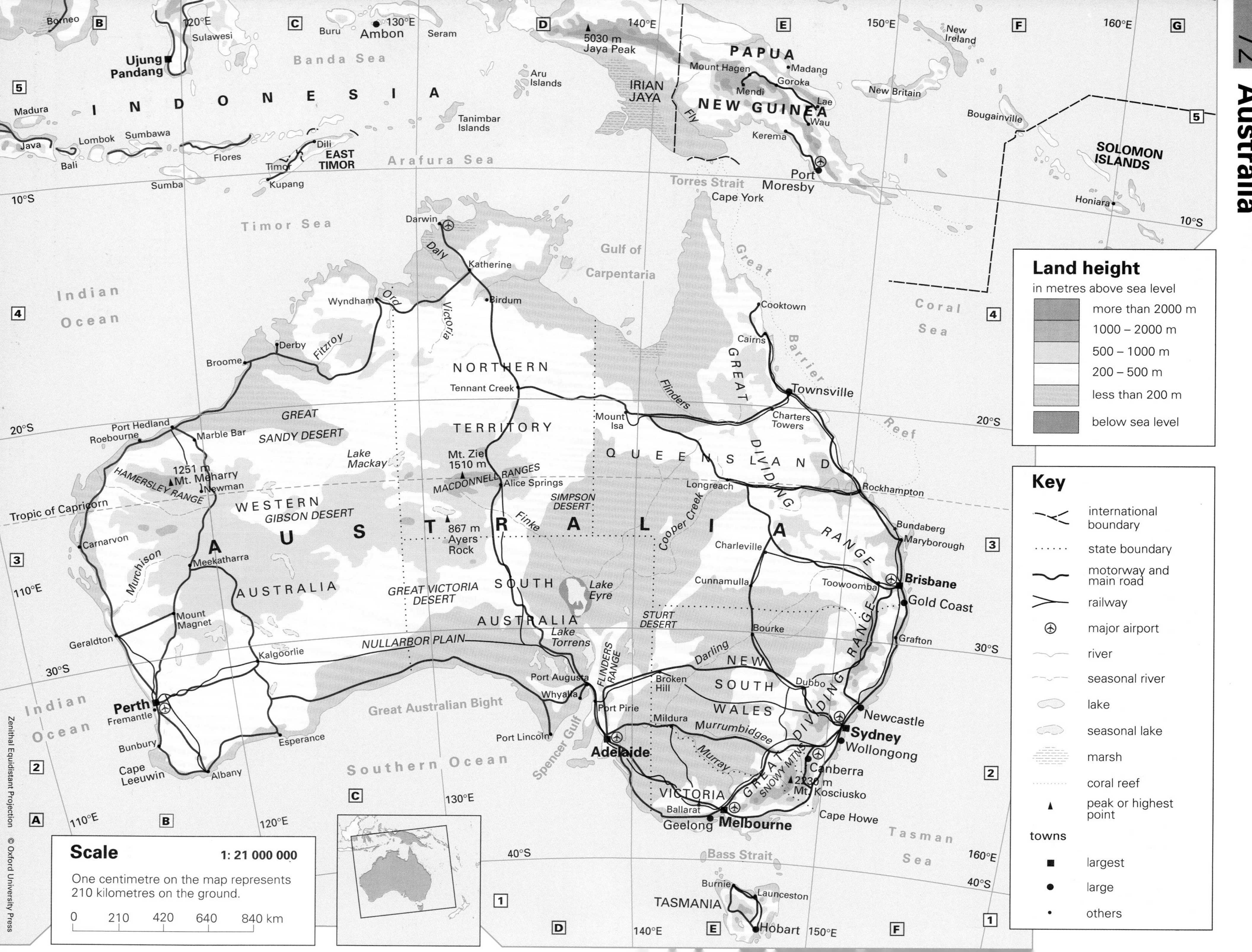

Land height
in metres above sea level

more than 2000 m
1000 – 2000 m
500 – 1000 m
200 – 500 m
less than 200 m
below sea level

Key

international boundary
state boundary
motorway and main road
railway
major airport
river
seasonal river
lake
seasonal lake
marsh
coral reef
peak or highest point

towns
largest
large
others

Scale   1: 21 000 000

One centimetre on the map represents 210 kilometres on the ground.

0   210   420   640   840 km

Zenithal Equidistant Projection   © Oxford University Press

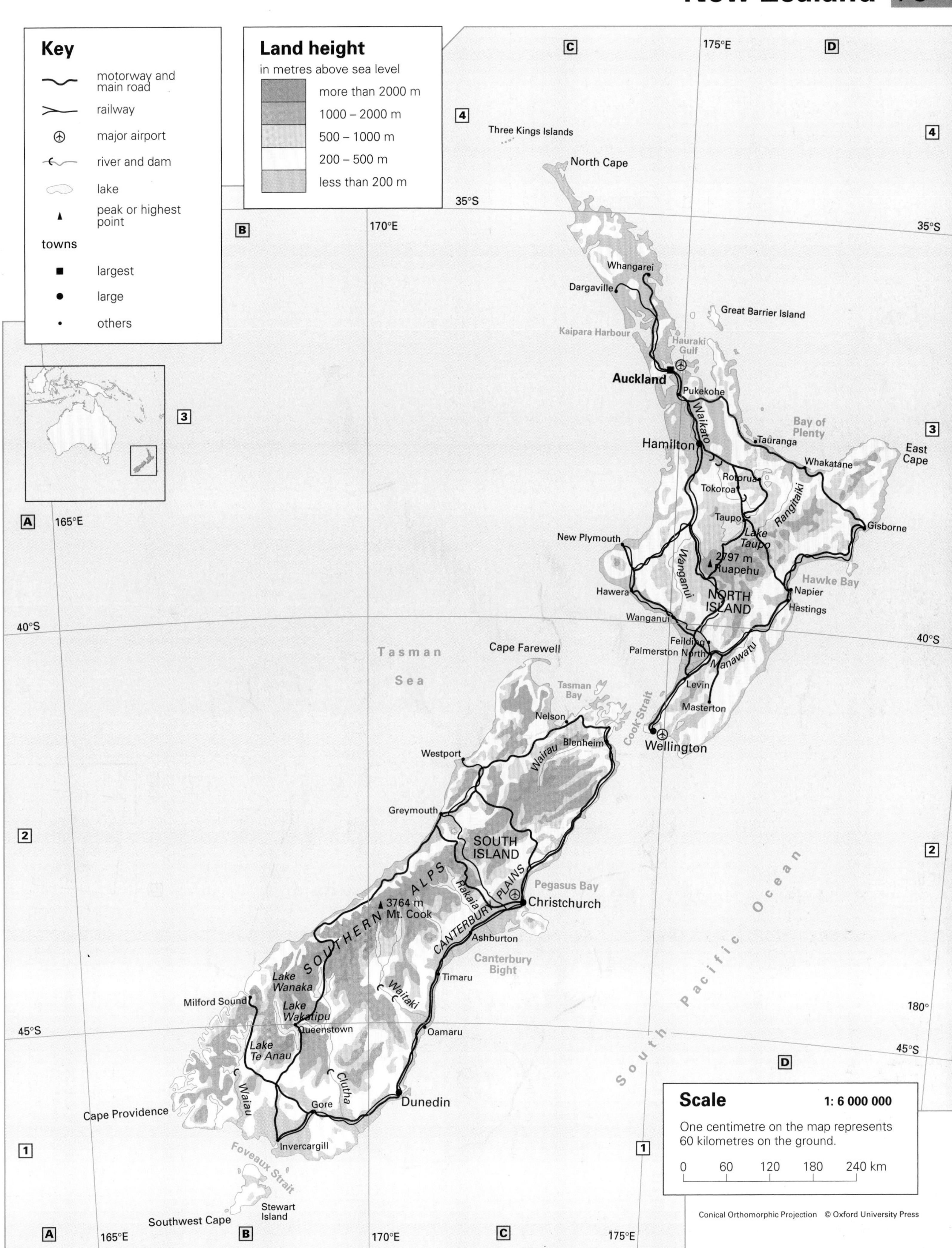

Key

- 〰 motorway and main road
- ⌁ railway
- ⊕ major airport
- ⤙ river and dam
- ⬭ lake
- ▲ peak or highest point

towns
- ■ largest
- ● large
- · others

Land height

in metres above sea level

- more than 2000 m
- 1000 – 2000 m
- 500 – 1000 m
- 200 – 500 m
- less than 200 m

Three Kings Islands

North Cape

North Cape

Whangarei

Dargaville

Great Barrier Island

Kaipara Harbour

Hauraki Gulf

Auckland

Pukekohe

Bay of Plenty

Hamilton

Tauranga

Waikato

Whakatane

East Cape

Rotorua

Tokoroa

Rangitaiki

Taupo

Gisborne

New Plymouth

Lake Taupo

2797 m ▲ Ruapehu

Wanganui

Hawke Bay

Hawera

NORTH ISLAND

Napier

Wanganui

Hastings

Feilding

Palmerston North

Manawatu

Levin

Masterton

Tasman Sea

Cape Farewell

Tasman Bay

Nelson

Cook Strait

Wellington

Westport

Wairau

Blenheim

Greymouth

SOUTH ISLAND

SOUTHERN ALPS

3764 m ▲ Mt. Cook

Rakaia

CANTERBURY PLAINS

Pegasus Bay

Christchurch

Ashburton

Canterbury Bight

Lake Wanaka

Milford Sound

Waitaki

Lake Wakatipu

Timaru

Queenstown

Oamaru

Lake Te Anau

Clutha

South Pacific Ocean

Cape Providence

Waiau

Gore

Dunedin

Invercargill

Foveaux Strait

Southwest Cape

Stewart Island

Scale

1: 6 000 000

One centimetre on the map represents 60 kilometres on the ground.

0   60   120   180   240 km

Conical Orthomorphic Projection   © Oxford University Press

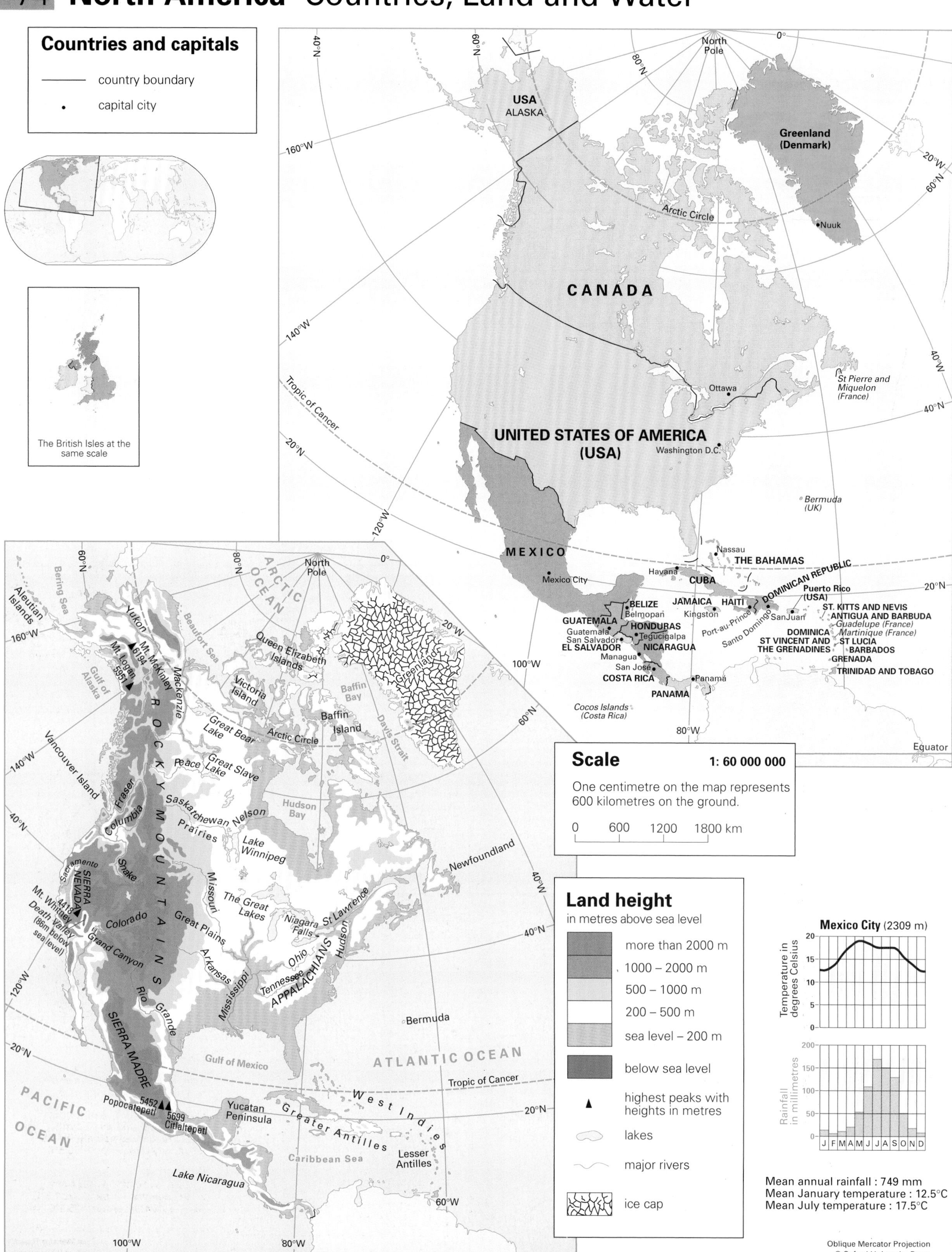

Countries and capitals

— country boundary

• capital city

The British Isles at the same scale

USA ALASKA

Greenland (Denmark)

• Nuuk

Arctic Circle

CANADA

Ottawa

St Pierre and Miquelon (France)

Tropic of Cancer

UNITED STATES OF AMERICA (USA)

Washington D.C.

Bermuda (UK)

MEXICO

Mexico City

Nassau

THE BAHAMAS

Havana

CUBA

DOMINICAN REPUBLIC

Puerto Rico (USA)

BELIZE

Belmopan

JAMAICA

HAITI

ST. KITTS AND NEVIS

GUATEMALA

Guatemala

Kingston

Port-au-Prince

Santo Domingo

San Juan

ANTIGUA AND BARBUDA

Guadelupe (France)

HONDURAS

DOMINICA

Martinique (France)

San Salvador

Tegucigalpa

ST VINCENT AND

ST LUCIA

EL SALVADOR

NICARAGUA

THE GRENADINES

BARBADOS

Managua

San José

GRENADA

COSTA RICA

Panama

TRINIDAD AND TOBAGO

PANAMA

Cocos Islands (Costa Rica)

Equator

Scale   1 : 60 000 000

One centimetre on the map represents 600 kilometres on the ground.

0   600   1200   1800 km

Aleutian Islands

Bering Sea

Yukon

Mt McKinley 6194

Mt Logan 5951

Gulf of Alaska

ARCTIC OCEAN

North Pole

Queen Elizabeth Islands

Greenland

Baffin Bay

Vancouver Island

Mackenzie

Victoria Island

Baffin Island

Arctic Circle

Davis Strait

Beaufort Sea

Great Bear Lake

Fraser

Columbia

Peace

Great Slave Lake

R O C K Y   M O U N T A I N S

Saskatchewan

Prairies

Nelson

Hudson Bay

Snake

Lake Winnipeg

Newfoundland

SIERRA NEVADA 4418

Missouri

Mt Whitney

Death Valley (86m below sea level)

Colorado

Grand Canyon

Great Plains

The Great Lakes

St Lawrence

Niagara Falls

Sacramento

Arkansas

Ohio

Hudson

Tennessee

APPALACHIANS

Rio Grande

SIERRA MADRE

Mississippi

Bermuda

PACIFIC OCEAN

Gulf of Mexico

ATLANTIC OCEAN

West Indies

Tropic of Cancer

Popocatepetl 5452

Citlaltepetl 5699

Yucatan Peninsula

Greater Antilles

Lesser Antilles

Caribbean Sea

Lake Nicaragua

Land height

in metres above sea level

more than 2000 m

1000 – 2000 m

500 – 1000 m

200 – 500 m

sea level – 200 m

below sea level

▲ highest peaks with heights in metres

lakes

major rivers

ice cap

Mexico City (2309 m)

Temperature in degrees Celsius

Rainfall in millimetres

J F M A M J J A S O N D

Mean annual rainfall : 749 mm
Mean January temperature : 12.5°C
Mean July temperature : 17.5°C

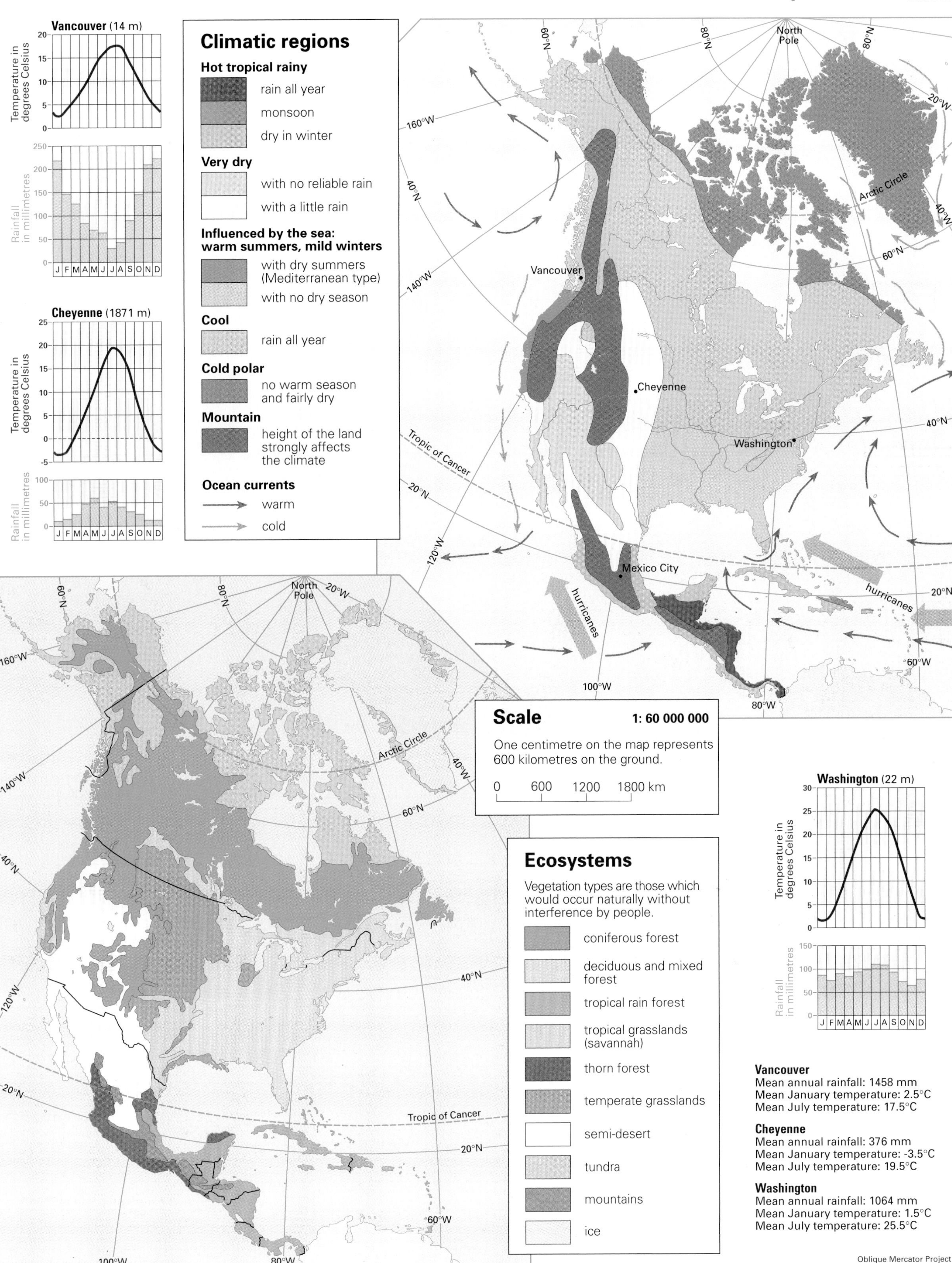

Vancouver (14 m)

Temperature in degrees Celsius

Rainfall in millimetres

J F M A M J J A S O N D

Cheyenne (1871 m)

Temperature in degrees Celsius

Rainfall in millimetres

J F M A M J J A S O N D

Climatic regions

Hot tropical rainy

- rain all year
- monsoon
- dry in winter

Very dry

- with no reliable rain
- with a little rain

Influenced by the sea: warm summers, mild winters

- with dry summers (Mediterranean type)
- with no dry season

Cool

- rain all year

Cold polar

- no warm season and fairly dry

Mountain

- height of the land strongly affects the climate

Ocean currents

- → warm
- → cold

Scale

1: 60 000 000

One centimetre on the map represents 600 kilometres on the ground.

0   600   1200   1800 km

Ecosystems

Vegetation types are those which would occur naturally without interference by people.

- coniferous forest
- deciduous and mixed forest
- tropical rain forest
- tropical grasslands (savannah)
- thorn forest
- temperate grasslands
- semi-desert
- tundra
- mountains
- ice

Washington (22 m)

Temperature in degrees Celsius

Rainfall in millimetres

J F M A M J J A S O N D

Vancouver
Mean annual rainfall: 1458 mm
Mean January temperature: 2.5°C
Mean July temperature: 17.5°C

Cheyenne
Mean annual rainfall: 376 mm
Mean January temperature: -3.5°C
Mean July temperature: 19.5°C

Washington
Mean annual rainfall: 1064 mm
Mean January temperature: 1.5°C
Mean July temperature: 25.5°C

Oblique Mercator Projection
© Oxford University Press

Farming, forestry, and fishing

main farming types

little or no farming : because the area is too cold or otherwise harsh.	
trapping and fishing : for family food. Furs and surplus fish sold for profit.	
shifting cultivation : small areas farmed until soils exhausted, then family moves.	
mixed subsistence : crops and animals for family food.	
subsistence crops : mostly intensive with the aid of irrigation. Family food only.	
grazing and stock rearing : on a large scale, for profit.	
mixed farming : animals and crops for profit.	
grain farming : mostly wheat, on a large scale, for profit.	
plantation : well organised, specializing in one crop for profit, e.g. cotton.	
mediterranean farming : cereals, animals, vegetables, fruit, wine, surplus for profit.	
specialized horticulture : often supported by irrigation.	
dairy farming : milk, butter, and cheese for profit.	

forestry

cutting and replacement of timber for profit

cash crops

- cocoa
- coffee
- cotton
- tobacco
- fruit
- sugar
- groundnuts

animal products

- meat
- fish

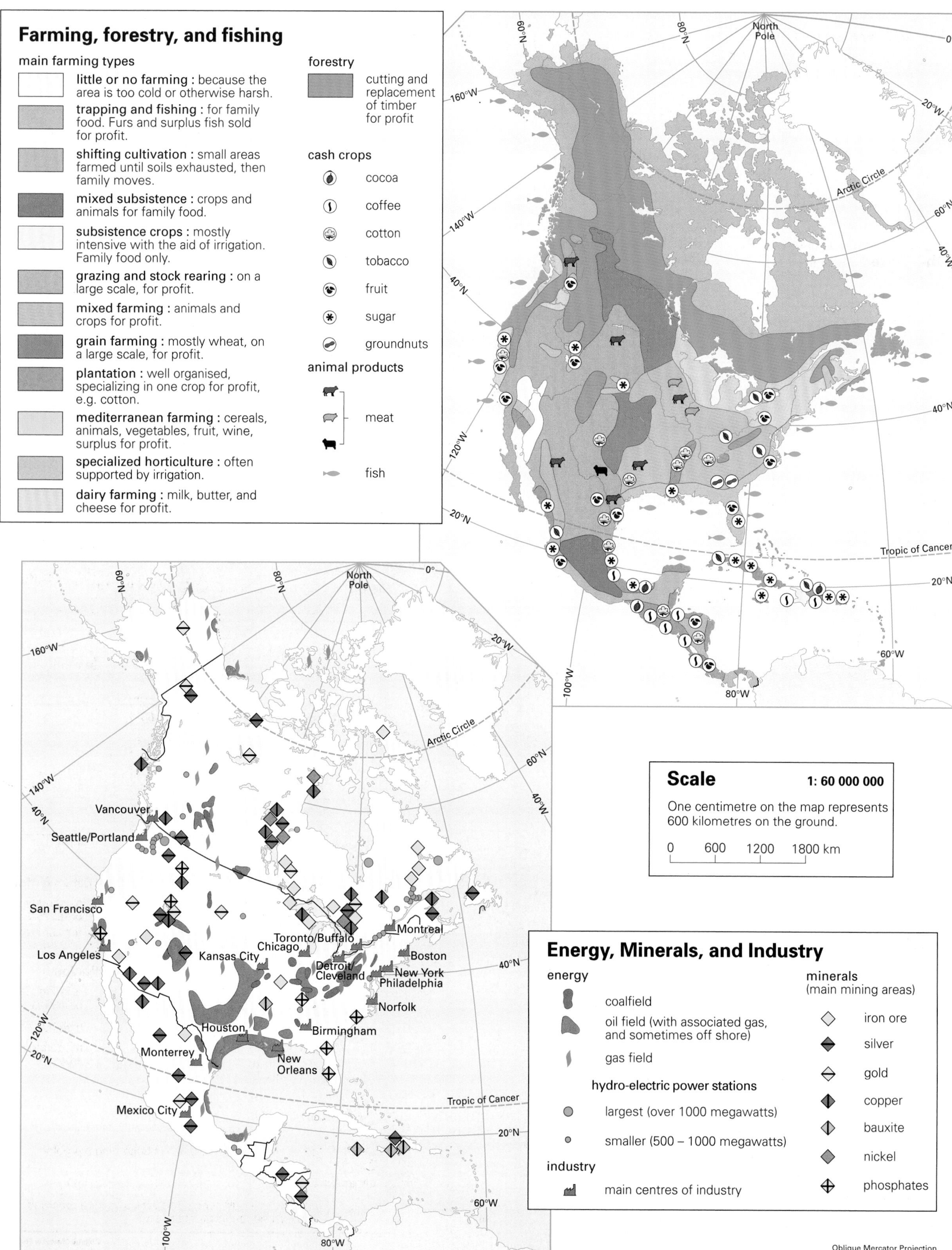

Scale 1: 60 000 000

One centimetre on the map represents 600 kilometres on the ground.

0   600   1200   1800 km

Energy, Minerals, and Industry

energy

- coalfield
- oil field (with associated gas, and sometimes off shore)
- gas field

hydro-electric power stations

- largest (over 1000 megawatts)
- smaller (500 – 1000 megawatts)

industry

- main centres of industry

minerals (main mining areas)

- iron ore
- silver
- gold
- copper
- bauxite
- nickel
- phosphates

Oblique Mercator Projection
© Oxford University Press

Population density

number of people per square kilometre

high	more than 100
moderate	10 – 100
sparse	1 – 10
very low	less than 1

■ major cities and built up areas of at least 3 million people

□ cities with 1 – 3 million people

Population structure of the United States

Age

Males   Females

80
70
60
50
40
30
20
10
0

5 4 3 2 1 0   0 1 2 3 4 5

percent of the population in 2000

Total population : 275.6 million

Population structure of Mexico

Age

Males   Females

80
70
60
50
40
30
20
10
0

7 6 5 4 3 2 1 0   0 1 2 3 4 5 6 7

percent of the population in 2000

Total population : 100.3 million

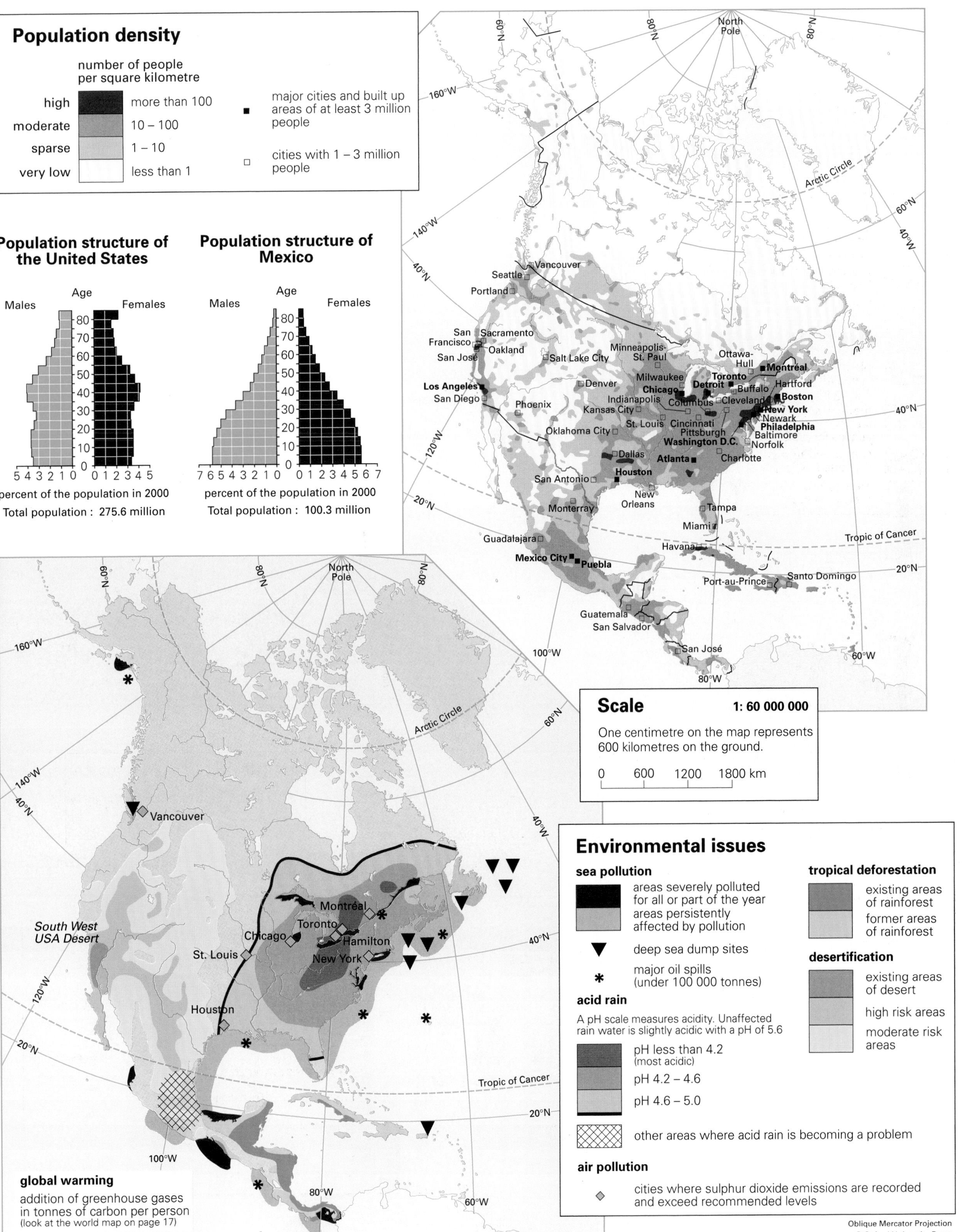

Scale

1 : 60 000 000

One centimetre on the map represents 600 kilometres on the ground.

0   600   1200   1800 km

Environmental issues

sea pollution

■	areas severely polluted for all or part of the year
	areas persistently affected by pollution
▼	deep sea dump sites
✳	major oil spills (under 100 000 tonnes)

acid rain

A pH scale measures acidity. Unaffected rain water is slightly acidic with a pH of 5.6

	pH less than 4.2 (most acidic)
	pH 4.2 – 4.6
	pH 4.6 – 5.0

⊠ other areas where acid rain is becoming a problem

air pollution

◈ cities where sulphur dioxide emissions are recorded and exceed recommended levels

tropical deforestation

	existing areas of rainforest
	former areas of rainforest

desertification

	existing areas of desert
	high risk areas
	moderate risk areas

global warming

addition of greenhouse gases in tonnes of carbon per person (look at the world map on page 17)

South West USA Desert

Oblique Mercator Projection

© Oxford University Press

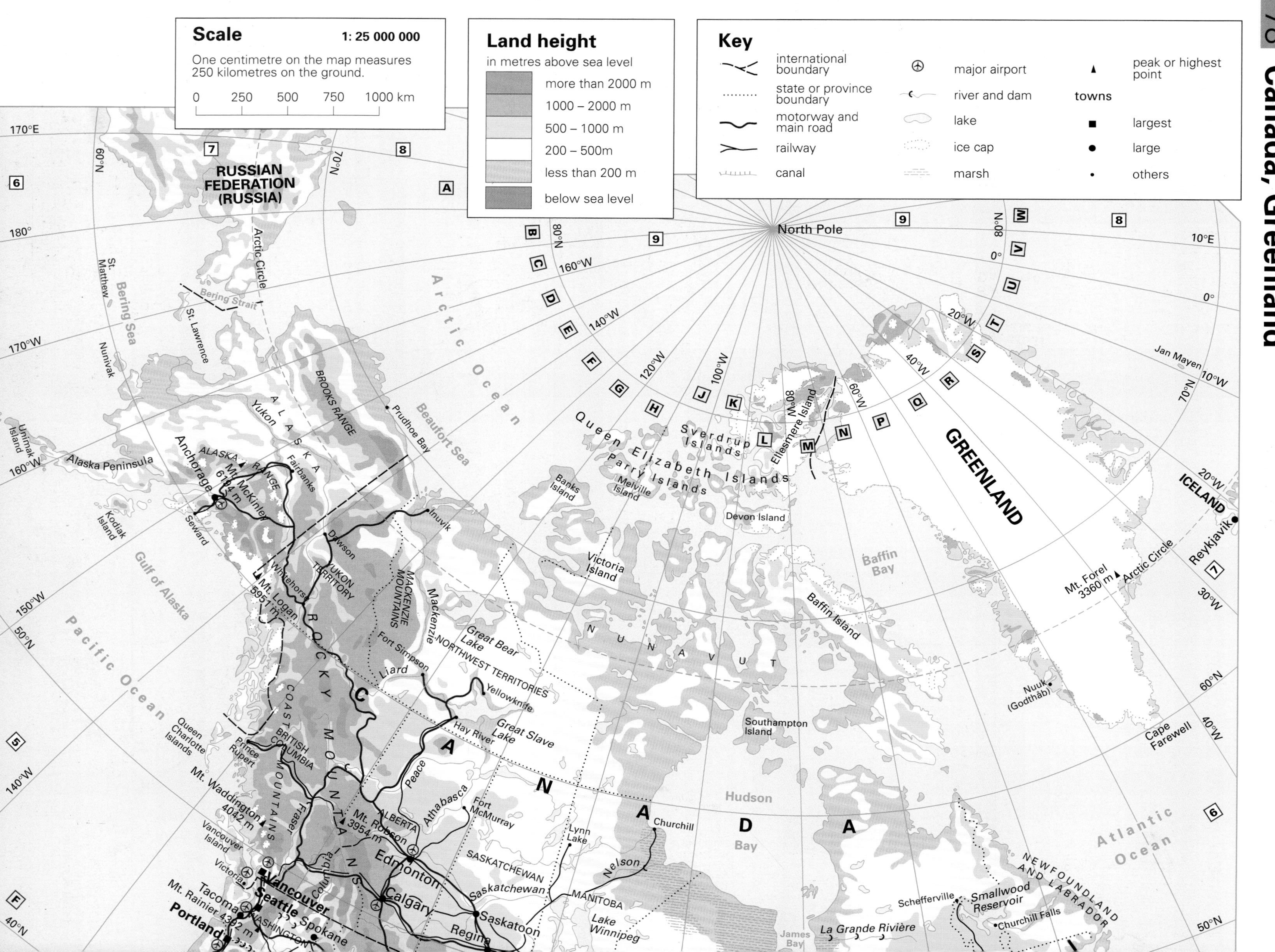

Key

international boundary
state or province boundary
motorway and main road
railway
canal

major airport
river and dam
lake
ice cap
marsh

peak or highest point

towns
largest
large
others

Land height
in metres above sea level

more than 2000 m
1000 – 2000 m
500 – 1000 m
200 – 500m
less than 200 m
below sea level

Scale 1: 25 000 000

One centimetre on the map measures 250 kilometres on the ground.

0   250   500   750   1000 km

ICELAND
Reykjavík
Arctic Circle
Mt. Forel 3360 m

GREENLAND

Atlantic Ocean

Cape Farewell

NEWFOUNDLAND AND LABRADOR

Schefferville
Smallwood Reservoir
Churchill Falls
La Grande Rivière

Baffin Bay

Nuuk (Godthåb)

James Bay

Baffin Island

Hudson Bay

Southampton Island

CANADA

Churchill

Ellesmere Island

Devon Island

Queen Elizabeth Islands
Sverdrup Islands
Parry Islands

Melville Island

Banks Island

Victoria Island

N U N A V U T

Nelson

MANITOBA
Lake Winnipeg

Lynn Lake

Arctic Ocean

Beaufort Sea

Prudhoe Bay

Inuvik

Mackenzie

Great Bear Lake

Great Slave Lake

Yellowknife

Hay River

NORTHWEST TERRITORIES

Fort Simpson

Fort McMurray

Liard

Peace

Athabasca

SASKATCHEWAN
Saskatoon
Regina

ALBERTA
Edmonton
Calgary

MACKENZIE MOUNTAINS

Dawson

YUKON TERRITORY

BROOKS RANGE

ALASKA
Yukon
Fairbanks

ALASKA RANGE

Mt. McKinley 6194 m

Anchorage

Seward

Whitehorse

Mt. Logan 5959 m

ROCKY MOUNTAINS

Mt. Robson 3954 m

BRITISH COLUMBIA

Fraser

COAST MOUNTAINS

Prince Rupert

Mt. Waddington 4042 m

Queen Charlotte Islands

Vancouver Island

Victoria

Vancouver

Seattle
Spokane

Tacoma
WASHINGTON
Mt. Rainier 4392 m

Portland

RUSSIAN FEDERATION (RUSSIA)

Arctic Circle

Bering Strait

St. Lawrence

St. Matthew

Nunivak

Kodiak Island

Gulf of Alaska

Bering Sea

Unimak Island

Alaska Peninsula

Pacific Ocean

North Pole

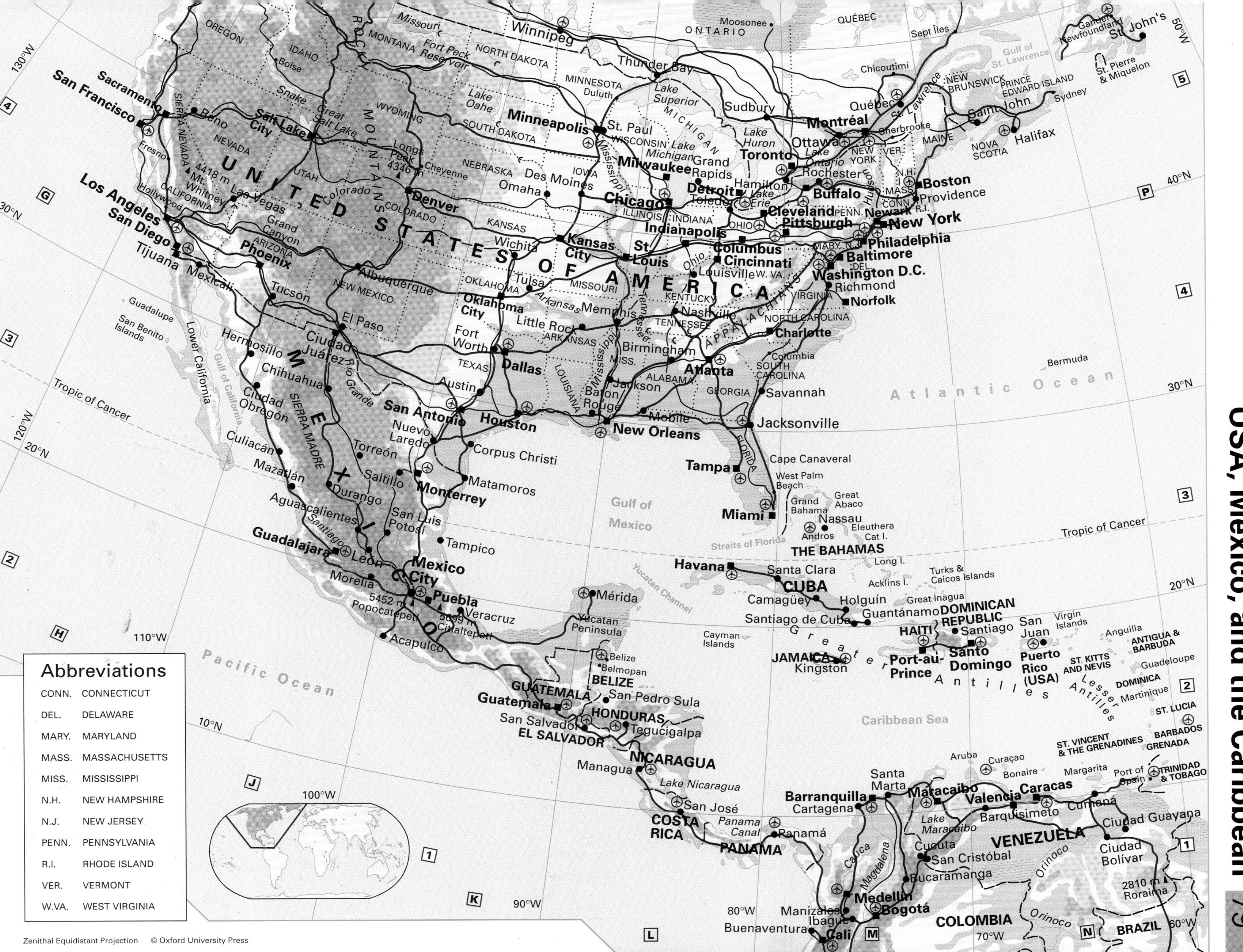
UNITED STATES OF AMERICA
MEXICO
CUBA
THE BAHAMAS
JAMAICA
HAITI
DOMINICAN REPUBLIC
Puerto Rico (USA)
BELIZE
GUATEMALA
HONDURAS
EL SALVADOR
NICARAGUA
COSTA RICA
PANAMA
COLOMBIA
VENEZUELA
BRAZIL
Atlantic Ocean
Pacific Ocean
Gulf of Mexico
Caribbean Sea
Gulf of California
Gulf of St. Lawrence
Greater Antilles
Lesser Antilles
Tropic of Cancer
Yucatan Channel
Straits of Florida
ROCKY MOUNTAINS
SIERRA NEVADA
SIERRA MADRE
APPALACHIANS
Mississippi
Missouri
Rio Grande
Colorado
Orinoco
Magdalena
Washington D.C.
New York
Philadelphia
Boston
Chicago
Los Angeles
San Francisco
San Diego
Houston
Dallas
New Orleans
Miami
Atlanta
Denver
Mexico City
Guadalajara
Monterrey
Havana
Kingston
Port-au-Prince
Santo Domingo
Caracas
Bogotá
Montréal
Toronto
Ottawa
Québec
Halifax
Winnipeg
Mt. Whitney 4418 m
Longs Peak 4346 m
Popocatépetl 5452 m
Citlaltépetl 5699 m
Roraima 2810 m
Abbreviations
CONN. CONNECTICUT
DEL. DELAWARE
MARY. MARYLAND
MASS. MASSACHUSETTS
MISS. MISSISSIPPI
N.H. NEW HAMPSHIRE
N.J. NEW JERSEY
PENN. PENNSYLVANIA
R.I. RHODE ISLAND
VER. VERMONT
W.VA. WEST VIRGINIA
Zenithal Equidistant Projection

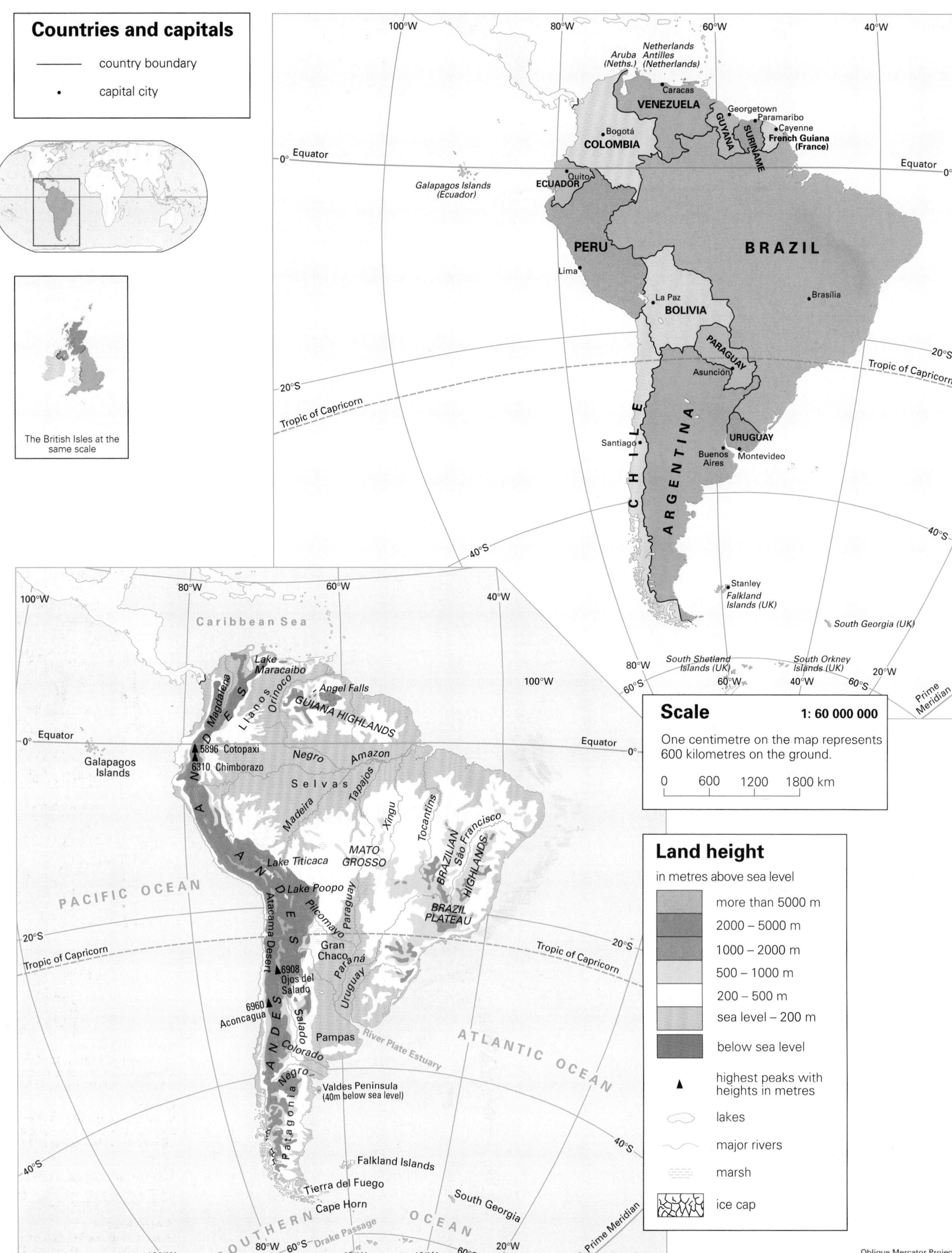

Countries and capitals

— country boundary

• capital city

The British Isles at the same scale

Scale 1: 60 000 000

One centimetre on the map represents 600 kilometres on the ground.

0   600   1200   1800 km

Land height

in metres above sea level

more than 5000 m

2000 – 5000 m

1000 – 2000 m

500 – 1000 m

200 – 500 m

sea level – 200 m

below sea level

▲ highest peaks with heights in metres

lakes

major rivers

marsh

ice cap

Oblique Mercator Projection
© Oxford University Press

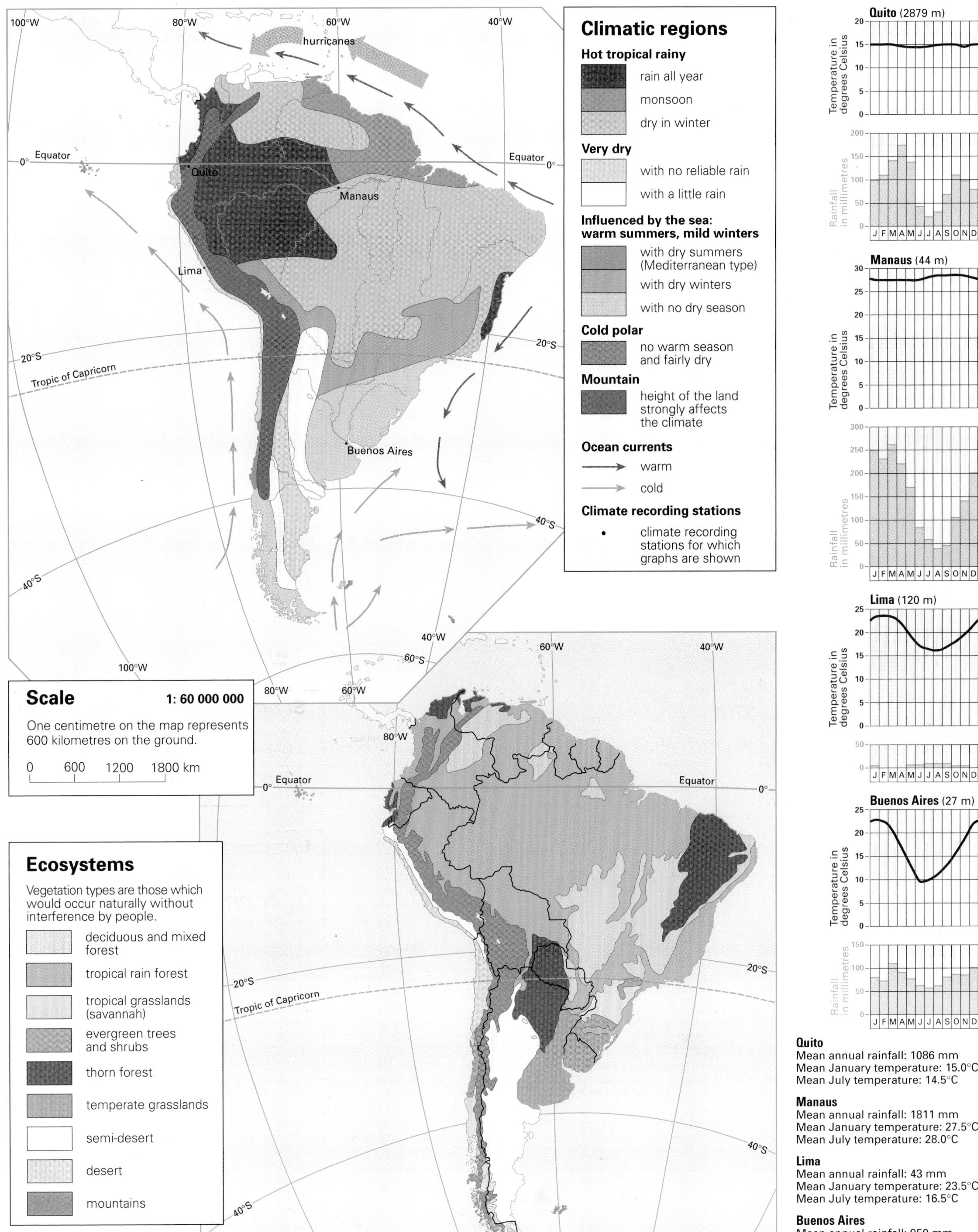

Climatic regions

Hot tropical rainy
- rain all year
- monsoon
- dry in winter

Very dry
- with no reliable rain
- with a little rain

Influenced by the sea: warm summers, mild winters
- with dry summers (Mediterranean type)
- with dry winters
- with no dry season

Cold polar
- no warm season and fairly dry

Mountain
- height of the land strongly affects the climate

Ocean currents
- → warm
- → cold

Climate recording stations
- • climate recording stations for which graphs are shown

Scale   1: 60 000 000

One centimetre on the map represents 600 kilometres on the ground.

0   600   1200   1800 km

Ecosystems

Vegetation types are those which would occur naturally without interference by people.

- deciduous and mixed forest
- tropical rain forest
- tropical grasslands (savannah)
- evergreen trees and shrubs
- thorn forest
- temperate grasslands
- semi-desert
- desert
- mountains

Oblique Mercator Projection
© Oxford University Press

Quito (2879 m)

Manaus (44 m)

Lima (120 m)

Buenos Aires (27 m)

Quito
Mean annual rainfall: 1086 mm
Mean January temperature: 15.0°C
Mean July temperature: 14.5°C

Manaus
Mean annual rainfall: 1811 mm
Mean January temperature: 27.5°C
Mean July temperature: 28.0°C

Lima
Mean annual rainfall: 43 mm
Mean January temperature: 23.5°C
Mean July temperature: 16.5°C

Buenos Aires
Mean annual rainfall: 950 mm
Mean January temperature: 23.0°C
Mean July temperature: 10.0°C

Farming, forestry, and fishing

main farming types

little or no farming : because the area is too dry or otherwise harsh.

shifting and marginal cultivation : small areas of forest cleared and farmed until soils exhausted, then family moves. Some hunting and gathering. Some timber cutting, no replacement. In mountains, families try to grow food on the same soil for many years.

mixed subsistence : crops and animals for family food.

subsistence crops : mostly intensive. Family food only.

grazing and stock rearing : on a large scale, for profit.

mixed farming : animals and cereal crops for profit.

grain farming : mostly wheat and maize, on a large scale, for profit.

plantation : well organised, specializing in one crop for profit, e.g. coffee or sugar.

mediterranean farming : cereals, animals, vegetables, fruit, wine, surplus for profit.

specialized horticulture : often supported by irrigation.

dairy farming : milk, butter, and cheese for profit.

forestry

cutting and replacement of timber for profit

cash crops

- cocoa
- coffee
- cotton
- tobacco
- fruit
- sugar
- groundnuts

animal products

- wool
- meat
- fish

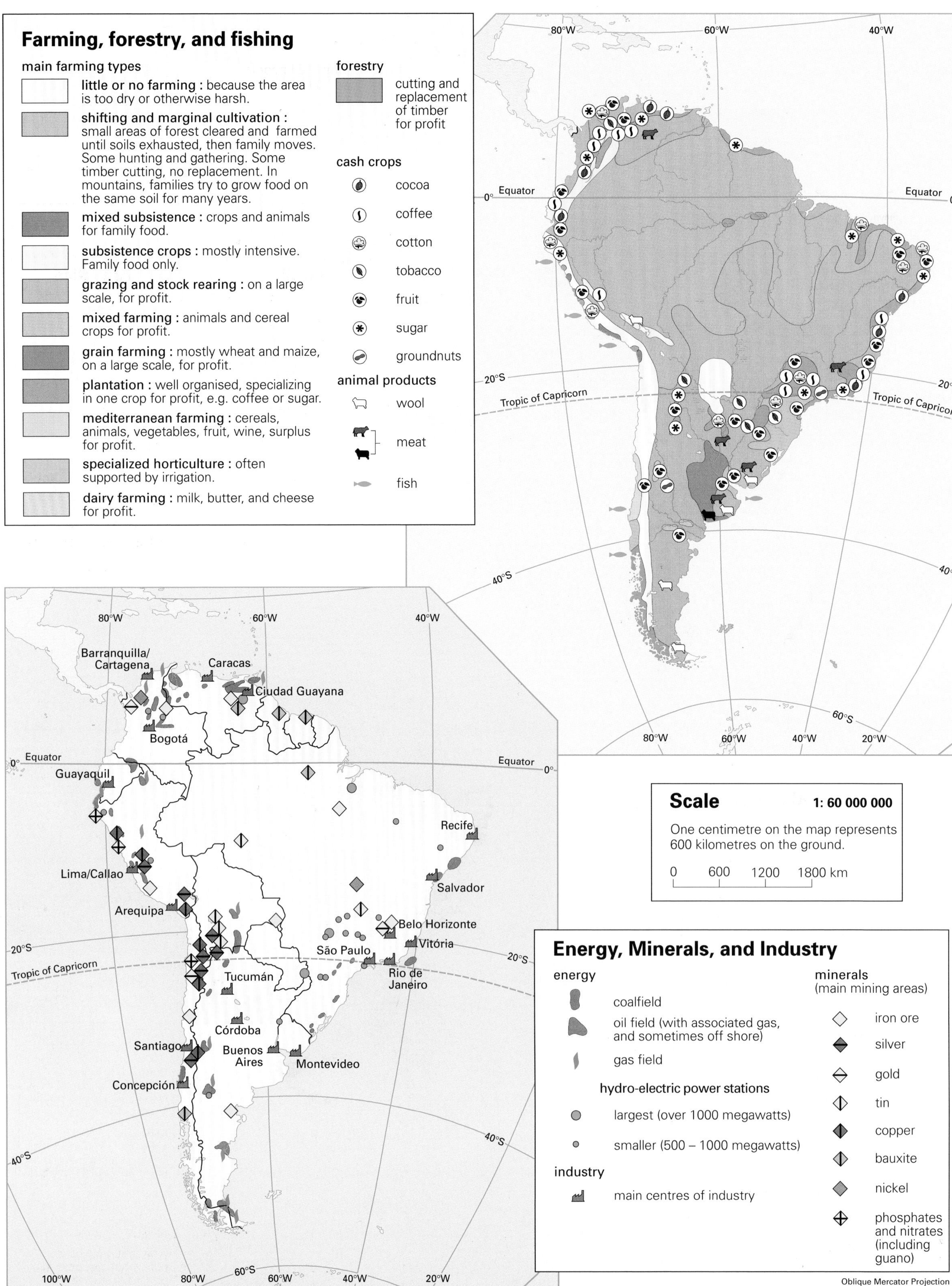

Scale   1: 60 000 000

One centimetre on the map represents 600 kilometres on the ground.

0   600   1200   1800 km

Energy, Minerals, and Industry

energy

- coalfield
- oil field (with associated gas, and sometimes off shore)
- gas field

hydro-electric power stations

- largest (over 1000 megawatts)
- smaller (500 – 1000 megawatts)

industry

- main centres of industry

minerals (main mining areas)

- iron ore
- silver
- gold
- tin
- copper
- bauxite
- nickel
- phosphates and nitrates (including guano)

Barranquilla/Cartagena
Caracas
Ciudad Guayana
Bogotá
Guayaquil
Lima/Callao
Arequipa
Tucumán
Córdoba
Santiago
Concepción
Buenos Aires
Montevideo
São Paulo
Rio de Janeiro
Belo Horizonte
Vitória
Salvador
Recife

Population density

number of people
per square kilometre

high	more than 100
moderate	10 – 100
sparse	1 – 10
very low	less than 1

■ major cities and built up areas of at least 3 million people

□ cities with 1 – 3 million people

Population structure of Brazil

Age

Males — Females

80
70
60
50
40
30
20
10

6 5 4 3 2 1 0   0 1 2 3 4 5 6

percent of the population in 2000

Total population : 172.9 million

Population structure of Argentina

Age

Males — Females

80
70
60
50
40
30
20
10

6 5 4 3 2 1 0   0 1 2 3 4 5 6

percent of the population in 2000

Total population : 37.0 million

Scale

1: 60 000 000

One centimetre on the map represents 600 kilometres on the ground.

0   600   1200   1800 km

Environmental issues

sea pollution

areas severely polluted for all or part of the year

areas persistently affected by pollution

✻ major oil spills (over 100 000 tonnes)

✱ major oil spills (under 100 000 tonnes)

acid rain

areas where acid rain is becoming a problem

air pollution

◆ cities where sulphur dioxide emissions are recorded and exceed recommended levels

tropical deforestation

existing areas of rainforest

former areas of rainforest

desertification

existing areas of desert

high risk areas

moderate risk areas

global warming

addition of greenhouse gases in tonnes of carbon per person
(look at the world map on page 17)

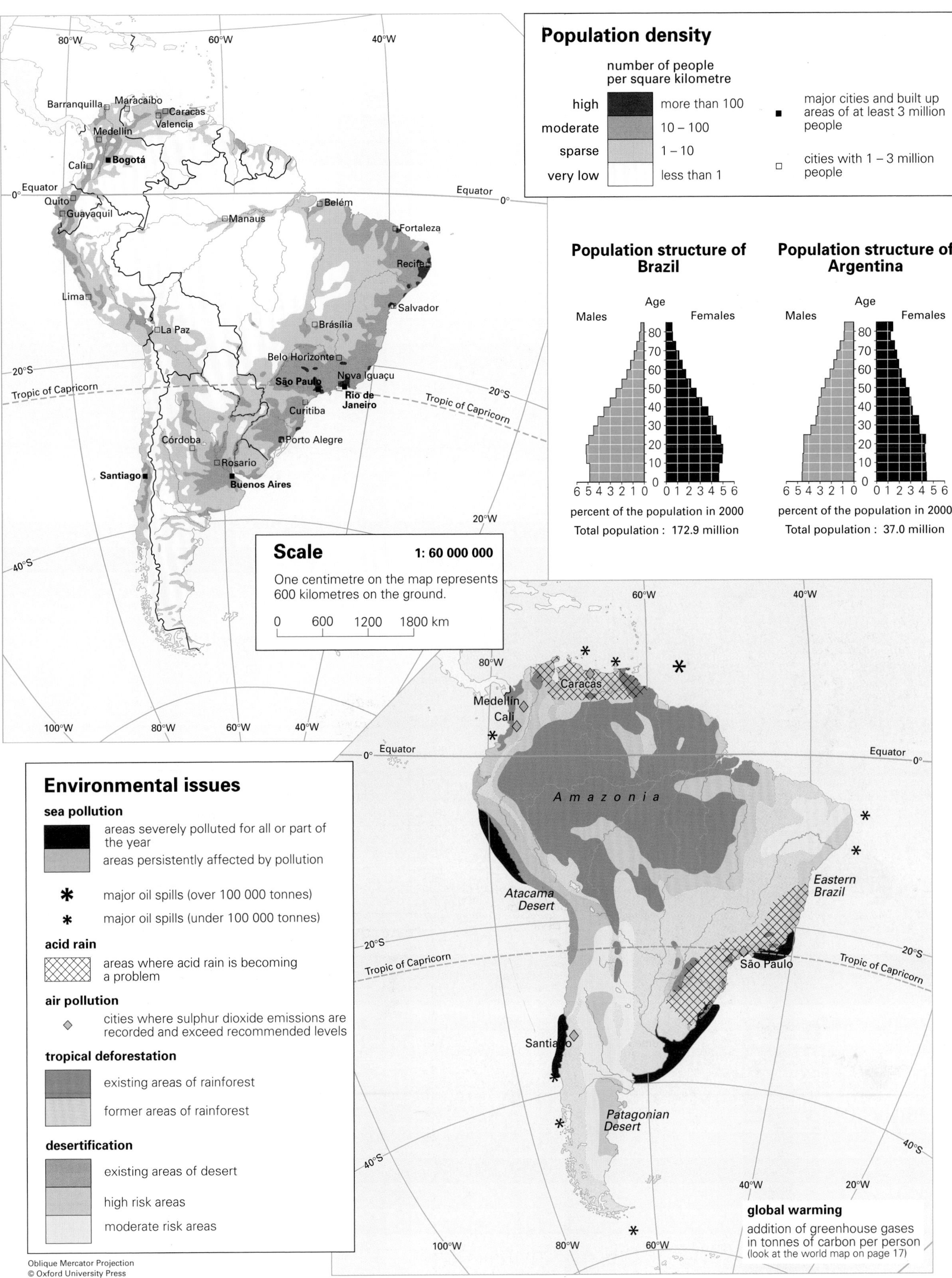

Oblique Mercator Projection
© Oxford University Press

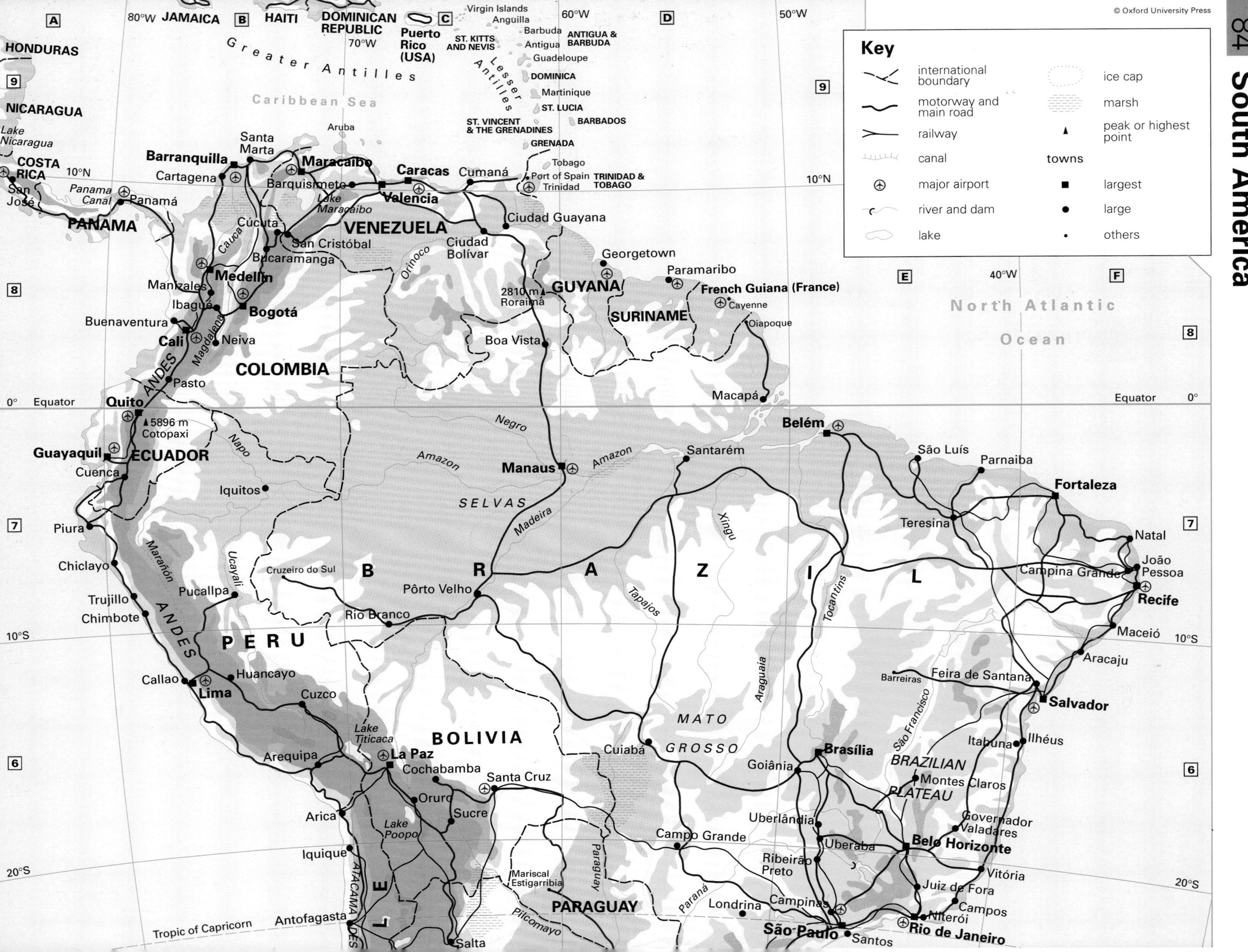
© Oxford University Press
Key
international boundary
motorway and main road
railway
canal
major airport
river and dam
lake
ice cap
marsh
peak or highest point
towns
largest
large
others
North Atlantic Ocean
Caribbean Sea
Greater Antilles
Lesser Antilles
Equator
Tropic of Capricorn
80°W
70°W
60°W
50°W
40°W
10°N
0°
10°S
20°S
HONDURAS
NICARAGUA
Lake Nicaragua
COSTA RICA
San José
Panama Canal
Panamá
PANAMA
JAMAICA
HAITI
DOMINICAN REPUBLIC
Puerto Rico (USA)
Virgin Islands
Anguilla
ST. KITTS AND NEVIS
Barbuda
Antigua
ANTIGUA & BARBUDA
Guadeloupe
DOMINICA
Martinique
ST. LUCIA
BARBADOS
ST. VINCENT & THE GRENADINES
GRENADA
Tobago
Port of Spain
Trinidad
TRINIDAD & TOBAGO
Aruba
Santa Marta
Barranquilla
Cartagena
Maracaibo
Barquisimeto
Lake Maracaibo
Caracas
Valencia
Cumaná
VENEZUELA
Ciudad Guayana
Ciudad Bolívar
Orinoco
Cúcuta
San Cristóbal
Bucaramanga
Cauca
Medellín
Manizales
Ibagué
Bogotá
Buenaventura
Cali
Neiva
Magdalena
COLOMBIA
ANDES
Pasto
Quito
5896 m Cotopaxi
Guayaquil
ECUADOR
Cuenca
Napo
Iquitos
Georgetown
GUYANA
2810 m Roraima
Paramaribo
SURINAME
French Guiana (France)
Cayenne
Oiapoque
Boa Vista
Macapá
Negro
Amazon
Manaus
SELVAS
Madeira
Santarém
Belém
São Luís
Parnaiba
Fortaleza
Teresina
Natal
João Pessoa
Campina Grande
Recife
Maceió
Aracaju
Piura
Chiclayo
Trujillo
Chimbote
Marañón
Ucayali
Pucallpa
Cruzeiro do Sul
B R A Z I L
Pôrto Velho
Rio Branco
Xingu
Tapajos
Tocantins
Araguaia
PERU
Callao
Lima
Huancayo
Cuzco
Lake Titicaca
La Paz
BOLIVIA
Cochabamba
Santa Cruz
Oruro
Sucre
Lake Poopo
Arequipa
Arica
Iquique
ATACAMA DESERT
Antofagasta
Salta
Mariscal Estigarribia
Pilcomayo
Paraguay
PARAGUAY
Paraná
MATO GROSSO
Cuiabá
Barreiras
Feira de Santana
Salvador
São Francisco
Itabuna
Ilhéus
Brasília
Goiânia
BRAZILIAN PLATEAU
Montes Claros
Governador Valadares
Belo Horizonte
Uberlândia
Uberaba
Campo Grande
Ribeirão Preto
Vitória
Juiz de Fora
Campos
Londrina
Campinas
Niterói
São Paulo
Santos
Rio de Janeiro
CHILE

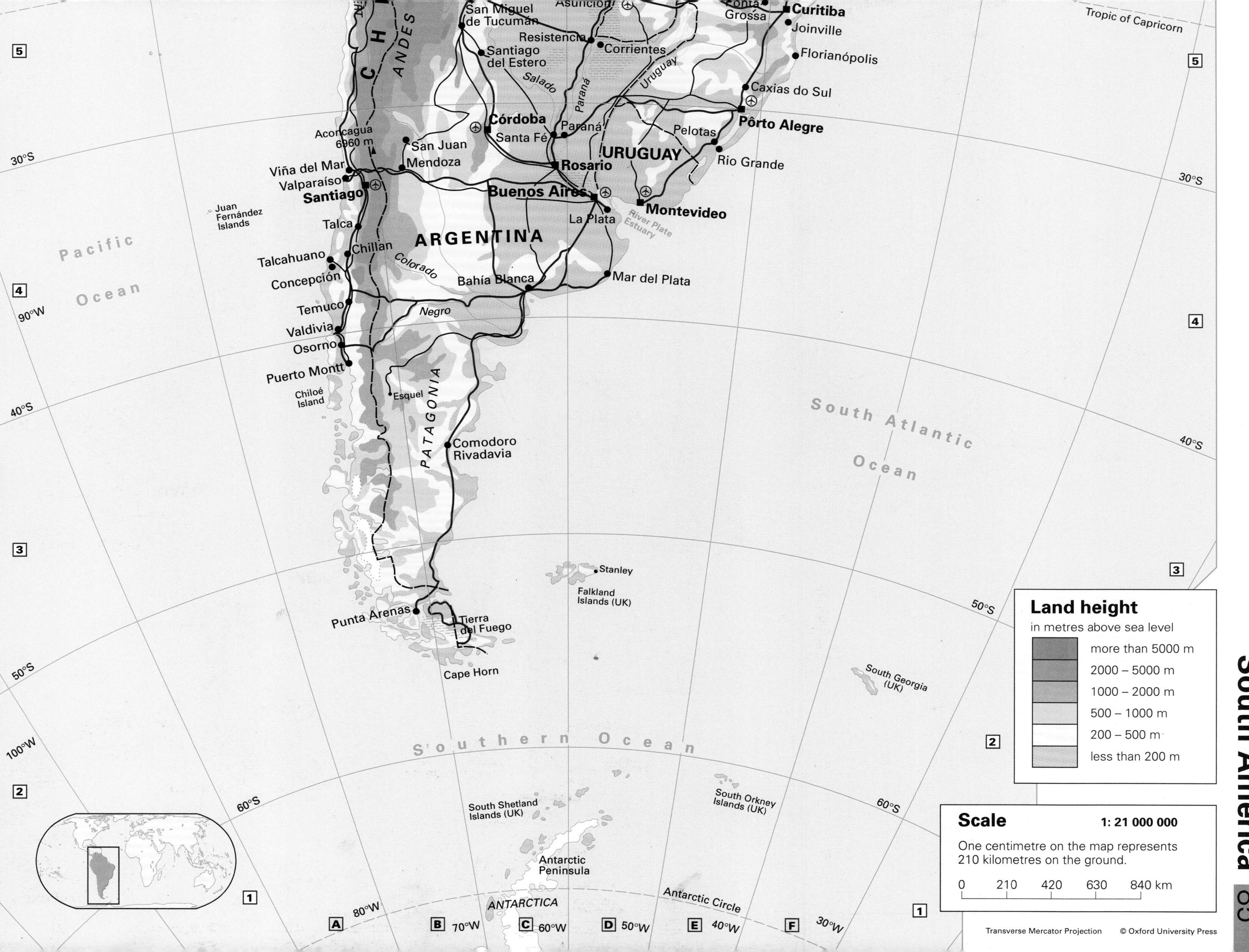

Land height
in metres above sea level

more than 5000 m
2000 – 5000 m
1000 – 2000 m
500 – 1000 m
200 – 500 m
less than 200 m

Scale   1: 21 000 000

One centimetre on the map represents
210 kilometres on the ground.

0   210   420   630   840 km

Transverse Mercator Projection   © Oxford University Press

South Georgia
(UK)

South Atlantic
Ocean

Southern Ocean

South Orkney
Islands (UK)

Antarctic Circle

Antarctic
Peninsula

South Shetland
Islands (UK)

ANTARCTICA

Stanley
Falkland
Islands (UK)

Cape Horn
Tierra
del Fuego

Punta Arenas

PATAGONIA

Esquel

Comodoro
Rivadavia

Curitiba
Joinville
Florianópolis
Grossa
Caxias do Sul
Porto Alegre
Rio Grande
Pelotas

URUGUAY
Montevideo

Uruguay

Corrientes
Asunción
Resistencia
Paraná
Salado
Santiago
del Estero
San Miguel
de Tucumán

Córdoba
Santa Fé
Rosario
Paraná

Buenos Aires
La Plata
River Plate
Estuary
Mar del Plata

Bahía Blanca

ARGENTINA

Negro
Colorado

San Juan
Mendoza

Aconcagua
6960 m
Viña del Mar
Valparaíso
Santiago
Talca
Chillán
Talcahuano
Concepción
Temuco
Valdivia
Osorno
Puerto Montt
Chiloé
Island

C H I L E
A N D E S

Juan
Fernández
Islands

Pacific
Ocean

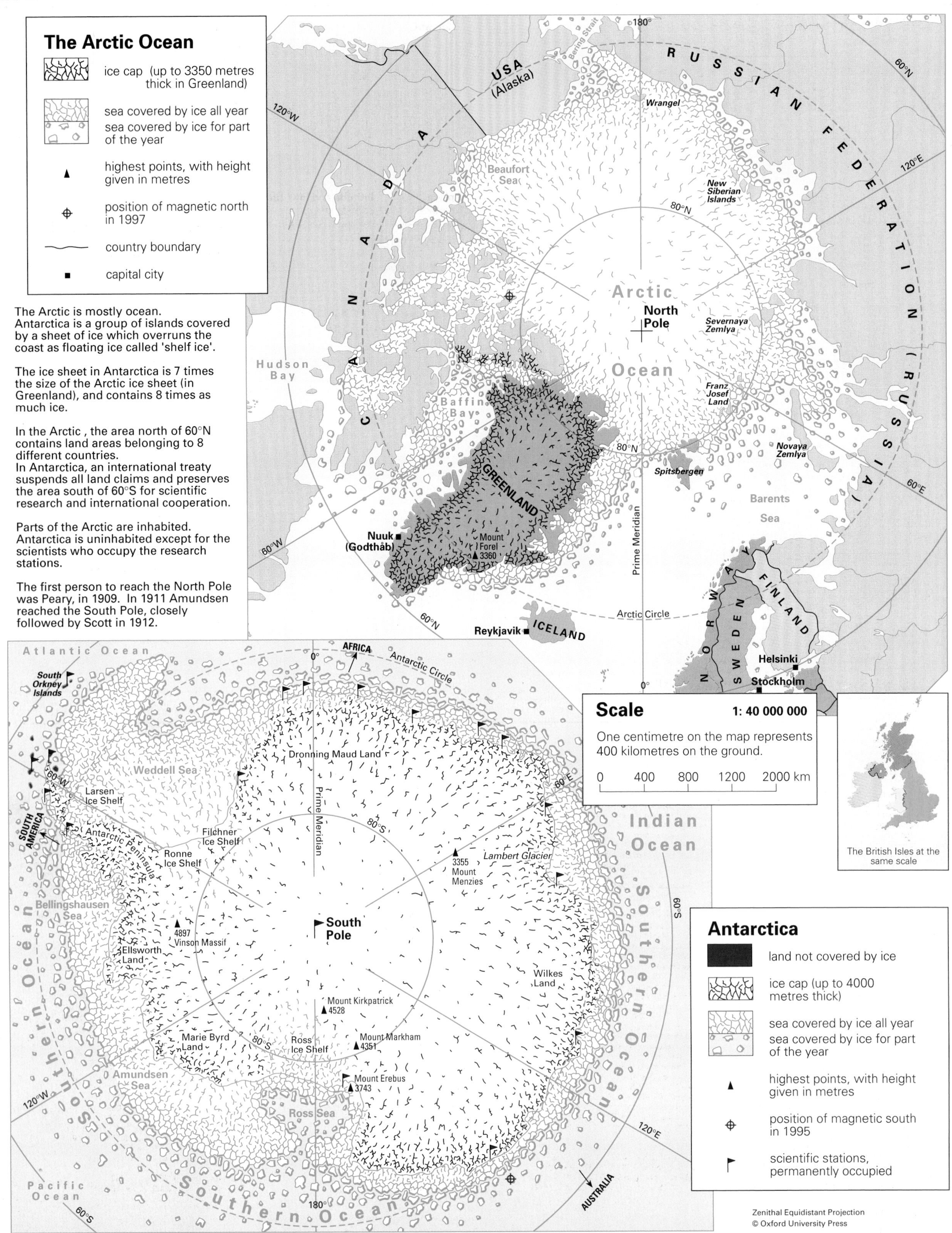

The Arctic Ocean

ice cap (up to 3350 metres thick in Greenland)

sea covered by ice all year
sea covered by ice for part of the year

▲ highest points, with height given in metres

⊕ position of magnetic north in 1997

country boundary

■ capital city

The Arctic is mostly ocean.
Antarctica is a group of islands covered by a sheet of ice which overruns the coast as floating ice called 'shelf ice'.

The ice sheet in Antarctica is 7 times the size of the Arctic ice sheet (in Greenland), and contains 8 times as much ice.

In the Arctic, the area north of 60°N contains land areas belonging to 8 different countries.
In Antarctica, an international treaty suspends all land claims and preserves the area south of 60°S for scientific research and international cooperation.

Parts of the Arctic are inhabited. Antarctica is uninhabited except for the scientists who occupy the research stations.

The first person to reach the North Pole was Peary, in 1909. In 1911 Amundsen reached the South Pole, closely followed by Scott in 1912.

Scale

1: 40 000 000

One centimetre on the map represents 400 kilometres on the ground.

0   400   800   1200   2000 km

The British Isles at the same scale

Antarctica

land not covered by ice

ice cap (up to 4000 metres thick)

sea covered by ice all year
sea covered by ice for part of the year

▲ highest points, with height given in metres

⊕ position of magnetic south in 1995

▶ scientific stations, permanently occupied

Zenithal Equidistant Projection
© Oxford University Press

How to use the index

To find a place on an atlas map use either the grid code or latitude and longitude.

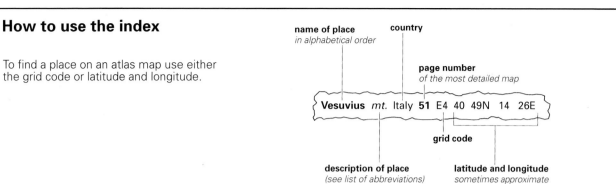

name of place *in alphabetical order*

country

page number *of the most detailed map*

Vesuvius *mt.* Italy **51** E4 40 49N 14 26E

grid code

description of place *(see list of abbreviations)*

latitude and longitude *sometimes approximate*

Grid code

Vesuvius is in grid square E4

Vesuvius *mt.* Italy **51** E4 40 49N 14 26E

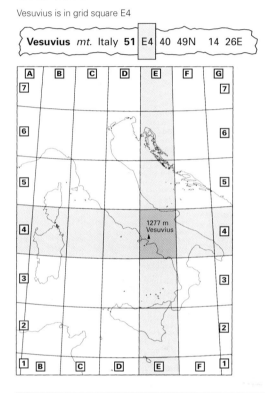

Latitude and longitude

Vesuvius is at latitude 40 49N longitude 14 26E

Vesuvius *mt.* Italy **51** E4 40 49N 14 26E

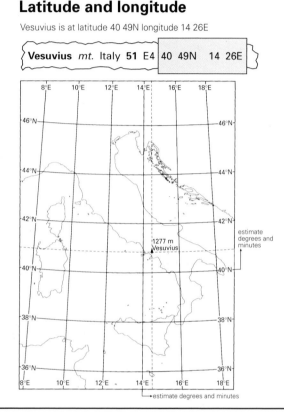

Abbreviations used in the index

admin.	administrative area
b.	bay or harbour
bor.	borough
c.	cape, point or headland
co.	county
est.	estuary
geog.reg.	geographical region
i.	island
is.	islands
l.	lake, lakes, lagoon
mt.	mountain
mts.	mountains
p.	peninsula
pk.	peak
plat.	plateau
pt.	point
r.	river
res.	reservoir
sd.	sound, strait or channel
sum.	summit
tn.	town
u.a.	unitary authority
vol.	volcano

A

Aachen Germany **49** D4 50 46N 6 06E
Aare *r.* Switzerland **49** D2 47 15N 7 30E
Abadan Iran **61** E4 30 20N 48 15E
Abbeville France **48** D5 50 06N 1 51E
Aberaeron Wales **36** C2 52 49N 44 43W
Aberchirder Scotland **31** G2 57 33N 2 38W
Aberdare Wales **36** D1 51 43N 3 27W
Aberdeen Scotland **31** G2 57 10N 2 04W
Aberdeen City *u.a.* Scotland **31** G2 57 10N 2 00W
Aberdeenshire *u.a.* Scotland **31** G2 57 10N 2 50W
Aberfeldy Scotland **31** F1 56 37N 3 54W
Abergavenny Wales **36** D1 51 50N 3 00W
Abertillery Wales **36** D1 51 45N 3 09W
Aberystwyth Wales **36** C2 52 25N 4 05W
Abha Saudi Arabia **61** E2 18 14N 42 31E
Abidjan Côte d'Ivoire **66** B3 5 19N 4 01W
Abingdon England **38** C2 51 41N 1 17W
Aboyne Scotland **31** G2 57 05N 2 50W
Abu Dhabi United Arab Emirates **61** F3 24 28N 54 25E
Abuja Nigeria **66** C3 9 10N 7 11E
Acapulco Mexico **79** K2 16 51N 99 56W
Accra Ghana **66** B3 5 33N 0 15W
Acklins Island The Bahamas **79** M3 22 30N 74 30W
Aconcagua *mt.* Argentina **85** B4 32 40S 70 02W
Adamawa Highlands Africa **66** D3 7 00N 13 00E
Adana Turkey **43** P3 37 00N 35 19E
Addis Ababa Ethiopia **61** D1 9 03N 38 42E
Adelaide Australia **72** D2 34 55S 138 36E
Aden Yemen Republic **61** E2 12 50N 45 03E
Aden, Gulf of Indian Ocean **61** E2 12 30N 47 30E
Adour *r.* France **48** C1 43 45N 0 30W
Adriatic Sea Mediterranean Sea **51** E5 43 00N 15 00E
Aegean Sea Mediterranean Sea **42** L3 39 00N 24 00E
AFGHANISTAN 58 B4
Agadez Niger **66** C4 17 00N 7 56E
Agadir Morocco **66** B6 30 30N 9 40W
Agra India **58** C3 27 09N 78 00E
Aguascalientes Mexico **79** J3 21 51N 102 18W
Ahmadabad India **58** C3 23 03N 72 40E
Ahvaz Iran **61** E4 31 17N 48 43E
Ailsa Craig *i.* Scotland **32** D3 55 16N 5 07W

Aïn Sefra Algeria **42** F2 32 45N 0 35W
Airdrie Scotland **33** F3 55 52N 3 59W
Aire *r.* England **34** C2 54 00N 2 05W
Aix-en-Provence France **48** F1 43 31N 5 27E
Ajaccio Corsica **51** B4 41 55N 8 43E
Ajdabiya Libya **66** E6 30 46N 20 14E
Akita Japan **59** N2 39 44N 140 05E
Akureyri Iceland **42** C9 65 41N 18 04W
Alabama *state* USA **79** L4 32 00N 87 00W
Alaska *state* USA **78** D7 63 00N 150 00W
Alaska, Gulf of USA **78** E6 58 00N 147 00W
Alaska Peninsula USA **78** D6 56 30N 159 00W
Alaska Range *mts.* USA **78** D7/E7 62 30N 152 30W
Albacete Spain **50** E3 39 00N 1 52W
ALBANIA 42 L4
Albany Australia **72** B2 35 00S 117 53E
Alberta *province* Canada **78** H6 55 00N 115 00W
Albert, Lake Congo Dem. Rep./Uganda **67** D5 2 00N 31 00E
Ålborg Denmark **42** H7 57 05N 9 50E
Albuquerque USA **79** J4 35 05N 106 38W
Alcalá de Henares Spain **50** D4 40 28N 3 22W
Alcudia Balearic Islands **50** G3 39 51N 3 06E
Aldabra Islands Indian Ocean **67** E4 9 00S 46 00E
Aldeburgh England **39** F3 52 09N 1 35E
Alderney *i.* Channel Islands British Isles **41** E2 49 43N 2 12W
Aldershot England **38** D2 51 15N 0 47W
Aleppo Syria **61** D4 36 14N 37 10E
Alessándria Italy **51** B6 44 55N 8 37E
Alexandria Egypt **61** C4 31 13N 29 55E
Alexandria Scotland **33** E3 55 59N 4 36W
Algarve *geog. reg.* Portugal **50** A2 37 30N 8 00W
ALGERIA 66 C5
Algiers Algeria **66** C6 36 50N 3 00E
Al Hoceima Morocco **50** D1 35 14N 3 56W
Alicante Spain **50** E3 38 21N 0 29W
Alice Springs Australia **72** D3 23 41S 133 52E
Al Jawf Libya **66** E5 24 12N 23 18E
Allahabad India **58** D3 25 27N 81 50E
Allier *r.* France **48** E3 46 15N 3 15E
Alloa Scotland **33** F4 56 07N 3 49W
Almanzor *mt.* Spain **50** C4 40 15N 5 18W
Almaty Kazakhstan **56** H2 43 19N 76 55E

Almería Spain **50** D2 36 50N 2 26W
Al Mukha Yemen Republic **61** E2 13 20N 43 16E
Aln *r.* England **33** H3 55 30N 1 50W
Alnwick England **33** H3 55 25N 1 42W
Alps *mts.* Europe **49** D2/G2 46 00N 7 30E
Altai Mountains Mongolia **57** K2 47 00N 92 30E
Alton England **38** D2 51 09N 0 59W
Alyth Scotland **31** F1 56 37N 3 13W
Amazon *r.* Brazil **84** D7 2 30S 65 30W
Amble England **33** H3 55 20N 1 34W
Ambleside England **34** C3 54 26N 2 58W
Ambon Indonesia **60** D2 3 41S 128 10E
Amesbury England **38** C2 51 10N 1 47W
Amiens France **48** E4 49 54N 2 18E
Amlwch Wales **36** C3 53 25N 4 20W
Amman Jordan **61** D4 31 04N 46 17E
Ammanford Wales **36** D1 51 48N 3 58W
Amritsar India **58** C4 31 35N 74 56E
Amsterdam Netherlands **49** C5 52 22N 4 54E
Amu Darya *r.* Asia **56** G2 41 00N 61 00E
Amundsen Sea Southern Ocean **86** 72 00S 130 00W
Amur *r.* Asia **57** N4 54 00N 122 00E
Anchorage USA **78** E7 61 10N 150 00W
Ancona Italy **51** D5 43 37N 13 31E
Andaman Islands India **58** E2 12 00N 94 00E
Andaman Sea Indian Ocean **58** E2 13 00N 95 00E
Andes *mts.* South America **84/85** B8/C5 10 00S 77 00W
Andizhan Uzbekistan **56** H2 40 40N 72 12E
ANDORRA 50 F5
Andover England **38** C2 51 13N 1 28W
Andros *i.* The Bahamas **79** M3 24 00N 78 00W
Aneto *mt.* Spain **50** F5 42 37N 0 40E
Angara *r.* Russia **57** K3 59 00N 97 00E
Angeles The Philippines **60** D4 15 09N 120 33E
Angers France **48** C3 47 29N 0 32W
Anglesey *i.* Wales **36** C3 53 13N 4 23W
ANGOLA 67 B3
Angoulême France **48** D2 45 40N 0 10E
Anguilla *i.* Leeward Islands **79** N2 18 14N 63 05W
Angus *u.a.* Scotland **31** F1/G1 56 45N 3 00W
Ankara Turkey **43** N3 39 55N 32 50E
'Annaba Algeria **66** C6 36 55N 7 47E
An Najaf Iraq **61** E4 31 59N 44 19E

Annam Range *mts.* Laos/Vietnam **60** B4 19 00N 104 00E
Annan Scotland **33** F2 54 59N 3 16W
Annan *r.* Scotland **33** F3 55 05N 3 20W
Annapurna *mt.* Nepal **58** D3 28 34N 83 50E
Annecy France **48** G2 45 54N 6 07E
Anshan China **59** D4 41 05N 122 58E
Anstruther Scotland **33** G4 56 14N 2 42W
Antalya Turkey **43** N3 36 53N 30 42E
Antananarivo Madagascar **67** E3 18 52S 47 30E
Antarctic Peninsula Antarctica **86** 68 00S 65 00W
Antibes France **48** G1 43 35N 7 07E
Antigua *i.* Antigua & Barbuda **84** C9 17 09N 61 49W
ANTIGUA AND BARBUDA 79 N2
Antofagasta Chile **84** B5 23 40S 70 23W
Antrim Northern Ireland **32** C2 54 43N 6 13W
Antrim *district* Northern Ireland **32** C2 54 45N 6 25W
Antrim Mountains Northern Ireland **32** C3/D2 55 00N 6 10W
Antwerp Belgium **49** C4 51 13N 4 25E
Anxi China **59** A5 40 32N 95 57E
Aomori Japan **59** N3 40 50N 140 43E
Aosta Italy **51** A6 45 43N 7 19E
Aparri The Philippines **60** D4 18 22N 121 40E
Apeldoorn Netherlands **49** C5 52 13N 5 57E
Appalachians *mts.* USA **79** L4 37 00N 82 00W
Appennines *mts.* Italy **51** C6/F4 44 30N 10 00E
Appleby-in-Westmorland England **34** C3 53 36N 2 29W
Aqaba Jordan **61** D3 29 32N 35 00E
Arabian Sea Indian Ocean **7** 17 00N 60 00E
Aracaju Brazil **84** F6 10 54S 37 07W
Arafura Sea Australia **72** D5 9 00S 133 00E
Arak Iran **61** E4 34 05N 49 42E
Araks *r.* Asia **61** E4 39 30N 48 00E
Aral Sea Asia **56** G2 45 00N 60 00E
Aran Fawddy *mt.* Wales **36** D2 52 47N 3 41W
Ararat, Mount Turkey **43** Q3 39 44N 44 15E
Arbil Iraq **61** E4 36 12N 44 01E
Arbroath Scotland **31** G1 56 34N 2 35W
Arctic Ocean 86
Ardabil Iran **61** E4 38 15N 48 18E
Ardbeg Scotland **32** C3 55 39N 6 05W

Ardennes *mts.* Belgium **49** C4 50 10N 5 45E
Ardminish Scotland **32** D3 55 42N 5 44W
Ardres France **39** F1 50 51N 1 59E
Ards *district* Northern Ireland **32** D2 54 30N 5 30W
Ards Peninsula Northern Ireland **32** D2 54 25N 5 30W
Arequipa Peru **84** B6 16 25S 71 32W
Arezzo Italy **51** C5 43 28N 11 53E
ARGENTINA 85 C4
Argyll and Bute *u.a.* Scotland **32/33** D4/E4 56 10N 5 00W
Århus Denmark **42** J7 56 15N 10 10E
Arica Chile **84** B6 18 30S 70 20W
Arisaig Scotland **30** D1 56 51N 5 51W
Arisaig, Sound of Scotland **30** D1 56 50N 5 50W
Arizona *state* USA **79** H4 34 00N 112 00W
Arkansas *r.* USA **79** K4 35 00N 93 00W
Arkansas *state* USA **79** K4 34 00N 93 00W
Arkhangel'sk Russia **56** E4 64 32N 40 40E
Arklow Republic of Ireland **36** A2 52 48N 6 09W
Arles France **48** F1 43 41N 4 38E
Armagh Northern Ireland **32** C2 54 21N 6 39W
Armagh *district* Northern Ireland **32** C2 54 20N 6 40W
ARMENIA 43 Q4
Armentières France **39** G1 50 41N 2 53E
Arnhem Netherlands **49** C4 52 00N 5 53E
Arno *r.* Italy **51** C5 43 45N 11 00E
Arnold England **37** F2 53 00N 1 09W
Arran *i.* Scotland **32** D3 55 35N 5 15W
Arras France **48** E5 50 17N 2 46E
Artá Balearic Islands **50** G3 39 42N 3 20E
Aruba *i.* Netherlands **79** N2 12 20N 70 00W
Aru Islands Indonesia **60** E2 6 00S 134 30E
Arun *r.* England **38** D2 51 05N 0 30W
Arundel England **38** D1 50 51N 0 34W
Asahikawa Japan **59** N3 43 46N 142 23E
Asahi, Mount Japan **59** N3 43 42N 142 54E
Asansol India **58** D3 23 40N 86 59E
Ascension Island Atlantic Ocean **5** 7 57S 14 22W
Ashbourne England **37** F3 53 01N 1 43W
Ashburton New Zealand **73** C2 43 54S 171 45E
Ashford England **39** E2 51 09N 0 53E
Ashgabat Turkmenistan **56** F1 37 58N 58 24E
Ashington England **33** H3 55 11N 1 34W
Asmara Eritrea **61** D2 15 20N 38 58E
Assisi Italy **51** D5 43 04N 12 37E
Astana Kazakhstan **56** H3 51 10N 71 28E
Astrakhan Russia **56** E2 46 22N 48 04E
Asunción Paraguay **85** D5 25 15S 57 40W
Aswan Egypt **61** D3 24 05N 32 56E
Asyut Egypt **61** D3 27 14N 31 07E
Atacama Desert Chile **84/85** B5 22 30S 70 00W
Atbara Sudan **61** D2 17 42N 34 00E
Atbara *r.* Sudan **61** D2 17 00N 35 00E
Athabasca *r.* Canada **78** H6 57 30N 112 00W
Athens Greece **42** L3 38 00N 23 44E
Atlanta USA **79** L4 33 45N 84 23W
Atlantic Ocean 79 N4
Atlas Mountains Morocco **66** B6 32 00N 2 00W
Atrek *r.* Iran/Turkmenistan **61** F4 38 00N 57 00E
Atyrau Kazakhstan **56** F2 47 08N 51 59E
Auchterarder Scotland **31** F1 56 18N 3 43W
Auchtermuchty Scotland **33** F4 56 17N 3 15W
Auckland New Zealand **73** C3 36 51S 174 46E
Auderville France **41** F2 49 43N 1 56W
Augsburg Germany **49** F3 48 21N 10 54E
Austin USA **79** K4 30 18N 97 47W
AUSTRALIA 72
AUSTRIA 42 J5
Auxerre France **48** E3 47 48N 3 35E
Aveiro Portugal **50** A4 40 38N 8 40W
Aviemore Scotland **31** F2 57 12N 3 50W
Avignon France **48** F1 43 56N 4 48E
Avon *r.* Warwickshire/Worcestershire England **37** F2 52 15N 1 55W
Avon *r.* Wiltshire/Bath and North East Somerset/North Somerset England **38** B2 51 20N 2 05W
Avon *r.* Wiltshire/Hampshire/Dorset England **38** C1 50 55N 1 50W
Axe *r.* England **41** E3 50 50N 2 50W
Axminster England **41** E3 50 47N 3 00W
Ayaguz Kazakhstan **56** J2 47 59N 80 27E
Ayers Rock *mt.* Australia **72** D3 25 20S 131 01E
Aylesbury England **38** D2 51 50N 0 50W
Ayr Scotland **33** E3 55 28N 4 38W
Ayr *r.* Scotland **33** E3 55 30N 4 20W
Ayre, Point of *c.* Isle of Man British Isles **33** E2 54 25N 4 22W
AZERBAIJAN 56 E2
Azores *is.* Atlantic Ocean **4** 38 30N 28 00W
Azov, Sea of Asia **43** P5 46 00N 36 00E

B

Bacolod The Philippines **60** D4 10 38N 122 58E
Badajoz Spain **50** B3 38 53N 6 58W
Baden-Baden Germany **49** E3 48 45N 8 15E
Baffin Bay Canada **78** N8 72 00N 64 00W
Baffin Island Canada **78** M8 70 00N 75 00W
Baghdad Iraq **61** E4 33 20N 44 26E
BAHAMAS, THE 79 M3
Bahía Blanca Argentina **85** C4 38 45S 62 15W
BAHRAIN 61 F3
Baie de la Seine *b.* France **41** G2 49 40N 0 30W
Bakewell England **37** F3 53 13N 1 40W
Baku Azerbaijan **56** E2 40 22N 49 53E
Bala Wales **36** D2 52 54N 3 35W
Bala Lake Wales **36** D2 52 53N 3 38W
Balearic Islands Spain **50** F3/H4 40 00N 2 00E
Bali *i.* Indonesia **60** C2 8 30S 115 00E
Balikesir Turkey **42** M3 39 37N 27 51E
Balikpapan Indonesia **60** C2 1 15S 116 50E
Balkhash, Lake Kazakhstan **56** H2 46 00N 75 00E
Ballantrae Scotland **32** D3 55 06N 5 00W
Ballarat Australia **72** E2 37 33S 143 52E
Ballater Scotland **31** F2 57 03N 3 03W
Ballybofey Republic of Ireland **32** B2 54 48N 7 47W
Ballycastle Northern Ireland **32** C3 55 12N 6 15W
Ballymena Northern Ireland **32** C2 54 52N 6 17W
Ballymena *district* Northern Ireland **32** C2 54 55N 6 20W
Ballymoney Northern Ireland **32** C3 55 04N 6 31W
Ballymoney *district* Northern Ireland **32** C3 55 00N 6 30W
Ballyshannon Republic of Ireland **32** A2 54 30N 8 11W
Baltic Sea Europe **42** K7 55 15N 17 00E
Baltimore USA **79** M4 39 18N 76 38W
Bamako Mali **66** B4 12 40N 7 59W
Bamberg Germany **49** F3 49 54N 10 54E
Bamburgh England **33** H3 55 36N 1 42W
Banbridge Northern Ireland **32** C2 54 21N 6 16W
Banbridge *district* Northern Ireland **32** C2 54 20N 6 20W
Banbury England **38** C3 52 04N 1 20W
Banchory Scotland **31** G2 57 30N 2 30W
Banda Aceh Indonesia **60** A3 5 30N 95 20E
Bandar-e 'Abbas Iran **61** F3 27 12N 56 15E
Bandar Seri Begawan Brunei **60** C3 4 53N 114 57E
Banda Sea Indonesia **60** D2 5 50S 126 00E
Bandung Indonesia **60** B2 6 57S 107 34E
Banff Scotland **31** G2 57 40N 2 33W
Bangalore India **58** C2 12 58N 77 35E
Bangka *i.* Indonesia **60** B2 2 30S 107 00E
Bangkok *(Krung Thep)* Thailand **60** B4 13 44N 100 30E
BANGLADESH 58 D3/E3
Bangor Northern Ireland **32** D2 54 40N 5 40W
Bangor Wales **36** C3 53 13N 4 08W
Bangui Central African Republic **67** B5 4 23N 18 37E
Bangweulu, Lake Zambia **67** C3 11 15S 29 45E
Banjarmasin Indonesia **60** C2 3 22S 114 33E
Banjul The Gambia **66** A4 13 28N 16 39W
Banks Island Canada **78** G8 73 15N 121 30W
Bann *r.* Northern Ireland **32** C2 54 55N 6 30W
Baotou China **59** B4 40 38N 109 59E
BARBADOS 79 P2
Barbuda *i.* Antigua & Barbuda **84** C9 17 41N 61 48W
Barcelona Spain **50** G4 41 25N 2 10E
Bareilly India **58** C3 28 20N 79 24E
Barents Sea Arctic Ocean **86** 75 00N 40 00E
Barfleur France **41** F2 49 40N 1 16W
Bari Italy **51** F4 41 07N 16 52E
Barito *r.* Indonesia **60** C2 2 00S 115 00E
Barking England **39** E2 51 33N 0 06E
Barletta Italy **51** F4 41 20N 16 17E
Barmouth Wales **36** C2 52 43N 4 03W
Barnard Castle England **34** D3 54 33N 1 55W
Barnaul Russia **56** J3 53 21N 83 45E
Barnet England **38** D2 51 39N 0 12W
Barnoldswick England **34** C2 53 56N 2 16W
Barnsley England **35** D2 53 34N 1 28W
Barnstaple England **40** C4 51 05N 4 04W
Barquisimeto Venezuela **84** C9 10 03N 69 18W
Barra *i.* Scotland **30** B1/2 57 00N 7 25W
Barranquilla Colombia **84** B9 11 10N 74 50W
Barreiras Brazil **84** E6 12 09S 44 58W
Barrow-in-Furness England **34** B3 54 07N 3 14W
Barry Wales **36** D1 51 24N 3 18W
Barton-upon-Humber England **35** E2 53 41N 0 27W
Basel Switzerland **49** D2 47 33N 7 36E
Basildon England **39** E2 51 34N 0 25W
Basingstoke England **38** C2 51 16N 1 05W
Basra Iraq **61** E4 30 30N 47 50E
Bassein Myanmar **58** E2 16 46N 94 45E
Bass Strait Australia **72** E2 39 51S 145 53E
Bastia France **51** B5 42 14N 9 26E
Bata Equatorial Guinea **66** C3 1 51N 9 49E
Batang China **59** A3 30 02N 99 01E
Batangas The Philippines **60** D4 13 46N 121 01E
Bath England **38** B2 51 23N 2 22W
Bath and North East Somerset *u.a.* England **38** B2 51 25N 2 30W
Bathgate Scotland **33** F3 55 55N 3 39W
Baton Rouge USA **79** K4 30 30N 91 10W
Batumi Georgia **56** E2 41 37N 41 36E
Bavaria *admin.* Germany **49** F3/G3 49 00N 12 00E
Bayeux France **48** C4 49 16N 0 42W
Baykal, Lake Russia **57** L3 54 00N 109 00E
Bayonne France **48** C1 43 30N 1 28W
Bayreuth Germany **49** F3 49 27N 11 35E
Beachy Head *c.* England **39** E1 50 44N 0 16E
Bearsden Scotland **33** E3 55 56N 4 20W
Beaufort Sea Arctic Ocean **78** E7 72 00N 140 00W
Beauly *r.* Scotland **31** E2 57 30N 4 30W
Beauvais France **48** E4 49 26N 2 05E
Beccles England **39** F3 52 28N 1 34E
Bechar Algeria **66** B6 31 35N 2 17W
Bedford England **38** D3 52 08N 0 29W
Bedfordshire *co.* England **38** D3 52 08N 0 29W
Bedworth England **37** F2 52 29N 1 28W
Beersheba Israel **43** N2 31 15N 34 47E
Beida Libya **66** E6 32 00N 21 30E
Beijing China **59** C3 39 55N 116 26E
Beinn Dearg *mt.* Scotland **31** E2 57 47N 4 56W
Beira Mozambique **67** D3 19 49S 34 52E
Beirut Lebanon **61** D4 33 52N 35 30E
Beja Portugal **50** B3 38 01N 7 52W
Bejaïa Algeria **42** H3 36 49N 5 03E
BELARUS 56 C3
Belém Brazil **84** E7 1 27S 48 29W
Belfast Northern Ireland **32** D2 54 35N 5 55W
Belfast *district* Northern Ireland **32** C2/D2 54 30N 5 58W
Belfast Lough *est.* Northern Ireland **32** D2 54 40N 5 45W
Belfort France **48** G3 47 38N 6 52E
Belgaum India **58** C2 15 54N 74 36E
BELGIUM 49
Belgrade Yugoslavia **42** L4 44 50N 20 30E
Belitung *i.* Indonesia **60** B2 2 30S 107 30E
BELIZE 79 L2
Belize Belize **79** L2 17 29N 88 10W
Belle Isle *i.* France **48** B3 47 20N 3 10W
Bellingshausen Sea Southern Ocean **86** 71 00S 85 00W
Belmopan Belize **79** L2 17 13N 88 48W
Belo Horizonte Brazil **84** E6 19 54S 43 54W
Ben Alder *mt.* Scotland **31** E1 56 49N 4 28W
Benavente Spain **50** C5 42 00N 5 40W
Benbecula *i.* Scotland **30** B2 57 25N 7 20W
Ben Cruachan *mt.* Scotland **30** D1 56 26N 5 09W
Bengal, Bay of Indian Ocean **58** D2 17 00N 88 00E
Benghazi Libya **66** E6 32 07N 20 04E
Benguela Angola **67** B3 12 34S 13 24E
Ben Hope *mt.* Scotland **31** E3 58 24N 4 37W
BENIN 66 C4
Ben Klibreck *mt.* Scotland **31** E3 58 14N 4 22W
Ben Lawers *mt.* Scotland **31** E1 56 33N 4 15W
Ben Lomond *mt.* Scotland **33** E4 56 12N 4 38W
Ben More *mt.* Argyll and Bute Scotland **30** C1 56 25N 6 02W
Ben More *mt.* Stirling Scotland **31** E1 56 25N 6 02W
Ben More Assynt *mt.* Scotland **31** E3 58 07N 4 52W
Ben Nevis *mt.* Scotland **31** D1 56 48N 5 00W
Benue *r.* Nigeria/Cameroon **66** C3/D3 9 00N 10 00E
Ben Wyvis *mt.* Scotland **31** E2 57 40N 4 35W
Berbera Somalia **66** E6 10 28N 45 02E
Berezniki Russia **43** T7 59 26N 56 49E
Bérgamo Italy **51** B6 45 42N 9 40E
Bergen Norway **42** H8 60 23N 5 20E
Bergerac France **48** D2 44 50N 0 29E
Bering Sea Pacific Ocean **57** S3 58 00N 170 00W
Bering Strait Russia/USA **78** C7 69 00N 169 00W
Berlin Germany **49** G5 52 32N 13 25E
Bermuda *i.* Atlantic Ocean **79** N4 32 50N 64 20W
Bern Switzerland **49** D2 46 57N 7 26E
Berneray *i.* Scotland **30** B2 57 45N 7 10W
Bernina *mt.* Europe **49** E2 46 23N 9 54E
Berwick-upon-Tweed England **33** G3 55 46N 2 00W
Besançon France **48** F3 47 14N 6 02E
Bethesda Wales **36** C3 53 11N 4 03W
Béthune France **48** E5 50 32N 2 38E
Beverley England **35** E2 53 51N 0 26W
Bewdley England **37** E2 52 22N 2 19W
Bexley England **39** E2 51 27N 0 09E
BHUTAN 58 D3/E3
Białystok Poland **42** L6 53 09N 23 10E
Biarritz France **48** C1 43 29N 1 33W
Bicester England **38** C2 51 54N 1 09W
Bideford England **40** C4 51 01N 4 13W
Bideford Bay England **40** C4 51 05N 4 25W
Bielefeld Germany **49** E5 52 02N 8 32E
Bigbury Bay England **40** D3 50 17N 4 00W
Biggar Scotland **33** F3 55 38N 3 32W
Biggleswade England **38** D3 52 05N 0 17W
Bikaner India **58** C3 28 01N 73 22E
Bilbao Spain **50** D5 43 15N 2 56W
Bintan *i.* Indonesia **60** B3 0 50N 104 30E
Birdum Australia **72** D4 15 39S 133 13E
Birkenhead England **34** B2 53 24N 3 02W
Birmingham England **37** F2 52 30N 1 50W
Birmingham USA **79** L4 33 30N 86 55W
Biscay, Bay of Atlantic Ocean **48** B2 45 30N 2 50W
Bishkek Kyrgyzstan **56** H2 42 53N 74 46E
Bishop Auckland England **34** D3 54 40N 1 40W
Bishop's Stortford England **39** E2 51 53N 0 09E
Biskra Algeria **42** H2 34 50N 5 41E
Bissau Guinea-Bissau **66** A4 11 52N 15 39W
Biwa, Lake Japan **59** M2 35 20N 135 20E
Bizerte Tunisia **51** B2 37 18N 9 52E
Blackburn England **34** C2 53 45N 2 29W
Blackburn with Darwen *u.a.* England **34** C2 53 43N 2 25W
Black Forest *mts.* Germany **49** E3 47 00N 8 00E
Black Mountains Wales **36** D1 51 55N 3 10W
Blackpool England **34** B2 53 50N 3 03W
Blackpool *u.a.* England **34** B2 53 51N 3 10W
Black Sea Europe **43** P4 43 00N 35 00E
Black Volta *r.* Africa **66** B3/4 10 00N 3 00W
Blackwater *r.* Northern Ireland **32** C2 54 30N 6 45W
Blackwater Reservoir Scotland **30** E1 56 41N 4 46W
Blaenau Ffestiniog Wales **36** D2 52 59N 3 56W
Blaenau Gwent *u.a.* Wales **36** D1 51 45N 3 10W
Blagoveshchensk Russia **57** N3 50 19N 127 30E
Blairgowrie Scotland **31** F1 56 36N 3 21W
Blandford Forum England **41** E3 50 52N 2 11W
Blantyre Malawi **67** D3 15 46S 35 00E
Blenheim New Zealand **73** C2 41 31S 173 57E
Blida Algeria **42** G3 36 30N 2 50E
Blois France **48** D3 47 36N 1 20E
Bloomfontein Republic of South Africa **67** C2 29 07S 26 14E
Blue Nile *r.* Ethiopia/Sudan **61** D2 12 00N 33 00E
Blyth England **33** H3 55 07N 1 30W
Blyth *r.* England **33** H3 55 10N 1 45W
Boa Vista Brazil **84** C8 3 23S 55 30W
Bobo Dioulasso Burkina **66** B4 11 11N 4 18W
Bochum Germany **49** D4 51 28N 7 11E
Bodele Depression Chad **66** D4 17 00N 17 50E
Bodmin England **40** C3 50 29N 4 43W
Bodmin Moor England **40** C3 50 35N 4 40W
Bodø Norway **42** J9 67 18N 14 26E
Bognor Regis England **38** D1 50 47N 0 41W
Bogor Indonesia **60** B2 6 34S 106 45E
Bogotá Colombia **84** B8 4 38N 74 05W
Boise USA **79** H5 43 38N 116 12W
BOLIVIA 84 C6
Bologna Italy **51** C6 44 30N 11 20E
Bolton England **34** C2 53 35N 2 26W
Bolzano Italy **51** C7 46 30N 11 22E
Bombay *see* Mumbai
Bonaire *i.* Lesser Antilles **79** N2 12 15N 68 27W
Bonar Bridge *tn.* Scotland **31** E2 57 53N 4 21W
Bo'ness Scotland **33** F4 56 01N 3 37W
Bonifacio Corsica **51** B4 41 23N 9 10E
Bonn Germany **49** D4 50 44N 7 06E
Bootle England **34** B2 53 28N 3 00W
Bordeaux France **48** C2 44 50N 0 34W
Borneo *i.* Indonesia/Malaysia **60** C3 1 00N 113 00E
Bornholm *i.* Denmark **49** H6 55 02N 15 00E
Boscastle England **40** C3 50 41N 4 42W
BOSNIA-HERZEGOVINA 42 K4
Boston England **35** E1 52 29N 0 01W
Boston USA **79** M5 42 20N 71 05W
Bothnia, Gulf of Finland/Sweden **42** L8 61 00N 19 10E
BOTSWANA 67 C2
Bouaké Côte d'Ivoire **66** B3 7 42N 5 00W
Bougainville *i.* Papua New Guinea **72** F5 6 15S 155 00E
Boulogne-sur-Mer France **48** D5 50 43N 1 37E
Bourges France **48** E3 47 05N 2 23E
Bourke Australia **72** E2 30 05S 145 58E
Bournemouth England **41** F3 50 43N 1 54W
Bournemouth *u.a.* England **41** F3 50 46N 1 52W
Bou Saâda Algeria **42** G3 35 10N 4 09E
Bovey Tracey England **40** D3 50 36N 3 40W
Boyoma Falls Congo Dem.Rep. **67** C5 0 18N 25 30E
Bracknell England **38** D2 51 26N 0 46W
Bracknell Forest *u.a.* England **38** D2 51 22N 0 43W
Bradford England **34** D2 53 48N 1 45W
Braemar Scotland **31** F2 57 01N 3 23W
Brahmaputra *r.* India/Bangladesh **58** E3 27 00N 94 00E
Brăila Romania **42** M5 45 17N 27 58E
Braintree England **39** E2 51 53N 0 32E
Brampton England **34** C3 54 57N 2 43W
Brandenburg Germany **49** G5 52 25N 12 34E
Branderburgh Scotland **31** F2 57 43N 3 18W
Brásília Brazil **84** E6 15 45S 47 57W
Bra∞ov Romania **42** M5 45 39N 25 35E
Bratislava Slovakia **42** K5 48 10N 17 10E
Bratsk Russia **57** L3 56 20N 101 50E
Braunton England **40** C4 51 07N 4 10W
Bray Republic of Ireland **36** A3 53 12N 6 06W
BRAZIL 84 C7/E7
Brazilian Plateau Brazil **84** E6 17 00S 44 00W
Brazzaville Congo **66** D2 4 14S 15 14E
Brechin Scotland **31** G1 56 44N 2 40W
Brecon Wales **36** D1 51 57N 3 24W
Brecon Beacons *mts.* Wales **36** D1 51 53N 3 30W
Breda Netherlands **49** C4 51 35N 4 46E
Bremen Germany **49** E5 53 05N 8 48E
Bremerhaven Germany **49** E5 53 33N 8 35E
Brenner Pass Austria/Italy **49** F2 47 02N 11 32E
Brent England **38** D2 51 34N 0 17W
Brentwood England **39** E2 51 38N 0 18E
Bréscia Italy **51** C6 45 33N 10 13E
Bressay *i.* Scotland **29** D3 60 08N 1 05W
Brest Belarus **42** L6 52 08N 23 40E
Brest France **48** A4 48 23N 4 30W
Bridgend Wales **36** D1 51 31N 3 35W
Bridgend *u.a.* Wales **36** D1 51 32N 3 35W
Bridgnorth England **37** E2 52 33N 2 25W
Bridgwater England **41** E4 51 08N 3 00W
Bridgwater Bay England **41** D4 51 15N 3 20W
Bridlington England **35** D3 54 05N 0 12W
Bridport England **41** E3 50 44N 2 46W
Brigg England **35** E2 53 34N 0 30W
Brighouse England **34** D2 53 42N 1 47W
Brighton England **38** D1 50 50N 0 10W
Brighton & Hove *u.a.* England **38** D1 50 52N 0 13W
Bríndisi Italy **51** F4 40 37N 17 57E
Brisbane Australia **72** F3 27 28S 153 03E
Bristol England **38** B2 51 27N 2 35W
Bristol England *u.a.* **38** B2 51 30N 2 30W
Bristol Channel United Kingdom **36** C1/D1 51 20N 3 50W
British Columbia *province* Canada **78** G6 55 00N 128 00W
Brittany *geog. reg.* France **48** B4 48 00N 3 00W
Brive France **48** D2 45 09N 1 32E
Brixham England **40** D3 50 23N 3 30W
Brno Czech Republic **42** K5 49 13N 16 40E
Broad Bay Scotland **30** C3 58 15N 6 10W
Broadford Scotland **30** D2 57 14N 5 54W
Broad Law *mt.* Scotland **33** F3 55 30N 3 22W
Broadway England **37** F2 52 02N 1 50W
Brodick Scotland **32** D3 55 35N 5 09W
Broken Hill *tn.* Australia **72** E2 31 57S 141 28E
Bromley England **39** E2 51 31N 0 01W
Bromsgrove England **37** E2 50 20N 2 03W
Bromyard England **37** E2 52 11N 2 30W
Brooks Range *mts.* U.S.A. **78** D7/E7 67 55N 155 00W
Broome Australia **72** C4 17 57S 122 13E
Brora Scotland **31** F3 58 01N 3 51W
Brough England **34** C3 54 32N 2 19W
Brough Head Scotland **29** B2 59 09N 3 19W
Brown Clee Hill England **37** E2 52 27N 2 35W
Brown Willy *sum.* England **40** C3 50 35N 4 36W
Brugge Belgium **49** B4 51 13N 3 14E
BRUNEI 60 C3
Brunswick Germany **49** F5 52 15N 10 30E
Brussels Belgium **49** C4 50 50N 4 21E
Bryansk Russia **56** D3 53 15N 34 09E
Bryher *i.* England **40** A2 49 57N 6 21W
Bucaramanga Colombia **84** B8 7 08N 73 10W
Buchan Ness *c.* Scotland **31** H2 57 28N 1 47W
Bucharest Romania **42** M4 44 25N 26 07E
Buckfastleigh England **40** D3 50 29N 3 46W
Buckhaven Scotland **33** F4 56 11N 3 03W
Buckie Scotland **31** G2 57 40N 2 58W
Buckingham England **38** D2 52 00N 1 00W
Buckinghamshire *co.* England **38** D2 51 50N 0 50W
Budapest Hungary **42** K5 47 30N 19 03E
Bude England **40** C3 50 50N 4 33W
Bude Bay England **40** C3 50 50N 4 40W
Buenaventura Colombia **84** B8 3 54N 77 02W
Buenos Aires Argentina **85** D4 34 40S 58 30W
Buffalo USA **79** M5 42 52N 78 55W
Builth Wells Wales **36** D2 52 09N 3 24W
Bujumbura Burundi **67** C4 3 22S 29 19E
Bukavu Congo Dem. Rep. **67** C4 2 30S 28 50E
Bukhara Uzbekistan **56** G1 39 47N 64 26E
Bulawayo Zimbabwe **67** C2 20 10S 28 43E
BULGARIA 42 M4
Bunbury Australia **72** B2 33 20S 115 39E
Buncrana Republic of Ireland **32** B3 55 08N 7 27W
Bundaberg Australia **72** F3 24 53S 152 21E
Bungay England **39** F3 52 28N 1 26E
Buraida Saudi Arabia **61** E3 26 20N 43 59E
Bure *r.* England **39** F3 52 47N 1 20E
Burgas Bulgaria **42** M4 42 30N 27 29E
Burghead *tn.* Scotland **31** F2 57 42N 3 30W
Burgos Spain **50** D5 42 21N 3 41W
Burgundy *geog. reg.* France **48** F3 47 00N 5 00E
BURKINA 66 B4
BURMA *see* MYANMAR
Burnie Australia **72** E1 41 03S 145 55E
Burnley England **34** C2 53 48N 2 14W
Burry Port Wales **36** C1 51 42N 4 15W

Bursa Turkey **42** M4 40 12N 29 04E
Burton upon Trent England **37** F2 52 48N 1 36W
Buru *i.* Indonesia **60** D2 3 30S 126 30E
BURUNDI 67 C4
Bury England **34** C2 53 36N 2 17W
Bury St. Edmunds England **39** E3 52 15N 0 43E
Bush *r.* Northern Ireland **32** C3 55 10N 6 30W
Bute *i.* Scotland **32** D3 55 50N 5 05W
Bute, Sound of Scotland **32** D3 55 45N 5 10W
Buton *i.* Indonesia **60** D2 5 00S 122 45E
Butt of Lewis *c.* Scotland **30** C3 58 30N 6 20W
Butuan The Philippines **60** D3 8 56N 125 31E
Buxton England **37** F3 53 15N 1 55W
Bydgoszcz Poland **42** K6 53 16N 18 00E

C

Cabanatuan The Philippines **60** D4 15 30N 120 58E
Cabinda *province* Angola **66** D2 5 00S 12 00E
Cabora Bassa, Lake Mozambique **67** D3 15 40S 31 40E
Cabrera *i.* Balearic Islands **50** G3 39 00N 2 59E
Cader Idris *mt.* Wales **36** D2 52 42N 3 54W
Cádiz Spain **50** B2 36 32N 6 18W
Caen France **48** C4 49 11N 0 22W
Caernarfon Wales **36** C3 53 08N 4 16W
Caernarfon Bay Wales **36** C3 53 05N 4 30W
Caerphilly Wales **36** D1 51 35N 3 14W
Caerphilly *u.a.* Wales **36** D1 51 37N 3 5W
Cagayan de Oro The Philippines **60** D3 8 29N 124 40E
Cágliari Italy **51** B3 39 13N 9 08E
Cairn Gorm *mt.* Scotland **31** F2 57 07N 3 40W
Cairngorms *mts.* Scotland **31** F2 57 10N 3 30W
Cairns Australia **72** E4 16 54S 145 45E
Cairo Egypt **61** D4 30 03N 31 15E
Calais France **48** D5 50 57N 1 52E
Cala Ratjada Balearic Islands **50** G3 39 43N 3 27E
Calatayud Spain **50** E4 41 21N 1 39W
Calbayog The Philippines **60** D4 12 04N 124 38E
Calcutta *see* Kolkata
Calgary Canada **78** H6 51 05N 114 05W
Cali Colombia **84** B8 3 24N 76 30W
Calicut India **58** C2 11 15N 75 45E
California *state* USA **79** H4 35 00N 119 00W
California, Gulf of Mexico **79** H3 27 00N 111 00W
Callander Scotland **33** E4 56 15N 4 13W
Callao Peru **84** B6 12 05S 77 08W
Calligarry Scotland **30** D2 57 02N 5 58E
Calne England **38** B2 51 27N 2 00W
Cam *r.* England **39** E3 52 15N 0 15W
Camagüey Cuba **79** M3 21 25N 77 55W
Camberley England **38** D2 51 21N 0 45W
CAMBODIA 60 B4
Camborne England **40** B3 50 12N 5 19W
Cambrai France **48** E5 50 10N 3 14E
Cambrian Mountains Wales **36** D2 52 15N 3 45W
Cambridge England **39** E3 52 12N 0 07E
Cambridgeshire *co.* England **38/39** D3/E3 52 30N 0 00
Camel *r.* England **40** C3 50 30N 4 45W
CAMEROON 66 D3
Cameroun, Mount Cameroon **66** C3 4 13N 9 10E
Campbeltown Scotland **32** D3 55 26N 5 36W
Campina Grande Brazil **84** F7 7 15S 35 50W
Campinas Brazil **84** E5 22 54S 47 06W
Campo Grande Brazil **84** D5 20 24S 54 35W
Campos Brazil **84** E5 21 46S 41 21W
Campsie Fells *hills* Scotland **33** E4 56 00N 4 15W
CANADA 78
Canary Islands Spain **66** A5 28 30N 15 10W
Canaveral, Cape USA **79** L3 28 28N 80 28W
Canberra Australia **72** E2 35 17S 149 09E
Canisp *mt.* Scotland **31** D3 58 07N 5 03W
Canna *i.* Scotland **30** C2 57 05N 6 35W
Cannes France **48** G1 43 33N 7 00E
Cannock England **37** E2 52 42N 2 01W
Cantabrian Mountains Spain **50** B5/C5 43 00N 5 30W
Canterbury England **39** F2 51 17N 1 05E
Canterbury Bight *b.* New Zealand **73** C2 44 00S 172 00E
Canterbury Plains New Zealand **73** C2 43 45S 171 56E
Can Tho Vietnam **60** B4 10 03N 105 46E
Cap de la Hague *c.* France **41** F2 49 44N 1 56W
Cape Town Republic of South Africa **67** B1 33 56S 18 28E
CAPE VERDE 4
Cap Gris-Nez *c.* France **39** F1 50 52N 1 35E
Caracas Venezuela **84** C9 10 35N 66 56W
Carcassonne France **48** E1 43 13N 2 21E
Cardiff Wales **36** D1 51 30N 3 13W
Cardiff *u.a.* Wales **36** D1 51 32N 3 14W
Cardigan Wales **36** C2 52 06N 4 40W
Cardigan Bay Wales **36** C2 52 30N 4 30W
Carentan France **41** F2 49 18N 1 14W
Caribbean Sea Central America **79** M2 15 00N 75 00W
Carlingford Lough *est.* Northern Ireland/ Republic of Ireland **32** C2 54 05N 6 10W
Carlisle England **34** C3 54 54N 2 55W
Carmarthen Wales **36** C1 51 51N 4 20W
Carmarthen Bay Wales **36** C1 51 40N 4 30W
Carmarthenshire *u.a.* Wales **36** C1/D1 51 55N 4 00W
Carmel Head Wales **36** C3 53 24N 4 34W
Carnarvon Australia **72** B3 24 53S 113 40E
Carn Eige *mt.* Scotland **31** D2 57 22N 5 07W
Carnforth England **34** C3 54 08N 2 46W
Carnoustie Scotland **31** G1 56 30N 2 44W
Carpathians *mts.* Europe **42** L5/M5 49 00N 22 00E
Carpentaria, Gulf of Australia **72** D4 14 39S 139 11E
Carrickfergus Northern Ireland **32** D2 54 43N 5 49W
Carrickfergus *district* Northern Ireland **32** D2 54 40N 5 50W
Cartagena Colombia **84** B9 10 24N 75 33W
Cartagena Spain **50** E2 37 36N 0 59W
Carteret France **41** F2 49 22N 1 48W
Casablanca Morocco **66** B6 33 39N 7 35W
Caspian Sea Asia **56** F2 41 00N 50 00E
Cassel France **39** G1 51 40N 2 28E
Cassino Italy **51** D4 41 29N 13 50E
Castlebay Scotland **30** B1 56 57N 7 28W
Castleblaney Republic of Ireland **32** C2 54 07N 6 44W
Castle Douglas Scotland **33** F2 54 57N 3 56W
Castleford England **35** D2 43 44N 1 21W
Castlereagh *district* Northern Ireland **32** D2 54 35N 5 50W
Castletown Isle of Man British Isles **33** E2 54 04N 4 38W
Castrovillari Italy **51** F3 39 48N 16 12E
Catánia Italy **51** E2 37 31N 15 06E
Catanzaro Italy **51** F3 38 54N 16 36E
Cat Island The Bahamas **79** M3 24 30N 75 30W
Cauca *r.* Colombia **84** B8 7 40N 75 00W
Caucasus *mts.* Asia **56** E2 43 00N 43 00E
Cavan Republic of Ireland **32** B1 53 58N 7 21W
Caxias do Sul Brazil **85** D5 29 14S 51 10W
Cayenne French Guiana **84** D8 4 55N 52 18W
Cayman Islands Caribbean Sea **79** L2 19 20N 81 15W
Cebollera *mt.* Spain **50** D4 42 00N 2 40W
Cebu The Philippines **60** D4 10 17N 123 56E
Celebes Sea Indonesia **60** D3 3 00N 122 00E
Cemaes Head Wales **36** C2 53 10N 4 50W
CENTRAL AFRICAN REPUBLIC 67 B5/C5
Central Siberian Plateau Russia **57** L4 65 00N 110 00E
Ceredigion *u.a.* Wales **36** C2/D2 52 20N 4 00W
Ceuta *territory* Spain **50** C1 35 53N 5 19W
CHAD 66 D4
Chad, Lake West Africa **66** D4 13 50N 14 00E
Chagos Archipelago *is.* Indian Ocean **5** 6 00S 72 00E
Châlons-sur-Marne France **48** F4 48 58N 4 22E
Chalon-sur-Saône France **48** F3 46 47N 4 51E
Chambéry France **48** F2 45 34N 5 55E
Changchun China **59** D4 43 50N 125 20E
Chang Jiang *(Yangtze) r.* China **59** C3 30 00N 116 00E
Changsha China **59** C2 28 10N 113 00E
Channel Islands British Isles **41** E2 49 30N 2 30W
Channel Tunnel United Kingdom/France **39** F1/2 5 00N 1 30E
Chard England **41** E3 50 53N 2 58W
Chardzhev Turkmenistan **56** G1 39 09N 63 34E
Chari *r.* Chad/Sudan **66** D4 11 00N 16 00E
Charleroi Belgium **49** C4 50 25N 4 27E
Charlestown of Aberlour Scotland **31** F2 57 28N 3 14W
Charleville Australia **72** E3 26 24S 146 14E
Charleville France **48** F4 49 46N 4 43E
Charlotte USA **79** L4 35 03N 80 50W
Charters Towers Australia **72** E3 20 04S 146 16E
Chartres France **48** D4 48 27N 1 30E
Châteauroux France **48** D3 46 49N 1 41E
Chatham England **39** E2 51 23N 0 32E
Cheadle England **34** C2 53 24N 2 13W
Cheb Czech Republic **49** G4 50 08N 12 28E
Cheboksary Russia **56** E3 56 08N 47 12E
Chelmsford England **39** E2 51 44N 0 28E
Cheltenham England **38** B2 51 54N 2 04W
Chelyabinsk Russia **56** G3 55 12N 61 25E
Chemnitz Germany **49** G4 50 50N 12 55E
Chengdu China **59** B3 30 37N 104 06E
Chennai *(Madras)* **58** D2 13 05N 80 18E
Chepstow Wales **37** E1 51 39N 2 41W
Cher *r.* France **48** D3 47 15N 1 30E
Cherbourg France **48** B4 49 38N 1 37W
Chernivtsi Ukraine **42** M5 48 19N 25 52E
Cherwell *r.* England **38** C2 51 55N 1 20W
Cheshire *co.* England **34** C2 53 30N 2 30W
Cheshunt England **38** D2 51 43N 0 02W
Chester England **34** C2 53 12N 2 54W
Chesterfield England **37** F3 53 15N 1 25W
Chester-le-Street England **34** D3 54 52N 1 34W
Cheviot Hills England/Scotland **33** G3 55 25 N2 20W
Cheviot, The *sum.* England **33** G3 55 29N 2 20W
Cheyenne USA **79** J5 41 08N 104 50W
Chiang Mai Thailand **60** A4 18 48N 98 59E
Chiba Japan **59** N2 35 38N 140 07E
Chicago USA **79** L5 41 50N 87 45W
Chichester England **38** D1 50 50N 0 48W
Chiclayo Peru **84** B7 6 47S 79 47W
Chicoutimi Canada **79** M5 48 26N 71 06W
Chieti Italy **51** E5 42 21N 14 10E
Chihuahua Mexico **79** J3 28 40N 106 06W
CHILE 84/85 B6/C2
Chillán Chile **85** B4 36 37S 72 10W
Chiloé Island Chile **85** B3 42 30S 74 00W
Chiltern Hills England **38** C2/D2 51 40N 1 00W
Chimbote Peru **84** B7 9 04S 78 34W
CHINA 59
Chippenham England **38** B2 51 28N 2 07W
Chipping Norton England **38** C2 51 56N 1 32W
Chipping Sodbury England **38** B2 51 33N 2 24W
Chi~inău Moldova **42** M5 47 00N 28 50E
Chita Russia **57** M3 52 03N 113 35E
Chittagong Bangladesh **58** E3 22 20N 91 48E
Cholet France **48** C3 47 04N 0 53W
Chongjin North Korea **59** D4 41 50N 129 55E
Chongqing China **59** B2 29 30N 106 35E
Chorley England **34** C2 53 40N 2 38W
Christchurch England **41** F3 50 44N 1 45W
Christchurch New Zealand **73** C2 43 32S 172 38E
Christmas Island Indian Ocean **60** B1 10 28S 105 35E
Churchill Canada **78** K6 58 45N 94 00W
Churchill Falls *tn.* Canada **78** N6 53 35N 64 00W
Cincinnati USA **79** L4 39 10N 83 30W
Cirencester England **38** C2 51 44N 1 59W
Citlaltépetl *mt.* Mexico **79** K2 19 00N 97 18W
City of Edinburgh *u.a.* Scotland **33** F3 55 55N 3 15W
City of Kingston upon Hull *u.a.* England **35** E2 53 45N 0 25W
Ciudad Bolívar Venezuela **84** C8 8 06N 63 36W
Ciudadela Balearic Islands **50** G3 40 00N 3 50E
Ciudad Guayana Venezuela **84** C8 8 22N 62 37W
Ciudad Juárez Mexico **79** J4 31 42N 106 29W
Ciudad Obregón Mexico **79** J3 27 28N 109 59W
Ciudad Rodrigo Spain **50** B4 40 36N 6 33W
Clachan Scotland **32** D3 55 45N 5 34W
Clackmannanshire *u.a.* England **33** F4 56 10N 3 40W
Clacton on Sea England **39** F2 51 48N 1 09E
Claonaig Scotland **32** D3 55 46N 5 22W
Cleethorpes England **35** E2 53 34N 0 02W
Clermont-Ferrand France **48** E2 45 47N 3 05E
Clevedon England **38** B2 51 27N 2 51W
Cleveland Hills England **35** D3 54 25N 1 15W
Clisham *mt.* Scotland **30** C2 57 58N 6 50W
Clitheroe England **34** C2 53 53N 2 23W
Clones Republic of Ireland **32** B2 54 11N 7 15W
Cluj-Napoca Romania **42** L5 46 47N 23 37E
Clutha *r.* New Zealand **73** B1 46 00S 169 30E
Clwyd *r.* Wales **36** D3 53 15N 3 25W
Clyde *r.* Scotland **33** F3 55 45N 3 55W
Clydebank Scotland **33** E3 55 54N 4 24W
Coalisland Northern Ireland **32** C2 54 32N 6 42W
Coalville England **37** F2 52 44N 1 20W
Coast Mountains Canada **78** G6 58 10N 132 40W
Coatbridge Scotland **33** E3 55 52N 4 01W
Coburg Germany **49** F4 50 15N 10 58E
Cochabamba Bolivia **84** C6 17 26S 66 10W
Cochin India **58** C1 9 56N 76 15E
Cockermouth England **34** B3 54 40N 3 21W
Cognac France **48** C2 45 42N 0 19W
Coimbatore India **58** C2 11 00N 76 57E
Coimbra Portugal **50** A4 40 12N 8 25W
Colchester England **39** E2 51 54N 0 54E
Coldstream *tn.* Scotland **33** G3 55 39N 2 15W
Coleraine Northern Ireland **32** C3 55 08N 6 40W
Coleraine *district* Northern Ireland **32** C3 55 00N 6 40W
Coll *i.* Scotland **30** C1 56 40N 6 35W
Colmar France **48** G4 48 05N 7 21E
Colne England **34** C2 53 32N 2 09W
Colne *r.* England **39** E2 51 54N 0 45E
Cologne Germany **49** D4 50 56N 6 57E
COLOMBIA 84 B8
Colombo Sri Lanka **58** C1 6 55N 79 52E
Colonsay *i.* Scotland **32** C4 56 05N 6 15W
Colorado *r.* Argentina **85** C4 37 30S 69 00W
Colorado *r.* USA/Mexico **79** J4 38 00N 109 00W
Colorado *state* USA **79** J4 39 00N 106 00W
Columbia USA **79** L4 34 00N 81 00W
Columbia *r.* Canada/USA **78** H6 50 30N 119 00W
Columbus USA **79** L4 39 59N 83 03W
Colwyn Bay *tn.* Wales **36** D3 53 18N 3 43W
Communism Peak Tajikistan **56** H1 38 59N 72 01E
Como Italy **51** B6 45 48N 9 05E
Comodoro Rivadavia Argentina **85** C3 45 50S 67 30W
Como, Lake Italy **51** B6/7 46 00N 9 00E
COMOROS 67 E3
Conakry Guinea **66** A3 9 30N 13 43W
Concepción Chile **85** B4 36 50S 73 03W
Conejara *i.* Balearic Islands **50** G3 39 11N 2 58E
CONGO 66 D2
Congo *r.* Africa **67** B4 3 00S 16 00E
CONGO DEMOCRATIC REPUBLIC 67 C4
Coniston Water *l.* England **34** B3 54 20N 3 05W
Connecticut *state* USA **79** M5 41 00N 73 00W
Consett England **34** D3 54 51N 1 49W
Constance, Lake Europe **49** E2 47 40N 9 30E
Constanța Romania **42** M4 44 12N 28 40E
Constantine Algeria **66** C6 36 22N 6 40E
Conwy Wales **36** D3 53 17N 3 50W
Conwy *r.* Wales **36** D3 53 20N 3 55W
Conwy *u.a.* Wales **36** D3 53 10N 3 50W
Cook Islands Pacific Ocean **4** 19 30S 159 50W
Cook, Mount New Zealand **73** C2 43 36S 170 09E
Cookstown Northern Ireland **32** C2 54 39N 6 45W
Cookstown *district* Northern Ireland **32** C2 54 35N 6 55W
Cook Strait New Zealand **73** C2 41 24S 174 36E
Cooktown Australia **72** E4 15 28S 145 15E
Cooper Creek Australia **72** E3 26 10S 142 20E
Copenhagen Denmark **42** J7 55 43N 12 34E
Coquet *r.* England **33** H3 55 20N 1 50W
Coral Sea Pacific Ocean **72** F4 15 00S 154 00E
Corby England **38** D3 52 49N 0 32W
Córdoba Argentina **85** C4 31 25S 64 11W
Córdoba Spain **50** C2 37 53N 4 46W
Corfu *i.* Greece **42** K3 39 00N 19 00E
Cornwall *co.* England **40** B3/C3 50 25N 4 50W
Corpus Christi USA **79** K3 27 47N 97 26W
Corrientes Argentina **85** D5 27 30S 58 48W
Corsewall Point Scotland **32** D3 55 00N 5 10W
Corsica *i.* France **51** B5 42 00N 9 00E
Cosenza Italy **51** F3 39 17N 16 16E
Costa Brava *geog. reg.* Spain **50** G4/5 41 40N 3 50E
Costa del Sol *geog. reg.* Spain **50** C2/D2 36 40N 4 40W
COSTA RICA 79 L1
CÔTE D'IVOIRE 66 B3
Cotonou Benin **66** C3 6 24N 2 31E
Cotopaxi *vol.* Ecuador **84** B7 0 40S 78 28W
Cotswold Hills England **38** B2/C2 51 40N 2 10W
Cottbus Germany **49** H4 51 43N 14 21E
Coupar Angus Scotland **31** F1 56 33N 3 17W
Coutainville France **41** F2 49 03N 1 34W
Coutances France **41** F2 49 03N 1 29W
Coventry England **37** F2 52 25N 1 30W
Cowes England **38** C1 50 45N 1 18W
Craigavon Northern Ireland **32** C2 54 28N 6 25W
Craigavon *district* Northern Ireland **32** C2 54 30N 6 30W
Craighouse Scotland **32** D3 55 51N 5 57W
Craignure Scotland **30** D1 56 28N 5 42W
Crail Scotland **33** G4 56 16N 2 38W
Craiova Romania **42** L4 44 18N 23 47E
Cramlington England **33** H3 55 05N 1 35W
Crawley England **38** D2 51 07N 0 12W
Crediton England **40** D3 50 47N 3 39W
Cree *r.* Scotland **33** E3 55 00N 4 30W
Creeslough Republic of Ireland **32** B3 55 07N 7 55W
Cremona Italy **51** C6 45 08N 10 01E
Crete *i.* Greece **42** M3 35 00N 25 00E
Crewe England **34** C2 53 05N 2 27W
Crewkerne England **41** E3 50 53N 2 48W
Crianlarich Scotland **31** E1 56 23N 4 37W
Crieff Scotland **31** F1 56 23N 3 52W
Crimea *p.* Ukraine **43** N5 46 00N 34 00E
CROATIA 42 K5
Cromarty Scotland **31** E2 57 40N 4 02W
Cromarty Firth *est.* Scotland **31** E2 57 40N 4 20W
Cromer England **39** F3 52 56N 1 18E
Cross Fell *sum.* England **34** C3 54 43N 2 29W
Crossmaglen Northern Ireland **32** C2 54 05N 6 37W
Crotone Italy **51** F3 39 05N 17 08E
Croydon England **38** D2 51 23N 0 06W
Crumlin Northern Ireland **32** C2 54 37N 6 14W
Cruzeiro do Sul Brazil **84** B7 7 40S 72 39W
Cuanza *r.* Angola **67** B4 9 40S 15 00E
CUBA 79 M3
Cubango *r.* Southern Africa **67** B3 17 00S 18 00E
Cúcuta Colombia **84** B8 7 55N 73 31W
Cuenca Ecuador **84** B7 2 54S 79 00W
Cuiabá Brazil **84** D6 15 32S 56 05W
Cuillin Hills Scotland **30** C2 57 15N 6 15W
Culiacán Mexico **79** J3 24 50N 107 23W
Cullen Scotland **31** G2 57 41N 2 49W
Cullompton England **40** D3 50 52N 3 24W
Cumaná Venezuela **84** C9 10 29N 64 12W
Cumbernauld Scotland **33** F3 55 57N 4 00W
Cumbria *co.* England **34** B3/C3 54 30N 2 50W
Cumnock Scotland **33** E3 55 27N 4 16W
Cunene *r.* Angola/Namibia **67** B3 17 00S 15 00E
Cuneo Italy **51** A6 44 24N 7 33E
Cunnamulla Australia **72** E3 28 03S 145 43E
Cupar Scotland **33** F4 56 19N 3 01W
Curaçao *i.* Lesser Antilles **79** N2 12 20N 68 20W
Curitiba Brazil **85** E5 25 25S 49 25W
Cuttack India **58** D3 20 26N 85 56E
Cuzco Peru **84** B6 13 32S 1 57W
Cwmbran Wales **36** D1 51 39N 3 00W
Cyclades *is.* Greece **42** L3/L4 36 00N 25 00E
CYPRUS 43 N2
CZECH REPUBLIC 42 K5
Częstochowa Poland **42** K6 50 49N 19 07E

D

Daer Reservoir Scotland **33** F3 55 25N 3 30W
Dakar Senegal **66** A4 14 38N 17 27W
Dalbeattie Scotland **33** F2 54 56N 3 49W
Dalian China **59** D3 38 53N 121 37E
Dallas USA **79** K4 32 47N 96 48W
Dalmally Scotland **31** E1 56 24N 4 58W
Dalton-in-Furness England **34** B3 54 09N 3 11W
Daly *r.* Australia **72** D4 13 30S 130 30E
Damascus Syria **61** D4 33 30N 36 19E
Dammam Saudi Arabia **61** F3 26 25N 50 06E
Da Nang Vietnam **60** B4 16 04N 108 14E
Danube *r.* Europe **42** L4 44 00N 25 00E
Dar es Salaam Tanzania **67** D4 6 51S 39 18E
Darfur *mts.* Sudan **61** C2 12 40N 24 20E
Dargaville New Zealand **73** C3 35 56S 173 52E
Darling *r.* Australia **72** E2 31 00S 144 00E
Darlington England **34** D3 54 31N 1 34W
Darlington *u.a.* England **34** D3 54 35N 1 34W
Darmstadt Germany **49** E3 49 52N 8 39E
Darnah Libya **42** L2 32 46N 22 39E
Dart *r.* England **40** D3 50 30N 3 50W
Dartford England **39** E2 51 27N 0 13E
Dartmoor *geog. reg.* England **40** D3 50 35N 3 50W
Dartmouth England **40** D3 50 21N 3 35W
Darvel Scotland **33** E3 55 37N 4 18W
Darwin Australia **72** D4 12 24S 130 52E
Daugava *r.* Belarus **42** M7 55 00N 29 00E
Daugavpils Latvia **42** M7 55 52N 26 31E
Dauphine *geog. reg.* France **48** F2 45 00N 5 00E
Davao The Philippines **60** D3 7 05N 125 38E
Daventry England **38** C3 52 16N 1 09W
Dawlish England **40** D3 50 35N 3 28W
Dawson Canada **78** F7 64 04N 139 24W
Deal England **39** F2 51 14N 1 24E
Debrecen Hungary **42** L5 47 30N 21 37E
Deccan *plat.* India **58** C2 18 00N 78 00E
Dee *r.* Aberdeenshire/AberdeenCity Scotland **31** G2 57 05N 2 10W
Dee *r.* Dumfries and Galloway Scotland **33** E2/F2 54 55N 4 00W
Dee *r.* England/Wales **36** D3 53 20N 3 10W
Deeps, The *b.* Scotland **29** D3 60 10N 1 25W
Delaware *state* USA **79** M4 39 00N 75 00W
Delhi India **58** C3 28 40N 77 14E
Demavand, Mount Iran **61** F4 35 56N 52 08E
Denbigh Wales **36** D3 53 11N 3 25W
Denbighshire *u.a.* Wales **36** D3 53 10N 3 10W
DENMARK 42 H7
Denver USA **79** J4 39 45N 105 00W
De Panne Belgium **39** G2 51 06N 2 35E
Derby Australia **72** C4 17 18S 123 37E
Derby England **37** F2 52 55N 1 30W
Derby City *u.a.* England **37** F2 52 53N 1 30W
Derbyshire *co.* England **37** F3 52 55N 1 30W
Derg *r.* Northern Ireland **32** B2 54 40N 7 45E
Derwent *r.* Cumbria England **34** B3 54 40N 3 30W
Derwent *r.* Derbyshire England **37** F3 53 20N 1 40W
Derwent *r.* Northumberland/Durham/Tyne and Wear England **34** C3 54 50N 2 05W
Derwent *r.* North Yorkshire/York/East Riding of Yorkshire England **35** E2 53 50N 0 55W
Derwent Water *l.* England **34** B3 54 35N 3 09W
Des Moines USA **79** K5 41 35N 93 35W
Dessau Germany **49** G4 51 51N 12 15E
Detroit USA **79** L5 42 23N 83 05W
Deveron *r.* Scotland **31** G2 57 35N 2 40W
Devizes England **38** C2 51 22N 1 59W
Devon *co.* England **40** C3/D3 50 45N 3 50W
Devon Island Canada **78** L8 75 47N 88 00W
Dewsbury England **34** D2 53 42N 1 37W
Dezful Iran **61** E4 32 23N 48 28E
Dhaka Bangladesh **58** E3 23 42N 90 22E
Dibrugarh India **58** E3 27 29N 94 56E
Didcot England **38** C2 51 37N 1 15W
Dieppe France **48** D4 49 55N 1 05E
Dijon France **48** F3 47 20N 5 02E
Dili East Timor **60** D2 8 33S 125 34E
Dingwall Scotland **31** E2 57 35N 4 29W
Dire Dawa Ethiopia **61** E1 9 35N 41 50E
Diss England **39** F3 52 23N 1 06W
Diyarbakir Turkey **43** Q3 37 55N 40 14E
Djelfa Algeria **42** G2 34 43N 3 14E
DJIBOUTI 61 E2
Djibouti Djibouti **61** E2 11 35N 43 11E
Dnieper *r.* Ukraine/Belarus **56** D3 51 00N 30 00E
Dniester *r.* Europe **42** M5 48 00N 27 00E
Dnipropetrovsk Ukraine **56** D2 48 29N 35 00E

Dodoma Tanzania 67 D4 6 10S 35 40E
Doha Qatar 61 F3 25 15N 51 36E
Dolgellau Wales 36 D2 52 44N 3 53W
Dolomites mts. Italy 49 F2 46 00N 12 00E
DOMINICA 79 N2
DOMINICAN REPUBLIC 79 M2
Don r. Russia 56 E3 50 00N 40 30E
Don r. Scotland 31 G2 57 15N 2 10W
Donaghadee Northern Ireland 32 D2 54 39N 5 33W
Doncaster England 35 D2 53 32N 1 07W
Donegal Republic of Ireland 32 A2 54 39N 8 07W
Donegal co. Republic of Ireland 32 A2/B2 54 55N 8 00W
Donetsk Ukraine 56 D2 48 00N 37 50E
Dongting Hu l. China 59 C2 29 00N 113 30E
Doon r. Scotland 33 E3 55 20N 4 30W
Dorchester England 41 E3 50 43N 2 26W
Dordogne r. France 48 D2 45 00N 1 30E
Dordrecht Netherlands 49 C4 51 48N 4 40E
Dorking England 38 D2 51 14N 0 20W
Dornoch Scotland 31 E2 57 52N 4 02W
Dornoch Firth est. Scotland 31 E2 57 55N 3 55W
Dorset co. England 41 E3 50 50N 2 20W
Dortmund Germany 49 D4 51 32N 7 27E
Douai France 48 E5 50 22N 3 05E
Douala Cameroon 66 C3 4 04N 9 43E
Douglas Isle of Man British Isles 33 E2 54 09N 4 29W
Douro r. Spain/Portugal 50 B4 41 30N 6 30W
Dove r. England 37 F3 53 10N 1 50W
Dover England 39 F2 51 08N 1 19E
Dover, Strait of English Channel 39 F1/2 51 00N 1 20W
Down district Northern Ireland 32 D2 54 25N 5 55W
Downham Market England 39 E3 52 36N 0 23E
Downpatrick Northern Ireland 32 D2 54 20N 5 43W
Drakensberg mts. Republic of South Africa 67 C2 30 00S 28 00E
Drava r. Europe 49 G2 46 45N 13 30E
Dresden Germany 49 G4 51 03N 13 45E
Droitwich England 37 E2 52 16N 2 09W
Dromore Northern Ireland 32 C2 54 25N 6 09W
Dronning Maud Land geog. reg. Antarctica 86 73 00S 10 00E
Drummore Scotland 32 E2 54 42N 4 54W
Drumnadrochit Scotland 31 E2 57 20N 4 30W
Dubai United Arab Emirates 61 F3 25 14N 55 17E
Dubbo Australia 72 E2 32 15S 148 38E
Dublin Republic of Ireland 36 A3 53 20N 6 15W
Dudley England 37 E2 52 30N 2 05W
Dufftown Scotland 31 F2 57 26N 3 08W
Duisburg Germany 49 D4 51 26N 6 45E
Duluth USA 79 K5 46 45N 92 10W
Dumbarton Scotland 33 E3 55 57N 4 35W
Dumfries Scotland 33 F3 55 04N 3 37W
Dumfries and Galloway u.a. Scotland 33 E3/F3 55 10N 4 00W
Dunbar Scotland 33 G4 56 00N 2 31W
Dunblane Scotland 33 F4 56 12N 3 59W
Duncansby Head c. Scotland 29 B1 58 39N 3 02W
Dundalk Republic of Ireland 32 C2 54 01N 6 25W
Dundee Scotland 31 G1 56 28N 3 00W
Dundee City u.a. Scotland 31 F1/G1 56 30N 2 55W
Dunedin New Zealand 73 C1 45 53S 170 30E
Dunfermline Scotland 33 F4 56 04N 3 29W
Dungannon Northern Ireland 32 C2 54 31N 6 46W
Dungannon district Northern Ireland 32 B2/C2 54 30N 7 00W
Dungeness c. England 39 E1 50 55N 0 58E
Dungiven Northern Ireland 32 C2 54 55N 6 55W
Dunkerque France 48 E5 51 02N 2 23E
Dunkery Beacon sum. England 40 D4 51 11N 3 35W
Dún Laoghaire Republic of Ireland 36 A3 53 17N 6 08W
Dunnett Head Scotland 29 B1 58 40N 3 25W
Dunoon Scotland 32 E3 55 57N 4 56W
Duns Scotland 33 G3 55 47N 2 20W
Dunstable England 38 D2 51 53N 0 32W
Dunvegan Scotland 30 C2 57 26N 6 35W
Durance r. France 48 F1 43 50N 5 15E
Durango Mexico 79 J3 24 01N 104 40W
Durban Republic of South Africa 67 D2 29 53S 31 00E
Durham England 34 D3 54 47N 1 34W
Durham co. England 34 C3/D3 54 40N 2 00W
Dursley England 37 E1 51 42N 2 21W
Dushanbe Tajikistan 56 G1 38 38N 68 51E
Düsseldorf Germany 49 D4 51 13N 6 47E
Dyce Scotland 31 G2 57 12N 2 11W
Dyfi r. Wales 36 D2 52 38N 3 50W

E

Ealing England 38 D2 51 31N 0 18W
Earn r. Scotland 31 F1 56 15N 3 40W
East Ayrshire u.a. Scotland 33 E3 55 35N 4 15W
Eastbourne England 39 E1 50 46N 0 17E
East Cape New Zealand 73 D3 37 41S 178 33E
East Dereham England 39 E3 52 41N 0 56E
East Dunbartonshire u.a. Scotland 33 E3 55 55N 4 15W
Eastern Rift Valley East Africa 67 D4/5 4 00N 36 00E
East Friesian Islands Netherlands 49 D5 53 00N 7 00E
East Kilbride Scotland 33 E3 55 46N 4 10W
Eastleigh England 38 C1 50 58N 1 22W
East London Republic of South Africa 67 C1 33 00S 27 54E
East Lothian u.a. Scotland 33 G3 55 56N 2 42W
East Renfrewshire u.a. Scotland 33 E3 55 45N 4 25E
East Riding of Yorkshire u.a. England 35 E2 53 54N 0 40W
East Sussex co. England 39 E1 50 55N 0 10E
EAST TIMOR 60 D2
Ebbw Vale Wales 36 D1 51 47N 3 12W
Ebro r. Spain 50 E4 42 00N 1 15W
Ech Cheliff Algeria 42 G3 36 05N 1 15E
ECUADOR 84 B7
Eday i. Scotland 29 C2 59 11N 2 47W
Eddrachillis Bay Scotland 30 D3 58 25N 5 15W
Eden r. Cumbria England 34 C3 54 45N 2 40W
Eden r. Surrey/Kent England 39 E2 51 10N 0 05E
Edinburgh Scotland 33 F3 55 57N 3 13W
Edmonton Canada 78 H6 53 34N 113 25W
Edward, Lake Congo Dem. Rep./Uganda 67 C4 0 30S 29 00E
EGYPT 61 C3
Eigg i. Scotland 30 C1 56 55N 6 10W
Eindhoven Netherlands 49 C4 51 26N 5 30E
Elba i. Italy 51 C5 42 00N 10 00E
El Bayadh Algeria 42 G2 33 40N 1 00E
Elbe r. Europe 49 F5 53 15N 11 00E
Elbrus, Mount Russia 43 Q4 43 21N 42 29E
Elche Spain 50 E3 38 16N 0 41W
Eleuthera i. The Bahamas 79 M3 25 05N 76 30W
El Faiyum Egypt 61 D3 29 19N 30 50E
El Fasher Sudan 61 C2 13 37N 25 22E
Elgin Scotland 31 F2 57 39N 3 20W
El Gîza Egypt 61 D4 30 01N 31 12E
Elgol Scotland 30 C2 57 09N 6 06W
El Kharga Egypt 61 D3 25 27N 30 32E
Ellen r. England 34 B3 54 45N 3 25W
Ellesmere Island Canada 78 L8 77 30N 82 30W
Ellesmere Port England 34 C2 53 17N 2 54W
Ellon Scotland 31 G2 57 22N 2 05W
Ellsworth Land geog. reg. Antarctica 86 75 00S 80 00W
El Minya Egypt 61 D3 28 06N 30 45E
El Paso USA 79 J4 31 45N 106 30W
EL SALVADOR 79 L2
Elvas Portugal 50 B3 38 53N 7 10W
Ely England 39 E3 52 24N 0 16E
Emden Germany 49 D5 53 23N 7 13E
Emi Koussi mt. Chad 66 D4 19 52N 18 31E
Ems r. Germany 49 D5 53 00N 7 00E
Enard Bay Scotland 30 D3 58 10N 5 25W
Enfield England 38 D2 51 39N 0 05W
Enggano i. Indonesia 60 B2 5 20S 102 20E
England country United Kingdom 28 53 00N 2 00W
English Channel United Kingdom/France 28 50 00N 2 00W
Enniskillen Northern Ireland 32 B2 54 21N 7 38W
Enschede Netherlands 49 D5 52 13N 6 55E
Entebbe Uganda 67 D5 0 04N 32 27E
Épinal France 48 G4 48 10N 6 28E
Epsom England 38 D2 51 20N 0 16W
EQUATORIAL GUINEA 66 D3
Erebus, Mount Antarctica 86 77 40S 167 20E
Erfurt Germany 49 F4 50 58N 11 02E
Erie, Lake Canada/U.S.A. 79 L5 42 15N 81 00W
Eriskay i. Scotland 30 B2 57 05N 7 10W
ERITREA 61 D2
Erlangen Germany 49 F3 49 36N 11 02E
Erne r. Northern Ireland/Republic of Ireland 32 B2 54 10N 7 30W
Errigal Mountain Republic of Ireland 32 A3 55 02N 8 07W
Erzurum Turkey 43 Q3 39 57N 41 17E
Esfahan Iran 61 F4 32 41N 51 41E
Esha Ness pt. Scotland 29 D3 60 29N 1 37W
Esk r. England 35 E3 54 30N 0 45W
Esk r. Scotland/England 33 F3 55 15N 3 05W
Eskisehir Turkey 43 N3 39 46N 30 30E
Esperance Australia 72 C2 33 51S 121 54E
Esquel Argentina 85 B3 42 55S 71 20W
Essen Germany 49 D4 51 27N 6 57E
Essex co. England 39 E2 51 46N 0 30E
ESTONIA 42 M7
ETHIOPIA 61 E1
Ethiopian Highlands Africa 61 D1 8 00N 37 00E
Etna, Mount Italy 51 E2 37 45N 15 00E
Etosha Pan salt l. Namibia 67 B3 18 30S 16 30E
Eyre, Lake Australia 72 D3 28 43S 137 11E
Euphrates r. Iraq/Syria/Turkey 61 D4/E4 35 00N 40 00E
Europa i. Mozambique Channel 67 E2 22 20S 40 20E
Everest, Mount China/Nepal 58 D3 27 59N 86 56E
Evesham England 37 F2 52 06N 1 56W
Evreux France 48 D4 49 03N 1 11E
Evvoia i. Greece 42 L3 38 00N 24 00E
Exe r. England 40 D4 51 10N 3 35W
Exeter England 40 D3 50 43N 3 31W
Exmoor geog. reg. England 40 D4 51 08N 3 40W
Exmouth England 40 D3 50 37N 3 25W
Eyemouth Scotland 33 G3 55 25N 2 06W
Eye Peninsula Scotland 30 C3 58 10N 6 10W

F

Faroe Islands Atlantic Ocean 42 E8 62 00N 7 00W
Fairbanks USA 78 E7 64 50N 147 50W
Fair Head c. Northern Ireland 32 C3 55 15N 6 10W
Fair Isle i. Shetland Islands Scotland 29 D2 59 32N 1 38W
Faisalabad Pakistan 58 C4 31 25N 73 09E
Fakenham England 39 E3 52 50N 0 51E
Fal r. England 40 C3 50 15N 4 55W
Falkirk Scotland 33 F3 55 59N 3 48W
Falkirk u.a. Scotland 33 F3/4 56 05N 3 53W
Falkland Islands South Atlantic Ocean 85 D2 52 30S 60 00W
Falmouth England 40 B3 50 08N 5 04W
Falster i. Denmark 49 F6/G6 54 00N 12 00E
Fareham England 38 C1 50 51N 1 10W
Farewell, Cape Greenland 78 Q6 60 00N 44 00W
Farewell, Cape New Zealand 73 C2 40 30S 172 41E
Faringdon England 38 C2 51 40N 1 35W
Farnborough England 38 D2 51 17N 0 46W
Farnham England 38 D2 51 13N 0 49W
Faro Portugal 50 B2 37 01N 7 56W
Fawley England 38 C1 50 49N 1 20W
FEDERATED STATES OF MICRONESIA 5
Fehmarn i. Germany 49 F6 54 00N 11 00E
Feilding New Zealand 73 D2 40 14S 175 34E
Feira de Santana Brazil 84 F6 12 17S 38 53W
Felixstowe England 39 F2 51 58N 1 20E
Fens, The geog. reg. England 35 E1/F1 52 45N 0 05E
Fergana Uzbekistan 56 H2 40 23N 71 19E
Fermanagh district Northern Ireland 32 B2 54 25N 7 45W
Ferrara Italy 51 C6 44 50N 11 38E
Fès Morocco 66 B6 34 05N 5 00W
Fethaland, Point of Scotland 29 D3 60 35N 1 18W
Fetlar i. Scotland 29 E3 60 37N 0 52W
Fife u.a. Scotland 33 F4/G4 56 10N 3 00W
FIJI 5
Filchner Ice Shelf Antarctica 86 80 00S 37 00W
Finke r. Australia 72 D3 25 00S 135 00E
FINLAND 42 M8
Finland, Gulf of Finland/Russia 42 L7 59 40N 23 30E
Finn r. Northern Ireland/Republic of Ireland 32 B2 54 50N 7 50W
Fionnphort Scotland 30 C1 56 19N 6 23W
Firth of Clyde est. Scotland 32 E3 55 45N 5 00W
Firth of Forth est. Scotland 33 F4/G4 56 05N 3 00W
Firth of Lorn est. Scotland 30 D1 56 15N 6 00W
Firth of Tay est. Scotland 31 F1 56 25N 3 00W
Fishguard Wales 36 C1 51 59N 4 59W
Fitzroy r. Australia 72 C4 17 00S 126 00E
Flamborough Head c. England 35 D3 54 06N 0 04W
Fleetwood England 34 B2 53 56N 3 01W
Flinders r. Australia 72 E3/4 20 00S 142 00E
Flinders Range Australia 72 D2 31 20S 138 45E
Flint Wales 36 D3 53 15N 3 07W
Flintshire u.a. Wales 36 D3 53 25N 3 10W
Florence Italy 51 C5 43 47N 11 15E
Flores i. Indonesia 60 D2 8 30S 121 00E
Flores Sea Indonesia 60 D2 7 00S 119 00E
Florianópolis Brazil 85 E5 27 35S 48 31W
Florida state USA 79 L3 28 00N 82 00W
Florida, Straits of sd. Cuba/USA 79 L3 24 00N 81 00W
Fly r. Papua New Guinea 72 E5 8 00S 142 00E
Fochabers Scotland 31 F2 57 37N 3 05W
Fóggia Italy 51 E4 41 28N 15 33E
Folkestone England 39 F2 51 05N 1 11E
Fontainebleau France 48 E4 48 24N 2 42E
Forel, Mount Greenland 86 67 00N 37 00W
Forest of Bowland hills England 34 C2 54 00N 2 35W
Forfar Scotland 31 G1 56 38N 2 54W
Forlí Italy 51 D6 44 13N 12 02E
Formby England 34 B2 53 34N 3 05W
Formentera i. Balearic Islands 50 F3 38 41N 1 30E
Fornells Balearic Islands 50 H3 40 04N 4 07E
Forres Scotland 31 F2 57 37N 3 38W
Fortaleza Brazil 84 F7 3 45S 38 35W
Fort Augustus Scotland 31 E2 57 09N 4 41W
Forth r. Scotland 33 E4 56 10N 4 10W
Fort McMurray Canada 78 H6 56 45N 111 27W
Fort Peck Reservoir USA 79 J5 48 01N 106 28W
Fort Simpson Canada 78 G7 61 46N 121 15W
Fort William Scotland 31 D1 56 49N 5 07W
Fort Worth U.S.A. 79 K4 32 45N 97 20W
Foula i. Scotland 29 C3 60 08N 2 05W
Foveaux Strait New Zealand 73 B1 46 42S 167 59E
Fowey England 40 C3 50 20N 4 38W
Fowey r. England 40 C3 50 25N 4 30W
Foyle r. Northern Ireland/Republic of Ireland 32 B2 54 58N 7 35W
FRANCE 48
Frankfurt Germany 49 E4 50 06N 8 41E
Franz Josef Land is. Russia 57 G6 80 00N 50 00E
Fraser r. Canada 78 G6 52 00N 122 00W
Fraserburgh Scotland 31 G2 57 42N 2 00W
Freetown Sierra Leone 66 A3 8 30N 13 17W
Freiburg Germany 49 D3 48 00N 7 52E
Fréjus France 48 G1 43 26N 6 44E
Fremantle Australia 72 B2 32 03S 115 46E
French Guiana territory France 84 D8 5 00N 53 00W
French Polynesia is. Pacific Ocean 4 21 00S 150 00W
Fresno USA 79 H4 36 41N 119 47W
Frome England 41 E4 51 14N 2 20W
Frome r. England 41 E3 50 40N 2 20W
Fuji, Mount Japan 59 M2 35 23N 138 42E
Fukui Japan 59 M2 36 04N 136 12E
Fukuoka Japan 59 L1 33 39N 130 21E
Fukushima Japan 59 N2 37 44N 140 28E
Fukuyama Japan 59 L1 34 29N 133 21E
Furnace Scotland 32 D4 56 09N 5 12W
Fushun China 59 D4 41 50N 123 54E
Fuzhou China 59 C2 26 09N 119 17E
Fyn i. Denmark 49 F6 55 30N 10 00E
FYROM see MACEDONIA, FORMER YUGOSLAV REPUBLIC OF

G

Gabès Tunisia 42 J2 33 52N 10 06E
GABON 66 D2
Gaborone Botswana 67 C2 24 45S 25 55E
Gafsa Tunisia 42 H2 34 28N 8 43E
Gainsborough England 35 E2 53 24N 0 48W
Gairloch tn. Scotland 30 D2 57 42N 5 40W
Galapagos Islands Pacific Ocean 4 12 00S 87 00W
Galashiels Scotland 33 G3 55 37N 2 49W
Galați Romania 42 M5 45 27N 28 02E
Gallipoli Italy 51 G4 40 03N 17 59E
GAMBIA, THE 66 A4
Gäncä Azerbaijan 56 E2 40 39N 46 20E
Gander Canada 79 P5 49 00N 54 15W
Ganges r. India/Bangladesh 58 D3 24 00N 88 00E
Gap France 48 G2 44 33N 6 05E
Garda, Lake Italy 51 C6 45 00N 10 00E
Garelochhead Scotland 33 E4 56 05N 4 50W
Garonne r. France 48 D2 44 45N 0 15E
Gatehouse of Fleet Scotland 33 E2 54 53N 4 11W
Gateshead England 34 D3 54 58N 1 35W
Gaziantep Turkey 43 P3 37 04N 37 21E
Gdańsk Poland 42 K6 54 22N 18 41E
Gdynia Poland 42 K6 54 31N 18 30E
Geelong Australia 72 E2 38 08S 144 20E
Gelsenkirchen Germany 49 D4 51 30N 7 05E
Geneva Switzerland 49 D2 46 13N 6 09E
Geneva, Lake France/Switzerland 49 D2 46 20N 6 20E
Genoa Italy 51 B6 44 24N 8 56E
Gent Belgium 49 B4 51 02N 3 42E
Georgetown Guyana 84 D8 6 46N 58 10W
George Town Malaysia 60 B3 5 25N 100 20E
GEORGIA 56 E2
Georgia state USA 79 L4 33 00N 83 00W
Gera Germany 49 G4 50 51N 12 11E
Geraldton Australia 72 B3 28 46S 114 36E
GERMANY 49
GHANA 66 B3
Gibraltar territory UK 50 C2 36 09N 5 21W
Gibraltar, Strait of Spain/Morocco 50 C1 35 58N 5 30W
Gibson Desert Australia 72 C3 24 00S 122 00E
Giessen Germany 49 E4 50 35N 8 42E
Gifu Japan 59 M2 35 27N 136 46E
Gigha is. Scotland 32 D3 55 40N 5 45W
Gijón Spain 50 C5 43 32N 5 40W
Gillingham England 39 E2 51 24N 0 33E
Gironde r. France 48 C2 45 30N 1 00W
Girvan Scotland 32 E3 55 15N 4 51W
Gisborne New Zealand 73 D3 38 40S 178 01E
Glasgow Scotland 33 E3 55 53N 4 15W
Glasgow City u.a. Scotland 33 E3 55 50N 4 20W
Glastonbury England 41 E4 51 09N 2 43W
Glenluce Scotland 33 E2 54 53N 4 49W
Glenrothes Scotland 33 F4 56 12N 3 10W
Gloucester England 38 B2 51 53N 2 14W
Gloucestershire co. England 38 B2 51 50N 2 20W
Goat Fell mt. Scotland 32 D3 55 39N 5 11W
Gobi Desert Mongolia 57 L2 48 30N 100 00E
Godavari r. India 58 C2/D2 19 00N 80 00E
Godthåb see Nuuk
Goiânia Brazil 84 E6 16 43S 49 18W
Gold Coast tn. Australia 72 F3 28 04S 153 25E
Gongga Shan mt. China 59 B2 29 34N 101 53E
Good Hope, Cape of Republic of South Africa 67 B1 34 30S 19 00E
Goole England 35 E2 53 42N 0 52W
Gore New Zealand 73 B1 46 06S 168 56E
Goroka Papua New Guinea 72 E5 6 02S 145 22E
Göteborg Sweden 42 J7 57 45N 12 00E
Gotland i. Sweden 42 K7 57 30N 18 40E
Göttingen Germany 49 E4 51 32N 9 57E
Governador Valadares Brazil 84 E6 18 51S 41 57W
Gower p. Wales 36 C1 51 35N 4 10W
Grafton Australia 72 F3 29 40S 152 58E
Grampian Mountains Scotland 31 E1/F1 56 45N 4 00W
Granada Spain 50 D2 37 10N 3 35W
Grand Bahama i. The Bahamas 79 M3 27 00N 78 00W
Grand Canyon USA 79 H4 36 04N 112 07W
Grand Rapids tn. USA 79 L5 42 57N 86 40W
Grangemouth Scotland 33 F4 56 01N 3 44W
Grantham England 35 E1 52 55N 0 39W
Grantown-on-Spey Scotland 31 F2 57 20N 3 58W
Gravesend England 39 E2 51 27N 0 24E
Grays England 39 E2 51 29N 0 20E
Graz Austria 42 K5 47 05N 15 22E
Great Abaco i. The Bahamas 79 M3 26 40N 77 00W
Great Australian Bight b. Australia 72 C2 32 31S 130 00E
Great Barrier Island New Zealand 73 D3 36 13S 175 24E
Great Barrier Reef Australia 72 E4/F3 15 00S 146 00E
Great Bear Lake Canada 78 H7 66 00N 120 00W
Great Dividing Range mts. Australia 72 E2/F3 35 00N 148 00E
Great Driffield England 35 E3 54 01N 0 26W
Greater Antilles is. West Indies 79 M2/N2 19 00N 78 00W
Greater London co. England 38 D2 51 30N 0 10W
Greater Manchester co. England 34 C2 53 30N 2 15W
Great Inagua i. The Bahamas 79 M3 21 40N 73 00W
Great Karoo mts. Republic of South Africa 67 C1 32 30S 22 30E
Great Malvern England 37 E2 52 07N 2 19W
Great Ouse r. England 39 E3 52 40N 0 20E
Great St. Bernard Pass France/Italy 48 G2 45 50N 7 10E
Great Salt Lake USA 79 H5 41 10N 112 40W
Great Sandy Desert Australia 72 C3 21 00S 121 00E
Great Slave Lake Canada 78 H7 62 00N 114 00W
Great Stour r. England 39 F2 51 20N 1 10E
Great Torrington England 40 C3 51 57N 4 09W
Great Victoria Desert Australia 72 C3/D3 28 00S 129 00E
Great Wall China 59 B3 39 00N 109 00E
Great Whernside sum. England 34 D3 54 10N 1 59W
Great Yarmouth England 39 F3 52 37N 1 44E
GREECE 42 L3
GREENLAND 78 Q8
Greenock Scotland 33 E3 55 57N 4 45W
Greenwich England 38 D2 51 29N 0 00
GRENADA 79 N2
Grenoble France 48 F2 45 11N 5 43E
Greta r. England 34 C3 54 10N 2 30W
Greymouth New Zealand 73 C2 42 27S 171 12E
Greystones Republic of Ireland 36 A3 53 09N 6 04W
Grimsby England 35 E2 53 35N 0 05W
Groningen Netherlands 49 D5 53 13N 6 35E
Grosseto Italy 51 C5 42 46N 11 07E
Gross Glockner mt. Austria 49 G2 47 05N 12 44E
Groznyy Russia 56 E2 43 21N 45 42E
Guadalajara Mexico 79 J3 20 40N 103 20W
Guadalquivir r. Spain 50 C2 37 45N 5 30W
Guadalupe i. Mexico 79 H3 29 00N 118 24W
Guadeloupe i. Lesser Antilles 79 N2 16 30N 61 30W
Guadiana r. Spain/Portugal 50 C3 39 00N 5 30W
GUAM 5
Guangzhou China 59 C2 23 08N 113 20E
Guantánamo Cuba 79 M3 20 09N 75 14W
Guarda Portugal 50 B4 40 32N 7 17W
GUATEMALA 79 K2
Guatemala Guatemala 79 K2 14 38N 90 22W
Guayaquil Ecuador 84 B7 2 13S 79 54W
Guernsey i. Channel Islands British Isles 41 E2 46 27N 2 35W
Guildford England 38 D2 51 14N 0 35W
GUINEA 66 A4
GUINEA-BISSAU 66 A4
Guinea, Gulf of Atlantic Ocean 66 C3 2 00N 2 30W
Guisborough England 35 D3 54 32N 1 04W
Guiyang China 59 B2 26 35N 106 40E
Gulf, The Middle East 61 F3 27 20N 51 00E
Guwahati India 58 E3 26 10N 91 45E
GUYANA 84 D8

Gwadar Pakistan **58** B3 25 07N 62 19E
Gwalior India **58** C3 26 12N 78 09E
Gwynedd *u.a.* Wales **36** D2 52 45N 3 55W

H

Haarlem Netherlands **49** C5 52 23N 4 39E
Hachinohe Japan **59** N3 40 30N 141 30E
Haifa Israel **61** D4 32 49N 34 59E
Hail Saudi Arabia **61** E3 27 31N 41 45E
Hainan *i.* China **59** B1 18 50N 109 50E
Hai Phong Vietnam **60** B5 20 50N 106 41E
HAITI 79 M2
Hakodate Japan **59** N3 41 46N 140 44E
Halesowen England **37** E2 52 26N 2 05W
Halifax Canada **79** N5 44 38N 63 35W
Halifax England **34** D2 53 44N 1 52W
Halkirk Scotland **31** F3 58 30N 3 30W
Halle Germany **49** F4 51 28N 11 58E
Halmahera *i.* Indonesia **60** D3 0 30S 127 00E
Halton *u.a.* England **34** C2 53 20N 2 40W
Haltwhistle England **34** C3 54 58N 2 27W
Hamadan Iran **61** E4 34 46N 48 35E
Hamah Syria **43** P3 35 10N 36 45E
Hamamatsu Japan **59** M1 34 42N 137 42E
Hamburg Germany **49** F5 53 33N 10 00E
Hamersley Range Australia **72** B3 22 04S 117 37E
Hami China **58** E5 42 37N 93 32E
Hamilton Canada **79** M5 43 15N 79 50W
Hamilton New Zealand **73** D3 37 47S 175 17E
Hamilton Scotland **33** E3 55 47N 4 03W
Hamm Germany **49** D4 51 40N 7 49E
Hampshire *co.* England **38** C2 51 10N 1 15W
Hampshire Downs *hills* England **38** C2 51 15N 1 10W
Hangzhou China **59** D3 30 18N 120 07E
Hannover Germany **49** E5 52 23N 9 44E
Hanoi Vietnam **60** B5 21 01N 105 52E
Harad Saudi Arabia **61** E3 24 12N 49 12E
Harare Zimbabwe **67** D3 17 50S 31 03E
Harbin China **59** D4 45 45N 126 41E
Hargeysa Somalia **67** E5 9 31N 44 02E
Harlech Wales **36** C2 52 52N 4 07W
Harlow England **39** E2 51 47N 0 08E
Haroldswick Scotland **29** E3 60 47N 0 50W
Harris *i.* Scotland **30** C2 57 50N 6 55W
Harris, Sound of Scotland **30** B2 57 45N 7 10W
Harrogate England **34** D2 54 00N 1 33W
Harrow England **38** D2 51 34N 0 20W
Hartland Point England **40** C4 51 02N 4 31W
Hartlepool England **35** D3 54 41N 1 13W
Hartlepool *u.a.* England **35** D3 54 41N 1 13W
Harwich England **39** F2 51 57N 1 17E
Harz *mts.* Europe **49** F4 52 00N 10 00E
Haslemere England **38** D2 51 06N 0 43W
Hassi Messaoud Algeria **66** C6 31 52N 5 43E
Hastings England **39** E1 50 51N 0 36E
Hastings New Zealand **73** D3 39 39S 176 51E
Hatherleigh England **40** C3 50 49N 4 04W
Hauraki Gulf New Zealand **73** D3 36 38S 175 04E
Havana Cuba **79** L3 23 07N 82 25W
Havant England **38** D1 50 51N 0 59W
Haverfordwest Wales **36** C1 51 49N 4 58W
Haverhill England **39** E3 52 05N 0 26E
Havering England **39** E2 51 34N 0 14E
Hawaiian Islands Pacific Ocean **4** 20 00N 156 00W
Hawera New Zealand **73** C3 39 35S 174 17E
Hawick Scotland **33** G3 55 25N 2 47W
Hawke Bay New Zealand **73** D3 39 23S 177 12E
Hay-on-Wye Wales **36** D2 52 04N 3 07W
Hay River *tn.* Canada **78** H7 60 51N 115 42W
Haywards Heath England **38** D2 51 00N 0 06W
Hefei China **59** C3 31 55N 117 18E
Hegang China **59** E4 47 36N 130 30E
Heidelberg Germany **49** E3 49 25N 8 42E
Heilbronn Germany **49** E3 49 08N 9 14E
Helensburgh Scotland **33** E4 56 01N 4 44W
Hellín Spain **50** E3 38 31N 1 43W
Helmsdale Scotland **31** F3 58 07N 3 40W
Helmsdale *r.* Scotland **31** F3 58 10N 3 50W
Helsinki Finland **42** L8 60 08N 25 00E
Helston England **40** B3 50 05N 5 16W
Helvellyn *mt.* England **34** B3 54 32N 3 02W
Hemel Hempstead England **38** D2 51 46N 0 28W
Hemsworth England **35** D2 53 38N 1 21W
Hengelo Netherlands **49** D5 52 16N 6 46E
Henley-on-Thames England **38** D2 51 32N 0 56W
Herat Afghanistan **58** B4 34 20N 62 12E
Hereford England **37** E2 52 04N 2 43W
Herefordshire *u.a.* England **37** E2 52 12N 2 40W
Herma Ness *c.* Scotland **29** E3 60 50N 0 54W
Hermosillo Mexico **79** H3 29 15N 110 59W
Hertfordshire *co.* England **38** D2 51 50N 0 05W
Hexham England **34** C3 54 58N 2 06W
Heysham England **34** C3 54 02N 2 54W
Highland *u.a.* Scotland **30/31** D2/E2 57 00N 5 00W
High Veld *mts.* Republic of South Africa **67** C2 28 00S 28 00E
High Wycombe England **38** D2 51 38N 0 46W
Hilla Iraq **61** E4 32 28N 44 29E
Hillingdon England **38** D2 51 32N 0 27W
Hilversum Netherlands **49** C5 52 14N 5 10E
Himalayas *mts.* Asia **58** D3 28 00N 85 00E
Himeji Japan **59** L1 34 50N 134 40E
Hinckley England **37** F2 52 33N 1 21W
Hindu Kush *mts.* Afghanistan **58** B4 35 00N 70 00E
Hiroshima Japan **59** L1 34 23N 132 27E
Hitchin England **38** D2 51 57N 0 17W
Hobart Australia **72** E1 42 53S 147 19E
Ho Chi Minh City Vietnam **60** B4 10 46N 106 43E
Hodeida Yemen Republic **61** E2 14 50N 42 58E
Höfn Iceland **42** C8 64 16N 15 10W
Hoggar *mts.* Algeria **66** C5 23 50N 6 00E
Hohhot China **59** C4 40 49N 117 37E
Hokkaido *i.* Japan **59** N3 43 30N 143 00E
Holderness *p.* England **35** E2 53 45N 0 05W
Holguín Cuba **79** M3 20 54N 76 15W
Hollywood USA **79** H4 34 05N 118 21W
Holsworthy England **40** C3 50 49N 4 21W
Holyhead Wales **36** C3 53 19N 4 38W
Holy Island England **33** H3 55 41N 1 48W
Holy Island Wales **36** C3 53 16N 4 39W
Homs Syria **61** D4 34 42N 36 40E
Homyel' Belarus **56** D3 52 25N 31 00E
HONDURAS 79 L2
Hong Kong China **59** C2 23 00N 114 00E
Honiara Solomon Islands **72** F5 9 28S 159 57E
Honiton England **41** D3 50 48N 3 13W
Honshu *i.* Japan **59** M2 37 15N 139 00E
Horn, Cape Chile **85** C2 56 00S 67 15W
Horncastle England **35** E2 53 13N 0 07W
Hornsea England **35** E2 53 55N 0 10W
Horsham England **38** D2 51 04N 0 21W
Hospitalet Spain **50** G4 41 21N 2 06E
Hounslow England **38** D2 51 28N 0 21W
Houston USA **79** K3 29 45N 95 25W
Hove England **38** D1 50 49N 0 11W
Howe, Cape Australia **72** E2 37 29S 149 59E
Howth Republic of Ireland **36** A3 53 23N 6 04W
Hoy *i.* Scotland **29** B1 58 48N 3 20W
Huainan China **59** C3 32 41N 117 06E
Huambo Angola **67** B3 12 44S 15 47E
Huancayo Peru **84** B6 12 05S 75 12W
Huang He *r.* China **59** C3 36 00N 116 00E
Hubli India **58** C2 15 20N 75 14E
Huddersfield England **34** D2 53 39N 1 47W
Hudson *r.* USA **79** M5 43 20N 73 50W
Hudson Bay Canada **78** L6/7 60 00N 89 00W
Hue Vietnam **60** B4 16 28N 107 35E
Huelva Spain **50** B2 37 15N 6 56W
Hufuf Saudi Arabia **61** E3 25 20N 49 34E
Hugh Town England **40** A2 49 55N 6 19W
Hull *r.* England **35** E2 53 50N 0 25W
Humber *r.* England **35** E2 53 40N 0 10W
HUNGARY 42 K5
Hungnam North Korea **59** D3 39 49N 127 40E
Hunstanton England **39** E3 52 57N 0 30E
Huntingdon England **38** D3 52 20N 0 12W
Huntly Scotland **31** G2 57 27N 2 47W
Huron, Lake Canada/USA **79** L5 45 00N 83 00W
Hyderabad India **58** C2 17 22N 78 26E
Hyderabad Pakistan **58** B3 25 22N 68 22E

I

Iaș**i** Romania **42** M5 47 09N 27 38E
Ibadan Nigeria **66** C3 7 23N 3 56E
Ibagué Colombia **84** B8 4 25N 75 20W
Ibiza Balearic Islands **50** F3 38 54N 1 26E
Ibiza *i.* Balearic Islands **50** F3 39 00N 1 20E
ICELAND 42 C9
Idaho *state* USA **79** H5 44 00N 115 00W
Ieper *(Ypres)* Belgium **39** G1 50 51N 2 53E
IJsselmeer *l.* Netherlands **49** C5 52 50N 5 15E
Ilchester England **41** E3 51 01N 2 41W
Ilebo Congo Dem. Rep. **67** C4 4 20S 20 35E
Ilfracombe England **40** C4 51 13N 4 08W
Ilhéus Brazil **84** F6 14 50S 39 06W
Ilkeston England **37** F2 52 59N 1 18W
Ilkley England **34** D2 53 55N 1 50W
Illinois *state* USA **79** L5 40 00N 89 00W
Ilminster England **41** E3 50 56N 2 55W
Iloilo The Philippines **60** D4 10 41N 122 33E
Immingham England **35** E2 53 36N 0 11W
Imphal India **58** E3 24 47N 93 55E
Inca Balearic Islands **50** G3 39 43N 2 54E
Inchon South Korea **59** D3 37 30N 126 38E
INDIA 58 C3
Indiana *state* USA **79** L5 40 00N 86 00W
Indianapolis USA **79** L4 39 45N 86 10W
Indian Ocean 7
INDONESIA 60 A3/D2
Indore India **58** C3 22 42N 75 54E
Indus *r.* Asia **58** B3 27 00N 68 00E
Ingleborough *sum.* England **34** C3 54 10N 2 23W
Ingolstadt Germany **49** F3 48 46N 11 27E
Inishowen Peninsula Republic of Ireland **32** B3 55 15N 7 15W
Inland Sea *sd.* Japan **59** L1 34 00N 132 30E
Inn *r.* Europe **49** G3 48 15N 12 30E
Inner Hebrides *is.* Scotland **30** C1/2 56 45N 6 45W
Innerleithen Scotland **33** F3 55 38N 3 05W
Inner Sound Scotland **30** D2 57 25N 5 55W
Innsbruck Austria **42** J5 47 17N 11 25E
Inuvik Canada **78** F7 68 16N 133 40W
Inveraray Scotland **32** D4 56 13N 5 05W
Inverbervie Scotland **31** G1 56 51N 2 17W
Invercargill New Zealand **73** B1 46 25S 168 22E
Inverclyde *u.a.* Scotland **33** E3 55 50N 4 45W
Invergarry Scotland **31** E2 57 02N 4 47W
Invergordon Scotland **31** E2 57 42N 4 10W
Inverkeithing Scotland **33** F4 56 02N 3 25W
Invermoriston Scotland **31** E2 57 13N 4 38W
Inverness Scotland **31** E2 57 27N 4 15W
Inverurie Scotland **31** G2 57 17N 2 23W
Iona *i.* Scotland **30** C1 56 19N 6 25W
Ionian Island Greece **42** L3 39 40N 20 51E
Ionian Sea Mediterranean Sea **42** K3 38 00N 27 00E
Iowa *state* USA **79** K5 42 00N 94 00W
Ipoh Malaysia **60** B3 4 36N 101 05E
Ipswich England **39** F3 52 04N 1 10E
Iquique Chile **84** B5 20 15S 70 08W
Iquitos Peru **84** B7 3 51S 73 13W
Iraklion Greece **42** M3 35 20N 25 08E
IRAN 61 F4
IRAQ 61 E4
Irbid Jordan **43** P2 32 33N 35 51E
Irian Jaya *admin.* Indonesia **72** D5 3 00S 133 00E
Irish Sea British Isles **28** 53 30N 5 30W
Irkutsk Russia **57** L3 52 18N 104 15E
Irrawaddy *r.* Myanmar **58** E3 26 00N 97 30E
Irthing *r.* England **34** C3 55 00N 2 40W
Irtysh *r.* Russia **56** H3 57 30N 72 30E
Irvine Scotland **33** E3 55 37N 4 40W
Ísafjördour Iceland **42** B9 66 05N 23 08W
Ishikari *r.* Japan **59** N3 43 30N 142 00E
Isigny-sur-Mer France **41** F2 49 18N 1 06W
Isla *r.* Scotland **31** F1 56 40N 3 15W
Islamabad Pakistan **58** C4 33 42N 73 10E
Island Magee *p.* Northern Ireland **32** D2 53 45N 5 45W
Islay *i.* Scotland **32** C3 55 48N 6 12W
Isle of Anglesey *u.a.* Wales **36** C3 53 18N 4 25W
Isle of Man British Isles **33** E2 54 15N 4 30W
Isle of Wight *u.a.* England **38** C1 50 40N 1 20W
ISRAEL 61 D4
Istanbul Turkey **42** M4 41 02N 28 57E
Istria *p.* Croatia **49** G1 45 00N 14 00E
Itabuna Brazil **84** F6 14 48S 39 18W
ITALY 51
Itchen *r.* England **38** C2 51 05N 1 15W
Ivanovo Russia **56** E3 57 00N 41 00E
Iwaki Japan **59** N2 37 03N 140 58E
Izhevsk Russia **43** S7 56 49N 53 11E
Izmir Turkey **42** M3 38 25N 27 10E
Izu Islands Japan **59** M1 34 20N 139 20E

J

Jabalpur India **58** C3 23 10N 79 59E
Jackson USA **79** K4 32 20N 90 11W
Jacksonville USA **79** L4 30 20N 81 40W
Jaffna Sri Lanka **58** D1 9 40N 80 01E
Jaipur India **58** C3 26 53N 75 50E
Jakarta Indonesia **60** B2 6 08S 106 45E
JAMAICA 79 M2
Jambi Indonesia **60** B2 1 34S 103 37E
James Bay Canada **78** L6 53 45N 81 00W
Jammu & Kashmir *state* Southern Asia **58** C4 29 40N 76 30E
Jamshedpur India **58** D3 22 47N 86 12E
JAPAN 59
Japan, Sea of Pacific Ocean **59** M3 39 00N 137 00E
Jauf Saudi Arabia **61** D3 29 49N 39 52E
Java *i.* Indonesia **60** B2/C2 7 00S 110 00E
Javalambre *mt.* Spain **50** E4 40 05N 1 02W
Java Sea Indonesia **60** C2 5 00S 112 00E
Jaya Peak Indonesia **72** D5 4 05S 137 09E
Jedburgh Scotland **33** G3 55 29N 2 34W
Jedda Saudi Arabia **61** D3 21 30N 39 10E
Jena Germany **49** F4 50 56N 11 35E
Jerez de la Frontera Spain **50** B2 36 41N 6 08W
Jersey *i.* Channel Islands British Isles **41** E2 49 13N 2 07W
Jerusalem Israel/Jordan **61** D4 31 47N 35 13E
Jiamusi China **59** E4 46 59N 130 29E
Jiayuguan China **59** A4 39 47N 98 14E
Jilin China **59** D4 43 53N 126 35E
Jinan China **59** C3 36 41N 117 00E
Jinsha Jiang *(Yangtze) r.* China **59** B2 27 30N 103 00E
Jixi China **59** E4 45 17N 131 00E
Jizan Saudi Arabia **61** E2 16 56N 42 33E
João Pessoa Brazil **84** F7 7 06S 34 53W
Johannesburg Republic of South Africa **67** C2 26 10S 28 02E
John o'Groats Scotland **31** F3 58 38N 3 05W
Johnstone Scotland **33** E3 55 50N 4 31W
Johor Bahru Malaysia **60** B3 1 27N 103 45E
Joinville Brazil **85** E5 26 20S 48 55W
Jönköping Sweden **42** J7 57 45N 14 10E
JORDAN 61 D4
Jos Plateau Nigeria **66** C3/4 9 30N 8 55E
Juan Fernández Islands Chile **85** B4 33 30S 80 00W
Juba Sudan **61** D1 4 50N 31 35E
Juba *r.* Somalia/Ethiopia **67** E5 5 00N 41 00E
Juiz de Fora Brazil **84** E5 21 47S 43 23W
Jungfrau *mt.* Switzerland **49** D2 46 33N 7 58E
Jura *i.* Scotland **32** D3/D4 55 55N 6 00W
Jura *mts.* France/Switzerland **48** F3 46 30N 6 00E
Jura, Sound of Scotland **32** D3/4 56 00N 5 45W
Jutland *p.* Denmark **49** E6 55 00N 9 00E

K

Kabul Afghanistan **58** B4 34 30N 70 00E
Kabwe Zambia **67** C3 14 29S 28 25E
Kaduna Nigeria **66** C4 10 28N 7 25E
Kaesong South Korea **59** D3 37 59N 126 30E
Kagoshima Japan **59** L1 31 37N 130 32E
Kainji Reservoir Nigeria **66** C4 10 25N 4 56E
Kaipara Harbour New Zealand **73** C3 36 12S 174 06E
Kaiserslautern Germany **49** D3 49 27N 7 47E
Kalahari Desert Southern Africa **67** C2 23 30S 23 00E
Kalemie Congo Dem. Rep. **67** C4 5 57S 29 10E
Kalgoorlie Australia **72** C2 30 49S 121 29E
Kaliningrad Russia **56** C3 54 40N 20 30E
Kamchatka Peninsula Russia **57** R3 57 30N 160 00E
Kampala Uganda **67** D5 0 19N 32 35E
Kananga Congo Dem. Rep. **67** C4 5 53S 22 26E
Kanazawa Japan **59** M2 36 35N 136 38E
Kandahar Afghanistan **58** B4 31 35N 65 45E
Kandalaksha Russia **42** N9 67 09N 32 31E
Kandla India **58** C3 23 03N 70 11E
Kandy Sri Lanka **58** D1 7 17N 80 40E
Kankan Guinea **66** B4 10 22N 9 11W
Kano Nigeria **66** C4 12 00N 8 31E
Kanpur India **58** D3 26 27N 80 14E
Kansas *state* USA **79** K4 38 00N 98 00W
Kansas City USA **79** K4 39 02N 94 33W
Kaohsiung Taiwan **59** D2 22 36N 120 17E
Kapuas *r.* Indonesia **60** C3 0 30N 112 00E
Karachi Pakistan **58** B3 24 52N 67 03E
Karaganda Kazakhstan **56** H2 49 53N 73 07E
Karbala Iraq **61** E4 32 37N 44 03E
Kariba, Lake Zambia/Zimbabwe **67** C3 17 00S 28 00E
Karlovac Croatia **51** E6 45 30N 15 34E
Karlsruhe Germany **49** E3 49 00N 8 24E
Karun *r.* Iran **61** E4 32 00N 48 00E
Kasai *r.* Angola/Congo Dem. Rep. **67** B4 4 00S 19 00E
Kashi China **58** C4 39 29N 76 02E
Kassala Sudan **61** D2 15 24N 36 30E
Kassel Germany **49** E4 51 18N 9 30E
Kasserine Tunisia **51** B1 35 13N 8 43E
Katherine Australia **72** D4 14 27S 132 15E
Kathmandu Nepal **58** D3 27 42N 85 19E
Katowice Poland **42** K6 50 15N 18 59E
Kaunas Lithuania **42** L6 54 52N 23 55E
Kayes Mali **66** A4 14 26N 11 28W
Kayseri Turkey **43** P3 38 42N 35 28E
KAZAKHSTAN 56 G2
Kazan' Russia **56** E3 55 45N 49 10E
Keady Northern Ireland **32** C2 54 15N 6 42W
Keighley England **34** D2 53 52N 1 54W
Keith Scotland **31** G2 57 32N 2 57W
Kelso Scotland **33** G3 55 36N 2 25W
Kemerovo Russia **56** J3 55 25N 86 05E
Kendal England **34** C3 54 20N 2 45W
Kenilworth England **37** F2 52 21N 1 34W
Kenitra Morocco **66** B6 34 20N 6 34W
Kennet *r.* England **38** C2 51 30N 1 45W
Kent *co.* England **39** E2 51 15N 0 09E
Kentucky *state* USA **79** L4 37 00N 85 00W
KENYA 67 D5
Kenya, Mount Kenya **67** D4 0 10S 37 19E
Kerema Papua New Guinea **72** E5 7 59S 145 46E
Kerguelen *is.* Indian Ocean **5** 49 15N 69 10E
Kerman Iran **61** F4 30 18N 57 05E
Kermanshah Iran **61** E4 34 19N 47 04E
Kerrera *i.* Scotland **32** D1 56 24N 5 33W
Keswick England **34** B3 54 37N 3 08W
Kettering England **38** D3 52 24N 0 44W
Keynsham England **38** B2 51 26N 2 30W
Khabarovsk Russia **57** P2 48 32N 135 08E
Khaniá Greece **42** L3 35 31N 24 01E
Khanka, Lake Asia **57** P2 45 00N 132 30E
Kharkiv Ukraine **56** D2 50 00N 36 15E
Khartoum Sudan **61** D2 15 33N 32 35E
Kherson Ukraine **56** D2 46 39N 32 38E
Khulna Bangladesh **58** D3 22 49N 89 34E
Khyber Pass Afghanistan/Pakistan **58** C4 34 06N 71 05E
Kidderminster England **37** E2 52 23N 2 14W
Kidsgrove England **37** E3 53 05N 2 14W
Kidwelly Wales **36** C1 51 45N 4 18W
Kiel Germany **49** F6 54 20N 10 08E
Kielder Water *res.* England **33** G3 55 10N 2 30W
Kiev Ukraine **56** D3 50 25N 30 30E
Kigali Rwanda **67** D4 1 56S 30 04E
Kigoma Tanzania **67** C4 4 52S 29 36E
Kikwit Congo Dem. Rep. **67** B4 5 02S 18 51E
Kilbrannan Sound Scotland **32** D3 55 30N 5 30W
Kilimanjaro, Mount Tanzania **67** D4 3 04S 37 22E
Kilkeel Northern Ireland **32** C2 54 04N 6 00W
Kilmacrenan Republic of Ireland **32** B3 55 02N 7 47W
Kilmaluag Scotland **30** C2 57 41N 6 17W
Kilmarnock Scotland **33** E3 55 36N 4 30W
Kilmory Scotland **32** D3 55 55N 5 41W
Kimberley Republic of South Africa **67** C2 28 45S 24 46E
Kinabalu, Mount Malaysia **60** C3 6 03N 116 32E
Kinbrace Scotland **31** F3 58 15N 3 56W
Kingsbridge England **40** D3 50 17N 3 46W
King's Lynn England **39** E3 52 45N 0 24E
Kingston Jamaica **79** M2 17 58N 76 48W
Kingston upon Hull England **35** E2 53 45N 0 20W
Kingston upon Thames England **38** D2 51 25N 0 18W
Kingswood England **38** B2 51 28N 2 30W
Kington England **36** D2 52 12N 3 01W
Kingussie Scotland **31** E2 57 05N 4 03W
Kinloch Scotland **30** C2 57 01N 6 17W
Kinross Scotland **31** F1 56 13N 3 27W
Kinshasa Congo Dem. Rep. **67** B4 4 18S 15 18E
Kintyre *p.* Scotland **32** D3 55 30N 5 35W
KIRIBATI 4/5
Kirkbean Scotland **33** F2 54 55N 3 36W
Kirkby England **34** C2 53 29N 2 54W
Kirkby Stephen England **34** C3 54 28N 2 20W
Kirkcaldy Scotland **33** F4 56 07N 3 10W
Kirkcudbright Scotland **33** E2 54 50N 4 03W
Kirkintilloch Scotland **33** E3 55 57N 4 10W
Kirk Michael Isle of Man British Isles **33** E2 54 17N 4 35W
Kirkpatrick, Mount Antarctica **86** 84 25S 165 30E
Kirkuk Iraq **61** E4 35 28N 44 26E
Kirkwall Scotland **29** C1 58 59N 2 58W
Kirov Russia **56** E3 58 00N 49 38E
Kirriemuir Scotland **31** F1 56 41N 3 01W
Kisangani Congo Dem. Rep. **67** C5 0 33N 25 14E
Kisumu Kenya **67** D4 0 08S 34 47E
Kitakami *r.* Japan **59** N2 39 00N 141 20E
Kita Kyushu Japan **59** L1 33 52N 130 49E
Kitwe Zambia **67** C3 0 08S 30 30E
Kitzbühel Austria **51** D7 47 27N 12 23E
Kivu, Lake Congo Dem. Rep./Rwanda **67** C4 2 00S 29 00E
Klagenfurt Austria **49** H2 46 38N 14 20E
Klaipėda Lithuania **42** L7 55 43N 21 07E
Knaresborough England **35** D3 54 00N 1 27W
Knighton England **36** D2 52 21N 3 03W
Kobe Japan **59** M1 34 40N 135 12E
Koblenz Germany **49** D4 50 21N 7 36E
Kochi Japan **59** L1 33 33N 133 32E
Kodiak Island USA **78** D6 57 20N 153 40W
Kokand Uzbekistan **56** H2 40 33N 70 55E
Kola Peninsula Russia **42** P9 67 00N 39 00E
Kolhapur India **58** C2 16 40N 74 20E
Kolkata *(Calcutta)* India **58** D3 22 30N 88 20E
Kolyma *r.* Russia **57** R4 68 00N 152 00E
Komsomolsk-on-Amur Russia **57** P3 50 32N 136 59E
Konya Turkey **43** N3 37 51N 32 30E
Koriyama Japan **59** N2 37 23N 140 22E
Kosciusko, Mount Australia **72** E2 36 27S 148 17E
Kota Bharu Malaysia **60** B3 6 08N 102 14E
Kota Kinabalu Malaysia **60** C3 5 59N 116 04E
Kotlas Russia **43** R8 61 15N 46 35E
Kragujevac Yugoslavia **42** L4 44 01N 20 55E
Kra, Isthmus of Myanmar/Thailand **60** A4 10 20N 99 00E
Kraków Poland **42** K6 50 03N 19 55E
Kranj Slovenia **51** E7 46 15N 14 20E
Krasnodar Russia **56** D2 45 02N 39 00E
Krasnovodsk Turkmenistan **56** F2 40 01N 53 00E
Krasnoyarsk Russia **57** K3 56 05N 92 46E
Kratie Cambodia **60** B4 12 30N 106 03E
Krefeld Germany **49** D4 51 20N 6 32E
Krishna *r.* India **58** C2 16 00N 79 00E
Kryvyy Rih Ukraine **56** D2 47 55N 33 24E

Kuala Lumpur Malaysia 60 B3 3 09N 101 42E
Kuala Terengganu Malaysia 60 B3 5 20N 103 09E
Kuantan Malaysia 60 B3 3 48N 103 19E
Kuching Malaysia 60 C3 1 35N 110 21E
Kuh-e-Hazaran *mt.* Iran 61 F3 29 35N 57 20E
Kumamoto Japan 59 L1 32 50N 130 42E
Kumasi Ghana 66 B3 6 45N 1 35W
Kunlun Shan *mts.* China 58 D4 36 30N 85 00E
Kunming China 59 B2 25 04N 102 41E
Kupang Indonesia 60 D1 10 13S 123 38E
Kurgan Russia 56 G3 55 30N 65 20E
Kuril Islands Russia 57 R2 50 00N 155 00E
Kursk Russia 56 D3 51 45N 36 14E
Kushiro Japan 59 N3 42 58N 144 24E
Kutaisi Georgia 43 Q4 42 15N 42 44E
KUWAIT 61 E3
Kuwait Kuwait 61 E3 29 20N 48 00E
Kwangju South Korea 59 D3 35 07N 126 52E
Kyle of Lochalsh Scotland 30 D2 57 17N 5 43W
Kyoga, Lake Uganda 67 D5 2 00N 34 00E
Kyoto Japan 59 M2 35 02N 135 45E
KYRGYZSTAN 56 H2
Kyushu *i.* Japan 59 L1 32 20N 131 00E

L

Laâyoune Western Sahara 66 A5 27 10N 13 11W
La Coruña Spain 50 A5 43 22N 8 24W
Ladoga, Lake Russia 56 D4 61 00N 30 00E
Lae Papua New Guinea 72 E5 6 45S 147 00E
Lagos Nigeria 66 C3 6 27N 3 28E
La Grande Rivière *r.* Canada 78 L6 53 34N 74 36W
Lahore Pakistan 58 C4 31 35N 74 18E
Lairg Scotland 31 E3 58 01N 4 25W
Lake District *geog. reg.* England 34 B3/C3 54 30N 3 00W
Lakshadweep *(Laccadive Islands)* India 58 C2 9 30N 73 00E
Lambert Glacier Antarctica 86 73 00S 70 00E
Lambourn *r.* England 38 C2 51 30N 1 30W
Lammermuir Hills Scotland 33 G3 55 50N 2 45W
Lampedusa *i.* Italy 51 D1 35 00N 12 00E
Lampeter Wales 36 C2 52 07N 4 05W
Lanark Scotland 33 F3 55 41N 3 48W
Lancang Jiang *(Mekong) r.* China/Myanmar/Laos/Cambodia 59 A3 32 00N 98 00E
Lancashire *co.* England 34 C2 53 50N 2 30W
Lancaster England 34 C3 54 03N 2 48W
Land's End *c.* England 40 B3 50 03N 5 44W
Langholm Scotland 33 G3 55 09N 3 00W
Languedoc *geog. reg.* France 48 E1/F2 44 00N 4 00E
Lanzhou China 59 B3 36 01N 103 45E
LAOS 60 B4
La Paz Bolivia 84 C6 16 30S 68 10W
La Plata Argentina 85 D4 34 52S 57 55W
La Puebla Balearic Islands 50 G3 39 46N 3 01E
Largs Scotland 32 E3 55 48N 4 52W
Lárisa Greece 42 L3 39 38N 22 25E
Larne Northern Ireland 32 D2 54 51N 5 49W
Larne *district* Northern Ireland 32 D2 54 50N 5 50W
la Rochelle France 48 C3 46 10N 1 10W
Larsen Ice Shelf Antarctica 86 67 00S 62 00W
La Sagra *mt.* Spain 50 D2 37 57N 2 34W
Las Palmas Canary Islands 66 A5 28 08N 15 27W
La Spezia Italy 51 B6 44 07N 9 48E
Las Vegas USA 79 H4 36 10N 115 10W
Latakia Syria 61 D4 35 31N 35 47E
Latina Italy 51 D4 41 28N 12 53E
LATVIA 42 M7
Launceston Australia 72 E1 41 27S 147 09E
Launceston England 40 C3 50 38N 4 21W
Laurencekirk Scotland 31 G1 56 50N 2 29W
Lausanne Switzerland 49 D2 46 32N 6 39E
Laval France 48 C4 48 04N 0 45W
Leader Water *r.* Scotland 33 G3 55 45N 2 50W
LEBANON 61 D4
Ledbury England 37 E2 52 02N 2 25W
Leeds England 34 D2 53 50N 1 35W
Leeuwin, Cape Australia 72 B2 34 21S 115 08E
le Havre France 48 D4 49 30N 0 06E
Leicester England 37 F2 52 38N 1 05W
Leicester City *u.a.* England 37 F2 52 36N 1 08W
Leicestershire *co.* England 37 F2/G2 52 30N 1 00W
Leiden Netherlands 49 C5 52 10N 4 30E
Leighton Buzzard England 38 D2 51 55N 0 41W
Leipzig Germany 49 G4 51 20N 12 25E
Leith Hill England 38 D2 51 11N 0 23W
Leitrim *co.* Republic of Ireland 32 A2 54 05N 8 00W
le Mans France 48 D4 48 00N 0 12E
Lena *r.* Russia 57 N4 64 30N 127 00E
Lens France 48 E5 50 26N 2 50E
Leominster England 37 E2 52 14N 2 45W
León Mexico 79 J3 21 10N 101 42W
León Spain 50 C5 42 35N 5 34W
le Puy France 48 E2 45 03N 3 53E
Lerwick Scotland 29 D3 60 09N 1 09W
LESOTHO 67 C2
Lessay France 41 F2 49 13N 1 32W
Lesser Antilles *is.* West Indies 79 N2 18 00N 65 00W
Letchworth England 38 D2 51 58N 0 14W
le Touquet-Paris-Plage France 39 F1 50 13N 1 36E
Letterkenny Republic of Ireland 32 B2 54 57N 7 44W
Leverkusen Germany 49 D4 51 02N 6 59E
Levin New Zealand 73 D2 40 37S 175 17E
Lewes England 38 E1 50 52N 0 01E
Lewis *i.* Scotland 30 C3 58 15N 6 30W
Leyburn England 34 D3 54 19N 1 49W
Leyland England 34 C2 53 42N 2 42W
Leyte *i.* The Philippines 60 D4 11 00N 125 00E
Lhasa China 58 E3 29 08N 87 43E
Lianyungang China 59 C3 34 37N 119 10E
Liao He *r.* China 59 D4 42 30N 122 00E
Liard *r.* Canada 78 G7 61 00N 122 00W
LIBERIA 66 B3
Libreville Gabon 66 C3 0 30N 9 25E
LIBYA 66 D5
Libyan Desert North Africa 61 C3 25 00N 25 00E
Lichfield England 37 F2 52 42N 1 48W
Liddel Water *r.* England/Scotland 33 G3 55 15N 2 50W
LIECHTENSTEIN 49 E2
Liège Belgium 49 C4 50 38N 5 35E
Liepāja Latvia 42 L7 56 30N 21 00E
Likasi Congo Dem. Rep. 67 C3 10 58S 26 47E
Lille France 48 E5 50 39N 3 05E
Lillers France 39 G1 50 34N 2 29E
Lilongwe Malawi 67 D3 13 58S 33 49E
Lima Peru 84 B6 12 06S 8 40W
Limassol Cyprus 43 N2 34 04N 33 03E
Limavady Northern Ireland 32 C3 55 03N 6 57W
Limavady *district* Northern Ireland 32 B2/C2 54 50N 7 00W
Limoges France 48 D2 45 50N 1 15E
Limpopo *r.* Southern Africa 67 C2 22 30S 28 00E
Lincoln England 35 E2 53 14N 0 33W
Lincolnshire *co.* England 35 E2 53 10N 0 20W
Lincoln Wolds *hills* England 35 E2 53 25N 0 05W
Lingga *i.* Indonesia 60 B2 0 10S 104 40E
Linköping Sweden 42 K7 58 25N 15 35E
Linlithgow Scotland 33 F3 55 59N 3 37W
Linz Austria 42 J5 48 19N 14 18E
Lipetsk Russia 56 D3 52 37N 39 36E
Lisbon Portugal 50 A3 38 44N 9 08W
Lisburn Northern Ireland 32 C2 54 31N 6 03W
Lisburn *district* Northern Ireland 32 C2 54 30N 6 10W
Lisieux France 48 D4 49 09N 0 14E
Liskeard England 40 C3 50 28N 4 28W
Lismore *i.* Scotland 30 D1 56 30N 5 30W
LITHUANIA 42 L7
Littlehampton England 38 D1 50 48N 0 33W
Little Minch *sd.* Scotland 30 C2 57 45N 6 30W
Little Ouse *r.* England 39 E3 52 30N 0 30E
Little Rock USA 79 K4 34 42N 92 17W
Liuzhou China 59 B2 24 17N 109 15E
Liverpool England 34 C2 53 25N 2 55W
Livingston Scotland 33 F3 55 53N 3 32W
Livorno Italy 51 C5 43 33N 10 18E
Lizard England 40 B2 49 57N 5 13W
Lizard Point England 40 B2 49 56N 5 13W
Ljubljana Slovenia 51 E7 46 04N 14 30E
Llandeilo Wales 36 D1 51 53N 3 59W
Llandovery Wales 36 D1 51 59N 3 48W
Llandrindod Wells Wales 36 D2 52 15N 3 23W
Llandudno Wales 36 D3 53 19N 3 49W
Llanelli Wales 36 C1 51 42N 4 10W
Llangollen Wales 36 D2 52 58N 3 10W
Llanidloes Wales 36 D2 52 27N 3 32W
Lleida Spain 50 F4 41 37N 0 38E
Lleyn Peninsula Wales 36 C2 52 53N 4 30W
Lobito Angola 67 B3 12 20S 13 34E
Lochaline *tn.* Scotland 30 D1 56 32N 5 47W
Loch Arkaig *l.* Scotland 30 D1 56 59N 5 10W
Loch Awe *l.* Scotland 30/31 D1 56 15N 5 17W
Lochdon *tn.* Scotland 30 D1 56 25N 5 35W
Loch Doon *l.* Scotland 33 E3 55 26N 4 38W
Loch Earn *l.* Scotland 31 E1 56 25N 4 10W
Loch Eishort *est.* Scotland 30 D2 57 08N 6 00W
Loch Eriboll *b.* Scotland 31 E3 58 31N 4 41W
Loch Ericht *l.* Scotland 31 E1 56 48N 4 25W
Loch Etive *l.* Scotland 30/31 D1 56 30N 5 10W
Loch Fyne *b.* Scotland 32 D4 56 10N 5 05W
Lochgilphead *tn.* Scotland 32 D4 56 03N 5 26W
Loch Katrine *l.* Scotland 33 E4 56 16N 4 30W
Loch Ken *l.* Scotland 33 E3 55 02N 4 07W
Loch Leven *l.* Scotland 31 F1 56 15N 3 23W
Loch Linnhe *b.* Scotland 30 D1 56 35N 5 25W
Loch Lochy *l.* Scotland 31 E1 56 58N 4 55W
Loch Lomond *l.* Scotland 33 E4 56 10N 4 35W
Loch Long *l.* Scotland 32/33 E4 56 10N 4 50W
Lochmaben *tn.* Scotland 33 F3 55 08N 3 27W
Lochmaddy *tn.* Scotland 30 B2 57 36N 7 08W
Loch Nan Clar *l.* Scotland 31 E3 58 30N 4 00W
Loch Maree *l.* Scotland 30 D2 57 40N 5 30W
Loch Mullardoch *l.* Scotland 31 E2 57 27N 4 58W
Lochnagar *mt.* Scotland 31 F1 56 57N 3 16W
Loch Ness *l.* Scotland 31 E2 57 02N 4 30W
Loch Rannoch *l.* Scotland 31 E1 56 41N 4 18W
Lochranza *tn.* Scotland 32 D3 55 42N 5 18W
Loch Shiel *l.* Scotland 30 D1 56 45N 5 35W
Loch Shin *l.* Scotland 31 E3 58 05N 4 30W
Loch Snizort *b.* Scotland 30 C2 57 30N 6 30W
Loch Tay *l.* Scotland 31 E1 56 31N 4 10W
Loch Torridon *b.* Scotland 30 D2 57 35N 5 46W
Lockerbie Scotland 33 F3 55 07N 3 22W
ŁódΩPoland 42 K6 51 49N 19 28E
Logan, Mount Canada 78 E7 60 34N 140 25W
Logroño Spain 50 D5 42 28N 2 26W
Loire *r.* France 48 D3 47 30N 1 00E
Lolland *i.* Denmark 49 F6 54 45N 12 20E
Lombok *i.* Indonesia 60 C2 8 30S 116 30E
Lomé Togo 66 C3 6 10N 1 21E
London England 38 D2 51 30N 0 10W
Londonderry Northern Ireland 32 B2 54 59N 7 19W
Londonderry *district* Northern Ireland 32 B2 54 55N 7 20W
Londrina Brazil 84 D5 23 18S 51 13W
Long Eaton England 37 F2 52 54N 1 15W
Long Island The Bahamas 79 M3 23 20N 75 00W
Long Mynd *sum.* England 37 E2 52 32N 2 52W
Longreach Australia 72 E3 23 26S 144 15E
Longs Peak USA 79 J5 40 20N 105 50W
Looe England 40 C3 51 21N 4 27W
Lorient France 48 B3 47 45N 3 21W
Los Angeles USA 79 H4 34 00N 118 15W
Lossiemouth Scotland 31 F2 57 43N 3 18W
Lostwithiel England 40 C3 50 25N 4 40W
Lot *r.* France 48 E2 44 30N 2 15E
Louangphrabang Laos 60 B4 19 53N 102 10E
Lough Allen *l.* Republic of Ireland 32 A2 54 15N 8 00W
Lough Beg *l.* Northern Ireland 32 C2 54 48N 6 16W
Loughborough England 37 F2 52 47N 1 11W
Lough Derg *l.* Republic of Ireland 32 B2 52 55N 8 15W
Lough Foyle *est.* Northern Ireland/Republic of Ireland 32 B3 55 10N 7 10W
Lough Macnean Lower *l.* Northern Ireland 32 B2 54 17N 7 50W
Lough Macnean Upper *l.* Northern Ireland/Republic of Ireland 32 B2 54 18N 7 55W
Lough Melvin *l.* Northern Ireland/Republic of Ireland 32 A2 54 25N 8 05W
Lough Neagh *l.* Northern Ireland 32 C2 54 35N 6 30W
Lough Oughter *l.* Republic of Ireland 32 B2 54 00N 7 30W
Lough Swilly *b.* Republic of Ireland 32 B3 55 20N 7 35W
Louisiana *state* USA 79 K4 32 00N 92 00W
Louisville USA 79 L4 38 13N 85 48W
Lourdes France 48 C1 43 06N 0 02W
Louth England 35 E2 53 22N 0 01W
Louth *co.* Republic of Ireland 32 C1/2 53 55N 6 25W
Lower California *p.* Mexico 79 H3 27 30N 113 00W
Lower Lough Erne *l.* Northern Ireland 32 B2 54 25N 7 45W
Lowestoft England 39 F3 52 29N 1 45E
Lowther Hills Scotland 33 F3 55 25N 3 45W
Lualaba *r.* Congo Dem. Rep 67 C4 4 00S 26 30E
Luanda Angola 67 B4 8 50S 13 15E
Lubango Angola 67 B3 14 55S 13 30E
Lübeck Germany 49 F5 53 52N 10 40E
Lublin Poland 42 L6 51 18N 22 31E
Lubumbashi Congo Dem. Rep 67 C3 11 41S 27 29E
Luce Bay Scotland 32/33 E2 54 47N 4 50W
Lucerne Switzerland 49 E2 47 03N 8 17E
Lucknow India 58 D3 26 50N 80 54E
Lüderitz Namibia 67 B2 26 38S 15 10E
Ludhiana India 58 C4 30 56N 75 52E
Ludlow England 37 E2 52 22N 2 43W
Ludwigshafen Germany 49 E3 49 29N 8 27E
Lugano Switzerland 49 E2 46 01N 8 57E
Luhans'k Ukraine 56 D2 48 35N 39 20E
Luleå Sweden 42 L9 65 35N 22 10E
Lundy *i.* England 40 C4 51 11N 4 40W
Lune *r.* England 34 C3 54 15N 2 40W
Luoyang China 59 C3 34 47N 112 26E
Lurgan Northern Ireland 32 C2 54 28N 6 20W
Lusaka Zambia 67 C3 15 26S 28 20E
Luton England 38 D2 51 53N 0 25W
Luton *u.a.* England 38 D2 51 53N 0 30W
LUXEMBOURG 49 C3/D3
Luxembourg Luxembourg 49 D3 49 37N 6 08E
Luxor Egypt 61 D3 25 41N 32 24E
Luzon *i.* The Philippines 60 D4 15 00N 122 00E
L'viv Ukraine 56 C2 49 50N 24 00E
Lybster Scotland 31 F3 58 18N 3 13W
Lyme Bay England 41 E3 50 40N 2 55W
Lyme Regis England 41 E3 50 44N 2 57W
Lymington England 38 C1 50 46N 1 33W
Lynn Lake *tn.* Canada 78 J6 56 51N 101 01W
Lynton England 40 D4 51 15N 3 50W
Lyons France 48 F2 45 46N 4 50E
Lys *r.* France 39 G1 50 40N 2 10E
Lytham St. Anne's England 34 B2 53 45N 3 01W

M

Maas *r.* Netherlands 49 C4 51 50N 5 45E
Maastricht Netherlands 49 C4 50 51N 5 42E
Mablethorpe England 35 F2 53 21N 0 15E
Macao China 59 C2 22 10N 113 40E
Macapá Brazil 84 D8 0 04N 51 04W
Macclesfield England 34 C2 53 16N 2 07W
Macdonnell Ranges Australia 72 D3 23 42S 128 42E
Macduff Scotland 31 G2 57 40N 2 29W
MACEDONIA, FORMER YUGOSLAV REPUBLIC OF (FYROM) 42 L4
Maceió Brazil 84 F7 9 40S 35 44W
Machynlleth Wales 36 D2 52 35N 3 51W
Mackay, Lake Australia 72 C3 22 25S 128 42E
Mackenzie *r.* Canada 78 G7 64 00N 123 00 W
Mackenzie Mountains Canada 78 G7 66 00N 132 00W
McKinley, Mount USA 78 E7 62 02N 151 01W
Mâcon France 48 F3 46 18N 4 50E
MADAGASCAR 67 E2/3
Madang Papua New Guinea 72 E5 5 14S 145 45E
Madeira *r.* Brazil 84 C7 6 00S 61 30W
Madeira Islands Atlantic Ocean 5 32 45N 17 00W
Madras *see* Chennai
Madrid Spain 50 D4 40 25N 3 43W
Madura *i.* Indonesia 60 C2 7 00S 113 00E
Madurai India 58 C1 9 55N 78 07E
Maebashi Japan 59 M2 36 24N 139 04E
Magadan Russia 57 R3 59 38N 150 50E
Magdalena *r.* Colombia 84 B8 3 00N 75 40W
Magdeburg Germany 49 F5 52 08N 11 37E
Maggiore, Lake Italy 51 B6/7 46 00N 8 00E
Maghera Northern Ireland 32 C2 54 51N 6 40W
Magherafelt Northern Ireland 32 C2 54 45N 6 36W
Magherafelt *district* Northern Ireland 32 C2 54 45N 6 50W
Magnitogorsk Russia 56 F3 53 28N 59 06E
Mahajanga Madagascar 67 E3 15 40S 46 20E
Mahakam *r.* Indonesia 60 C3 0 30N 116 00E
Mahilyow Belarus 56 D3 53 54N 30 20E
Mahón Balearic Islands 50 H3 39 54N 4 15E
Maidenhead England 38 D2 51 32N 0 44W
Maidstone England 39 E2 51 17N 0 32E
Maiduguri Nigeria 66 D4 11 53N 13 16E
Main *r.* Germany 49 F4 50 00N 10 30E
Main *r.* Northern Ireland 32 C2 54 50N 6 25W
Mai-Ndombe, Lake Congo Dem. Rep. 67 B4 2 00S 18 20E
Maine *state* USA 79 N5 45 00N 70 00W
Mainland *i.* Orkney Islands Scotland 29 B1/B2 59 00N 3 15W
Mainland *i.* Shetland Islands Scotland 29 D3 60 15N 1 20W
Mainz Germany 49 D3 50 00N 8 16E
Makassar Strait Indonesia 60 C2 0 00 119 00E
Makeyevka Ukraine 56 D2 48 01N 38 00E
Makhachkala Russia 56 E2 42 59N 47 30E
Malabo Equatorial Guinea 66 C3 3 45N 8 48E
Malacca, Strait of Indonesia 60 B3 4 00N 100 00E
Málaga Spain 50 C2 36 43N 4 25W
Malahide Republic of Ireland 36 A3 53 27N 6 09W
Malakal Sudan 61 D1 9 31N 31 40E
Malang Indonesia 60 C2 7 59S 112 45E
Malanje Angola 67 B4 9 32S 16 20E
Malatya Turkey 43 P3 38 22N 38 18E
MALAWI 67 D3
Malawi, Lake *see* Nyasa, Lake
Malaya *admin.* Malaysia 60 B3 5 00N 102 00E
MALAYSIA 60 B3/C3
MALDIVES 58 C1
MALI 66 B4
Malin Head *c.* Republic of Ireland 32 B3 55 30N 7 20W
Mallaig Scotland 30 D2 57 00N 5 50W
Mallorca *i.* Balearic Islands 50 G3 39 50N 2 30E
Malmesbury England 38 B2 51 36N 2 06W
Malmö Sweden 42 J7 55 35N 13 00E
MALTA 51 E1
Malton England 35 E3 54 08N 0 48W
Manacor Balearic Islands 50 G3 39 35N 3 12E
Manado Indonesia 60 D3 1 32N 124 55E
Managua Nicaragua 79 L2 12 06N 86 18W
Manaus Brazil 84 D7 3 06S 60 00W
Manawatu *r.* New Zealand 73 D2 40 30S 176 00E
Manchester England 34 C2 53 30N 2 15W
Mandalay Myanmar 58 E3 21 57N 96 04E
Manfredonia Italy 51 E4 41 37N 15 55E
Mangalore India 58 C2 12 54N 74 51E
Mangotsfield England 38 B2 51 29N 2 31W
Manila The Philippines 60 D4 14 37N 120 58E
Manitoba *province* Canada 78 K6 55 00N 98 00W
Manizales Colombia 84 B8 5 03N 75 32W
Mannheim Germany 49 E3 49 30N 8 28E
Mansfield England 37 F3 53 09N 1 11W
Manzanares Spain 50 D3 39 00N 3 23W
Maputo Mozambique 67 D2 25 58S 32 35E
Maracaibo Venezuela 84 B9 10 44N 71 37W
Maracaibo, Lake Venezuela 84 B8 9 50N 71 30W
Marañon *r.* Peru 84 B7 7 00S 77 40W
Marbella Spain 50 C2 36 31N 4 53W
Marble Bar Australia 72 B3 21 10S 119 43E
Mar del Plata Argentina 85 D4 38 00S 57 32W
Marden England 39 E2 51 11N 0 30E
Margarita *i.* Venezuela 79 N2 11 30N 64 00W
Margate England 39 F2 51 24N 1 24E
Maribor Slovenia 51 E7 46 34N 15 38E
Marie Byrd Land *geog. reg.* Antarctica 86 77 00S 130 00W
Mariscal Estigarribia Paraguay 84 C5 22 03S 60 35W
Mariupol Ukraine 56 D2 47 05N 37 34E
Market Drayton England 37 E2 52 54N 2 29W
Market Harborough England 37 G2 52 29N 0 55W
Market Rasen England 35 E2 53 24N 0 21W
Markham, Mount Antarctica 86 82 45S 160 25E
Marlborough England 38 C2 51 26N 1 43W
Marlow England 38 D2 51 35N 0 48W
Marne *r.* France 48 E4 49 00N 4 00E
Marrakesh Morocco 66 B6 31 49N 8 00W
Marsala Italy 51 D2 37 48N 12 27E
Marseille France 48 F1 43 18N 5 22E
MARSHALL ISLANDS 5
Martinique *i.* Lesser Antilles 79 N2 14 30N 61 00W
Maryborough Australia 72 F3 25 33S 152 42E
Maryland *state* USA 79 M4 39 00N 77 00W
Maryport England 34 B3 54 43N 3 30W
Maseru Lesotho 67 C2 29 19S 27 29E
Mashhad Iran 61 F4 36 16N 59 34E
Massachusetts *state* USA 79 M5 42 00N 72 00W
Massawa Eritrea 61 D2 15 42N 39 25E
Massif Central *mts.* France 48 E2 45 00N 3 30E
Masterton New Zealand 73 D2 40 57S 175 39E
Matadi Congo Dem. Rep. 67 B4 5 50S 13 32E
Matamoros Mexico 79 K3 25 33N 103 51W
Matlock England 37 F3 53 08N 1 32W
Mato Grosso *geog. reg.* Brazil 84 D6 14 00S 56 00W
Matsue Japan 59 L2 35 29N 133 04E
Matsuyama Japan 59 L1 33 50N 132 47E
Matterhorn *mt.* Switzerland 49 D1 45 59N 7 39E
MAURITANIA 66 A5
MAURITIUS 5
Maybole Scotland 33 E3 55 21N 4 41W
Mazatlán Mexico 79 J3 23 11N 106 25W
Mbandaka Congo Dem. Rep. 67 B5 0 03N 18 28E
Mbuji-Mayi Congo Dem. Rep. 67 C4 6 10S 23 39E
Mecca Saudi Arabia 61 D3 21 26N 39 49E
Medan Indonesia 60 A3 3 35N 98 39E
Medellín Colombia 84 B8 6 15N 75 36W
Medina Saudi Arabia 61 D3 24 30N 39 35E
Mediterranean Sea Africa/Europe 42/43 35 00N 15 00E
Medway *r.* England 39 E2 51 24N 0 30E
Medway *u.a.* England 39 E2 51 28N 0 35E
Meekatharra Australia 72 B3 26 35S 118 30E
Meerut India 58 C3 29 00N 77 42E
Mega Ethiopia 61 D1 4 02N 38 19E
Meharry, Mount Australia 72 B3 22 58S 118 35E
Meig *r.* Scotland 31 E2 57 40N 4 50W
Meknes Morocco 66 B6 33 53N 5 37W
Mekong *(Lancang Jiang) r.* Cambodia/Laos/Myanmar/China 59 B1 15 00N 105 00E
Melbourne Australia 72 E2 37 49S 144 58E
Melrose Scotland 33 G3 55 36N 2 44W
Melton Mowbray England 37 G2 52 46N 0 53W
Melville Island Canada 78 H8 75 30N 112 00W
Memphis USA 79 K4 35 10N 90 00W
Menam *r.* Thailand 60 B4 15 00N 100 00E
Mendip Hills England 41 E4 51 18N 2 45W
Mendoza Argentina 85 C4 32 48S 68 52W
Menorca *i.* Balearic Islands 50 H3 39 45N 4 15E
Mentawai Islands Indonesia 60 A2 2 00N 99 00E
Menzies, Mount Antarctica 86 73 30S 62 00E
Meon *r.* England 38 C1 50 55N 1 10W
Mere England 38 B2 51 06N 2 16W
Mérida Mexico 79 L3 20 59N 89 39W
Mersey *r.* England 34 C2 53 20N 2 55W
Merseyside *co.* England 34 C2 53 30N 3 20W
Mersin Turkey 43 N3 36 47N 34 37E
Merthyr Tydfil Wales 36 D1 51 46N 3 23W
Merthyr Tydfil *u.a.* Wales 36 D1 51 48N 3 20W
Merton England 38 D2 51 25N 0 12W
Messina Italy 51 E3 38 13N 15 33E
Metz France 48 G4 49 07N 6 11E
Meuse *r.* Belgium/France 49 C4 50 30N 5 00E
Mexicali Mexico 79 H4 32 36N 115 30W
MEXICO 79 H4/K2

Mexico City Mexico **79** K2 19 25N 99 10W
Mexico, Gulf of Mexico **79** L3 25 00N 90 00W
Miami U.S.A. **79** L3 25 45N 80 15W
Michigan state USA **79** L5 45 00N 85 00W
Michigan, Lake Canada/USA **79** L5 45 00N 87 00W
Mickle Fell sum. England **34** C3 54 38N 2 18W
Middlesbrough England **35** D3 54 35N 1 14W
Middlesbrough u.a. England **35** D3 54 33N 1 04W
Midlothian u.a. Scotland **33** F3 55 50N 3 05W
Milan Italy **51** B6 45 28N 9 12E
Mildenhall England **39** E3 52 21N 0 30E
Mildura Australia **72** E2 34 12S 142 09E
Milford Haven Wales **36** B1 51 44N 5 02W
Milford Sound New Zealand **73** B2 44 41S 167 56E
Milton Keynes England **38** D3 52 02N 0 42W
Milton Keynes u.a. England **38** D3 52 00N 0 40W
Milton Ness c. Scotland **31** G1 56 40N 2 20W
Milwaukee USA **79** L5 43 03N 87 56W
Minch, The sd. Scotland **30** C3/D3 58 00N 6 00W
Mindanao i. The Philippines **60** D3 8 00N 125 00E
Mindoro i. The Philippines **60** D4 13 00N 121 00E
Minehead England **40** D4 51 13N 3 29W
Mingulay i. Scotland **30** B1 56 49N 7 38W
Minneapolis USA **79** L5 45 00N 93 15W
Minnesota state USA **79** K5 47 00N 95 00W
Minsk Belarus **42** L5 53 51N 27 30E
Miskolc Hungary **42** L5 48 07N 20 47E
Misool i. Indonesia **60** E2 1 50S 129 55E
Misratah Libya **66** D4 32 23N 15 06E
Mississippi r. USA **79** K4 33 00N 90 30W
Mississippi state USA **79** K4 32 00N 90 00W
Missouri r. USA **79** J5 48 00N 109 00W
Missouri state USA **79** K4 38 00N 93 00W
Miyazaki Japan **59** L1 31 56N 131 27E
Mobile USA **79** L4 30 40N 88 05W
Moçambique Mozambique **67** E3 15 03S 40 45E
Módena Italy **51** C6 44 39N 10 55E
Moffat Scotland **33** F3 55 20N 3 27W
Mogadishu Somalia **67** E5 2 02N 45 21E
Mold Wales **36** D3 53 10N 3 08W
Moldau r. Czech Republic **49** H3 49 30N 14 15E
MOLDOVA **42** M5
Moluccas is. Indonesia **60** D3/E2 4 00S 127 00E
Molucca Sea Indonesia **60** D2 0 30S 125 30E
Mombasa Kenya **67** D4 4 04S 39 40E
MONACO **48** G1
Monadhliath Mountains Scotland **31** E2 57 10N 4 00W
Monaghan Republic of Ireland **32** C2 54 15N 6 58W
Monaghan co. Republic of Ireland **32** B2/C2 54 10N 7 00W
Monforte Spain **50** B5 42 32N 7 30W
MONGOLIA **57** L2
Monmouth Wales **37** E1 51 50N 2 43W
Monmouthshire u.a. Wales **37** E1 51 47N 2 55W
Monopoli Italy **51** F4 40 57N 17 18E
Monrovia Liberia **66** A3 6 20N 10 46W
Montana state USA **79** H5 47 00N 111 00W
Montauban France **48** D2 44 01N 1 20E
Montbéliard France **48** G3 47 31N 6 48E
Mont Blanc mt. France/Italy **48** G2 45 50N 6 52E
Monte Carlo Monaco **48** G1 43 44N 7 25E
Montenegro admin. Yugoslavia **42** K4 42 30N 19 00E
Monterrey Mexico **79** J3 25 40N 100 20W
Montes Claros tn. Brazil **84** E6 16 45S 43 52W
Montevideo Uruguay **85** D4 34 55S 56 10W
Montgomery Wales **36** D2 52 34N 3 10W
Montluçon France **48** E3 46 20N 2 36E
Montpellier France **48** E1 43 36N 3 53E
Montréal Canada **79** M5 45 32N 73 36W
Montreux Switzerland **49** D2 46 27N 6 55E
Montrose Scotland **31** G1 56 43N 2 29W
Monza Italy **51** B6 45 35N 9 16E
Moosonee Canada **79** L6 51 18N 80 39W
Moray u.a. Scotland **31** F2 57 20N 3 10W
Moray Firth est. Scotland **31** F2 57 45N 3 45W
Morecambe England **34** C3 54 04N 2 53W
Morecambe Bay England **34** B3/C3 54 00N 3 00W
Morelia Mexico **79** J2 19 40N 101 11W
Moreton-in-Marsh England **38** C2 51 59N 1 42W
Morioka Japan **59** N2 39 43N 141 08E
Morlaix France **48** B4 48 35N 3 50W
MOROCCO **66** B6
Moroni Comoros **67** E3 11 40S 43 16E
Morotai i. Indonesia **60** D3 2 30N 128 30E
Morven mt. Scotland **31** F3 58 14N 3 42W
Moscow Russia **56** D3 55 45N 37 42E
Mosel r. Germany/France **49** D3 50 00N 7 00E
Móstoles Spain **50** D4 40 19N 3 53W
Mosul Iraq **61** E4 36 21N 43 08E
Motherwell Scotland **33** E3 55 48N 3 59W
Moulmein Myanmar **58** E2 16 30N 97 39E
Mount Hagen tn. Papua New Guinea **72** E5 5 54S 114 13E
Mount Isa tn. Australia **72** D3 20 44S 139 29E
Mount Magnet tn. Australia **72** B3 28 02S 117 50E
Mounts Bay England **40** B3 50 05N 5 30W
Moyale Kenya **66** D5 3 31N 39 04E
Moyle district Northern Ireland **32** C3 55 10N 6 10W
MOZAMBIQUE **67** D3
Mozambique Channel Mozambique/Madagascar **67** E3 18 00S 42 00E
Muck i. Scotland **30** C1 56 50N 6 15W
Muckle Roe i. Scotland **29** D3 60 22N 1 26W
Mudanjiang China **59** D4 44 36N 129 42E
Mukalla Yemen Republic **61** E2 14 34N 49 09E
Mulhacén mt. Spain **50** D2 37 04N 3 19W
Mulhouse France **48** G3 47 45N 7 21E
Mull i. Scotland **30** C1/D1 56 25N 6 00W
Mullion England **40** B3 50 01N 5 14W
Mull Head c. Scotland **29** C2 59 20N 2 58W
Mull of Galloway c. Scotland **32** E2 54 38N 4 50W
Mull of Kintyre c. Scotland **32** D3 55 17N 5 55W
Mull of Oa c. Scotland **32** C3 55 35N 6 20W
Mull, Sound of Scotland **30** D1 56 30N 6 00W
Multan Pakistan **58** C4 30 10N 71 36E
Mumbai (Bombay) India **58** C2 18 56N 72 51E
München Gladbach Germany **49** D4 51 12N 6 25E
Munich Germany **49** F3 48 08N 11 35E
Münster Germany **49** D4 51 58N 7 37E

Mur r. Europe **49** H2 47 00N 14 00E
Murchison r. Australia **72** B3 26 00S 117 00E
Murcia Spain **50** E2 37 59N 1 08W
Murmansk Russia **56** D4 68 59N 33 08E
Muroran Japan **59** N3 42 21N 140 59E
Murray r. Australia **72** E2 35 40S 144 00E
Murrumbidgee r. Australia **72** E2 35 00S 145 00E
Muscat Oman **61** F3 23 37N 58 38E
Musi r. Indonesia **60** B2 3 00S 104 00E
Musselburgh Scotland **33** F3 55 57N 3 04W
Mwanza Tanzania **67** D4 2 31S 32 56E
Mweru, Lake Congo Dem. Rep./Zambia **67** C4 8 30S 28 30E
MYANMAR (BURMA) **58** E3
Mykolayiv Ukraine **56** D2 46 57N 32 00E
Mynydd Eppynt hills Wales **36** D2 52 02N 3 35W
Mynydd Preseli hills Wales **36** C1 51 58N 4 45W
Mysore India **58** C2 12 18N 76 37E

N

Naberezhnyye Chelny Russia **56** F3 55 42N 52 19E
Nabeul Tunisia **42** J3 36 30N 10 44E
Nador Morocco **50** D1 35 10N 3 00W
Nagano Japan **59** M2 36 39N 138 10E
Nagasaki Japan **59** K1 32 45N 129 52E
Nagoya Japan **59** M3 35 08N 136 53E
Nagpur India **58** C3 21 10N 79 12E
Nairn Scotland **31** F2 57 35N 3 53W
Nairn r. Scotland **31** E2 57 28N 4 10W
Nairobi Kenya **67** D4 1 17S 36 50E
Najran Saudi Arabia **61** E2 17 37N 44 40E
Namangan Uzbekistan **56** H2 40 59N 71 41E
Namib Desert Namibia **67** B2 22 00S 14 00E
NAMIBIA **67** B2
Nampo North Korea **59** D3 38 51N 125 10E
Nampula Mozambique **66** D3 15 09S 39 14E
Namur Belgium **49** C4 50 28N 4 52E
Nanchang China **59** C2 28 33N 115 58E
Nancy France **48** G4 48 42N 6 12E
Nanjing China **59** C3 32 03N 118 47E
Nanning China **59** B2 22 50N 108 19E
Nan Shan mts. China **59** A3 38 00N 99 00E
Nantes France **48** C3 47 14N 1 35W
Napier New Zealand **73** D3 39 30S 176 54E
Naples Italy **51** E4 40 50N 14 15E
Napo r. Ecuador/Peru **84** B7 1 30S 74 30W
Narbonne France **48** E1 43 11N 3 00E
Narmada r. India **58** C3 22 00N 78 00E
Narvik Norway **42** K9 68 26N 17 25E
Nassau The Bahamas **79** M3 25 05N 77 20W
Nasser, Lake Egypt **61** D3 22 35N 31 40E
Natal Brazil **84** F7 5 46S 35 15W
NAURU **5**
Ndjamena Chad **66** D4 12 10N 14 59E
Ndola Zambia **67** C3 13 00S 28 39E
Neath Wales **36** D1 51 40N 3 48W
Neath Port Talbot u.a. Wales **36** D1 51 40N 3 45W
Nebraska state USA **79** J5 42 00N 102 00W
Negro r. Argentina **85** C4 39 39S 67 30W
Negro r. Bolivia/Brazil **84** C7 1 00S 62 20W
Negros i. The Philippines **60** D3 10 00N 123 00E
Neiva Colombia **84** B8 2 58N 75 15W
Nelson England **34** C2 53 51N 2 13W
Nelson New Zealand **73** C2 41 30S 172 30E
Nelson r. Canada **78** K6 57 00N 94 00W
Nemuro Japan **59** P3 43 22N 145 36E
Nene r. England **39** E3 52 45N 0 10E
Nen Jiang r. China **59** D4 45 00N 124 00E
NEPAL **58** D3
Nevada state USA **79** H4 39 00N 118 00W
Nevers France **48** E3 47 00N 3 09E
Nevis i. St. Kitts and Nevis **79** N2 17 00N 62 30W
Newark USA **79** M5 40 43N 74 11W
Newark-on-Trent England **37** G3 53 05N 0 49W
New Britain i. Papua New Guinea **72** F5 4 45S 150 30E
New Brunswick province Canada **79** N5 47 30N 66 00W
Newburgh Scotland **33** F4 57 18N 2 00W
Newbury England **38** C2 51 25N 1 20W
New Caledonia i. Pacific Ocean **5** 22 00S 165 00E
Newcastle Australia **72** F2 32 57S 151 43E
Newcastle Northern Ireland **32** D2 54 12N 5 54W
Newcastle Emlyn Wales **36** C2 52 02N 4 28W
Newcastle-under-Lyme England **37** E3 53 00N 2 14W
Newcastle upon Tyne England **34** D3 54 59N 1 35W
New Cumnock Scotland **33** E3 55 24N 4 12W
Newfoundland i. Canada **79** P5 53 51N 56 56W
Newfoundland and Labrador province Canada **78** P6 56 00N 60 00W
New Galloway Scotland **33** E3 55 05N 4 10W
New Hampshire state USA **79** M5 43 00N 72 00W
New Ireland i. Papua New Guinea **72** F5 3 15S 152 30E
New Jersey state USA **79** M4 40 00N 75 00W
Newman Australia **72** B3 23 22S 119 43E
Newmarket England **39** E3 52 15N 0 25E
New Mexico state USA **79** J4 35 00N 107 00W
New Orleans USA **79** K3 30 00N 90 03W
New Plymouth New Zealand **73** C3 39 04S 174 04E
Newport Isle of Wight England **38** C1 50 42N 1 18W
Newport Telford and Wrekin England **37** E2 52 47N 2 22W
Newport Wales **36** D1 51 35N 3 00W
Newport u.a. Wales **36** D1/E1 51 33N 3 00W
Newquay England **40** B3 50 25N 5 05W
New Quay Wales **36** C2 52 13N 4 22W
Newry Northern Ireland **32** C2 54 11N 6 20W
Newry and Mourne district Northern Ireland **32** C2 54 10N 6 20W
New Siberian Islands Russia **57** Q5 75 00N 145 00E
New South Wales state Australia **72** E2 32 00S 145 00E
Newton Abbot England **40** D3 50 32N 3 36W
Newton Aycliffe England **34** D3 54 37N 1 34W
Newtonmore Scotland **31** E2 57 04N 4 08W
Newton Stewart Scotland **33** E2 54 57N 4 29W
Newtown Wales **36** D2 52 32N 3 19W

Newtownabbey Northern Ireland **32** D2 54 40N 5 54W
Newtownabbey district Northern Ireland **32** D2 54 45N 5 55W
Newtownards Northern Ireland **32** D2 54 36N 5 41W
Newtownhamilton Northern Ireland **32** C2 54 12N 6 35W
Newtownstewart Northern Ireland **32** B2 54 43N 7 24W
New York USA **79** M5 40 40N 73 50W
New York state USA **79** M5 43 00N 76 00W
NEW ZEALAND **73**
Ngaoundéré Cameroon **66** D3 7 20N 13 35E
Nguru Nigeria **66** D4 12 53N 10 30E
Nha-Trang Vietnam **60** B4 12 15N 109 10E
Niamey Niger **66** C4 13 32N 2 05E
Nias i. Indonesia **60** A3 1 00N 97 30E
NICARAGUA **79** L2
Nicaragua, Lake Nicaragua **79** L2 11 50N 86 00W
Nice France **48** G1 43 42N 7 16E
Nicobar Islands India **58** E1 8 30N 94 00E
Nicosia Cyprus **43** N3 35 11N 33 23E
Nidd r. England **34** D2 54 05N 1 40W
Nieuwpoort Belgium **39** G2 51 08N 2 45E
NIGER **66** C4
Niger r. Africa **66** B4 11 00N 5 00W
NIGERIA **66** C3
Niigata Japan **59** M2 37 58N 139 02E
Nijmegen Netherlands **49** C4 51 50N 5 52E
Nile r. Sudan/Egypt **61** D3 28 00N 31 00E
Nimba, Mount Guinea/Liberia **66** B3 7 39N 8 30W
Nîmes France **48** F1 43 50N 4 21E
Niort France **48** C3 46 19N 0 27W
Ni≠ Yugoslavia **42** L4 43 20N 21 54E
Niteroi Brazil **84** E5 22 54S 43 06W
Nith r. Scotland **33** F3 55 15N 3 50W
Nizhniy Novgorod Russia **56** E3 56 20N 44 00E
Nizhniy Tagil Russia **56** G3 58 00N 59 58E
Norfolk USA **79** M4 36 54N 76 18W
Norfolk co. England **39** E3/F3 52 45N 1 00E
Norfolk Broads geog. reg. England **39** F3 52 45N 1 30E
Norilsk Russia **57** J4 69 21N 88 02E
Normandy geog. reg. France **48** C4/D4 49 00N 0 00
Norrköping Sweden **42** K7 58 35N 16 10E
Northallerton England **35** D3 54 20N 1 26W
Northampton England **38** D3 52 14N 0 54W
Northamptonshire co. England **38** C3/D3 52 20N 1 00W
North Ayrshire u.a. Scotland **32/33** D3/E3 55 30N 5 05W
North Berwick Scotland **33** G4 56 04N 2 44W
North Cape New Zealand **73** C4 34 25S 173 03E
North Carolina state USA **79** M4 36 00N 80 00W
North Channel British Isles **32** D2/3 55 20N 5 50W
North Dakota state USA **79** J5 47 00N 102 00W
North Down district Northern Ireland **32** D2 54 35N 5 50W
North Downs hills England **38/39** D2/E2 51 15N 0 30E
North Dvina r. Russia **56** E4 63 00N 43 00E
North East Lincolnshire u.a. England **35** E3 53 30N 0 10W
Northern Ireland province United Kingdom **32** B2 54 40N 7 00W
NORTHERN MARIANAS **5**
Northern Territory Australia **72** D4 19 00S 132 00E
North Esk r. Scotland **31** G1 56 50N 2 50W
North Foreland c. England **39** F2 51 23N 1 27E
North Friesian Islands Germany **49** E6 54 00N 8 00E
North Island New Zealand **73** D3 39 00N 176 00E
NORTH KOREA **59** D4
North Lanarkshire u.a. Scotland **33** F3 55 50N 3 55W
North Lincolnshire u.a. England **35** E3 53 40N 0 40W
North Pole Arctic Ocean **86** 90 00N
North Ronaldsay i. Scotland **29** C2 59 23N 2 26W
North Sea Atlantic Ocean **42** G7 57 00N 4 00E
North Shields England **35** D4 55 01N 1 26W
North Uist i. Scotland **30** B2 57 04N 7 16W
Northumberland co. England **33** G3/H3 55 10N 2 00W
Northwest Highlands Scotland **30/31** D2/E3 58 00N 5 00W
North West Somerset u.a. England **38** B2 51 25N 2 50W
Northwest Territories territory Canada **78** H7 64 00N 110 30W
Northwich England **34** C2 53 16N 2 32W
North York Moors England **35** E3 55 23N 0 45W
North Yorkshire co. England **34/35** D3/E3 54 05N 1 20W
Norton England **35** E3 54 08N 0 48W
NORWAY **42** H7/M9
Norwich England **39** F3 52 38N 1 18E
Nottingham England **37** F2 52 58N 1 10W
Nottingham City u.a. England **37** F2 52 58N 1 10W
Nottinghamshire co. England **37** F3/G3 53 20N 1 00W
Nouadhibou Mauritania **66** A5 20 54N 17 01W
Nouakchott Mauritania **66** A4 18 09N 15 58W
Novara Italy **51** B6 45 27N 8 37E
Nova Scotia province Canada **79** N5 45 30N 63 00W
Novaya Zemlya i. Russia **56** F5 74 00N 55 00E
Novgorod Russia **42** N7 58 30N 31 20E
Novokuznetsk Russia **57** J3 53 45N 87 12E
Novosibirsk Russia **56** J3 55 04N 83 05E
Nuevo Laredo Mexico **79** K3 27 39N 99 30W
Nu Jiang (Salween) r. China/Myanmar **58** E4 31 30N 94 00E
Nullarbor Plain Australia **72** C2 30 30S 129 00E
Nunavut territory Canada **78** K7 67 30N 95 30W
Nuneaton England **37** F2 52 32N 1 28W
Nunivak i. USA **78** C6 60 00N 166 00W
Nuremberg Germany **49** F3 49 27N 11 05E
Nuuk (Godthåb) Greenland **78** P7 64 10N 51 40W
Nyala Sudan **61** C2 12 01N 24 50E
Nyasa, Lake (Lake Malawi) Malawi/Mozambique **67** D3 12 00S 35 00E

O

Oahe, Lake USA **79** J5 45 00N 100 00W

Oamaru New Zealand **73** C1 45 06S 170 58E
Ob r. Russia **56** G4 64 00N 65 00E
Oban Scotland **30** D1 56 25N 5 29W
Oberammergau Germany **49** F2 47 35N 11 07E
Obihiro Japan **59** N3 42 56N 143 10E
Obi Islands i. Indonesia **60** D3 1 30S 127 30E
Ochil Hills Scotland **31** F1 56 15N 3 30W
Odense Denmark **42** H7 55 24N 10 25E
Oder r. Europe **49** H5 53 00N 14 30E
Odessa Ukraine **56** D2 46 30N 30 46E
Ogbomoso Nigeria **66** C3 8 05N 4 11E
Ohio r. USA **79** L4 39 00N 85 00W
Ohio state USA **79** L5 40 00N 83 00W
Oiapoque Brazil **84** D8 3 54N 51 46W
Oise r. France **48** E4 49 30N 3 00E
Oita Japan **59** L1 33 15N 131 36E
Okavango Swamp Botswana **67** C3 19 00S 23 00E
Okayama Japan **59** L1 34 40N 133 54E
Okehampton England **40** C3 50 44N 4 00W
Okhotsk, Sea of Russia **57** Q3 56 00N 145 00E
Oki Islands Japan **59** L2 36 05N 133 00E
Oklahoma state USA **79** K4 36 00N 98 00W
Oklahoma City USA **79** K4 35 28N 97 33W
Öland i. Sweden **42** K7 56 45N 51 50E
Olbia Italy **51** B4 40 56N 9 30E
Oldenburg Germany **49** E5 53 08N 8 13E
Oldham England **34** C2 53 33N 2 07W
Oldmeldrum Scotland **31** G2 57 20N 2 20W
Olongapo The Philippines **60** D4 14 49N 120 17E
Olympus, Mt. Greece **42** L4 40 05N 22 21E
Omagh Northern Ireland **32** B2 54 36N 7 18W
Omagh district Northern Ireland **32** B2 54 30N 7 30W
Omaha USA **79** K5 41 15N 96 00W
OMAN **61** F3
Oman, Gulf of Iran/Oman **61** F3 24 30N 58 30E
Omdurman Sudan **61** D2 15 37N 32 29E
Omsk Russia **56** H3 55 00N 73 24E
Onega, Lake l. Russia **56** D4 62 00N 40 00E
Onitsha Nigeria **66** C3 6 10N 6 47E
Ontario province Canada **79** L6 51 00N 85 00W
Ontario, Lake Canada/USA **79** M5 43 45N 78 00W
Oostende Belgium **49** B4 51 13N 2 55E
Oporto Portugal **50** A4 41 09N 8 37W
Oran Algeria **66** B6 35 45N 0 38W
Orange France **48** F2 44 08N 4 48E
Orange r. Southern Africa **67** B2 29 00S 19 00E
Ord r. Australia **72** C4 15 00S 129 00E
Örebro Sweden **42** K7 59 17N 15 13E
Oregon state USA **79** G5 44 00N 120 00W
Orel Russia **56** D3 52 58N 36 04E
Orenburg Russia **56** F3 51 50N 55 00E
Orford Ness c. England **39** F2 52 05N 1 34E
Orinoco r. Venezuela/Colombia **84** C8 6 40N 64 30W
Oristano Italy **51** B3 39 54N 8 36E
Orkney Islands u.a. Scotland **29** B1/C2 59 00N 3 00W
Orléans France **48** D3 47 54N 1 54E
Orne r. France **41** G1/2 49 00N 1 30W
Oronsay i. Scotland **32** C4 56 00N 6 15W
Orsk Russia **56** F3 51 13N 58 35E
Ortles mt. Italy **49** F2 46 31N 10 33E
Oruro Bolivia **84** C6 17 59S 67 08W
Osaka Japan **59** M1 34 40N 135 30E
Osh Kyrgyzstan **56** H2 40 37N 72 49E
Oslo Norway **42** J7 59 56N 10 45E
Osnabrück Germany **49** E5 52 17N 8 03E
Osorno Chile **85** B3 40 35S 73 14W
Ostrava Czech Republic **42** K5 49 50N 18 15E
Osumi Islands Japan **59** L1 30 30N 130 30E
Oswestry England **36** D2 52 52N 3 03W
Otranto Italy **51** G4 40 08N 18 30E
Ottawa Canada **79** M5 46 00N 77 00W
Ouagadougou Burkina **66** B4 12 20N 1 40W
Oubangui r. Central Africa **67** C5 4 00N 21 00E
Oujda Morocco **66** B6 34 41N 1 45W
Oulu Finland **42** M9 65 02N 25 27E
Oundle England **38** D3 52 29N 0 29W
Ouse r. England **35** D2 53 40N 1 05W
Outer Hebrides is. Scotland **30** B1/C3 58 00N 7 00W
Out Skerries is. Scotland **29** E3 60 25N 0 46W
Oviedo Spain **50** C5 43 21N 7 18W
Oxford England **38** C2 51 46N 1 15W
Oxfordshire co. England **38** C2 51 50N 1 25W

P

Pabbay i. Scotland **30** B2 57 47N 7 14W
Pacific Ocean **79** J2
Padang Indonesia **60** B2 1 00S 100 21E
Paderborn Germany **49** E4 51 43N 8 44E
Padstow England **40** C3 50 33N 4 56W
Padua Italy **51** C6 45 24N 11 53E
Paisley Scotland **33** E3 55 50N 4 26W
Pakanbaru Indonesia **60** B3 0 33N 101 30E
PAKISTAN **58** B3
Palau Islands Pacific Ocean **60** E3 7 30N 134 30E
Palawan i. The Philippines **60** C3 10 00N 119 00E
Palembang Indonesia **60** B2 2 59S 104 45E
Palermo Italy **51** D3 38 08N 13 23E
Palma Balearic Islands **50** G3 39 35N 2 39E
Palmerston North New Zealand **73** D2 40 22S 175 37E
Pamirs mts. Asia **58** C4 38 00N 74 00E
Pamplona Spain **50** E5 42 49N 1 39W
PANAMA **79** L1
Panamá Panama **79** M1 8 57N 19 30W
Panama Canal Panama **79** L1 9 00N 80 00W
Panay i. The Philippines **60** D4 11 00N 122 00E
Pantelleria i. Italy **51** D2 36 00N 12 00E
Papa Stour i. Scotland **29** D3 60 20N 1 42W
Papa Westray i. Scotland **29** C2 59 22N 2 54W
PAPUA NEW GUINEA **72** E5
PARAGUAY **84** D5
Paraguay r. South America **84** D5 21 20S 58 20W
Paramaribo Suriname **84** D8 5 52N 55 14W
Paraná Argentina **85** C4 31 45S 60 30W
Paraná r. South America **85** D5 30 00S 59 50W
Paris France **48** E4 48 52N 2 20E

Parma Italy **51** C6 44 48N 10 19E
Parnaiba Brazil **84** E7 2 58S 41 46W
Parrett *r.* England **41** E4 51 05N 2 55W
Parry Islands Canada **78** J8 75 15N 109 00W
Pasto Colombia **84** B8 1 12N 77 17W
Patagonia *geog. reg.* Argentina **85** C3 48 00S 70 00W
Patna India **58** D3 25 37N 85 12E
Patra Greece **42** L3 38 14N 21 44E
Pau France **48** C1 43 18N 0 22W
Peace *r.* Canada **78** H6 57 30N 117 00W
Pechora Russia **43** T9 65 14N 57 18E
Pechora *r.* Russia **43** S9 66 00N 53 00E
Peebles Scotland **33** F3 55 39N 3 12W
Peel Isle of Man British Isles **33** E2 54 14N 4 42W
Peel Fell *sum.* Scotland/England **33** G3 55 17N 2 35W
Pegasus Bay New Zealand **73** C2 43 22S 172 55E
Pegu Myanmar **58** E2 17 18N 96 31E
Peipus, Lake Estonis/Russia **42** M7 58 00N 27 45E
Peloponnese *geog. reg.* Greece **42** L3 37 00N 22 00E
Pelotas Brazil **85** D4 31 45S 52 20W
Pematangsiantar Indonesia **60** A3 2 59N 99 01E
Pembroke Wales **36** C1 51 41N 4 55W
Pembrokeshire *u.a.* Wales **36** B1/C1 51 50N 5 00W
Peñalara *mt.* Spain **50** D4 40 51N 3 58W
Penicuik Scotland **33** F3 55 50N 3 14W
Pennines *hills* England **34** C3 54 30N 2 10W
Pennsylvania *state* USA **79** M5 41 00N 78 00W
Penrith England **34** C3 54 40N 2 44W
Penryn England **40** B3 50 09N 5 06W
Pentland Firth *sd.* Scotland **29** B1 58 45N 3 10W
Pentland Hills Scotland **33** F3 55 45N 3 30W
Pen-y-ghent *sum.* England **34** C3 54 10N 2 14W
Penza Russia **56** E3 53 11N 45 00E
Penzance England **40** B3 50 07N 5 33W
Perm Russia **56** F3 58 01N 56 10E
Perpignan France **48** E1 42 42N 2 54E
Perth Australia **72** B2 31 57S 115 52E
Perth Scotland **31** F1 56 42N 3 28W
Perth and Kinross *u.a.* Scotland **31** E1/F1 56 45N 3 50W
PERU **84** B6
Perugia Italy **51** D5 43 07N 12 23E
Pescara Italy **51** E5 42 27N 14 13E
Peshawar Pakistan **58** C4 34 01N 71 33E
Peterborough England **38** D3 52 35N 0 15W
Peterborough *u.a.* England **38** D3 52 40N 0 15W
Peterhead Scotland **31** H2 57 30N 1 46W
Peterlee England **35** D3 54 46N 1 19W
Petersfield England **38** D2 51 00N 0 56W
Petropavlovsk Kazakhstan **56** G3 54 53N 69 13E
Petropavlovsk-Kamchatskiy Russia **57** R3 53 03N 158 43E
Petrozavodsk Russia **42** N8 61 46N 34 19E
Pforzheim Germany **49** E3 48 53N 8 41E
Philadelphia USA **79** M4 40 00N 75 10W
PHILIPPINES **60** D3/4
Phnom Penh Cambodia **60** B4 11 35N 104 55E
Phoenix USA **79** H4 33 30N 112 03W
Piacenza Italy **51** B6 45 03N 9 41E
Pickering England **35** E3 54 14N 0 46W
Pickering, Vale of England **35** E3 54 10N 0 45W
Pietermaritzburg Republic of South Africa **67** D2 29 36S 30 24E
Pilcomayo *r.* South America **84** C5 24 00S 61 00W
Piraeus Greece **42** L3 37 57N 23 42E
Pisa Italy **51** C5 43 43N 10 24E
Pitcairn Islands Pacific Ocean **4** 25 04S 130 06W
Pitlochry Scotland **31** F1 56 43N 3 45W
Piura Peru **84** A7 5 15S 80 38W
Plenty, Bay of New Zealand **73** D3 37 48S 177 12E
Ploieşti Romania **42** M4 44 57N 26 01E
Plovdiv Bulgaria **42** L4 42 08N 24 45E
Plymouth England **40** C3 50 23N 4 10W
Plymouth *u.a.* England **40** C3 50 24N 4 10W
Plynlimon *mt.* Wales **36** D2 52 28N 3 47W
Po *r.* Italy **51** C6/D6 45 00N 12 00E
Pobeda Peak Kyrgyzstan **56** J2 42 25N 80 15E
Pointe Noire *tn.* Congo **66** D2 4 46S 11 53E
Poitiers France **48** D3 46 35N 0 20E
POLAND **42** K6
Ponta Grossa Brazil **85** D5 25 07S 50 09W
Pontardulais Wales **36** C1 51 43N 4 02W
Pontefract England **35** D2 53 42N 1 18W
Pontianak Indonesia **60** B2 0 05S 109 16E
Pontypool Wales **36** D1 51 43N 3 02W
Pontypridd Wales **36** D1 51 37N 3 22W
Poole England **41** F3 50 43N 1 59W
Poole England *u.a.* **41** F3 50 45N 1 58W
Poolewe Scotland **30** D2 57 45N 5 37W
Poopo, Lake Bolivia **84** C6 18 30S 67 20W
Popocatepetl *vol.* Mexico **79** K2 19 02N 98 38W
Porbandar India **58** B3 21 04N 69 40E
Portadown Northern Ireland **32** C2 54 26N 6 27W
Port Askaig Scotland **32** C3 55 51N 6 07W
Port Augusta Australia **72** D2 32 30S 137 48E
Port-au-Prince Haiti **79** M2 18 33N 72 20W
Port Elizabeth Republic of South Africa **67** C1 33 58S 25 36E
Port Ellen Scotland **32** C3 55 39N 6 12W
Port Gentil Gabon **66** C2 0 40S 8 50E
Port Glasgow Scotland **33** E3 55 56N 4 41W
Port Harcourt Nigeria **66** C3 4 43N 7 05E
Port Hedland Australia **72** B3 20 18S 118 35E
Porthmadog Wales **36** C2 52 55N 4 08W
Portknockie Scotland **31** G2 57 42N 2 52W
Portland USA **78** G5 45 32N 122 40W
Portland Bill *c.* England **41** E3 50 31N 2 27W
Port Lincoln Australia **72** D2 34 44S 135 52E
Port Moresby Papua New Guinea **72** E5 9 30S 147 07E
Portnahaven Scotland **32** C3 55 41N 6 31W
Pôrto Alegre Brazil **85** D4 30 03S 51 10W
Port of Ness Scotland **30** C3 58 29N 6 13W
Port of Spain Trinidad and Tobago **79** N2 10 38N 61 31W
Porto Novo Benin **66** C3 6 30N 2 47E
Pôrto Velho Brazil **84** C7 8 45S 63 54W
Portpatrick Scotland **32** D2 54 51N 5 07W
Port Pirie Australia **72** D2 33 10S 138 02E
Portree Scotland **30** C2 57 24N 6 12W
Portrush Northern Ireland **32** C3 55 12N 6 40W
Port Said Egypt **61** D4 31 17N 32 18E
Portsmouth England **38** C1 50 48N 1 05W
Portsmouth *u.a.* England **38** C1 50 50N 1 04W
Portsoy Scotland **31** G2 57 41N 2 41W
Portstewart Northern Ireland **32** C3 55 11N 6 43W
Port Sudan Sudan **61** D2 19 38N 37 07E
Port Talbot Wales **36** D1 51 36N 3 47W
PORTUGAL **50** A3
Potenza Italy **51** E4 40 38N 15 48E
Potsdam Germany **49** G5 52 24N 13 04E
Powys *u.a.* Wales **36** D2 52 10N 3 30W
Poyang Hu *l.* China **59** C2 29 00N 116 30E
Poznań Poland **42** K6 52 25N 16 53E
Prague Czech Republic **42** J6 50 06N 14 26E
Prato Italy **51** C5 43 53N 11 06E
Preston England **34** C2 53 46N 2 42W
Prestwick Scotland **33** E3 55 30N 4 37W
Pretoria Republic of South Africa **67** C2 25 45S 28 12E
Prijedor Bosnia-Herzegovina **51** F6 45 00N 16 41E
Prince Edward Island *province* Canada **79** N5 46 30N 63 00W
Prince Rupert Canada **78** F6 54 09N 130 20W
Principe *i.* Gulf of Guinea **66** C3 1 37N 7 27E
Pripet *r.* Belarus **42** M6 52 00N 28 00E
Provence *geog. reg.* France **48** F1/G1 44 00N 6 00E
Providence USA **79** M5 41 50N 71 28W
Providence, Cape New Zealand **73** B1 46 01S 166 28E
Prudhoe Bay *tn.* USA **78** E7 70 05N 148 20W
Pskov Russia **42** M7 57 48N 28 26E
Pucallpa Peru **84** B7 8 21S 74 33W
Puebla Mexico **79** K2 19 03N 98 10W
Puerto Montt Chile **85** B3 41 28S 73 00W
PUERTO RICO **79** N2
Puig Mayor *mt.* Balearic Islands **50** G3 39 49N 2 47E
Pukekohe New Zealand **73** C3 37 12S 174 54E
Pune India **58** C2 18 34N 73 58E
Punta Arenas Chile **85** B2 53 10S 70 56W
Pusan South Korea **59** D3 35 05N 129 02E
Puy de Sancy *mt.* France **48** E2 45 32N 2 48E
Pwllheli Wales **36** C2 52 53N 4 25W
Pyongyang North Korea **59** D3 39 00N 125 47E
Pyrénées *mts.* France/Spain **50** F5 42 50N 0 30E

Q

Qaidam Pendi *(Qaidam Basin)* China **59** A4 37 30N 94 00E
QATAR **61** F3
Qattara Depression Egypt **61** C3 24 00N 27 30E
Qazvin Iran **61** E4 36 16N 50 00E
Qingdao China **59** D3 36 04N 120 22E
Qinghai Hu *l.* China **59** B3 37 00N 100 00E
Qiqihar China **59** D4 47 23N 124 00E
Qizil *r.* Iran **61** E4 36 00N 48 00E
Qom Iran **61** F4 34 39N 50 57E
Quantock Hills England **41** D4 51 05N 3 15W
Québec Canada **79** M5 46 50N 71 15W
Québec *province* Canada **79** M6 51 00N 75 00W
Queen Charlotte Islands Canada **78** F6 53 30N 131 50W
Queen Elizabeth Islands Canada **78** J8 77 30N 105 00W
Queensland *state* Australia **72** E3 22 00S 143 00E
Queenstown New Zealand **73** B1 45 02S 168 40E
Quetta Pakistan **58** B4 30 12N 67 00E
Quezon City The Philippines **60** D4 14 39N 121 02E
Qui Nhon Vietnam **60** B4 13 47N 109 11E
Quito Ecuador **84** B7 0 14S 78 30W

R

Raasay *i.* Scotland **30** C2 57 25N 6 05W
Rabat-Salé Morocco **66** B6 34 02N 6 51W
Rainier, Mount USA **78** G5 46 25N 121 45W
Raipur India **58** D3 21 16N 81 42E
Rajang *r.* Malaysia **60** C3 2 00N 114 00E
Rakaia *r.* New Zealand **73** C2 43 00S 172 00E
Ramsey Isle of Man British Isles **33** E2 54 19N 4 23W
Ramsgate England **39** F2 51 20N 1 25E
Randalstown Northern Ireland **32** C2 54 45N 6 19W
Rangitaiki *r.* New Zealand **73** D3 38 45S 177 00E
Ras Dashen *mt.* Ethiopia **61** D2 13 15N 38 27E
Rasht Iran **61** E4 37 18N 49 38E
Rathlin Island Northern Ireland **32** C3 55 20N 6 10W
Rathlin Sound Northern Ireland **32** C3 55 20N 6 25W
Rattray Scotland **31** F1 56 36N 3 20W
Ravenna Italy **51** D6 44 25N 12 12E
Rawalpindi Pakistan **58** C4 33 36N 73 04E
Reading England **38** D2 51 28N 0 59W
Reading *u.a.* England **38** D2 51 27N 0 59W
Recife Brazil **84** F7 8 06S 34 53W
Recklinghausen Germany **49** D4 51 37N 7 11E
Redbridge England **39** E2 51 34N 0 05E
Redcar England **35** D3 54 37N 1 04W
Redcar and Cleveland *u.a.* England **35** D3/E3 54 30N 1 00W
Redditch England **37** F2 52 19N 1 56W
Rede *r.* England **33** G3 55 15N 2 20W
Redhill *tn.* England **38** D2 51 14N 0 11W
Redruth England **40** B3 50 13N 5 14W
Red Sea Middle East **61** D3 27 00N 35 00E
Regensburg Germany **49** G3 49 01N 12 07E
Reggio di Calabria Italy **51** E3 38 06N 15 39E
Reggio nell'Emilia Italy **51** C6 44 42N 10 37E
Regina Canada **78** J6 50 30N 104 38W
Reigate England **38** D2 51 14N 0 13W
Reims France **48** F4 49 15N 4 02E
Remscheid Germany **49** D4 51 10N 7 11E
Renfrewshire *u.a.* Scotland **33** E3 55 50N 4 40W
Rennes France **48** C4 48 06N 1 40W
Reno USA **79** H4 39 32N 119 49W
REPUBLIC OF IRELAND **28**
REPUBLIC OF SOUTH AFRICA **67** C2
Resistencia Argentina **85** D5 27 28S 59 00W
Reutlingen Germany **49** E3 48 30N 9 13E
Reykjavík Iceland **42** B8 64 09N 21 58W
Rhayader Wales **36** D2 52 18N 3 30W
Rhine *r.* Europe **49** D4 50 30N 7 30E
Rhode Island *state* USA **79** M5 41 00N 71 00W
Rhodes *i.* Greece **42** M3 36 00N 28 00E
Rhondda Wales **36** D1 51 40N 3 30W
Rhondda Cynon Taff *u.a.* Wales **36** D1 51 40N 3 30W
Rhône *r.* Switzerland/France **48** F2 45 00N 4 50E
Rhum *i.* Scotland **30** C1/2 57 00N 6 20W
Rhyl Wales **36** D3 53 19N 3 29W
Ribble *r.* England **34** C2 53 45N 2 30W
Ribeirão Preto Brazil **84** E5 21 09S 47 48W
Richmond England **34** D3 54 24N 1 44W
Richmond USA **79** M4 37 34N 77 27W
Richmond upon Thames England **38** D2 51 28N 0 19W
Riga Latvia **42** L7 56 53N 24 08E
Rimini Italy **51** D6 44 03N 12 34E
Ringwood England **38** C1 50 51N 1 47W
Rio Branco *tn.* Brazil **84** C7 9 59S 67 49W
Rio de Janeiro *tn.* Brazil **84** E5 22 53S 43 17W
Rio Grande *r.* Mexico/USA **79** J3 29 30N 105 00W
Rio Grande *tn.* Brazil **85** D4 32 03S 52 08W
Ripon England **34** D3 54 08N 1 31W
River Plate Estuary Uruquay/Argentina **85** D4 35 00S 57 00W
Riyadh Saudi Arabia **61** E3 24 39N 46 46E
Roanne France **48** F3 46 02N 4 05E
Robson, Mount Canada **78** H6 53 08N 118 18W
Rochdale England **34** C2 53 38N 2 09W
Rochester England **39** E2 51 24N 0 30E
Rochester USA **79** M5 43 12N 77 37W
Rockhampton Australia **72** F3 23 22S 150 30E
Rocky Mountains Canada/USA **78/79** F7/J4 46 00N 110 00W
Roebourne Australia **72** B3 20 45S 117 08E
ROMANIA **42** L5
Rome Italy **51** D4 41 53N 12 30E
Romsey England **38** C1 50 59N 1 30W
Ronne Ice Shelf Antarctica **86** 77 00S 60 00W
Rora Head Scotland **29** B1 58 52N 3 26W
Roraima *mt.* Guyana **84** C8 5 14N 60 44W
Rosario Argentina **85** C4 33 00S 60 40W
Rosehearty Scotland **31** G2 57 42N 2 07W
Rosenheim Germany **51** D7 47 51N 12 09E
Rossano Italy **51** F3 39 35N 16 38E
Ross Ice Shelf Antarctica **86** 80 00S 180 00
Ross of Mull *p.* Scotland **30** C1 56 20N 6 10W
Ross-on-Wye England **37** E1 51 55N 2 35W
Ross Sea Antarctica **86** 75 00S 180 00
Rostock Germany **49** G6 54 06N 12 09E
Rostov-on-Don Russia **56** D2 47 15N 39 45E
Rotherham England **35** D2 53 26N 1 20W
Rothes Scotland **31** F2 57 31N 3 13W
Rothesay Scotland **32** D3 55 51N 5 03W
Rotorua New Zealand **73** D3 38 08S 176 14E
Rotterdam Netherlands **49** C4 51 54N 4 28E
Rouen France **48** D4 49 26N 1 05E
Rousay *i.* Scotland **29** B2 59 10N 3 00W
Royal Leamington Spa England **37** F2 52 18N 1 31W
Royal Tunbridge Wells England **39** E2 51 08N 0 16E
Royston England **38** D3 52 03N 0 01W
Ruapehu *mt.* New Zealand **73** D3 39 18S 175 34E
Rubha Hunish *c.* Scotland **30** C2 57 40N 6 20W
Rugby England **37** F2 52 23N 1 15W
Rugeley England **37** F2 52 46N 1 55W
Rügen *i.* Germany **49** G6 54 00N 14 00E
Rukwa, Lake Tanzania **67** D4 8 00S 33 00E
Runcorn England **34** C2 53 20N 2 44W
RUSSIA *see* RUSSIAN FEDERATION
RUSSIAN FEDERATION *(RUSSIA)* **56/57**
Rutland *u.a.* England **38** D3 52 42N 0 35W
Rutland Water *l.* England **38** D3 52 40N 0 37W
Ruvuma *r.* Tanzania/Mozambique **67** D3 11 00S 39 00E
Ruwenzori, Mount Congo Dem. Rep./Uganda **67** C5 0 23N 29 54E
RWANDA **67** C4
Ryazan Russia **56** D3 54 37N 39 43E
Rybinsk Russia **56** D3 58 03N 38 50E
Rybinsk Reservoir Russia **43** P7 59 00N 38 00E
Ryde England **38** C1 50 44N 1 10W
Rye England **39** E1 50 57N 0 44E
Ryukyu Islands Japan **59** D2 27 30N 127 30E

S

Saale *r.* Germany **49** F4 51 15N 12 00E
Saar *r.* Germany/France **49** D3 49 15N 6 30E
Saarbrücken Germany **49** D3 49 15N 6 58E
Sabadell Spain **50** G4 41 33N 2 07E
Sabah *admin.* Malaysia **60** C3 5 00N 115 00E
Sabhā Libya **66** D5 27 02N 14 26E
Sacramento USA **79** G4 38 32N 121 30W
Sado *i.* Japan **59** M2 38 20N 138 30E
Saffron Walden England **39** E3 52 01N 0 15E
Safi Morocco **66** B6 32 20N 9 17W
Sahara Desert North Africa **66** A5/E5 22 50N 0 00
St. Abb's Head *c.* Scotland **33** G3 55 55N 2 09W
St. Agnes England **40** B3 50 18N 5 13W
St. Albans England **38** D2 51 46N 0 21W
St. Albans Head *c.* England **41** E3 50 34N 2 04W
St. Andrews Scotland **33** G4 56 20N 2 48W
St. Anton Austria **49** F2 47 09N 10 17E
St. Austell England **40** C3 50 20N 4 48W
St. Bees Head England **34** B3 54 31N 3 39W
St. Bride's Bay Wales **36** B1 51 50N 5 15W
St. Brieuc France **48** B4 48 31N 2 45W
St. Catherine's Point England **38** C1 50 34N 1 18W
St. David's Wales **36** B1 51 54N 5 16W
St. David's Head Wales **36** B1 51 55N 5 19W
St-Denis France **48** E4 48 57N 2 22E
St-Dizier France **48** F4 48 38N 4 58E
Saintes France **48** C2 45 44N 0 38W
St-Étienne France **48** F2 45 26N 4 23E
St. Gallen Switzerland **51** B7 47 25N 9 23E
St. George's Channel British Isles **36** A1/B2 52 00N 6 00W
St. Germain France **48** E4 48 55N 2 08E
St. Gotthard Pass Switzerland **49** E2 46 34N 8 31E
St. Helena *i.* Atlantic Ocean **5** 15 58S 5 43W
St. Helens England **34** C2 53 28N 2 44W
St. Helier Jersey Channel Islands **41** E2 49 12N 2 07W
St. Ives Cambridgeshire England **38** D3 52 20N 0 05W
St. Ives Cornwall England **40** B3 50 12N 5 29W
Saint John Canada **79** N5 45 16N 66 03W
St. John's Canada **79** P5 47 34N 52 43W
St. John's Point Northern Ireland **32** D2 54 15N 5 40W
St. John's Town of Dalry Scotland **33** E3 55 07N 4 10W
St. Just England **40** B3 50 07N 5 41W
St. Kilda *i.* Scotland **30** A2 57 49N 8 34W
ST. KITTS AND NEVIS **79** N2
St. Lawrence *i.* Alaska **78** C7 63 15N 169 50W
St. Lawrence *r.* Canada/USA **79** M5 47 30N 70 00W
St. Lawrence, Gulf of Canada **79** N5 49 00N 62 30W
St-Lô France **41** F2 49 07N 1 05W
St. Louis Senegal **66** A4 16 01N 16 30W
St. Louis USA **79** K4 38 40N 90 15W
ST. LUCIA **79** N2
St. Magnus Bay Scotland **29** D3 60 25N 1 35W
St-Malo France **48** C4 48 39N 2 00W
St. Martin's *i.* England **40** A2 49 58N 6 17W
St. Mary's *i.* England **40** A2 49 55N 6 18W
St. Mary's Loch *l.* Scotland **33** F3 55 29N 3 12W
St. Matthew *i.* USA **78** B7 60 30N 172 30W
St. Moritz Switzerland **49** E2 46 30N 9 51E
St-Nazaire France **48** B3 47 17N 2 12W
St. Neots England **38** D3 52 14N 0 17W
St-Omer France **39** G1 50 45N 2 15E
St. Paul USA **79** K5 45 00N 93 10W
St. Peter-Port Guernsey Channel Islands **41** E2 49 27N 3 32W
St. Petersburg Russia **56** D3 59 55N 30 25E
Saint Pierre & Miquelon *is.* Atlantic Ocean **79** P5 47 00N 56 20W
St-Quentin France **48** E4 49 51N 3 17E
St-Tropez France **48** G1 43 16N 6 39E
ST. VINCENT AND THE GRENADINES **79** N2
Sakhalin *i.* Russia **57** Q3 50 00N 143 00E
Salado *r.* Argentina **85** C5 28 30S 62 30W
Salalah Oman **61** F2 17 00N 54 04E
Salamanca Spain **50** C4 40 58N 5 40W
Salcombe England **40** D3 50 13N 3 47W
Sale England **34** C2 53 26N 2 19W
Salem India **58** C2 11 38N 78 08E
Salerno Italy **51** E4 40 40N 14 46E
Salford England **34** C2 53 30N 2 16W
Salisbury England **38** C2 51 05N 1 48W
Salisbury Plain England **38** C2 51 10N 1 55W
Salta Argentina **84** C5 24 46S 65 28W
Saltash England **40** C3 50 24N 4 12W
Saltcoats Scotland **33** E3 55 38N 4 47W
Saltillo Mexico **79** J3 25 30N 101 00W
Salt Lake City USA **79** H5 40 45N 111 55W
Salvador Brazil **84** F6 12 58S 38 29W
Salween *r. see* Nu Jiang
Salzburg Austria **42** J5 47 48N 13 03E
Salzgitter Germany **49** F5 52 13N 10 20E
Samar *i.* The Philippines **60** D4 12 00N 125 00E
Samara Russia **56** F3 53 10N 50 10E
Samarinda Indonesia **60** C2 0 30S 117 09E
Samarkand Uzbekistan **56** G1 39 40N 66 57E
Sambre *r.* France **48** E5 50 15N 3 50E
SAMOA **4/5**
Samsun Turkey **43** P4 41 17N 36 22E
Sana Yemen Republic **61** E2 15 23N 44 14E
Sanaga *r.* Cameroon **66** D3 5 00N 14 00E
San Antonio *r.* USA **79** K3 29 00N 97 00W
San Antonio Abad Balearic Islands **50** F3 38 59N 1 19E
San Benito Islands Mexico **79** H3 28 00N 115 00W
San Cristobal Venezuela **84** B7 7 46N 72 15W
Sandakan Malaysia **60** C3 5 52N 118 04E
Sanday *i.* Scotland **29** C2 59 15N 2 30W
San Diego USA **79** H4 32 45N 117 10W
Sandown England **38** C1 50 39N 1 09W
San Francisco USA **79** G4 37 45N 122 27W
San Francisco Javier Balearic Islands **50** F3 38 43N 1 26E
San José Costa Rica **79** L1 9 59N 84 04W
San Juan Argentina **85** C4 31 33S 68 31W
San Juan Puerto Rico **79** N2 18 29N 66 08W
Sanliurfa Turkey **43** P3 37 09N 38 49E
San Luis Potosí Mexico **79** J3 22 10N 101 00W
SAN MARINO **51** D5
San Miguel de Tucumán Argentina **85** C5 26 47S 65 15W
San Pedro Sula Honduras **79** L2 15 26N 88 01W
Sanquhar Scotland **33** F3 55 22N 3 56W
San Salvador El Salvador **79** L2 13 40N 89 10W
San Sebastián Spain **50** E5 43 19N 1 59W
Santa Clara Cuba **79** M3 22 25N 79 58W
Santa Cruz Bolivia **84** C6 17 50S 63 10W
Santa Fé Argentina **85** C4 31 35S 60 50W
Santa Marta Colombia **84** B9 11 18N 74 10W
Santander Spain **50** D5 43 28N 3 48W
Santañy Balearic Islands **50** G3 39 22N 3 07E
Santarém Brazil **84** D7 2 26S 54 41W
Santarém Portugal **50** A3 39 14N 8 40W
Santiago Chile **85** B4 33 30S 70 40W
Santiago *r.* Mexico **79** J3 104 00W 21 30N
Santiago de Cuba Cuba **79** M3 20 00N 75 49W
Santiago del Estero Argentina **85** C5 27 47S 64 15W
Santo Domingo Dominican Republic **79** N2 18 30N 69 57W
Santos Brazil **84** E5 23 56S 46 22W
São Francisco *r.* Brazil **84** E6 13 40S 44 00W
São Luís Brazil **84** E7 2 34S 44 16W
Saône *r.* France **48** F3 47 30N 5 30E
São Paulo Brazil **84** E5 23 33S 46 39W

São Tomé *i.* Gulf of Guinea **66** C3 0 25N 6 35E
SÃO TOMÉ AND PRINCIPE 66 C3
Sapporo Japan **59** N3 43 05N 141 21E
Sarajevo Bosnia-Herzegovina **42** K4 43 52N 18 26E
Saratov Russia **56** E3 51 30N 45 55E
Sarawak *admin.* Malaysia **60** C3 1 00N 111 00E
Sardinia *i.* Italy **51** B4 40 00N 9 00E
Sarh Chad **66** D3 9 08N 18 22E
Sark *i.* Channel Islands British Isles **41** E2 49 26N 2 22W
Saskatchewan *province* Canada **78** J6 55 00N 105 00W
Saskatchewan *r.* Canada **78** J6 53 30N 105 00W
Saskatoon Canada **78** J6 52 10N 106 40W
Sassari Italy **51** B4 40 43N 8 34E
SAUDI ARABIA 61 E3
Saumur France **48** C3 47 16N 0 05W
Sava *r.* Europe **51** F6 45 45N 16 15E
Savannah USA **79** L4 32 04N 81 07W
Sawel *mt.* Northern Ireland **32** B2 54 49N 7 02W
Say'un Yemen Republic **61** E2 15 59N 48 44E
Scafell Pike *mt.* England **34** B3 54 27N 3 14W
Scalasaig Scotland **32** C4 56 04N 6 12W
Scalloway Scotland **29** D3 60 08N 1 17W
Scalpay *i.* Highland Scotland **30** D2 57 15N 6 00W
Scalpay *i.* Western Isles Scotland **30** C2 57 15N 6 00W
Scapa Scotland **29** C1 58 58N 2 59W
Scapa Flow *sd.* Scotland **29** B1 58 55N 3 00W
Scarba *i.* Scotland **32** D4 56 45N 5 50W
Scarborough England **35** E3 54 17N 0 24W
Scarp *i.* Scotland **30** B3 58 02N 7 08W
Schefferville Canada **78** N6 54 50N 67 00W
Schelde *r.* Netherlands **49** B4/C4 51 00N 4 00E
Schwerin Germany **49** F5 53 38N 11 25E
Scilly, Isles of England **40** A2 49 56N 6 20W
Scotland *country* United Kingdom **28** 56 10N 4 00W
Scottish Borders *u.a.* Scotland **33** F3/G3 55 30N 3 00W
Scunthorpe England **35** E2 53 35N 0 39W
Seascale England **34** B3 54 24N 3 29W
Seaton England **41** D3 50 43N 3 05W
Seattle USA **78** G5 47 35N 122 20W
Sedan France **48** F4 49 42N 4 57E
Seine *r.* France **48** D4 49 15N 1 15E
Sekondi Takoradi Ghana **66** B3 4 59N 1 43W
Selby England **35** D2 53 48N 1 04W
Selkirk Scotland **33** G3 55 33N 2 50W
Selsey Bill *p.* England **38** D1 50 43N 0 48W
Selvas *geog. reg.* South America **84** C7 7 00S 65 00W
Semarang Indonesia **60** C2 6 58S 110 29E
Semipalatinsk Kazakhstan **56** J3 50 26N 80 16E
Sendai Japan **59** N2 38 16N 140 52E
SENEGAL 66 A4
Senegal *r.* Senegal/Mauritania **66** A4 16 00N 15 00W
Sennar Sudan **61** D2 13 31N 33 38E
Sennen England **40** B3 50 03N 5 42W
Seoul South Korea **59** D3 37 32N 127 00E
Sept Îles *tn.* Canada **79** N6 50 10N 66 00W
Seram *i.* Indonesia **60** D2 3 30S 129 30E
Seram Sea Indonesia **60** D2 2 30S 130 00E
Serbia *admin.* Yugoslavia **42** L4 44 50N 21 00E
Seremban Malaysia **60** B3 2 43N 102 57E
Serov Russia **56** G3 59 42N 60 32E
Sétif Algeria **42** H3 36 11N 5 24E
Setúbal Portugal **50** A3 38 31N 8 54W
Sevastopol Ukraine **56** D2 44 36N 33 31E
Sevenoaks England **39** E2 51 16N 0 12E
Severn *r.* England **37** E1 51 30N 2 30W
Severnaya Zemlya *is.* Russia **57** K5 80 00N 95 00E
Severodvinsk Russia **43** P8 64 35N 39 50E
Seville Spain **50** C2 37 24N 5 59W
Seward USA **78** E7 60 05N 149 34W
SEYCHELLES 5
Sfax Tunisia **66** D6 34 45N 10 43E
Sgurr Mór *mt.* Scotland **31** D2 57 42N 5 03W
Shaftesbury England **41** E4 51 01N 2 12W
Shakhty Russia **43** Q5 47 43N 40 16E
Shanghai China **59** D3 31 06N 121 22E
Shanklin England **38** C1 50 38N 1 10W
Shannon *r.* Republic of Ireland **32** B2 54 15N 8 00W
Shapinsay *i.* Scotland **29** C2 59 03N 2 51W
Sheerness England **39** E2 51 27N 0 45E
Sheffield England **35** D2 53 23N 1 30W
Shenyang China **59** D4 41 50N 123 26E
Shepton Mallet England **41** E4 51 12N 2 33W
Sherborne England **41** E3 50 57N 2 31W
Sherbrooke Canada **79** M5 45 24N 71 54W
Sheringham England **39** F3 52 57N 1 12E
Shetland Islands *u.a.* Scotland **29** D3 60 00N 1 15W
Shiant Islands Scotland **30** C2 57 55N 6 20W
Shiel *r.* Scotland **30** D2 57 09N 5 25E
Shijiazhuang China **59** C3 38 04N 114 28E
Shikoku *i.* Japan **59** L1 33 40N 134 00E
Shilka *r.* Russia **57** M3 52 00N 118 00E
Shimonoseki Japan **59** L1 33 59N 130 58E
Shiraz Iran **61** F3 29 38N 52 34E
Shizuoka Japan **59** M1 34 59N 138 24E
Shrewsbury England **37** E2 52 43N 2 45W
Shropshire *co.* England **37** E2 52 35N 2 25W
Shymkent Kazakhstan **56** G2 42 16N 69 05E
Šiauliai Lithuania **42** L7 55 51N 23 20E
Siberian Lowland Russia **56** H4 60 00N 75 00E
Sibu Malaysia **60** C3 2 19N 111 50E
Sichuan Basin *see* Sichuan Pendi
Sichuan Pendi *(Sichuan Basin)* China **59** B3 32 00N 107 00E
Sicily *i.* Italy **51** E2 37 00N 14 00E
Sidi-Bel-Abbès Algeria **42** F3 35 15N 0 39W
Sidlaw Hills Scotland **31** F1/G1 56 30N 3 10W
Sidmouth England **41** D3 50 41N 3 15W
Siegen Germany **49** E4 50 52N 8 02E
Siena Italy **51** C5 43 19N 11 19E
SIERRA LEONE 66 A3
Sierra Madre *mts.* Mexico **79** J3 26 00N 108 00W
Sierra Nevada *mts.* Spain **50** D2 37 00N 3 20W
Sierra Nevada *mts.* USA **79** H4 37 00N 119 00W
Simferopol Ukraine **56** D2 44 57N 34 05E
Simplon Pass Europe **49** E2 46 15N 8 03E
Simpson Desert Australia **72** D3 25 00S 137 00E
Sinai, Mount Egypt **61** D3 28 32N 33 59E
SINGAPORE 60 B3
Singkep *i.* Indonesia **60** B2 0 20S 104 30E
Sinuiju North Korea **59** D4 40 04N 124 25E
Siracusa Italy **51** E2 37 04N 15 19E
Sirte Libya **42** K2 31 13N 16 35E
Sivas Turkey **43** P3 39 44N 37 01E
Skegness England **35** F2 53 10N 0 21E
Skelmersdale England **34** C2 53 55N 2 48W
Skiddaw *mt.* England **34** B3 54 40N 3 08W
Skikda Algeria **42** H3 36 53N 6 54E
Skipton England **34** C2 53 58N 2 01W
Skopje FYROM **42** L4 42 00N 21 28E
Skye *i.* Scotland **30** C2 57 20N 6 15W
Sleaford England **35** E1 53 00N 0 24W
Sleat, Sound of Scotland **30** D2 57 00N 5 55W
Slieve Donard *mt.* Northern Ireland **32** D2 54 11N 5 55W
Slieve Snaght *sum.* Republic of Ireland **32** B3 55 12N 7 20W
Slough England **38** D2 51 31N 0 36W
Slough *u.a.* England **38** D2 51 31N 0 36W
SLOVAKIA 42 K5
SLOVENIA 51 E7
Smallwood Reservoir Canada **78** N6 54 10N 63 50W
Smolensk Russia **56** D3 54 49N 32 04E
Snaefell *mt.* Isle of Man British Isles **33** E2 54 16N 4 28W
Snake *r.* USA **79** H5 43 00N 114 00W
Snowdon *mt.* Wales **36** C3 53 04N 4 05W
Snowy Mountains Australia **72** E2 36 24S 148 28E
Soar *r.* England **37** F2 52 40N 1 10W
Soay *i.* Scotland **30** C2 57 08N 6 14W
Sochi Russia **43** P4 43 35N 39 46E
Socotra *i.* Yemen Republic **61** F2 12 05N 54 10E
Sofia Bulgaria **42** L4 42 40N 23 18E
Sokhumi Georgia **43** Q4 43 01N 41 01E
Sokoto Nigeria **66** C4 13 02N 5 15E
Solapur India **58** C2 17 43N 75 56E
Solihull England **37** F2 52 25N 1 45W
Sóller Balearic Islands **50** G3 39 46N 2 42E
SOLOMON ISLANDS 72 F5
Solway Firth *est.* Scotland/England **34** B3 54 40N 3 40W
SOMALIA 67 E5
Somerset *co.* England **41** D4/E4 51 10N 3 00W
Somme *r.* France **48** E4 49 45N 2 30E
Songhua Hu *res.* China **59** D4 43 30N 126 51E
Songhua Jiang *r.* China **59** D4 46 30N 129 00E
Songkhla Thailand **60** B3 7 12N 100 35E
Song-koi *r.* China/Vietnam **59** B2 23 00N 102 00E
Sousse Tunisia **66** D6 35 50N 10 38E
Southampton England **38** C1 50 55N 1 25W
Southampton *u.a.* England **38** C1 50 54N 1 27W
Southampton Island Canada **78** L7 64 50N 85 00W
South Australia *state* Australia **72** D3 27 00S 135 00E
South Ayrshire *u.a.* Scotland **32/33** D2/E3 55 20N 4 40W
South Barrule *hill* Isle of Man British Isles **33** E2 54 09N 4 40W
South Benfleet England **39** E2 51 33N 0 34E
South Carolina *state* USA **79** L4 34 00N 81 00W
South China Sea Pacific Ocean **60** C4 15 00N 110 00E
South Dakota *state* USA **79** J5 45 00N 102 00W
South Downs *hills* England **38/39** D1/E 150 50N 0 45W
Southend Scotland **32** D3 55 20N 5 38W
Southend *u.a.* England **39** E2 51 33N 0 45E
Southend-on-Sea England **39** E2 51 33N 0 43E
Southern Alps *mts.* New Zealand **73** C2 43 07S 171 13E
Southern Ocean 86
Southern Uplands Scotland **33** E3/G3 55 30N 3 30W
South Esk *r.* Scotland **31** G1 56 40N 2 40W
South Georgia *i.* South Atlantic Ocean **85** F2 54 00S 36 00W
South Gloucestershire *u.a.* England **38** B2 51 30N 2 30W
South Island New Zealand **73** C2 42 30S 172 00E
SOUTH KOREA 59 D3
South Lanarkshire *u.a.* Scotland **33** E3/F3 55 35N 3 55W
South Molton England **40** D4 51 01N 3 50W
South Orkney Islands Southern Ocean **85** E1 60 00S 45 00W
South Pole Antarctica **86** 90 00S
Southport England **34** B2 53 39N 3 01W
South Ronaldsay *i.* Scotland **29** C1 58 47N 2 56W
South Shields England **35** D3 55 00N 1 25W
South Uist *i.* Scotland **30** B2 57 20N 7 15W
Southwest Cape New Zealand **73** B1 48 00S 168 00E
Southwold England **39** F3 52 20N 1 40E
South Yorkshire *co.* England **34/35** D2 53 30N 1 30W
Sovetskaya Gavan Russia **57** Q2 48 57N 140 16E
SPAIN 50 C3
Spalding England **35** E1 52 47N 0 10W
Spencer Gulf Australia **72** D2 34 16S 136 53E
Spennymoor *tn.* England **34** D3 54 42N 1 35W
Spey *r.* Scotland **31** F2 57 40N 3 10W
Spilsby England **35** F2 53 11N 0 05E
Spitsbergen *i.* Arctic Ocean **86** 79 00N 15 00E
Split Croatia **42** K4 43 31N 16 28E
Spokane USA **78** H5 47 40N 117 25W
Spurn Head England **35** F2 53 36N 0 07E
SRI LANKA 58 D1
Srinagar Jammu & Kashmir **58** C4 34 08N 74 50E
Stafford England **37** E2 52 48N 2 07W
Staffordshire *co.* England **37** E2/F2 52 50N 2 00W
Staines England **38** D2 51 26N 0 30W
Stamford England **35** E1 52 39N 0 29W
Stanley Falkland Islands **85** D2 51 45S 57 56W
Start Bay England **40** D3 50 16N 3 35W
Start Point England **40** D3 50 13N 3 38W
Stavanger Norway **42** H7 58 58N 5 45E
Stavropol Russia **43** Q5 45 03N 41 59E
Stevenage England **38** D2 51 55N 0 14W
Stewart Island New Zealand **73** B1 46 55S 167 55E
Stinchar *r.* Scotland **33** E3 55 10N 4 45W
Stirling Scotland **33** F4 56 07N 3 57W
Stirling *u.a.* Scotland **33** E4 56 10N 4 15W
Stockbridge England **38** C2 51 07N 1 29W
Stockholm Sweden **42** K7 59 20N 18 05E
Stockport England **34** C2 53 25N 2 10W
Stockton-on-Tees England **35** D3 54 34N 1 19W
Stockton-on-Tees *u.a.* England **35** D3 54 33N 1 24W
Stoke-on-Trent England **37** E3 53 00N 2 10W
Stoke-on-Trent *u.a.* England **37** E3 53 02N 2 10W
Stonehaven Scotland **31** G1 56 38N 2 13W
Stornoway Scotland **30** C3 58 12N 6 23W
Storr, The *mt.* Scotland **30** C2 57 30N 6 11W
Stour *r.* Dorset England **41** E3 50 50N 2 10W
Stour *r.* Suffolk/Essex England **39** E2/F2 51 55N 0 55E
Stourbridge England **37** E2 52 27N 2 09W
Stourport-on-Severn England **37** E2 52 21N 2 16W
Stowmarket England **39** F3 52 11N 1 00E
Stow-on-the-Wold England **38** C2 51 56N 1 44W
Strabane Northern Ireland **32** B2 54 49N 7 27W
Strabane *district* Northern Ireland **32** B2 54 45N 7 30W
Stralsund Germany **49** G6 54 18N 13 06E
Strangford Lough *inlet* Northern Ireland **32** D2 54 25N 5 45W
Stranraer Scotland **32** D2 54 55N 5 02W
Strasbourg France **48** G4 48 35N 7 45E
Stratford-upon-Avon England **37** F2 52 12N 1 41W
Strathy Point Scotland **31** E3 58 35N 4 02W
Stroma *i.* Scotland **31** F3 58 40N 3 08W
Stromness Scotland **29** B1 58 57N 3 18W
Stronsay *i.* Scotland **29** C2 59 07N 2 37W
Stronsay Firth *sd* Scotland **29** C2 59 00N 2 55W
Stroud England **38** B2 51 45N 2 12W
Strumble Head *c.* Wales **36** B2 52 02N 5 04W
Sturt Desert Australia **72** E3 27 00S 139 00E
Stuttgart Germany **49** E3 48 47N 9 12E
Sucre Bolivia **84** C6 19 05S 65 15W
SUDAN 61 C2
Sudbury Canada **79** L5 46 30N 81 01W
Sudbury England **39** E3 52 02N 0 44E
Suez Egypt **61** D3 29 59N 32 33E
Suez Canal Egypt **61** D4 31 30N 32 20E
Suffolk *co.* England **39** E3/F3 52 10N 1 00E
Sula Islands Indonesia **60** D2 1 50S 124 50E
Sulawesi *i.* Indonesia **60** D2 2 00S 120 00E
Sullom Voe *inlet* Scotland **29** D3 60 27N 1 20W
Sulu Sea The Philippines/Malaysia **60** D3 8 00N 120 00E
Sumatra *i.* Indonesia **60** A3/B2 0 00 100 00E
Sumba *i.* Indonesia **60** C2 10 00S 120 00E
Sumbawa *i.* Indonesia **60** C2 8 00S 118 00E
Sumburgh Head Scotland **29** D2 59 51N 1 16W
Sunda Strait Indonesia **60** B2 5 50S 105 30E
Sunderland England **35** D3 54 55N 1 23W
Superior, Lake Canada/USA **79** L5 48 00N 88 00W
Surabaya Indonesia **60** C2 7 14S 112 45E
Surakarta Indonesia **60** C2 7 32S 110 50E
Surat India **58** C3 21 10N 72 54E
SURINAME 84 D8
Surrey *co.* England **38** D2 51 25N 0 14W
Sutton England **38** D2 51 22N 0 12W
Sutton Coldfield England **37** F2 52 34N 1 48W
Sutton in Ashfield England **37** F3 53 08N 1 15W
Suzhou China **59** D3 31 21N 120 40E
Sverdrup Islands Canada **78** K8 79 00N 96 00W
Swaffham England **39** E3 52 39N 0 41E
Swale *r.* England **34** D3 54 30N 2 00W
Swanage England **41** F3 50 37N 1 58W
Swansea Wales **36** D1 51 38N 3 57W
Swansea *u.a.* Wales **36** C1 51 40N 4 05W
SWAZILAND 67 D2
SWEDEN 42 J7/L9
Swilly *r.* Republic of Ireland **32** B3 55 00N 7 30W
Swindon England **38** C2 51 34N 1 47W
Swindon *u.a.* England **38** C2 51 32N 1 46W
SWITZERLAND 49 D2/E2
Sydney Australia **72** F2 33 52S 151 13E
Sydney Canada **79** N5 46 10N 60 10W
Syktyvkar Russia **43** S8 61 42N 50 45E
Symbister Scotland **29** D3 60 21N 1 02W
Syr Darya *r.* Asia **56** G2 45 00N 66 00E
SYRIA 61 D4
Szczecin Poland **42** J6 53 25N 14 32E
Szeged Hungary **42** L5 46 15N 20 09E

T

Tabora Tanzania **67** D4 5 01S 32 48E
Tabriz Iran **61** E4 38 05N 46 18E
Tabuk Saudi Arabia **61** D3 28 33N 36 36E
Tacoma USA **78** G5 47 16N 122 30W
Tadcaster England **35** D2 53 53N 1 16W
Taegu South Korea **59** D3 35 52N 128 36E
Taejon South Korea **59** D3 36 20N 127 26E
Tagus *r.* Spain/Portugal **50** B3 39 30N 7 00W
Tahat, Mount Algeria **66** C5 23 18N 5 33E
Taibei Taiwan **59** D2 25 03N 121 30E
Taif Saudi Arabia **61** E3 21 15N 40 21E
Tai Hu *l.* China **59** D3 31 15N 120 10E
Tain Scotland **31** E2 57 48N 4 04W
TAIWAN 59 D2
Taiyuan China **59** C3 37 50N 112 30E
Ta'izz Yemen Republic **61** E2 13 35N 44 02E
TAJIKISTAN 56 H1
Takamatsu Japan **59** L1 34 20N 134 01E
Takazze *r.* Africa **61** D2 14 00N 38 00E
Talaud Islands Indonesia **60** D3 4 00N 127 00E
Talca Chile **85** B4 35 28S 71 40W
Talcahuano Chile **85** B4 36 40S 73 10W
Tamanrasset Algeria **66** C5 22 50N 5 28E
Tamar *r.* England **40** C3 50 35N 4 15W
Tambov Russia **43** Q6 52 44N 41 28E
Tampa USA **79** L3 27 58N 82 38W
Tampere Finland **42** L8 61 32N 23 45E
Tampico Mexico **79** K3 22 18N 97 52W
Tamworth England **37** F2 52 39N 1 40W
Tana, Lake Ethiopia **61** D2 12 20N 37 20E
Tanga Tanzania **67** D4 5 07S 39 05E
Tanganyika, Lake East Africa **67** C4 7 00S 30 00E
Tangier Morocco **66** B6 35 48N 5 45W
Tangshan China **59** C3 39 37N 118 05E
Tanimbar Islands Indonesia **60** E2 7 30S 131 30E
Tanjungkarang Indonesia **60** B2 5 28S 105 16E
TANZANIA 67 D4
Tapajós *r.* Brazil **84** D7 9 10S 56 20W
Taransay *i.* Scotland **30** B2 57 55N 7 00W
Táranto Italy **51** F4 40 28N 17 15E
Tarbat Ness *c.* Scotland **31** F2 57 50N 3 45W
Tarbert Argyll and Bute Scotland **32** D3 55 52N 5 26W
Tarbert Western Isles Scotland **30** C2 57 54N 6 49W
Tarbes France **48** D1 43 14N 0 05E
Tarbet Scotland **33** E4 56 12N 4 43W
Tarim Basin *see* Tarim Pendi
Tarim He *r.* China **58** C4 41 00N 77 00E
Tarim Pendi *(Tarim Basin)* China **58** D4/5 39 00N 84 00E
Tarn *r.* France **48** E1 44 00N 2 15E
Tarragona Spain **50** F4 41 07N 1 15E
Tashkent Uzbekistan **56** G2 41 16N 69 13E
Tasman Bay New Zealand **73** C2 41 00S 173 14E
Tasmania *state* Australia **72** E1 42 00S 143 00E
Tasman Sea Pacific Ocean **7** 39 00S 155 00E
Taunton England **41** D4 51 01N 3 06W
Taupo New Zealand **73** D3 38 42S 176 05E
Taupo, Lake New Zealand **73** D3 38 55S 175 49E
Tauranga New Zealand **73** D3 37 41S 176 10E
Tavistock England **40** C3 50 33N 4 08W
Tavy *r.* England **40** C3 50 35N 4 05W
Taw *r.* England **40** C4/D3 51 00N 4 00W
Tay *r.* Scotland **31** F1 56 30N 3 30W
T'bilisi Georgia **56** E2 41 43N 44 48E
Te Anau, Lake New Zealand **73** B1 45 13S 167 45E
Tébessa Algeria **42** H3 35 21N 8 06E
Tees *r.* England **35** D3 54 30N 1 25W
Tegucigalpa Honduras **79** L2 14 05N 87 14W
Tehran Iran **61** F4 35 40N 51 26E
Teifi *r.* Wales **36** C2 52 03N 4 30W
Teign *r.* England **40** D3 50 45N 3 40W
Teignmouth England **40** D3 50 33N 3 30W
Tel Aviv-Yafo Israel **61** D4 32 05N 34 46E
Telford England **37** E2 52 42N 2 28W
Telford and Wrekin *u.a.* England **37** E2 52 45N 2 30W
Teme *r.* England **37** E2 52 20N 2 30W
Temuco Chile **85** B4 38 45S 72 40W
Tenby Wales **36** C1 51 41N 4 43W
Tenerife *i.* Canary Islands **66** A5 28 15N 16 35W
Tennant Creek *tn.* Australia **72** D4 19 38S 134 12E
Tennessee *r.* USA **79** L4 36 00N 89 00W
Tennessee *state* USA **79** L4 35 00N 87 00W
Teramo Italy **51** D5 42 40N 13 43E
Teresina Brazil **84** E7 5 09S 42 46W
Terni Italy **51** D5 42 34N 12 39E
Terracina Italy **51** D4 41 17N 13 15E
Test *r.* England **38** C2 51 10N 1 30W
Tétouan Morocco **66** B6 35 34N 5 22W
Teviot *r.* Scotland **33** G3 55 30N 2 45W
Tewkesbury England **38** B2 51 59N 2 09W
Texas *state* USA **79** K4 31 00N 100 00W
THAILAND 60 B4
Thailand, Gulf of Asia **60** B4 10 50N 101 00E
Thame England **38** D2 51 45N 0 59W
Thame *r.* England **38** D2 51 45N 1 00W
Thames *r.* England **39** E2 51 30N 0 05E
Thar Desert India **58** C3 27 30N 72 00E
The Hague Netherlands **49** C5 52 05N 4 16E
The Needles *rocks* England **38** C1 50 39N 1 35W
The Peak *mt.* England **37** F3 53 24N 1 51W
The Solent *sd.* England **38** C1 50 45N 1 25W
Thessaloníki Greece **42** L4 40 38N 22 58E
Thetford England **39** E3 52 25N 0 45E
The Vale of Glamorgan *u.a.* Wales **36** D1 52 30N 3 30W
The Wrekin *pk.* England **37** E2 52 41N 2 32W
Thimphu Bhutan **58** D3 27 32N 89 43E
Thionville France **48** G4 49 22N 6 11E
Thirsk England **35** D3 54 14N 1 20W
Thornaby-on-Tees England **35** D3 54 34N 1 18W
Thornhill Scotland **33** F3 55 15N 3 46W
Three Kings Islands New Zealand **73** C4 34 10S 172 07E
Thunder Bay *tn.* Canada **79** L5 48 27N 89 12W
Thurrock England **39** E2 51 28N 0 20E
Thurrock *u.a.* England **39** E2 51 30N 0 23E
Thurso Scotland **31** F3 58 35N 3 32W
Thurso *r.* Scotland **31** F3 58 15N 3 35W
Tianjin China **59** C3 39 08N 117 12E
Tibetan Plateau Tibet **58** D4 33 00N 85 00E
Tibesti *mts.* Chad **66** D5 21 00N 17 00E
Tien Shan *mts.* China **58** C5/D5 41 00N 76 00E
Tierra del Fuego *i.* Chile/Argentina **85** C2 54 00S 67 30W
Tighnabruaich Scotland **32** D3 55 56N 5 14W
Tigris *r.* Iraq **61** E4 34 00N 43 00E
Tijuana Mexico **79** H4 32 29N 117 10W
Tilburg Netherlands **49** C4 51 34N 5 05E
Timaru New Zealand **73** C2 44 24S 171 15E
Timișoara Romania **42** L5 45 45N 21 15E
Timor *i.* Indonesia **60** D2 9 00S 125 00E
Timor Sea Australia **72** C4 12 30S 127 00E
Tiranë Albania **42** K4 41 20N 19 49E
Tiree *i.* Scotland **30** C1 56 30N 6 55W
Titicaca, Lake Peru/Bolivia **84** C6 16 00S 69 30W
Tiverton England **40** D3 50 55N 3 29W
Tivoli Italy **51** D4 41 58N 12 48E
Tizi Ouzou Algeria **50** H2 36 44N 4 05E
Toamasina Madagascar **67** E3 18 10S 49 23E
Tobago *i.* Trinidad and Tobago **84** C9 11 15N 60 40W
Tobermory Scotland **30** C1 56 37N 6 05W

Tobol *r.* Russia **56** G3 56 00N 66 00E
Tocantins *r.* Brazil **84** E7 8 40S 48 00W
TOGO **66** C3
Tokoroa New Zealand **73** D3 38 14S 175 52E
Tokyo Japan **59** M2 35 40N 139 45E
Toledo USA **79** L5 41 40N 83 35W
Toliara Madagascar **67** E2 23 20S 43 41E
Tol'yatti Russia **56** E3 53 32N 49 24E
Tombouctou Mali **66** B4 16 49N 2 59W
Tomsk Russia **56** J3 56 30N 85 05E
Tonbridge England **39** E2 51 12N 0 16E
Tone *r.* England **41** D4/E4 51 00N 3 00W
Tone *r.* Japan **59** N2 36 00N 140 00E
TONGA **5**
Toowoomba Australia **72** F3 27 34S 151 58E
Torbay England **40** D3 50 27N 3 30W
Torbay *u.a.* England **40** D3 50 26N 3 30W
Tordesillas Spain **50** C4 41 30N 5 00W
Torfean *u.a.* Wales **36** D1 51 45N 3 03W
Toronto Canada **79** M5 43 42N 79 46W
Toros DaΔlari *mts.* Turkey **43** N3 36 00N 33 00E
Torpoint *tn.* England **40** C3 50 22N 4 11W
Torre del Greco Italy **51** E4 40 46N 14 22E
Torrens, Lake Australia **72** D2 30 58S 137 52E
Torreón Mexico **79** J3 25 34N 103 25W
Torres Strait Australia **72** E5 9 30S 142 00E
Torridge *r.* England **40** C3 50 55N 4 15W
Tortosa Spain **50** F4 40 49N 0 31E
Tory Island Republic of Ireland **32** A3 55 16N 8 14W
Tory Sound Republic of Ireland **32** A3 55 15N 8 05W
Totnes England **40** D3 50 25N 3 41W
Totton England **38** C1 50 56N 3 06W1 29W
Tottori Japan **59** L2 35 32N 134 12E
Toubkal, Mount Morocco **66** B6 31 03N 7 57W
Touggourt Algeria **66** C6 33 08N 6 04E
Toulon France **48** F1 43 07N 5 55E
Toulouse France **48** D1 43 33N 1 24E
Tours France **48** D3 47 23N 0 42E
Towcester England **38** D3 52 08N 1 00W
Townsville Australia **72** E4 19 17S 146 48E
Toyama Japan **59** M2 36 42N 137 14E
Trabzona Turkey **43** P4 41 00N 39 43E
Trent *r.* England **37** G3 53 30N 0 50W
Trento Italy **51** C7 46 04N 11 08E
Tresco *i.* England **40** A2 49 57N 6 20W
Treviso Italy **51** D6 45 40N 12 15E
Trevose Head England **40** B3 50 33N 5 01W
Trier Germany **49** D3 49 45N 6 39E
Trieste Italy **51** D6 45 39N 13 47E
Trincomalee Sri Lanka **58** D1 8 34N 81 13E
Trinidad *i.* Trinidad and Tobago **84** C9 11 00N 61 30W
TRINIDAD AND TOBAGO **79** N2
Tripoli Lebanon **61** D4 34 27N 35 50E
Tripoli Libya **66** D6 32 54N 13 11E
Tristan da Cuhna *i.* Atlantic Ocean **5** 37 15S 12 30W
Trivandrum India **58** C1 8 30N 76 57E
Tromsø Norway **42** K9 69 42N 19 00E
Trondheim Norway **42** J8 63 36N 10 23E
Troon Scotland **33** E3 55 32N 4 40W
Trowbridge England **38** B2 51 20N 2 13W
Troyes France **48** F4 48 18N 4 05E
Trujillo Peru **84** B7 8 06S 79 00W
Trujillo Spain **50** C3 39 28N 5 53W
Truro England **40** B3 50 16N 5 03W
Tsimlyansk Reservoir Russia **43** Q5 47 30N 43 00E
Tsugaru Channel Japan **59** N3 41 30N 140 30E
Tubruq Libya **66** E6 32 05N 23 59E
Tucson USA **79** H4 32 15N 110 57W
Tula Russia **56** D3 54 11N 37 38E
Tulsa USA **79** K4 36 07N 95 58W
Tunis Tunisia **66** D6 36 50N 10 13E
TUNISIA **66** C6
Turin Italy **51** A6 45 04N 7 40E
Turkana, Lake Ethiopia/Kenya **67** D5 4 00N 36 00E
TURKEY **43** N3
TURKMENISTAN **56** F1
Turks and Caicos Islands West Indies **79** M3 21 30N 72 00W
Turku Finland **42** L8 60 27N 22 15E
Turpan Depression China **58** D5/E5 42 40N 89 30E
Turriff Scotland **31** G2 57 32N 2 28W
TUVALU **5**
Túy Spain **50** A5 42 03N 8 39W
Tver Russia **56** D3 56 49N 35 57E
Tweed *r.* Scotland/England **33** G3 55 45N 2 10W
Tynda Russia **57** N3 55 10N 124 35E
Tyndrum Scotland **31** E1 57 27N 4 44W
Tyne *r.* England **34** D3 54 58N 2 00W
Tyne and Wear *co.* England **35** D3 54 55N 1 20W
Tynemouth England **35** D4 55 01N 1 24W
Tyrrhenian Sea Europe **51** C4/D4 40 00N 12 00E
Tyumen Russia **56** G3 57 11N 65 29E
Tywi *r.* Wales **36** C1 51 45N 3 20W

U

Uberaba Brazil **84** E6 19 47S 47 57W
Uberlândia Brazil **84** E6 18 57S 48 17W
Ucayali *r.* Peru **84** B7 7 30S 75 00W
Udine Italy **51** D7 46 04N 13 14E
Uele *r.* Congo Dem. Rep. **67** C5 4 00N 26 00E
Ufa Russia **56** F3 54 45N 55 58E
'JGANDA **67** D5
jung Pandang Indonesia **60** C2 5 09S 119 28E
'ikhta Russia **43** S8 63 33N 53 44E
JKRAINE **56** D2
Ulan Bator Mongolia **57** L2 47 54N 106 52E
Ulan-Ude Russia **57** L3 51 55N 107 40E
Ullapool Scotland **30** D2 57 54N 5 10W
Ullswater *l.* England **34** C3 54 35N 2 55W
Ullung Island South Korea **59** L2 37 30N 132 00E
Ulm Germany **49** F3 48 24N 10 00E
Ulva *i.* Scotland **30** C1 56 30N 6 15W
Ul'yanovsk Russia **56** E3 54 19N 48 22E
Umeå Sweden **42** L8 63 50N 20 15E
Unimak Island USA **78** C6 55 00N 164 00W
UNITED ARAB EMIRATES **61** F3
UNITED KINGDOM **42** F6
UNITED STATES OF AMERICA *(USA)* **79**
Unst *i.* Scotland **29** E3 60 45N 0 55W
Upper Lough Erne *l.* Northern Ireland **32** B2 54 15N 7 30W
Uppsala Sweden **42** K7 59 55N 17 38E
Ural Mountains Russia **56** F3 57 00N 60 00E
Ural'sk Kazakhstan **56** F3 51 19N 51 20E
Ure *r.* England **34** D3 54 20N 2 00W
Urmia, Lake Iran **61** E4 37 20N 45 55E
URUGUAY **85** D4
Uruguay *r.* South America **85** D5 28 30S 55 30W
Ürümqi China **58** D5 43 43N 87 38E
Usk Wales **36** D1 51 59N 3 35W
Ustinov Russia **56** F3 56 49N 53 11E
Ust-Kut Russia **57** L3 56 48N 105 42E
Utah *state* USA **79** H4 39 0N 112 00W
Utrecht Netherlands **49** C5 52 05N 5 07E
Utsunomiya Japan **59** M2 36 33N 139 52E
Uttoxeter England **37** F2 52 54N 1 52W
UZBEKISTAN **56** G2

V

Vaal *r.* Republic of South Africa **67** C2 27 30S 25 00E
Vaasa Finland **42** L8 63 06N 21 36E
Vadodara India **58** C3 22 19N 73 14E
Vaduz Liechtenstein **49** E2 47 08N 9 32E
Valdepeñas Spain **50** D3 38 46N 3 24W
Valdivia Chile **85** B4 39 46S 73 15W
Valence France **48** F2 44 56N 4 54E
Valencia Spain **50** E3 39 29N 0 24W
Valencia Venezuela **84** C9 10 14N 67 59W
Valenciennes France **48** E5 50 22N 3 32E
Valladolid Spain **50** C4 41 39N 4 45W
Valletta Malta **51** E1 35 54N 14 32E
Valognes France **41** F2 49 31N 1 28W
Valparaíso Chile **85** B4 33 05S 71 40W
Vancouver Canada **78** G5 49 13N 123 06W
Vancouver Island Canada **78** G5 48 55N 124 33W
Vänern, Lake Sweden **42** J7 59 00N 13 30E
Van, Lake Turkey **43** Q3 38 33N 42 46E
Vannes France **48** B3 47 40N 2 44W
Vantaa Finland **42** L8 60 20N 24 50E
VANUATU **5**
Varanasi India **58** D3 25 20N 83 00E
Vara≈din Croatia **51** F7 46 18N 16 21E
Varna Bulgaria **42** M4 43 12N 27 57E
VENEZUELA **84** C8
Venice Italy **51** D6 45 26N 12 20E
Veracruz Mexico **79** K2 19 11N 96 10W
Verdun France **48** F4 49 10N 5 24E
Verkhoyansk Russia **57** P4 67 35N 133 25E
Vermont *state* USA **79** M5 44 00N 73 00W
Verona Italy **51** C6 45 26N 11 00E
Versailles France **48** E4 48 48N 2 07E
Vesuvius *mt.* Italy **51** E4 40 49N 14 26E
Veurne Belgium **39** G2 51 04N 2 40E
Vicenza Italy **51** C6 45 33N 11 32E
Vichy France **48** E3 46 07N 3 25E
Victoria Canada **78** G5 48 26N 123 20W
Victoria *r.* Australia **72** D4 17 00S 131 00E
Victoria *state* Australia **72** E2 47 00S 143 00E
Victoria Falls Zambia/Zimbabwe **67** C3 17 55S 25 51E
Victoria Island Canada **78** H8 70 45N 115 00W
Victoria, Lake East Africa **67** D4 2 00S 33 00E
Vienna Austria **42** K5 48 13N 16 22E
Vienne *r.* France **48** D3 46 30N 0 30E
Vientiane Laos **60** B4 17 59N 102 38E
Vierzon France **48** E3 47 14N 2 03E
VIETNAM **60** B4
Vigo Spain **50** A5 42 15N 8 44W
Vijayawada India **58** D2 16 34N 80 40E
Villach Austria **51** D7 46 37N 13 51E
Vilnius Lithuania **42** M6 54 40N 25 19E
Viña del Mar Chile **85** B4 33 02S 71 35W
Vinh Vietnam **60** B4 18 42N 105 41E
Vinnytsya Ukraine **56** C2 49 11N 28 30E
Vinson Massif *mts.* Antarctica **86** 78 02S 22 00W
Vire *r.* France **41** F2 49 15N 1 05W
Virginia *state* USA **79** M4 38 00N 77 00W
Virgin Islands West Indies **79** N2 18 00N 64 30W
Visakhapatnam India **58** D2 17 42N 83 24E
Vitória Brazil **84** E5 20 20S 40 18W
Vitoria Spain **50** D5 42 51N 2 40W
Vitsyebsk Belarus **56** D3 55 10N 30 14E
Vladikavkaz Russia **43** Q4 43 02N 44 43E
Vladimir Russia **56** E3 56 08N 40 25E
Vladivostok Russia **57** P2 43 09N 131 53E
Volga *r.* Russia **56** E3 51 30N 48 00E
Volgograd Russia **56** E2 48 45N 44 30E
Vologda Russia **56** D3 59 10N 39 55E
Volta, Lake Ghana **66** B3 7 30N 0 30W
Vorkuta Russia **56** G4 67 27N 64 00E
Voronezh Russia **56** D3 51 40N 39 13E
Vosges *mts.* France **48** G4 48 10N 6 50E
Vyrnwy *r.* Wales **36** D2 52 45N 3 10W
Vyrnwy, Lake Wales **36** D2 52 47N 3 30W

W

Waal *r.* Netherlands **49** C4 51 50N 5 00E
Waddington, Mount Canada **78** G6 51 22N 125 14W
Wadebridge England **40** C3 50 32N 4 50W
Wadi Halfa Sudan **61** D3 21 55N 31 20E
Wad Medani Sudan **61** D2 14 24N 33 30E
Waiau *r.* New Zealand **73** B1 46 00S 167 30E
Waigeo *i.* Indonesia **60** E2 0 15S 130 45E
Waikato *r.* New Zealand **73** D3 37 30S 175 30E
Wairau *r.* New Zealand **73** C2 42 00S 173 00E
Waitaki *r.* New Zealand **73** C2 44 45S 170 30E
Wakatipu, Lake New Zealand **73** B1 45 06S 168 31E
Wakayama Japan **59** M1 34 12N 135 10E
Wakefield England **35** D2 53 42N 1 29W
Wakkanai Japan **59** N4 45 26N 141 43E
Walbury Hill England **38** C2 51 25N 1 35W
Wales *country* United Kingdom **36** D2 52 40N 3 30W
Wallasey England **34** B2 53 26N 3 03W
Walls Scotland **29** D3 60 14N 1 34W
Walsall England **37** F2 52 35N 1 58W
Waltham Forest England **38** D2 51 36N 0 00
Walton on the Naze England **39** F2 51 51N 1 16E
Walvis Bay *tn.* Namibia **67** B2 22 59S 14 31E
Wanaka, Lake New Zealand **73** B2 44 28S 169 09E
Wanganui New Zealand **73** D3 39 56S 175 03E
Wanganui *r.* New Zealand **73** D3 39 30S 175 00E
Wansbeck *r.* England **33** H3 55 10N 1 50W
Wantage England **38** C2 51 36N 1 25W
Ward Hill Scotland **29** B1 58 54N 3 20W
Ward's Stone *hill* England **34** C3 54 03N 2 38W
Wareham England **41** E3 50 41N 2 07W
Warley England **37** F2 52 30N 1 59W
Warminster England **38** B2 51 13N 2 12W
Warrenpoint *tn.* Northern Ireland **32** C2 54 06N 6 15W
Warrington England **34** C2 53 24N 2 37W
Warrington *u.a.* England **34** C2 53 23N 2 37W
Warsaw Poland **42** L6 52 15N 21 00E
Warwick England **37** F2 52 17N 1 34W
Warwickshire *co.* England **37** F2 52 15N 1 40W
Washington England **33** D3 54 54N 1 31W
Washington *state* USA **78** G5/H5 47 00N 120 00W
Washington D.C. USA **79** M4 38 55N 77 00W
Wash, The *b.* England **35** F1 52 55N 0 10E
Waterlooville England **38** C1 50 53N 1 02W
Water of Luce *r.* Scotland **32/33** E2 54 55N 4 55W
Watford England **38** D2 51 39N 0 24W
Wau Papua New Guinea **72** E5 7 22S 146 40E
Waveney *r.* England **39** F3 52 30N 1 30E
Weald, The *geog. reg.* England **39** E2 51 05N 0 25E
Wear *r.* England **34** C3 54 40N 2 05W
Weddell Sea Southern Ocean **86** 71 00S 40 00W
Wei He *r.* China **59** B3 34 00N 106 00E
Welland *r.* England **38** D3 52 30N 0 40W
Wellingborough England **38** D3 52 19N 0 42W
Wellington England **41** D3 50 59N 3 15W
Wellington New Zealand **73** C2 41 17S 174 46E
Wells England **41** E4 51 13N 2 39W
Wells-next-the-Sea England **39** E3 52 58N 0 51E
Welshpool Wales **36** D2 52 40N 3 09W
Welwyn Garden City England **38** D2 51 48N 0 13W
Wenlock Edge *hills* England **37** E2 52 30N 2 45W
Wensum *r.* England **39** F3 52 45N 1 05E
Weser *r.* Germany **49** E5 52 30N 9 00E
West Berkshire *u.a.* England **38** C2 51 30N 1 17W
West Bromwich England **37** F2 52 31N 1 59W
Westbury England **38** B2 51 16N 2 11W
West Dunbartonshire *u.a.* Scotland **33** E3/4 56 03N 4 30W
Western Australia *state* Australia **72** 25 00S 123 00E
Western Ghats *mts.* India **58** C2 15 30N 74 00E
Western Isles *u.a.* Scotland **30** B2/C3 57 30N 7 00W
WESTERN SAHARA **66** A5
West Friesian Islands Netherlands **49** C5 53 25N 5 15E
West Lothian *u.a.* Scotland **33** F3 55 50N 3 36W
West Midlands *co.* England **37** E2/F2 52 28N 1 40W
Weston-super-Mare England **38** B2 51 21N 2 59W
West Palm Beach *tn.* USA **79** L3 26 42N 80 05W
Westport New Zealand **73** C2 41 45S 171 36E
Westray *i.* Scotland **29** B2/C2 59 18N 3 00W
Westray Firth *sd.* Scotland **29** B2/C2 59 15N 3 00W
West Rift Valley Africa **67** D4 0 00 30 00E
West Sussex *co.* England **38** D1 51 00N 0 25W
West Virginia *state* USA **79** L4 39 00N 81 00W
West Yorkshire *co.* England **34/35** D2 53 50N 1 30W
Wetherby England **35** D2 53 56N 1 23W
Weymouth England **41** E3 50 37N 2 25W
Whakatane New Zealand **73** D3 37 58S 176 59E
Whalsay *i.* Scotland **29** E3 60 22N 0 59W
Whangarei New Zealand **73** C3 35 43S 174 19E
Wharfe *r.* England **34** C3 54 10N 2 05W
Whernside *sum.* England **34** C3 54 14N 2 23W
Whitby England **35** E3 54 29N 0 37W
Whitchurch England **37** E2 52 58N 2 41W
Whiteadder Water *r.* Scotland/England **33** G3 55 50N 2 10W
Whitehaven England **34** B3 54 33N 3 35W
Whitehorse Canada **78** F7 60 41N 135 08W
White Nile *r.* Sudan **61** D2 11 00N 32 00E
White Sea Russia **42** P9 66 00N 37 30E
Whithorn Scotland **33** E2 54 44N 4 25W
Whitley Bay *tn.* England **33** H3 55 03N 1 25W
Whitney, Mount USA **79** H4 36 35N 118 17W
Whyalla Australia **72** D2 33 02S 137 35E
Wichita USA **79** K4 37 43N 97 20W
Wick Scotland **31** F3 58 26N 3 06W
Wicklow Republic of Ireland **36** A2 52 59N 6 03W
Widnes England **34** C2 53 22N 2 44W
Wiesbaden Germany **49** E4 50 05N 8 15E
Wigan England **34** C2 53 33N 2 38W
Wigston England **37** F2 52 36N 1 05W
Wigton England **34** B3 54 49N 3 09W
Wigtown Scotland **33** E2 54 52N 4 26W
Wigtown Bay Scotland **33** E2 54 10N 4 20W
Wilhelmshaven Germany **49** E5 53 32N 8 07E
Wilkes Land *geog. reg.* Antarctica **86** 68 00S 105 00E
Wiltshire *co.* England **38** B2/C2 51 30N 2 00W
Wimborne Minster England **41** F3 50 48N 1 59W
Wincanton England **41** E4 51 04N 2 25W
Winchester England **38** C2 51 04N 1 19W
Windermere England **34** C3 54 23N 2 54W
Windermere *l.* England **34** C3 54 20N 2 57W
Windhoek Namibia **67** B2 22 34S 17 06E
Windsor England **38** D2 51 29N 0 38W
Windsor & Maidenhead *u.a.* England **38** D2 51 30N 0 45W
Winnipeg Canada **79** K5 49 53N 97 10W
Winnipeg, Lake Canada **78** K6 53 00N 97 00W
Winsford England **34** C2 53 11N 2 31W
Winterthur Switzerland **49** E2 47 30N 8 45E
Wisbech England **39** E3 52 40N 0 10E
Wisconsin *state* USA **79** K5 45 00N 90 00W
Wishaw Scotland **33** F3 55 47N 3 56W
Witham England **39** E2 51 48N 0 38E
Witham *r.* England **35** E2 53 05N 0 10W
Witney England **38** C2 51 48N 1 29W
Wittenberg Germany **49** G5 51 53N 12 39E
Woking England **38** D2 51 20N 0 34W
Wokingham England **38** D2 51 25N 0 51W
Wokingham *u.a.* England **38** D2 51 24N 0 51W
Wolfsburg Germany **49** F5 52 27N 10 49E
Wollongong Australia **72** F2 34 25S 150 53E
Wolverhampton England **37** E2 52 36N 2 08W
Wonsan North Korea **59** D3 39 07N 127 26E
Woodbridge England **39** F3 52 06N 1 19E
Wooler England **33** G3 55 33N 2 01W
Worcester England **37** E2 52 11N 2 13W
Worcestershire *u.a.* England **37** E2 52 13N 2 13W
Workington England **34** B3 54 39N 3 33W
Worksop England **37** F3 53 18N 1 07W
Worms Head Wales **36** C1 51 34N 4 20W
Worthing England **38** D1 50 48N 0 23W
Wrangel *i.* Russia **57** U5 61 30N 180 00
Wrath, Cape Scotland **31** D3 58 37N 5 01W
Wrexham Wales **36** D3 53 03N 3 00W
Wrexham *u.a.* Wales **36** D3 53 00N 3 00W
Wrocław Poland **42** K6 51 05N 17 00E
Wuhan China **59** C3 30 35N 114 19E
Wuppertal Germany **49** D4 51 15N 7 10E
Würzburg Germany **49** E3 49 48N 9 57E
Wye *r.* England/Wales **37** E1 51 40N 2 40W
Wymondham England **39** F3 52 34N 1 07E
Wyndham Australia **72** C4 15 28S 128 06E
Wyoming *state* USA **79** J5 43 00N 108 00W
Wyre *r.* England **34** C2 53 50N 2 50W

X

Xi *r.* China **60** C5 23 00N 112 00E
Xi'an China **59** B3 34 16N 108 54E
Xi Jiang *r.* China **59** C2 22 00N 111 00E
Xingu *r.* Brazil **84** D7 5 30S 52 40W
Xining China **59** B3 36 35N 101 55E
Xuzhou China **59** C3 34 17N 117 18E

Y

Yakutsk Russia **57** N4 62 10N 129 50E
Yamagata Japan **59** N2 38 16N 140 16E
Yamoussoukro Côte d'Ivoire **66** B3 6 50N 5 20W
Yangon Myanmar **58** E2 16 47N 96 10E
Yangtze *r.* *see* Jinsha Jiang (upper course), Chang Jiang (lower course)
Yaoundé Cameroon **66** D3 3 51N 11 31E
Yarlung Zangbo Jiang *(Tsangpo)* *r.* China **58** D3 30 00N 90 00E
Yaroslavl Russia **56** D3 57 34N 39 52E
Yarrow Water *r.* Scotland **33** F3 55 35N 3 05W
Yazd Iran **61** F4 31 54N 54 22E
Yekaterinburg Russia **56** G3 56 52N 60 35E
Yell *i.* Shetland Islands Scotland **29** D3 60 35N 1 10W
Yellowknife Canada **78** H7 62 30N 114 29W
Yellow Sea China **59** D3 35 30N 122 30E
Yell Sound Scotland **29** D3 60 30N 1 15W
YEMEN REPUBLIC **61** E2
Yenisey *r.* Russia **57** J4 64 00N 88 00E
Yeo *r.* England **41** E4 51 00N 2 45W
Yeovil England **41** E3 50 57N 2 39W
Yerevan Armenia **43** Q4 40 10N 44 31E
Yes Tor *sum.* England **40** C3 50 42N 4 00W
Yogyakarta Indonesia **60** C2 7 48S 110 24E
Yokkaichi Japan **59** M1 34 58N 136 38E
Yokohama Japan **59** M2 35 27N 139 38E
York England **35** D2 53 58N 1 05W
York *u.a.* England **35** D2 53 56N 1 02W
York, Cape Australia **72** E4 10 41S 142 32E
Yorkshire Wolds *hills* England **35** E3 54 00N 0 45W
York, Vale of England **35** D3 54 10N 1 20W
Ypres *see* Ipres
Yucatan Channel Caribbean Sea **79** L3 21 00N 85 00W
Yucatan Peninsula Mexico **79** L2/3 19 00N 89 00W
YUGOSLAVIA **42** L4
Yukon *r.* Canada/USA **78** D7 65 00N 155 00W
Yukon Territory Canada **78** F7 62 00N 135 00W

Z

Zagreb Croatia **42** K5 45 48N 15 58E
Zagros Mountains Iran **61** E4/F3 32 45N 48 50E
Zahedan Iran **61** G3 29 32N 60 54E
Zahlé Lebanon **43** P2 33 50N 35 55E
Zambezi *r.* Southern Africa **67** D3 17 00S 34 00E
ZAMBIA **67** C3
Zamboanga The Philippines **60** D3 6 55N 122 05E
Zanzibar Tanzania **67** D4 6 10S 39 12E
Zaporizhzhya Ukraine **43** P5 47 50N 35 10E
Zaragoza Spain **50** E4 41 39N 0 54W
Zaria Nigeria **66** C4 11 01N 7 44E
Zarqa Jordan **43** P2 32 04N 36 05E
Zaysan, Lake Kazakhstan **56** J2 48 00N 84 00E
Zealand *i.* Denmark **49** F6 55 00N 12 00E
Zeebrugge Belgium **49** B4 51 20N 3 13E
Zhambyl Kazakhstan **56** H2 42 50N 71 25E
Zhangjiakou China **59** C4 40 51N 114 59E
Zhangye China **59** B3 38.58N 100.30E
Zhanjiang China **59** C2 21 10N 110 20E
Zhengzhou China **59** C3 34 45N 113 38E
Zhytomyr Ukraine **42** M6 50 18N 28 40E
Zibo China **59** C3 36 51N 118 01E
Ziel, Mount Australia **72** D3 23 30S 132 24E
ZIMBABWE **67** C3
Zinder Niger **66** C4 13 46N 8 58E
Zonguldak Turkey **43** N4 41 26N 31 47E
Zürich Switzerland **49** E2 47 23N 8 33E
Zwickau Germany **49** G4 50 43N 12 30E